T0173121

3D THINKING IN DESIGN AND ARCHITECTURE

FROM ANTIQUITY TO THE FUTURE

AUTHOR DEDICATION

Dedicated to my students — past, present and future — to my wife Lauren, my daughter Katy, my sons Nigel, Cam and Nick, and to all those who will read this book, in hope that they will benefit from the ideas contained within.

On the cover: Front: photograph courtesy of Valery Egorov / Shutterstock; drawing by the author. Back: image courtesy of the Compliant Mechanisms Research Group, Department of Mechanical Engineering, Brigham Young University.

First published in the United Kingdom in 2018 by Thames & Hudson Ltd, 181A High Holborn, London WC1V 7QX

3D Thinking in Design and Architecture © 2018 Thames & Hudson, London
Text © 2018 Roger Burrows
Artworks and diagrams © 2018 Roger Burrows
For all other illustrations, please see the picture credits list at the end of the book.

Designed by Peter Dawson, Namkwan Cho / GradeDesign.com

All Rights Reserved. No part of this publication may be reproduced or transmitted in any form or by any means, electronic or mechanical, including photocopy, recording or any other information storage and retrieval system, without prior permission in writing from the publisher.

British Library Cataloguing-in-Publication Data
A catalogue record for this book is available from the British Library

ISBN 978-0-500-51954-7

Printed in China by RR Donnelley

To find out about all our publications, please visit **www.thamesandhudson.com**. There you can subscribe to our e-newsletter, browse or download our current catalogue, and buy any titles that are in print.

3D THINKING
IN DESIGN AND
ARCHITECTURE
FROM ANTIQUITY
TO THE FUTURE

ROGER BURROWS

WITH 800 ILLUSTRATIONS, OVER 600 IN COLOUR

Thames & Hudson

CONTENTS

Nighttime exposure of the Perseids
meteor shower showing star trails
and meteor streaks

'Visual logic' is the process of thinking or reasoning to manipulate real or abstract forms. 'Geometry' is considered to be its more formalized, numerical counterpart.

Geometry may conjure thoughts of schoolbook exercises and trigonometry, but the essence of it is still that of visual logic – a creative means to explore, understand and control our environment. Geometry is a conceptual and visual language that has evolved to help us compensate for our limited human sensing and processing capabilities; to build architectural structures, navigate across the oceans and send spacecraft to distant planets. Geometry also serves to model physical events and observed phenomena, such as the motion of falling objects and the peculiarities of quantum effects.

This book traces the development of visual logic from Neolithic times through Indian, Egyptian, Babylonian, Chinese, native American, Greek, Celtic, Islamic and Renaissance cultures, to the present and the possible future. The intent of the book is not to repeat what is generally known but to reveal new insights and new ideas, with the objective of demonstrating that geometry, in particular, is something much more than how it is popularly conceived: it is a visual language that has evolved to meet new needs, to utilize new technologies and to change the way we think about what we observe in the world around us. *3D Thinking* introduces a type of mathematical archaeology that reveals how ideas interconnect across time and space, and how the past influences the present.

The manifestations of visual logic are highly influenced by culture and past traditions, and we can either learn from the past or be trapped by it. In many cases we treat our geometrical models and formulas with too much deference, sometimes to the point that we mistake our models for reality: there are no spheres, no cubes, no straight lines, these are just perfections conjured by our imagination. That does not mean that such concepts are bad, it is just to say that there is, or was, a time and place for the concept of a sphere – but, in the future, maybe there will not be.

Our visual logics have changed the way we perceive and experience the world in that, historically, the experience was not just intellectual but also physical, through dance, music, poetry and art. In the future new visual logics will help us perceive and experience the world in many new ways – hopefully for the betterment of humankind.

00.1 Auguste Rodin, *The Thinker*, Paris, 1904

00.2 Milton and Galileo, engraving by Kloss from a painting by Annibale Gatti, 1893

INTRODUCTION

3D Thinking started as a number of isolated ideas that seemed worth sharing but, as the work progressed, it became clear that there was more to communicate than originally intended – that there was a story to tell.

In one way the title of this book states the limitations of today's spatial thinking; in another way it sets a challenge for those who are attached to two-dimensional thinking without really knowing it.

Visual logic The main objectives of the first chapter are to show that our visual logic and associated geometries are products of our human imagination, of our limited sensing and processing capabilities, and of our cultural environments. This is meant literally, as our senses, the way we think, the way we build on past experiences, and our emotional drives, all provide the architecture of our visual logic (see fig. 00.4).

This introductory chapter will also show that our geometries, and the 3D forms we build, are dependent upon materials at hand, our abilities to select, shape and apply the materials, our physical and mental needs, and our imaginations.

Visual logic through time In the historical chapters – from the Neolithic to the Renaissance and beyond – we will see how abstract geometrical ideas evolved from path-like doodling, through representative line drawings, to the higher abstractions necessary to measure and to predict. Logical concepts were initially based on correspondences, visual representations and path logics, evolving in post-Neolithic cultures to measure lengths, areas, volumes and time; to predict crop cycles, seasons, food production, water availability and building material requirements.

The evolution of 3D thinking really starts with a 2D mindset, and, in many ways, 3D thought still retains a 2D mindset. Needs that are common to the various civilizations and cultures of the past will be evident, along with similar logical solutions, but the cultural bias of those solutions should be noted.

Whole numbers As the early civilizations developed, geometrical and numerical conventions limited 3D and 2D thinking – and designers, architects and artists had to work creatively within these limitations. A significant limitation was the concept of whole numbers and whole number ratios. These two concepts were the product of the way we generalized elements within our environment so that we could quantify them. The limitations are really philosophical, in that we chose to assign abstract qualities to events and objects so that we could simply count and measure them (see figs 00.3 and 00.5 to 00.11).

When it comes to measurement, the logic of the ancients allowed the multiplication and division of whole numbers by creating smaller or larger units, or by saying we have 'more' or 'less'. Thus, when a hand was a unit of measurement, fingers became a smaller unit – but there was no way to quantify spaces that could not be represented by whole numbers, such as, for example, the hypotenuse of a right isosceles triangle

'All our knowledge has its origins in our perceptions.'
LEONARDO DA VINCI
(1452–1519)

00.3 Mohenjo-daro, Indus Valley, 3000–1500 BCE

00.4 Roman mosaic with a cube pattern giving a three-dimensional effect

00.5 Classical labyrinth, Armenteira, Galicia, Spain, 2000 BCE

00.6 Stonehenge, England, 3000–2000 BCE

00.7 SilburyHill, Avebury, England, c.2400–2300 BCE

(see chapter 5). Cultural groups, up to the time of the ancient Greeks, were wedded to whole numbers and whole number ratios, even though many measurements in general could not be fully quantified with whole numbers. Eudoxus of Cnidus (408–355 BCE) developed the idea of magnitude and incommensurables as a means to jump across incommensurable gaps, and thereby avoided the problem.

Understanding the limit of 'whole number' thinking is critical to understanding the historical sections of this book. The limit is that whole numbers, and whole number ratios, are finite entities and their application is viable only when they are applied to finite things. Applying whole numbers and whole number ratios to finite things such as stone building blocks, coins or a number of sheep is effective, but applying them to dimensions requires a belief in a whole number universe – a belief in non-changing fundamentals, in absolutes and in indivisible particles. It is a pervasive belief and difficult to let go of even when you know that there are irrationals, infinite subdivisions, events that change constantly and even non-dimensional events. Letting go of a whole number and rational world is difficult even today: we tend to jump onto the nearest islands of stability – the nearest whole number ratio, the whole number line on a grid, approximations that take away the indeterminate nature of things.

A world of square grids From the belief in whole numbers we get whole number grids, particularly square grids, and then cubic grids (see chapters 3, 5

and 8). Whole number grids, and their associated whole number ratios, shaped the pyramids of Egypt, the fire altars of the Indus Valley and the geometries of the Pythagoreans. Whole number grids and ratios carried all the way through to the European Renaissance with its studies of perspective, and then influenced the development and conceptual format of Cartesian grids, structured as they are around whole numbers and whole number ratios.

From Cartesian x, y, z coordinate grids we created the logical concepts of calculus, where whole number ratios are used to harness infinity and compensate for it with ratios that are considered to be so small that they are negligible. Even our current 3D simulation and modelling software is based on x, y, z grids that are quantified with whole number ratios (finite approximations of irrationals). In fact we still, mostly, think of 3D using 2D geometric grids (planes) – thus we are the children of our ancestors, who have faithfully carried the baggage of the past into the present.

Many paths This book explores the many conceptual paths that developed through time and space, along with how different paths often converged and then divided again. For example, the ancient Egyptians developed concepts of pyramidal volume and also used progressions of whole number unit fractions to handle small quantities. In the Vedic texts of India, geometricians developed concepts of 'area-preserving transformations', such as transforming a square into a circle of the same area. The result of these two conceptual paths was that

theorems were generated using whole numbers, whole number ratios and long progressions of whole number unit fractions. The techniques developed by these two culturally influenced paths were similar but manifested differently. The convergence and unification of the two paths appear in Euclid's *Elements* (c.300 BCE), where formulas were rendered precisely and axiomatically in words and geometric diagrams.

After the decline of the Greek and Roman civilizations the paths diverged again, into the Middle East, southern Asia and Europe, with the evolution of concepts of zero, decimal placement and numeric symbols developed during the Gupta era of India (320–520 CE) and then refined by Islamic mathematicians. All this at a time when European innovation remained mostly dormant, or took steps backwards, until the Renaissance. The paths converged again, for the Europeans, during the Renaissance – and continued, more or less, on the same track until concepts of curved space and quantum effects and pairing changed the ballpark.

Enhancing the human experience
Developmental factors have tended to be materials at hand and functional objectives; proportional systems; symbolism and demonstrations of power and authority; and human needs, abuses and culture. To a much lesser degree a developmental factor has been that of enhancing the human experience and human behaviour. One of the key ideas put forward in this book relates to the use of geometrical concepts to enhance the human experience. Historically,

geometries have been used to measure, predict and 'control' people and populations. The means to measure were quickly used as the means to levy taxes, control land use and, often, to awe a population with 'protected' knowledge, such as an understanding of celestial events or the ability to construct a pyramid.

Major architectural structures were built as symbols, or to be purely functional and/or economical. Historically, the actual human and emotional needs of humankind were not designed for, other than to establish an individual's position in a social order or to dazzle with the power of an autocratic hierarchy – or with, today, the power of a large corporation or a government institution. Things have not really changed over the millennia.

There have been initiatives in the past to construct buildings or artworks designed to elevate the soul or enhance the human condition, with more than just symbols or decorations. Even in the labyrinths of Neolithic times we can see the possibility of altering human consciousness by creating meandering paths that an individual can spiritually follow, a function that eventually evolved into the use of labyrinths for chants and memory exercises in Gothic cathedrals. The layouts of many Buddhist temple complexes characterize an individual's path through life, as exemplified by the layout of the Taiyuin Mausoleum in Japan (see p.87).

Ancient Chinese scripts describe the use of music and dance to enhance the spirit, and similar ideas were pursued by the Pythagoreans and other cultures. We can see attempts to enhance perceptions with the use of proportionate systems and grids in the works of Vitruvius (c.70/80–c.15 BCE), for example, where the proportions of an idealized man were considered divine and, because of this, determined the proportions of many Greek and Roman temples and art forms. Leonardo da Vinci (1452–1519), and many other Renaissance artists and architects, followed the works of Vitruvius, and embellished them. A similar proportionate system – based on what was, and is, perceived as a geometry of nature – is that of the golden ratio, exemplified in the 20th century in the works of Le Corbusier (see chapters 5 and 8).

The acoustics of many Islamic domes were controlled with acoustic resonators, and the prayer niches of mosques were designed to direct and focus sounds (see chapter 7). The interiors of certain *tekkes* (Sufi shrines or halls) in Turkey were not only designed to enhance the spiritual experience of the Whirling Dervishes but also to focus sounds into specific areas and to communicate through numeric symbolism using the abjad system (see p.175).

In many ways spaces that connect one area with another, such as the cloisters of medieval monasteries, serve to enhance the human experience by providing areas of quiet reflection. More complex systems of enhancing perception were used by Islamic architects where the letters of words were used to generate numbers, which linked to geometric shapes, symbolic images, colours, reflected light patterns, movements, chants and architectural spaces (see chapter 7).

There are many examples of fragmented spaces created to enhance the human emotional and psychological experience, other than to entertain, but a disciplined science to create spaces that will enhance the human experience has not been developed. One of the hopes expressed in this book is that, with new technologies, architects and scientists can make progress in this area – particularly as new technologies offer the possibility of creating architectural spaces in almost any form with a huge multiplicity of characteristics.

New geometries The emphasis of the chapters relating to the present (chapters 9–12) is that, with a little help, the ideas of the past can be transformed into new ideas for both the present and the future – new ideas that can be applied with new technologies. In fact the author believes that there are many untapped concepts of the past that can have great value for the future and, if nothing else, provide us with a perspective from which we can take revolutionary conceptual leaps in the years ahead.

The Shape-Changers chapter describes the historical lineage of shape-changing polyhedra and then develops the concept, looking at how materials and constructs can change shape and size. The idea heralds an era in which our technologies can release us from the traditional limits of materials and traditional modular constructs and standardized sheet sizes. Moving into the future we can have materials that can be shipped flat and then either be constructed into shape-changers or be electrically transformed into 3D constructs.

The following chapter, 'Dynamic Circles and Spheres', is intended to encourage the reader to explore an idea that historically was static, and make it dynamic – and then to venture into a new universe of dynamic geometries. Applying this rationale to circles and spheres the reader will see that very new and different 3D constructs become possible, each with different

00.8 Pyramid of Khafre, Giza, Egypt, c.2570 BCE

spatial properties. The chapter contains many new discoveries, including a 3D close-packing of spheres that are in the golden ratio. It also opens the door, with the shape-changers, to an almost infinite number of 3D spaces – each with unique spatial properties. Applications for both the shape-changer and the dynamic circle and sphere geometries will also include cellular- and lattice-structured materials.

The chapters on modelling with equations (Cartesian geometry) and fractals cover concepts of the fairly recent past, and have been included because they have current software applications for 3D modelling – and also because the concepts are distinct and have been influential with regard to 2D and 3D thinking. As mentioned above, Cartesian geometry can be traced back to Egyptian and Vedic whole number grids; and, similarly, the concept of fractals can be traced back to Greek and Islamic geometries (see, for example, chapter 7, pp.190–94).

The future The chapter exploring the future is highly speculative – and readers might like to join in with speculations of their own. One idea expressed in the chapter is that, with the vastly increased sensing, memory storage and processing capabilities of computers, our algorithms might take on a very different form in the future, becoming much less wedded to our historic geometries and constructs. Equations designed to simulate events might disappear altogether, to be taken over by a sort of observed pattern-predictive system, based on our ever-increasing technological capability to sense subtle influences and link them to observed events, and thereby process data to create predictions of new events, of structural performance, material characteristics, and so on. In many ways this transformation has already started (see figs 00.12 and 00.13), with pattern-predictive algorithms for such things as the weather and the stock market.

As to how far we have progressed with three-dimensional logic to date,

we have, by definition, stayed wedded to dimensions – particularly two dimensions. To truly explore 'space', the author believes that we will need to leave behind the concept of dimensions and all the props we have so far used. Until we move away from linear and finite thinking and create models more aligned to the dynamics of energy and energy states we will not truly have a spatial logic.

00.9 Parthenon, Athens, Greece, 447–432 BCE

00.10 Dome of the Rock, Jerusalem, Israel, 7th century

00.11 Necropolis, Thatta, Pakistan, 14th century

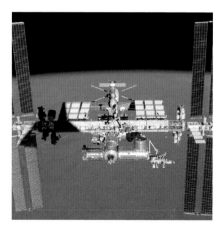

00.12 International Space Station, 2010

00.13 Himalaya water tower concept

SUMMARY OF THE CONCEPTUAL CONTENT

3D Thinking presents the conceptual development of visual logic through time, from the dawn of human history to the possible future. The key concepts covered are as follows:

(i) Correspondences: pictographic, symbolic and pre-numeric. See 'Visual Logic' and 'Neolithic Geometries'.

(ii) Human perception. See 'Visual Logic'.

(iii) Path logics: the development of circular, spiral, knot, irregular line and irregular polygonal visual logics. See 'Visual Logic', 'Neolithic Geometries' and 'European Tribal Geometry'.

(iv) Numbers: the development of measuring systems, and then of the abstractions of whole number concepts; the era of whole numbers and counting with units and number groups (e.g. bases two, ten and 60); the adoption of standards of measurement, mostly based on subdivisions or multiples (of parts) of the human body; the impact of number concepts on 3D applications. See 'The River Cultures' 'The Pythagoreans' and 'The Renaissance'.

(v) Simple polygonal and cursive structures: concepts and proportionate systems that use 2D square grids and simple polygonal and cursive structural forms, such as rectangular boxes, triangular frames, polygonal tessellations. See 'The River Cultures', 'The Pythagoreans' and 'The Renaissance'.

(vi) Divisions and quantifications of space: progressions of unit fractions, area-preserving transformations, 3D cubic grids, formulas for polygonal and circle-related volumes, development of regular 3D polygonal solids, and 3D tessellations of polygonal solids. See 'The River Cultures' and 'The Pythagoreans'.

(vii) Proportions, grids and dynamics: proportional systems and philosophies, and 3D projections in 2D (perspective drawings); the transformation of whole number 3D grids into Cartesian grids and the groundwork for calculus; cursive forms and paths, and correspondences with natural dynamics. See 'The River Cultures', 'The Pythagoreans' and 'The Renaissance'. Proportionate lattices, see the golden ratio sections in 'The Pythagoreans', 'The Renaissance' and 'Dynamic Circles and Spheres'.

(viii) Development of axiomatic and propositional logic: for example Euclidian logic. See 'The Pythagoreans' and descriptions of Euclid.

(ix) Circles, spheres and curves: the development of circle and sphere geometries; the concepts of close-packing and lattices; the development of cursive architectural geometries such as cylinders, domes and the Gothic arch. See 'The Pythagoreans' and 'The Renaissance'.

(x) Concepts of infinity: the development of decimals and place positioning; concepts of irrationals, zero and infinity; the later impact on visual logic – for example successive approximations and calculus, and applications for predicting physical events such as the motion of planetary bodies. See the Gupta section of 'The River Cultures', and 'Geometries of the Early Islamic Period' and 'The Renaissance'.

(xi) Shape-changers: fixed and shape-changing 3D polygonal forms and surfaces. See 'The Pythagoreans', 'Geometries of the Early Islamic Period' and 'Shape-Changers'.

(xii) Dynamic geometries: explorations of 3D space with close-packing and size- and position-changing circles and spheres, with corresponding regular and irregular polyhedral lattice sequences. See 'Dynamic Circles and Spheres'.

(xiii) Infinite subdivisions of space: nesting polygons, geometric progressions (such as the Fibonacci convergence with the golden ratio) and 3D fractal forms. See 'The Pythagoreans' and 'Fractals'.

(xiv) New technologies and new capabilities: as material availability and local technologies impacted the geometric applications of the past, so new technologies and new materials will transform the future – such as those that can map 3D forms with lasers and print 3D objects, and new material technologies that can form nano-structured or shape-changing materials; new possibilities of exploring 3D space, with enhanced sensor and computer-processing capabilities, will create a paradigm shift. See 'The Future of 3D Geometry'.

01. VISUAL LOGIC

A MEANS TO CREATE, TO THINK AND TO MODEL THE UNIVERSE

Visual logic has its origins in the distant past and may be variously seen as representing a search for perfection, a drive to model the universe, a way to think abstractly about two-dimensional and three-dimensional space, a means to navigate the universe, and a way to create new architectural forms.

It might be said that logic, as well as consciousness, is of the senses. We form mental representations that combine senses such as vision, hearing and touch with feelings such as pleasure and pain; and we encapsulate our needs and feelings within our minds in order to survive and excel in our experience of life. We communicate our mental representations with the logic of language and visual imagery (see figs 1.2 and 1.3). Subconscious memories may also impact our thought processes, as might a biological predisposition to awareness arising from our distant ancestral past.

It seems true to say that our visual sense provides the elements of one of our two most developed logical tools, that of 'visual logic' – the other being 'linguistic (and numeric) logic'. Clearly there are other sense-based logics, such as 'emotional logic' and 'musical logic', but such logics are not the subject of this book.

The discipline of visual logic originates with the concept of 'geometry', which derives from the ancient Greek words for 'earth' and 'measure'. Visual logic evolved from an observational and associationist logic to an increasingly abstract visual and symbolic logic. For example, humans progressed from pointing at a hilltop, at themselves and at a position of the sun, to abstracted concepts such as coordinates, measured lengths and time. The whole idea of number followed the same sort of path, from noticing a correspondence between, say, a number of fingers and a number of sheep, through counting in groups, to number symbols and bases.

The need for visual logic One of people's early needs would have been to establish the relative position of things in time and space – and this would require methods of calculating distance and measuring time, and, later, the adoption of standard measurements. At some point, probably as a result of the need to control field boundaries and crop yields, ways of measuring areas and volumes were added. Once the demands of building – such as creating structures with vertical supports and horizontal beams – required logical solutions, the tools of visual logic started to evolve. Constructing a true vertical would have been a structural necessity and although plumb-lines generally worked efficiently, other means would have been needed to calculate angular requirements and to plan and record the dimensions and layouts of stable structures.

A huge advance would have been the creation of a system of visual logic

1.1 Spiral galaxy M51

1.2 Engraved ochre stone, Blombos Cave, South Africa, c.70,000 BCE

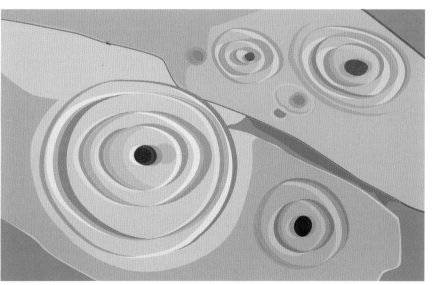

1.3 Petroglyph, Dingle Peninsula, Ireland, c.10,000 BCE

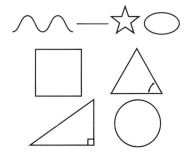

1.4 Perfections of visual logic

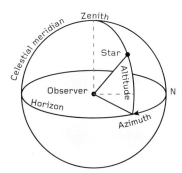

1.5 Spherical navigation and triangles

1.6 The Plimpton 322 tablet (c.1800 BCE)

where real structural problems could be represented in an abstract fashion to focus thought processes. It is quite a jump, conceptually, to start thinking of straight lines instead of flat or horizontal objects; angles instead of slopes; and even the idea of precise lengths using numbers. These abstractions, in their way, required as great a leap of imagination as thinking that one could fly. There are in real life no straight lines and no exact lengths, no spheres, and even no numbers: they are all abstractions, perfections in our imagination (see fig. 1.4). So to start thinking in terms of straight lines, geometrical curves and triangles was as major a step forward as the spoken and written language.

The abstract concept of a triangle, in a mathematical sense, would have been revolutionary as a true abstraction. The origin of the concept would probably have been structural – a means to fix a timber-built frame. Once abstract line drawings of triangles were created with a level of accuracy, using straight lines and measurable angles, the pace of the development of logical analysis must have accelerated greatly and with it the development of a true visual symbolic logic. The uniqueness of the triangle, in visual logic as much as in practical application, is not only that it is structurally sound but also, more importantly, that it is a great building

tool for exploring 2D and 3D space – because a triangle's characteristics can be quickly determined mathematically. If you can triangulate an object, or an event, then you can visually map it and improve your understanding of it. This is useful in everything from navigation and architecture to calculus and 3D modelling (see fig. 1.5).

A number of clay tablets survive from ancient Mesopotamia. One in particular, from the city of Larsa, known as the Plimpton 322 tablet and dating to c.1800 BCE (see fig. 1.6), appears to show a use of right-angled triangles and a knowledge of Pythagorean triples. On the tablet there is clear reference to the squared side of short lengths and diagonals with end calculations of ratios of squares. Whether or not the tablet shows evidence of a means to calculate Pythagorean ratios, it does show an everyday use of analytical mathematics.

Another concept was the mathematical proof. In many ways the idea of a proof is just as tenuous as the idea of a straight line, since a proof is based on many assumptions and abstractions. For the ancient Chinese a 'proof' was often given as something self-evident, such as the *Zhoubi Suanjing* proof of the Pythagorean theorem (see chapter 5). Euclidian geometry creates proofs using a deductive logic, for example showing that Pythagorean triples do encompass a

right-angled triangle and that the square of the hypotenuse equals the sum of the squares of the other two sides (see p.128). These sorts of abstract proofs exist only in their abstract worlds and apply broadly across the basic visual logic of polygons, polyhedra, geodesics and more modern geometries.

The quest When people looked at the sun, many thousands of years ago, they saw a circle. The act of drawing a circle was perhaps an attempt to capture, in a way, the wonder of the sun. When people looked at the number of petals on a flower and realized they corresponded with, say, the number of fingers on a hand, they likely believed that the correspondence was in some way special. When people started to create structured geometrical drawings, and wrote down symbols for numbers, they proceeded on the basis of a correspondence with their perception of the natural world. As abstract languages evolved, a belief developed that geometry and numerology were not created by man but 'through' man and represented something greater – something like the language of the gods. The 'resonance' between geometric forms and numbers with the divine has echoed through time. Ancient beliefs in the river valley cultures had it that whole number ratios and geometric forms such as circles, squares and triangles were not inventions of man but rather the result of glimpses into the mystical and harmonious nature of the universe (see chapter 3). This sort of concept came to maturity with the Pythagoreans, who looked at mathematics as an expression of the 'perfect', as captured by numbers, number sequences and geometric forms – for example, the harmonics of whole number divisions of a string, the spirals of a sunflower, the circular ripples in a pond. Even the wandering stars (the planets) followed their paths in a clockwork fashion, as did the stars in the night sky.

The 'quest' is the search for mathematical models that explain everything, from the movement of the stars (see fig. 1.7) to quantum effects (see fig. 1.8). The problem with the quest is that our models are only models, even though they are becoming increasingly predictive of events. The danger is that we can get too wedded to our models and think that they are real – and once we do that we try to squeeze our observations to fit the model. The alternative is take a mental leap and come up with a new type of model – a paradigm shift.

In particle physics, for example, the search for a particle known as the Higgs boson is part of an effort to support the Standard Model of particle physics, in which the fact that certain fundamental particles had mass could be hypothetically explained by the existence of another elementary particle. Experiments at the Large Hadron Collider at CERN (European Organization for Nuclear Research), using collisions between protons, aimed to prove the existence of this particle, and in 2013 the discovery of a particle with properties consistent with the Higgs boson was confirmed. The CERN image in fig. 1.8 shows a Higgs boson candidate – a particle quickly decaying into four muons (a type of heavy electron), shown by the four red tracks.

It may well be that the Standard Model can be extended and remain viable for many years, assuming that such things as gravity and dark energy can be explained; on the other hand, it may be that we are already misinterpreting observations to squeeze them into a model that is no longer viable. Maybe it is time for a new model to explain the universe. Conversely, we will often jump too quickly to a new model and miss the latent possibilities of an old one. In many ways, that is what this book is all about: the tremendous dynamics of new models and the latent possibilities of old ones.

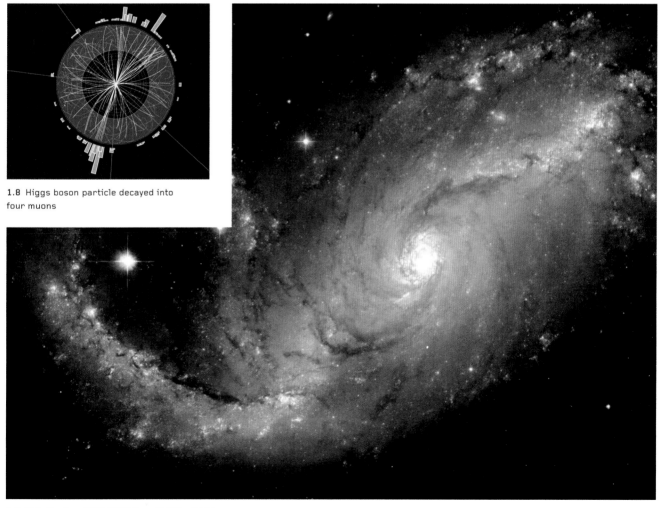

1.8 Higgs boson particle decayed into four muons

1.7 Spiral galaxy NGC 1672 from Hubble, NASA

CULTURAL GEOMETRY

In this book the terms 'geometry' and 'visual logic' are taken to mean, more or less, the same thing, but 'visual logic' has more of an association with the process of conceptual development while 'geometry' is more a formalized visual logic.

Historically, visual logic was used to measure, construct, navigate and model aspects of the world – aspects that are seen with the naked eye or through telescopes or microscopes. In the 6th century BCE the Pythagoreans believed that geometry was an expression of the perfect, of something eternal. Today, many people associate geometry with dull-looking textbooks and trigonometry exercises, although architects, designers and anyone who builds or models things make active use of the visual logic of geometry. Geometry, then, means different things to different people, depending upon their needs and circumstances.

Perhaps the best way to define visual logic is in terms of its applications, particularly its cultural applications. While people might use visual logic to build a structure in which they can live or to calculate the trajectory of a moving body in space, they have also used visual logic to create images and three-dimensional spaces that enhance perception or evoke certain thoughts or feelings. In this way visual logic is a part of another type of drive, to enhance who and what we are – whether such an enterprise is thought to be spiritual,

or just part of what is believed to be a natural evolutionary process.

As much as we might like to think that our visual logic is objective, or that it represents something eternal and pure, we do need to consider how our culture colours our thoughts and may prejudice our conceptual models. This is not necessarily a bad thing; in fact it can be quite the opposite, as an integrated cultural visual logic can help us explore our emotions, thoughts and beliefs. Yet cultural bias is something to be aware of when trying to be objective.

This line of thought, then, stretches the idea of what geometry is generally considered to be – a formalized and visual deductive logic or some sort of eternal language – to the true cultural visual logic that it is: and by clarifying the idea of what visual logic actually is, we can better understand the geometries that we have developed in the past and be better placed to create new geometries that meet future needs. In the historical chapters of this book cultural influence on the development of visual logic can clearly be seen, from a cultural need to square the circle for Indus Valley fire altar construction to the development of area and volume formulas in ancient Egypt to calculate potential crop yields or stone block requirements for the pyramids.

There are many examples of visual logics that are fully integrated into cultural environments – into a culture's symbolism, spirituality, material environment, needs of trade, dance,

music and art. An example of an integrated cultural geometry can be seen in the Bedouin culture as it existed before the 20th century. Historically, Bedouins travelled for trade and to find grazing for their animals. They lived in tents and trekked on camels across vast distances over arid terrain. Bedouins are tribal, following traditions handed down through generations. For these desert nomads, the stars in the night sky shone bright and clear and provided a means both to navigate and to measure time. Towns were visited for trade, but were also places where Bedouins could assimilate new knowledge, exchange ideas or revitalize old traditions.

The numeric logical systems of the Bedouins evolved from simple correspondence to tally marks, counting in groups, numeric symbols and basic algebra. Along the way, tally marks took the form of knots tied in small sections of rope, and letters were given numeric values (the abjad system; see p.175). Visual logic consisted of pictorial line drawings, pictographic stylizations and abstract symbols, as well as geometrical forms such as polygons, lines and angles. The use of numbers was a key part of the Bedouin culture, not only to keep track of goods and livestock, to trade and to navigate, but also as a tool that bridged symbolic and geometric forms and linguistic and spiritual ideas and concepts.

The geometries of the ancient Bedouins were applied to tents, rugs and garment design, as well as to navigation,

1.9 A traditional Bedouin tent

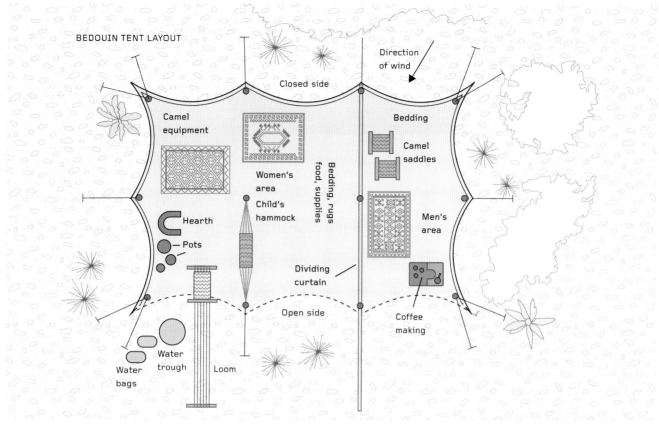

1.10 A traditional Bedouin tent layout (compare with a contemporary Western layout, p.289)

weaving and rope work. Efficiency and multifunctionality, in all things, were cornerstones of the Bedouin logic, as was a sense of the whole rather than the parts – in other words, everything was seen to interrelate and meanings in one medium corresponded with those in another.

An example of cultural geometry A description of Bedouin cultural geometry might be communicated in story form. Imagine a starlit night and a Bedouin man sitting in his *beit al-sha'r* ('house of hair') – a dwelling, little changed for about 4,000 years, consisting of short wooden posts supporting a framework of tightly stretched goat-hair ropes, over which is stretched a loosely woven goat-hair cloth to serve as walls and a roof. The cloth is composed of strips of varying lengths sewn together with black goat-hair thread to make up a single roof membrane. The goat hair's natural colour, mostly black, has been retained, since the black fabric absorbs heat but also provides deep shade, so that during the day temperatures inside are considerably lower than outside. The coarse weave allows heat to disperse,

and the covering provides good insulation in the cold desert night.

On this imagined night, in his house of hair, with the women occupying the rear section of the tent and separated by a woven divider, the man sits contemplating his day. Around him is the tent itself, cleverly and simply designed; and within the tent, there are the tent's dividers, storage bags and many rugs, all woven with tribal images that serve to define the man's lineage. Prayer rugs are rolled up in some special place; they are sacred to him and rich in symbolism and images that inspire him to reflect upon his humanity, as well as numeric messages woven into symbolic polygonal forms. Sequences of knots tied into the ropes supporting his tent, or in short lengths of cord, store messages and keep a tally of his animals and possessions.

In his mind the Bedouin recalls passages of the Qur'an, the poems of Omar Khayyam, the tales of Mullah Nasruddin or stories from the *Thousand and One Nights* – all rich in analogy, symbolism and multiple linguistic interpretations resulting from plays on the consonantal values of the Arabic root system. Perhaps, during the day,

the Bedouin had travelled across the desert to a nearby mosque, its dome, like an inverted heart, revealing itself to him above the horizon, an image impacting him as much as the messages woven into his prayer rug – that of a heart upside down, a reflection of his inner emotional self in the universe above. As he approached the walls of the mosque the shapes of the minarets reminded him that he had come for communal prayer. When the patterns on the walls became readable, new thoughts echoed through his mind. The geometrical systems used for the designs exercised his reason and visual logic; maybe the ray-method design system used by Islamic designers (see chapter 7), maybe the tessellations of the Pythagoreans. The colours of the designs also played a part: sandy desert-brown, the green ground of paradise, the blue of the protecting sky, black symbolizing the Kaaba in Mecca as well as being the colour of trust and respect. Standing in front of the mosque's mihrab (prayer niche) and listening to the prayers of the congregation resonate reminded him of a visit to a *tekke*, or Sufi shrine, when he passed through a door with a design of five- and ten-sided rosettes that symbolically described a dance within – that of the Whirling Dervishes.

The story of the imaginary Bedouin shows us that cultural geometry is something more than an abstract visual logic: it is a human language that has evolved to meet diverse cultural and functional needs.

Dividing space and enhancing perception

Family dwellings have been subdivided in many ways through time and according to culture. In a tipi, for example, there is only one space to share; a traditional Bedouin tent is divided by gender and age, with women and children living in one space and men in the other.

Possibly the need for group or individual spaces is a product of the amount of time spent indoors rather than outdoors. People of today tend to live in highly regulated spaces in densely populated areas, and therefore need interior connections and multiple interior spaces to compensate for the loss of external pathways and remote outdoor spaces.

Historically, cultural needs for communal prayer or worship, for political meetings, for sports and for entertainment led to the development of large enclosed spaces. Column-and-lintel construction was the primary means to enclose or cover large spaces for millennia – from Stonehenge to Greek and Roman temples. The development of the amphitheatre, the arch and the dome allowed far greater volumes to be enclosed – but with their development came problems of controlling sound. Whereas amphitheatres amplified and focused sounds, domed curvatures and large rectangular spaces created a scramble of reflected sound waves that made the spoken word difficult to comprehend at a distance. Various means were developed to dampen, focus and direct sound energy. To enhance certain sound frequencies in a dome, copper or ceramic sound resonators were embedded with openings aligning with interior surfaces. This type of sound control is described in Book 3 of *De architectura* (*On Architecture*) by the 1st-century BCE Roman author and architect Vitruvius (see p.155). In the Sultan Ahmed Mosque (1609–16) in

Istanbul, 75 resonators were found within three rings of the dome.

In Islamic architecture, architects used abutting half-domes, smaller lateral domes, windows and woven carpets to dampen overall sound levels. Muqarnas (honeycomb-type vaults, see pp. 197–200) were added to mihrabs in mosques to enhance and focus the spoken word and make readings from the Qur'an as clear as possible. Techniques to reflect, focus or dampen sounds, then, were known, and there is plenty of evidence to show that these were taken to a fairly high level in mosque construction. Often a whole space, or sequence of spaces, was designed to enhance specific sound properties, an example being the 16th-century Süleymaniye Mosque in Istanbul constructed by the Turkish master architect Mimar Sinan (see fig. 1.11).

To stimulate visual and linguistic logic, geometrical designs were developed. As well as creating a visual impact, these served to communicate messages through the constructional logic of the designs, through symbolism, through colour and through the 'abjad' system by which consonants represented numbers (see p.175).

Christian Gothic architecture used similar techniques of symbolism, pattern and spatial design to communicate and empower the faithful, but the approach was different from that of Islam – less thought was given towards preparing the minds of the faithful for prayer and more towards the idea of entering a space of spiritual transformation – the 'house of God'. Christian Gothic architecture is a showcase of two- and three-dimensional symbolism in iconographic form, such as biblically themed statues and images. The floor plans of Gothic churches are also symbolic, laid out as they generally are in the shape of a Christian cross. The cross shape consists of a long nave, a transept (which crosses the nave) and an apse (a circular or polygonal form at the opposite end to the nave). Religious spatial impacts result from the sequence of passing from the outside through the narthex (a porch or antechamber), into the nave (a large vaulted area that represents the human and heavenly 'body' of the church), to reach the transept (the 'arms' that cross the body) and to stand before the apse (the head).

Transitional spaces were also designed to create a physical and emotional impact, such as the aisles, corridors and staircases leading to crypts, cloisters and chapter houses. Polygonal forms were used symbolically: for example, chapter houses and baptismal fonts were often octagonal, representing the transition between Earth and Heaven. Traditionally, the apse of a church is aligned with the east. Two-dimensional geometric symbolism can also be seen in window tracery and in carved stone decorational elements where circular geometric constructions are common based on six-, eight-, twelve- and sixteen-fold symmetrical patterns – numbers that carry with them traditional Christian meanings (see chapter 2). Tiled floor designs are less common but when used they are often based on simple Archimedean tessellations, circle constructions and, in a few cases, labyrinthine logic (see chapter 2).

The Chapter House of Wells Cathedral, England (see fig. 1.12), is a good example of a medieval integrated cultural and functional space that utilizes light, sound and symbolism. The six-petalled shapes in the windows symbolize the Virgin Mary, as they do in Chartres Cathedral in France (see p.39). Voices carry well within the space and someone sitting on one side of the octagonal space can easily be heard on the other sides. The stone seats along the outer walls of the Chapter House contain niches that would have accommodated up to 40 priests, who presumably met to discuss the affairs of the cathedral.

1.11 Süleymaniye Mosque, Istanbul, Turkey, 1550–57

1.12 Wells Cathedral, England: the Chapter House, 1275–1310

VISUAL IMAGINATION

In many ways our visual logic has developed to compensate for our limited sensing, processing and communication capabilities. Our limited senses mean that we have a relatively fragmented and narrow awareness of our environment, so that we rely on our models to fill in the gaps or to give us the illusion of permanence, pattern or meaning. The modelling systems that succeed are the ones that best help us predict, control and communicate events.

Although we may be fairly conscious of our modelling systems, they mostly seem to function unconsciously and can, therefore, cause us to be surprised or even frightened – for example, when we suddenly glimpse a figure in a tree under a moonlit sky, only to realize that it is just the tree. We often complete images in our visual imagination with too little concrete information, whether accidentally or when we are actively trying to visually understand something. A rock might appear to be a sleeping man, but as we get more visual clues we realize that it is just a rock. We do the same sort of thing when we think we

recognize someone in the street and then find we are wrong.

Sometimes when we complete a visual image with insufficient information, the image stays with us and we find it hard to give it up even if it is an incorrect interpretation. A good example of this was the erroneous belief in the late 19th and early 20th centuries that there were canals on Mars, as famously depicted by American businessman and astronomer Percival Lowell (see fig. 1.13).

A reverse process occurs when we have a mindset for the way something is, such as the Earth being a sphere, or an atom looking like a mini solar system. The mindsets are only models that we create and although they can be very useful, they can also be limiting. Models of an atom range from the indivisible objects posited by Democritus in the 5th century BCE to 21st-century models that show electron cloud distributions or where electrons make instantaneous 'quantum leaps' from one orbit to another. Each model serves its purpose but none of them captures all of the properties of an atom. A measure of a model's success is the number of known

characteristics that it explains and the new phenomena that it leads us to observe (see fig. 1.14).

Perception, senses and time The McGurk effect is a sensory perception phenomenon in which an audio track of a constantly repeated sound, such as 'ba', is paired with a video of a mouth pronouncing that sound. The effect occurs when the video is changed to a mouth pronouncing a different sound, such as 'ga', without changing the audio track. Most people will then hear the new sound being pronounced, even though in reality the sound has not changed. Another sensory perception phenomenon is that of the rubber hand illusion discovered by researchers at Princeton University in the late 1990s. Participants viewed a dummy hand being stroked with a paintbrush, while at the same time a series of identical brushstrokes was applied to their own hand, which was hidden from view. They began to believe that the rubber hand was their own.

Illusions such as these show how one sense can override another and provide an indication of how the brain formulates concepts of reality from limited sensory input. The concepts thus formed are as efficient as possible for survival in the broadest sense of the word – so it is better that we misinterpret an image formed from incomplete information, such as seeing a tiger's face in the shadows under a tree, just in case the fragmented image really is a tiger. These multi-sensory concepts formed from fragmentary sensory information may provide an indication as to why we have distilled the building blocks of visual logic that we have, such as circles and straight lines. Other factors to consider are the architecture and biases of our optical system and the speed by which our brain processes information. For example, because our eyes respond to visible light and our perception of objects is primarily based on reflections from surfaces, we are biased to think in terms of objects defined by specific boundaries, of which line drawings or sculptures in stone become a good representation. If our eyes were receptive to heat then perceived object boundaries would be more diffuse, and if receptive to high-energy ionized radiation then our bias

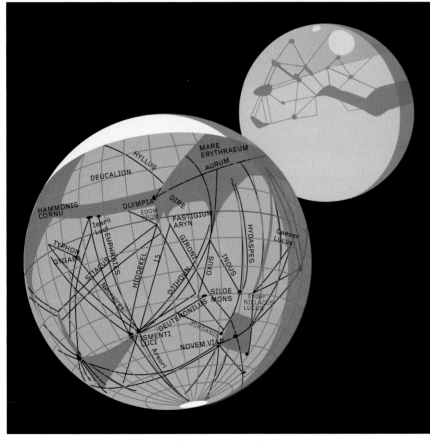

1.13 Percival Lowell's canals on Mars (early 20th century)

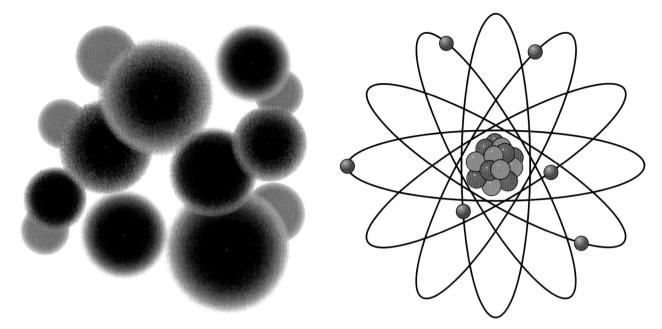

1.14 Left: Schrödinger–Heisenberg electron cloud model of the atom. Right: Rutherford–Bohr planetary model of the atom

would be more to do with how particles are deflected and absorbed, somewhat like multilayered x-rays.

Processing speeds have an impact on how we perceive the 'time' component of object recognition – meaning that our concepts of objects are determined by the rate at which we can process their presence. Our processing speed, as much as the time we devote to processing an object, determines the level of perception of it. Increasing our level of attention, with increased processing speeds, according to our senses, slows down our perception of time, and the reverse is also true. Modelling systems simplify objects, making them quicker to perceive, but limit the type of object processing that is possible.

Outcomes and platforms Whenever we define the axiomatic elements of a visual logic we also implicitly define an indeterminate set of possible outcomes for the logic. For example, when we create the proposition of a circle we are, whether we know it or not, also creating an outcome of the proposition that six equal-sized circles will close-pack around a seventh – so the definition of a circle creates the circumstance of the close-packing. Extending the idea, we could say that once we have defined the concept of a sphere we have simultaneously created all spherical

1.15 William Hogarth, *Satire on False Perspective*, 1754

events – even though such events might forever remain obscure. In other words, once we define a geometrical logic we are simultaneously creating possible outcomes. A proposition does not stand alone: it is part of a fabric of events.

Our visual logics create observational platforms from which we can observe, study and attempt to control our environments. The shape of the Earth appears to correspond with that of the Euclidian sphere – but if we treat the concept of 'sphere' as an observational platform, then we can debate the circumstances by which the Earth could find this state of mathematical perfection. It is only when we accept that the Earth is not the sphere of geometric invention that we can start to understand the forces in play – in other words the 'platform' that we adopted when creating the event of the Euclidian sphere needs to remain independent of the real-world event that it is being used to model.

We should be wary of our concepts and continually question their validity. At the moment we have no real, all-inclusive mindset for quantum physics, even though many are trying to create models to help us understand what

is going on. In some respects, it is wonderful that we do not have any set models for quantum effects, because it means that possibilities remain open. The same should be true for many of the established mindsets about gravity or the internal combustion engine – in fact, about almost everything – as fixed models can inhibit our thinking. Our visual imagination helps us survive and allows us to do wonderful things, but sometimes we are misled by it and it breeds prejudicial ideas. It is just a matter of how we direct our visual imagination.

The comic strip *B.C.* by American cartoonist Johnny Hart had a joke in which a caveman attempted to improve on the concept of a wheel by changing it from square to triangular. Conceptually the mindset is going the wrong way here. Instead of removing a bump, the better solution would be to add a bump, and more bumps, in fact an infinity of bumps. Eliminating bumps might have worked if conceptually one could envision moving from a square (four-bump wheel), to a three-bump, a two-bump, a one-bump and finally a no-bump wheel. Would a one-bump wheel be a perfect circle? Is a no-bump wheel possible?

There are many ways in which we can exercise our visual logic. We can step back from a mindset and try to visualize the focus of our imagination in a wholly new way. What, for example, are the alternatives to wheels for land vehicles? Or how can we visualize an atom in a way that helps us better understand its quantum states? What if we, for a moment, put away the idea that a plane has to fly by generating lift over its wings or body – what if there were a completely different way to generate lift?

A universe of possibilities The visual logic of lines, circles, spheres, triangles and the rest of our standard geometrical vocabulary is quite curious. As said, none of these forms actually exists, but there are many things that resemble them. Our sun and moon both look like perfect circles or spheres, but more precise observations reveal that they are not. Looking out to sea or across a desert, the horizon looks like a straight line, but more precise observations reveal that it is actually irregular and curved. The idea of a perpendicular, or a right angle, is quite abstract, and more of a deduction, possibly as a position of balance. The

1.16 Eliminating a bump (after Johnny Hart)

1.17 Planet Earth

triangle is even more abstract, as it is more of a discovery, linked to structure, than something that is observable. However, all of these standard geometric forms represent a means to break down what we see into logical building blocks, and because these abstractions are so perfect and controllable, they have become the foundations of visual and mathematical logic. Indeed, nature also seems to tend towards the efficiency of these geometric abstractions. Trees tend to grow vertically, bubbles form spherically, crystals triangulate, symmetries abound.

When we measure or construct something we mostly think in terms of straight lines, triangles, rectangles, perpendiculars, spheres and curves, and use algebra, trigonometry and calculus to calculate their properties. Combinations of these forms open up a universe of possibilities in a way similar to the spoken language and poetry – a universe that is not real, as such, but that seems to parallel the real universe in which we live. The geometrical universe is a universe of perfection that pushes us to question why the things we observe depart from the perfect, but also inclines us to find evidence of pure geometric structure in the things we see – atoms, molecules, planets, galaxies.

NEW OPPORTUNITIES FOR VISUAL LOGIC

With new generations of materials and new manufacturing techniques, including 3D printing, we have the opportunity to develop radically different structures, some that change shape, others that are rigid and flexible in different areas, still others that generate or dissipate energy, and so much more.

The development of architectural forms has been very much tied to the materials at hand. Early forms were constructed of branches, small rocks, ice, leaves, animal skins, fur, mud and anything else available. Natural or easily cut forms were also utilized, such as holes, caves, trenches and cavities. By trial and error, early structures made from natural materials became more structurally sound. Mud huts became circular, dome-like or conical, and twig, branch, leaf and ice structures followed similar paths. These architectural developments paralleled, and no doubt in some cases inspired, the development of visual logic.

Once techniques of weaving were discovered, the spaces between timber frames could be filled, creating a host of new possibilities. Weaving may have started by interlacing twigs and branches to fill gaps in fences or to create windbreaks for lean-to shelters, later evolving into weaving strands of wool, goat's hair or any fibrous material.

A major step forward was that of using 'modular' building materials, as primitive architects started to cut tree branches of similar length and cross-section, and match stones so that they stacked more uniformly. Along with this, the concepts of 'perpendicular' and 'horizontal' would have evolved as desirable characteristics for stable structures and assemblies. T-structures and A-structures would also have developed in pace with the uniformity of the selected building materials. Building blocks with straight edges and flat surfaces, whatever the material, are easier to fashion than curved shapes and surfaces, so there was a modular bias towards simple polygonal architectural forms.

Since woven materials, animal skins and more temporary materials, such as leaves, lacked natural structural integrity and relied more on tension

frameworks or something to hang from, they followed their own logical paths, resulting in such constructions as wigwams, tipis and lean-to shelters.

The concept of using modular construction materials greatly influenced the development of architectural form and, in some ways, squeezed out many other structural possibilities that might have evolved through, for example, woven, cast or heat-formable materials, such as clay (for example the mud buildings of Timbuktu, Mali).

The vast majority of contemporary architectural structures built with modular building blocks are rectangular (cuboid), combining perpendicular with horizontal. A smaller percentage are structured around regular polygons or other simple polyhedra, such as octagons and dodecahedrons; and an even smaller number are built around curves, cones and domes, which may have the possibility of higher levels of structural integrity and material efficiency. Historically and structurally we have seen developments from triangular lean-tos and triangular frames to post-and-lintel constructions, round arches, domes, vaults, buttresses and pointed arches. Rectangular and triangular constructional lattices have also evolved with the use of timber, stone, concrete, iron and steel.

The introduction of iron and steel girder lattices in the 19th and 20th centuries dramatically increased the number of structural possibilities, as did the use of steel cables for suspension bridges. New types of load-transferring structures were also developed in the 20th century, including geodesics, tension-based designs, inflatables and even plastic bubble structures (see chapter 13).

In the 21st century we have already seen the introduction of 'morphable' structures, which change shape or position. There are apartment towers where each floor can individually rotate to change the view, and greenhouses that are hydraulically powered to change their solar profiles. There are also space vehicles with solar arrays that are folded prior to launch and then unfolded after achieving orbit.

A completely new structural opportunity will be that of zero-gravity

1.18 Bigelow Aerospace inflatable Mars orbital space station

or low-gravity environments such as orbiting structures, or lunar, Mars or asteroid-based habitats (see fig. 1.18). Another game-changer will be the possibilities for new structures offered by carbon fibre, new resin lattices, nanomaterials and even self-replicating material composites.

With new materials bringing new structural opportunities, the question is: what will be the new parameters? Will we start to create structured spaces that are more than just aesthetic design statements or purely utilitarian; or will we start to explore, scientifically, how spaces can impact the way that we feel and behave?

It is important to match architectural design to building materials and construction technologies, something that does not always happen. With early constructions of geodesics, for example, rectangular building materials and techniques were used for structures composed of triangles, pentagons and hexagons. Beijing International Airport was designed with 23 different column sizes where the design objectives could have been met with one. The recently developed constructional methodology used for monolithic domes (see p.267) appears to match optimum design and constructional methodologies – and surely this should be a primary challenge of good architectural design.

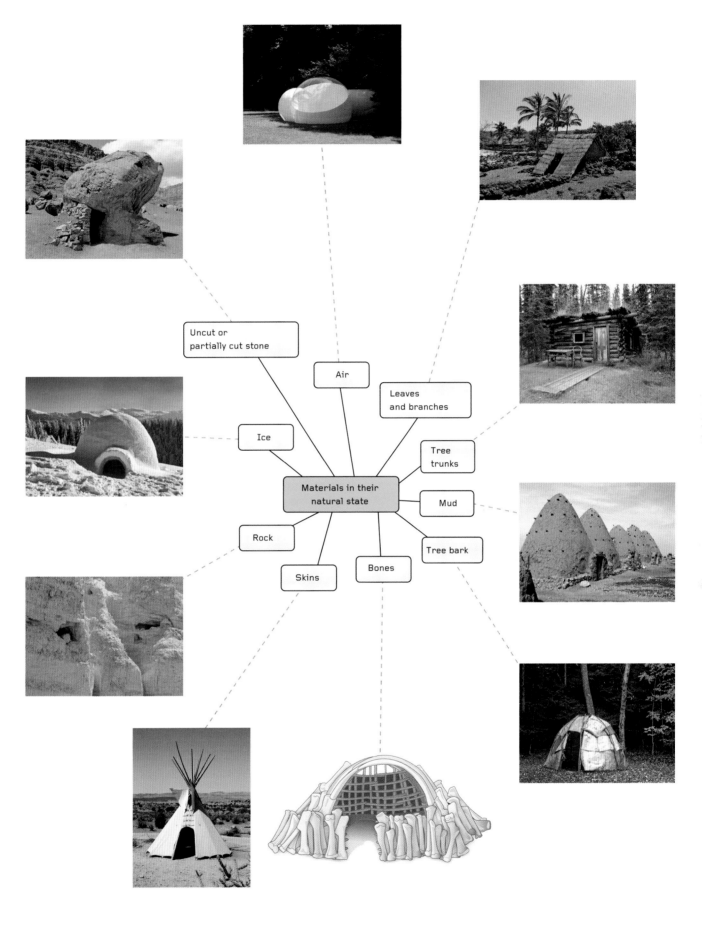

Uncut or partially cut stone

Air

Leaves and branches

Tree trunks

Ice

Mud

Materials in their natural state

Rock

Tree bark

Skins

Bones

1.19 Architecture based on available basic materials

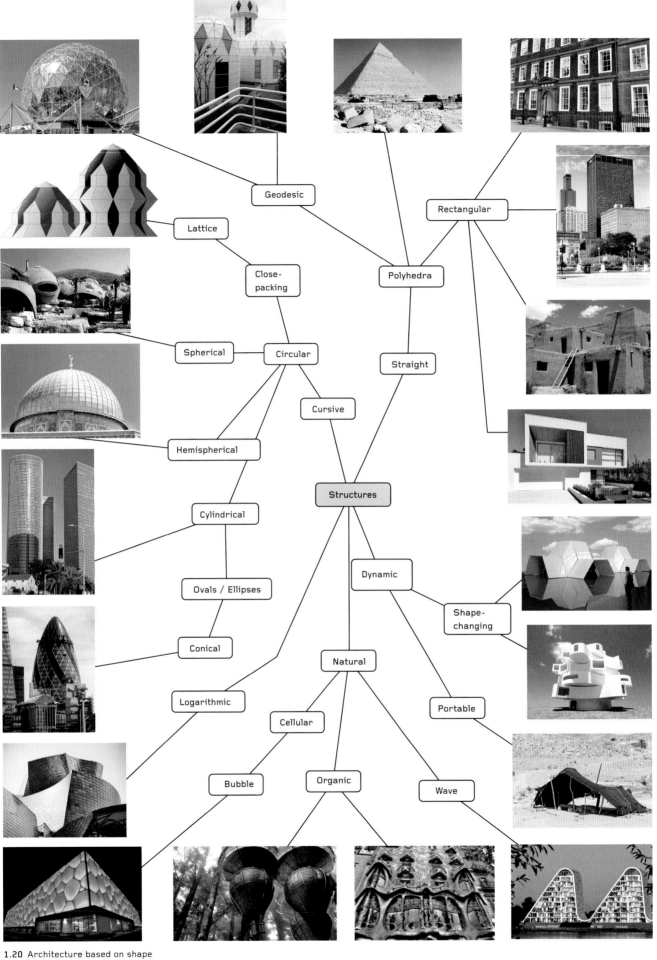

1.20 Architecture based on shape

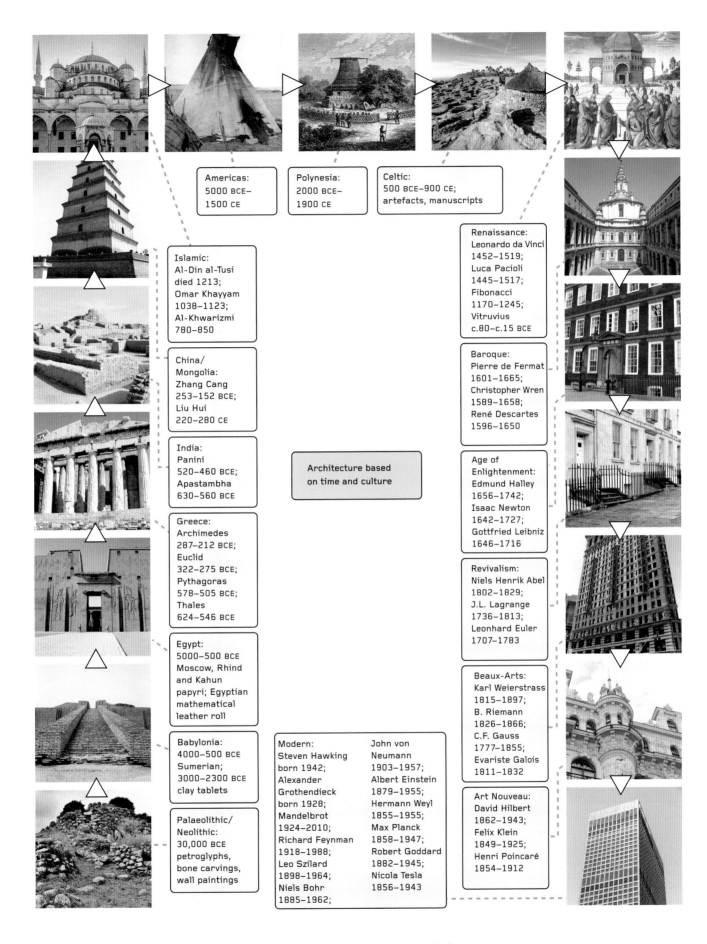

Americas:
5000 BCE–
1500 CE

Polynesia:
2000 BCE–
1900 CE

Celtic:
500 BCE–900 CE;
artefacts, manuscripts

Islamic:
Al-Din al-Tusi
died 1213;
Omar Khayyam
1038–1123;
Al-Khwarizmi
780–850

China/
Mongolia:
Zhang Cang
253–152 BCE;
Liu Hui
220–280 CE

India:
Panini
520–460 BCE;
Apastambha
630–560 BCE

Greece:
Archimedes
287–212 BCE;
Euclid
322–275 BCE;
Pythagoras
578–505 BCE;
Thales
624–546 BCE

Egypt:
5000–500 BCE
Moscow, Rhind
and Kahun
papyri; Egyptian
mathematical
leather roll

Babylonia:
4000–500 BCE
Sumerian;
3000–2300 BCE
clay tablets

Palaeolithic/
Neolithic:
30,000 BCE
petroglyphs,
bone carvings,
wall paintings

Architecture based
on time and culture

Modern:
Steven Hawking
born 1942;
Alexander
Grothendieck
born 1928;
Mandelbrot
1924–2010;
Richard Feynman
1918–1988;
Leo Szilard
1898–1964;
Niels Bohr
1885–1962;

John von
Neumann
1903–1957;
Albert Einstein
1879–1955;
Hermann Weyl
1855–1955;
Max Planck
1858–1947;
Robert Goddard
1882–1945;
Nicola Tesla
1856–1943

Renaissance:
Leonardo da Vinci
1452–1519;
Luca Pacioli
1445–1517;
Fibonacci
1170–1245;
Vitruvius
c.80–c.15 BCE

Baroque:
Pierre de Fermat
1601–1665;
Christopher Wren
1589–1658;
René Descartes
1596–1650

Age of
Enlightenment:
Edmund Halley
1656–1742;
Isaac Newton
1642–1727;
Gottfried Leibniz
1646–1716

Revivalism:
Niels Henrik Abel
1802–1829;
J.L. Lagrange
1736–1813;
Leonhard Euler
1707–1783

Beaux-Arts:
Karl Weierstrass
1815–1897;
B. Riemann
1826–1866;
C.F. Gauss
1777–1855;
Evariste Galois
1811–1832

Art Nouveau:
David Hilbert
1862–1943;
Felix Klein
1849–1925;
Henri Poincaré
1854–1912

1.21 Architecture based on time and culture; and the development of geometry, design and logic

VISUAL

LOGIC

THROUGH

TIME

To understand and explore any concept, including geometric concepts, it can help to go back to the time of their invention.

The geometries of the past have many stories associated with them – some known to us and others that we can only guess at. The geometries developed by our ancestors addressed the needs of their time, perhaps seeming strange to us even though they often form the foundations of today's logic. Looking at past geometries can help us better understand our present geometries and might also stimulate new ideas and reveal new possibilities and new directions.

Ancient architects approached challenges with as much thought and innovation as their modern counterparts. Moreover, ideas were developed and traded or shared all over the world between the great cultures of the past, including China, Babylonia, Egypt, Persia, the Indus Valley, Greece, and Celtic and Islamic cultures. Ideas were sometimes saved from loss and destruction by scribes copying older scripts and filing them away in libraries or personal collections, or by cultures that piggybacked those that were in decline.

Having evolved to provide us with efficient ways to control and shape our environment, geometrical concepts are powerful tools. Historically, such concepts have often been kept secret, with only initiates – such as the Freemasons, the Pythagoreans and the high priests of Egypt – being schooled in the axioms that underlie them. In fact, the concepts have never truly been secrets, as they have been protected only by the effort needed to understand them.

Geometrical concepts are not as objective as popular belief would have them. They are subjective, biased by human conceptual limitations as well as by cultural influences. When Chinese geometers developed geometric models to support the architectural ambitions of their communities, their culture influenced the models they created. For example, the axiomatic definitions of the point and the line given by the *Mo Jing* (c.5th century BCE) are philosophically different from those of Euclid (325–265 BCE), despite appearing the same at face value. The difference explains why the cultural applications of the geometrical concepts look so distinct. The cultural imprint as well as the nature of the visual logic creates unique geometrical footprints that can be followed through time and space.

02. NEOLITHIC GEOMETRIES

EARLY VISUAL LOGICS OF PATHWAYS

The Neolithic period is generally considered to have commenced around 10,000 BCE, and ended somewhere between 4500 and 2000 BCE in Europe and Asia (different terms are used in the Americas). Neolithic cultures saw the beginning of fairly complex geometries, generally tasked with measuring lengths and weights, with monitoring the times of the seasons, and with navigation. Geometries often became the domain of mysticism and rituals.

Stone carvings of line designs appear in Neolithic times and in many cultures throughout the world. Labyrinths are a type of line design often appearing to be based on a constructional methodology, making them easy to generate and communicate. The oldest surviving types of 'sequential' logic are those of the path logics of circular and spiral designs.

Palaeolithic and Neolithic designs were in the form of two-dimensional line patterns that were initially created without any formalized grids, proportions or symmetries, although the beginnings of these formalizations may be seen, and these carried over to such things as earthenware pottery designs in later periods. Spiral, zigzag, circle and polygonal designs, with some repetition of form, can be seen as early as 70,000 BCE in the Blombos Cave in South Africa (see p.15, fig. 1.2) and, much later, in Irish petroglyphs dating from around 3500 BCE.

Examples of these designs and patterns include the Westray Stone (c.3000–2000 BCE) (see fig. 2.2), found in Pierowall in Scotland's Orkney Islands, which is covered with carved spirals. The 1.3 m-long (4.3 ft) stone was once part of a Neolithic chambered cairn, which has not survived. Much like the Westray Stone, the Newgrange Entrance Stone (see figs 2.1 and 2.3) is carved with spirals. Dating to c.3200 BCE, Newgrange is a prehistoric tomb in Meath, Ireland, and the stone lies across its main entrance. Other decorated stones, including a lintel, have been found at Fourknocks Megalithic Tomb, Meath, a Neolithic passage chamber tomb built c.3000 BCE (see figs 2.5 and 2.6). The Gavrinis passage tomb on the island of Gavrinis in the Gulf of Morbihan, France, contains 23 slabs decorated with repeating arch-like shapes that resemble doorways (see fig. 2.4). Neolithic 'cup and ring' rock carvings (see fig. 2.7),

2.1 Newgrange, County Meath, Ireland, c. 3200 BCE

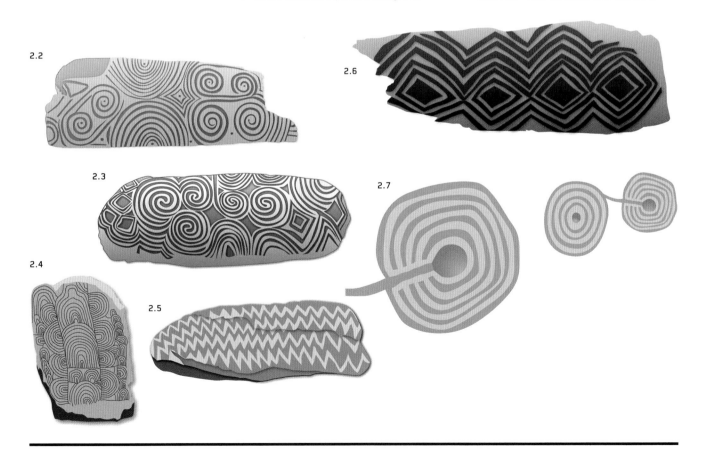

2.2

2.6

2.3

2.7

2.4

2.5

2.8 The classical labyrinth, Knossos coin, Crete, 350 BCE

2.9 A classical labyrinth at Armenteira, Galicia, Spain, 2000 BCE

2.10 A Bolshoi Zayatsky Island labyrinth, possibly 3000–2000 BCE

2.11 Hopi One and Hopi Two labyrinth designs, North America, 17th century

with cup-shaped central depressions, appear in many parts of Britain and Europe.

From spirals to labyrinths Labyrinthine logic is in the same family as that of early spiral designs but is more complex. Labyrinths are constructed with a single path that winds forwards and backwards, multiple times, before arriving at a central point. The oldest surviving labyrinths appear in Neolithic and Bronze Age rock carvings.

One of the most famous labyrinths is the one in Greek mythology designed by Daedalus for King Minos of Crete to hold the Minotaur – a creature that was part man, part bull. Coins found in Crete dating to the 4th century BCE often carry images of the Minotaur's labyrinth, with the result that the design is now known as the 'classical' labyrinth (see fig. 2.8).

Classical labyrinths, as well as many other designs, were constructed over a broad span of space and time, from Neolithic stone labyrinths in Europe (see fig. 2.9) to ancient labyrinths made of boulders on the Bolshoi Zayatsky Islands, Russia (see fig. 2.10, and see fig. 2.40 / key 12), to 400-year-old labyrinths in the Americas.

Labyrinths appear in the art forms of the Hopi culture of the American Southwest, where they have become a symbol of Mother Earth. There are two primary variations of the Hopi labyrinths (see fig. 2.11), which appear very similar but are, in fact, structurally different (see figs 2.17 and 2.19 / keys 10 and 11).

The Hopi One design is the same as the classical labyrinth, while the Hopi Two labyrinth seems to be unique to North America. How and why the labyrinth appeared in the Americas is unknown. Possibly the labyrinth designs were created independently by Hopi, Navajo or Pima tribes, or they could have been brought over to the Americas by the conquistadors or other European settlers. It is also conceivable that their presence might be evidence of the arrival of Norsemen in the 10th century

and of trade between them and Native Americans, who trafficked the design, eventually, down to the tribal territories of the Hopi.

It has been suggested that another variation of the classical labyrinth, from Neolithic times, appears to wind around Glastonbury Tor in England (see fig. 2.12). This hill, once an island surrounded by marshes, has many mythological and spiritual assocations, including with the legends of King Arthur and the Holy Grail. Some interpretation is needed to see a complete labyrinth in the seven paths that wind round the hill; it is possible that they might simply have been terraces for growing crops. The nearby hill Brent Knoll has earthwork features similar to those of the Tor but there is no indication that they were a labyrinth.

However, if Glastonbury Tor were indeed a classical labyrinth, then following the path would lead a person close to the top three times before their final arrival, and would rotate them

2.12 Glastonbury Tor, England

2.13 The Chakravyuha labyrinth, Hoysaleswara temple, Halebidu, India, 12th century

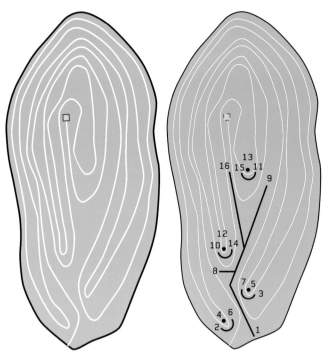

2.14 Glastonbury Tor possible labyrinth

about the top four times clockwise and three times counter-clockwise. Fig. 2.14 shows the possible Glastonbury labyrinth completed with some imagination and with the centre at the top of the Tor.

Labyrinths in ritual and defence

A labyrinth – unlike a maze, which may have many paths or branches – has only one path, so it should be impossible to get lost within its walls (making it a poor prison for a Minotaur). It is only when the path to reach the centre is as important as, or more important than, what is at the centre that using a labyrinth makes any sense. Homer describes the labyrinth as the ceremonial dancing ground of Ariadne, the daughter of King Minos and also perhaps an ancient Minoan goddess of nature's creativity. The legend of Theseus and the Minotaur may have had its origins in a fertility ritual of some sort. Some ancient Greek sources relate that King Minos, after his death, became a judge of the dead in the underworld. So was there a ritual where

a person walked, or danced, through the four seasons, represented by the four inner corners of the classical labyrinth, to ensure a good harvest? Or was a labyrinth, perhaps, a training ground for going to meet the god of the underworld after death?

One use of labyrinths is shown in a 12th-century carving in the Hoysaleswara temple, Halebidu, India, which shows the warrior Abhimanyu entering the 'Chakravyuha' (see fig. 2.13). The Chakravyuha was a spiral battle formation comprising hundreds of soldiers all moving in the same direction. The spinning wheel of warriors engulfed any soldier who entered the mouth of the labyrinth and conducted him to the centre, where the most experienced warriors were concentrated. The great Hindu epic the *Mahabharata* (400 CE) recounts that Abhimanyu knew how to breach this almost impenetrable formation, having learned the secret when he was still in his mother's womb, but unfortunately he did not know how to

exit the Chakravyuha, and was killed in battle while trying to escape.

As a labyrinth, the Chakravyuha shares some of the features of the classical labyrinth. The Hoysaleswara temple carving depicts it as having only five layers, including the centre (see figs 2.15 and 2.16), but other sources say that it usually consisted of seven layers.

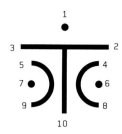

2.15 Key 5: the Chakravyuha labyrinth

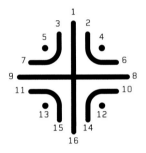

2.16 The Chakravyuha key connections

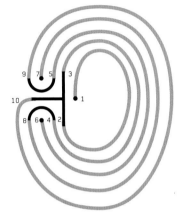

2.17 Key 10: the classical labyrinth

2.18 The classical key connections

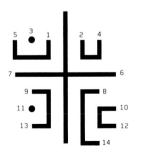

2.19 Key 11: Hopi Two labyrinth (see fig. 2.11)

KEYS TO THE LABYRINTH

Many labyrinths appear to be constructed around a central core of lines and dots, a design 'key' of sorts (also called 'seed logic' or a 'seed pattern'). This suggests that a labyrinth design methodology evolved to generate labyrinths of different types and of different levels of complexity. The key logic might have been used to communicate a particular labyrinth structure from one tribe to another, for example. There are a number of labyrinths ranging from 750 BCE to the 19th century that were clearly constructed with a keylike logic.

The key to the Chakravyuha labyrinth is in the shape of a capital T surrounded by two cups and three dots (see key 5, fig. 2.15). To create the Chakravyuha labyrinth, connect the line and cup end points in a sequential order: 1 to 2, 3 to 4, 5 to 6, and so on (see fig. 2.16).

The key to the classical labyrinth is shaped like a cross with four cups and four dots that represent the ends of lines (see key 10, fig. 2.17). Fig 2.18 shows how the contact points are connected.

The Hopi One key is the same as that of the classical labyrinth. The logic of the Hopi Two labyrinth key (see key 11, fig. 2.19) is significantly different, with only two connected line ends, 3 and 11, five cups, and one line-through connector, 7 to 6.

THE CHARTRES LABYRINTH

A more complex labyrinth can be found in the 13th-century Chartres Cathedral in France, which is about 12.8 m (42 ft) in diameter, with a path length of more than 245 m (800 ft). The labyrinth may well have been designed using a development of the Neolithic key method (see fig. 2.22). The Chartres Cathedral school was an important centre of scholarship from 1020 until it was overtaken by the University of Paris in the 12th century, and the cathedral itself is a good example of Gothic architecture.

While the Chartres labyrinth design may have been generated using a development of the key method (see fig. 2.22A), a simpler approach would have been to use a concentric grid methodology (see fig. 2.22B).

The craftsmen who were given the commission to design the Chartres labyrinth may have been given a project brief along the lines of the following:

(i) the labyrinth was to have 12 layers, including the centre, possibly to symbolize the 12 gates of the Kingdom of God, or the Virgin Mary surrounded by 12 stars (the 12 tribes of Israel);

(ii) the circle was to be used, possibly to symbolize God's act of creation and eternal life;

(iii) the cross was to be represented, with its symbology of a vertical line ascending to Heaven and a horizontal line associated with the horizon of the Earth.

2.20 Chartres Cathedral labyrinth, France

2.21 Chartres labyrinth schematic

If the application of the labyrinth was primarily for meditation and prayer, then the brief might also have included a requirement for the design to accommodate a number of chants, prayers or recitations, of various lengths. For example, a chant might be: 'Let air above and cloud (and) rain (be) true', followed by, after a turn, 'Reveal earth and spring, the deliverer' (chanted, of course, in Latin). Thus, the labyrinth's turns and paths of different lengths may correspond with the number and duration of the chants to be recited. The completed Chartres design has turning points for half- and quarter-turn traverses, in clockwise and anti-clockwise directions, and movements towards and away from the centre. According to this line of reasoning, the Chartres labyrinth is about ascending and descending, and, ultimately, about arriving at a meeting-point of Heaven and Earth.

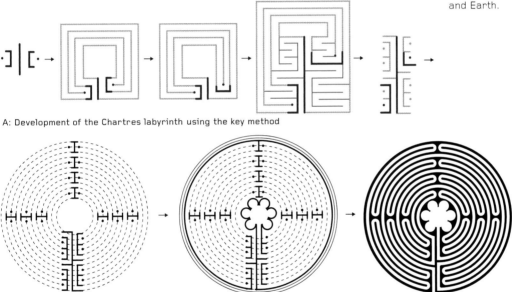

A: Development of the Chartres labyrinth using the key method

B: Alternative development of the Chartres labyrinth using a simpler concentric grid methodology, see fig. 2.49

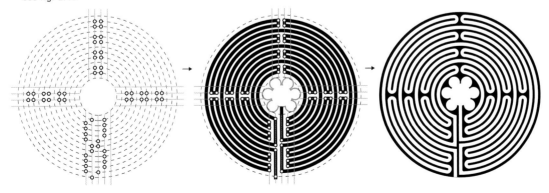

2.22 Possible developments of the Chartres labyrinth from keys A and B

2.23 Labyrinth in the Basilica of Saint-Quentin, France, 1495

2.24 Labyrinth in the Basilica of San Vitale, Ravenna, Italy, 1500, and schematic (right)

We can speculate about the numbers that appear in the Chartres labyrinth.

12 There are 12 layers, perhaps representing the 12 disciples, the 12 lunar months or the 12 gates of Heaven.

112 and 114 There are 112 foils (cups) around the perimeter of the labyrinth, but if the foils had been extended across its entrance, there would have been 114. The number 112 has many multiples with numbers that could have been used symbolically, while 114 has fewer multiples but they include 6 x 19. Here, 19 might have represented the Metonic cycle – a period of 19 years that is a common multiple of the solar year and the synodic (lunar) month – which was a cycle used in numerous traditional calendars including the Babylonian, Greek, Hebrew and Runic calendars.

6 The central flower shape has six petals. The number six has been used to symbolize the Virgin Mary and the Holy Spirit; it is also the number of days of creation. It would be interesting to discover if there were six eminent members who would be given the privilege of standing on the six central 'petals' of the labyrinth.

8 There are eight 90° and 180° traverses clockwise: eight often refers to regeneration or resurrection, and for this reason the baptismal font in many churches has eight sides. Eight can also refer to the eight phases of the moon, the octave, and the second cubic number after one.

10 There are ten 90° traverses anti-clockwise. In the Bible there are ten Commandments. Ten was considered to be the number of the universe by the Greeks, an expression of the golden ratio; the sum of 1, 2, 3 and 4; the fourth triangular number after 1, 3 and 6; and a number of infinite potential.

5 There are five 180° traverses anti-clockwise. Christ supposedly had five wounds on the cross.

Walking the Chartres labyrinth
In Chartres it is easy to imagine six monks, pilgrims or students of the cathedral school chanting as they followed the path of the labyrinth, until they came to stand on one of the six petals of the central flower. One cannot help thinking of Homer's description of the labyrinth as Ariadne's ceremonial dancing ground, where maybe she danced along the spirals of the labyrinth in a celebration of the grace of life. Whether or not the numbers associated with the labyrinth had symbolic significance in this context, the monks were probably aware of their potential meanings.

The labyrinths of the Basilica of Saint-Quentin and of Amiens Cathedral (see figs 2.23 and 2.25) share the same logic as the labyrinth of Chartres. The labyrinth of San Vitale, Ravenna, is very similar but simpler (see fig. 2.24).

2.25 Amiens Cathedral labyrinth, France, 12th century

LABYRINTH KEY LOGIC

On cave walls in northern Spain, we can see Stone Age renderings of bison and deer. We can also see Neolithic line drawings of circles and spirals carved into rocks or painted on cave walls. These ancient images show an evolving visual logic where spiral and circle designs transitioned from the very basic to the more complex.

Spirals can be drawn freehand, but a more structured way is to draw straight lines, or dots, and then connect them (see fig. 2.26). A variation creates a double spiral similar to one seen in the Nazca Lines in the desert of southern Peru (see fig. 2.27). It appears that labyrinth keys developed in a similar way to spirals and possibly out of similar techniques.

Connecting the lines in a slightly different way creates a very simple labyrinth (see fig. 2.28). A few more variations in the way the lines connect creates the classical labyrinth (see fig. 2.30), although not in the more classical key form of lines and dots.

The key logic allows dots and end points of lines to be connected only once, so, within the logic, only one line connects to a dot or to a line end. The logic limits what can be done with a key arrangement, but the keys themselves can be configured in many ways – by adding more lines and dots for example. Figs 2.26 to 2.30 show a possible evolution of labyrinth key designs.

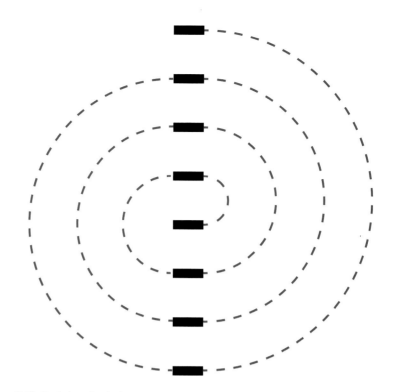

2.26 First stage key logic

2.27 Nazca Lines spiral

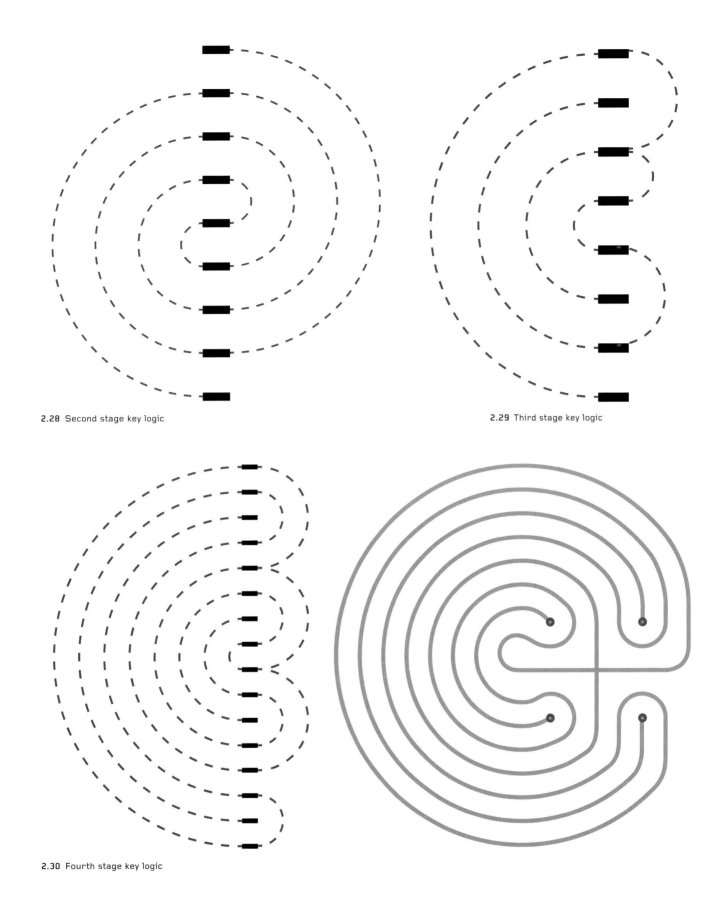

2.28 Second stage key logic

2.29 Third stage key logic

2.30 Fourth stage key logic

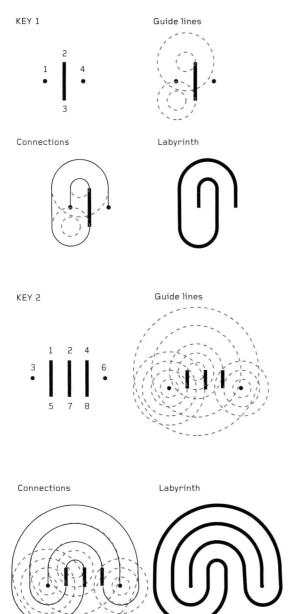

2.31 Key logic development keys 1 and 2

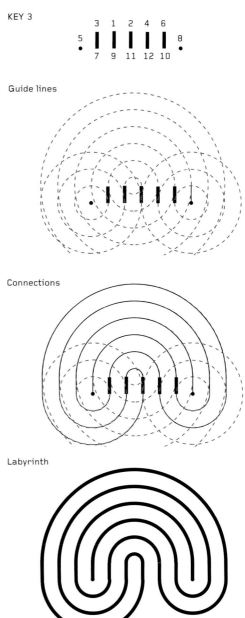

2.32 Key logic development key 3

Figs 2.31 to 2.43 show a possible evolution of key logic, starting with the simplest conceivable connecting structure of lines and dots, shown as key 1. The lines that connect line end points and dots can be of any type or shape. For convenience, in this case, circular arcs have been used.

Key 1 has four connection positions and creates a very simple two-turn spiral.

Key 2 extends key 1 with two additional lines, although a natural progression would have used two lines only.

Key 3 shows a similar jump in the progression as key 2.

Keys 2 and 3 produce labyrinths with characteristic backwards and forwards path directions.

Key 4 has six connection positions and has a three-end centred line structure. The hexagonal symmetry applied to the key is just a convenient choice. The key could have been mapped on to other symmetries.

Key 5 is an extension of key 4 and is, essentially, the same key as that used for the Chakravyuha labyrinth, where the paths are curved rather than drawn in straight lines (see p.35).

Key 6 adds another level to key 5, extending the labyrinth to a design with five layers.

The turn angles for each change of direction in the keys shown are 180°, 120° and 60°.

End points and dots of keys do not always have to be connected in the same way. Variations can be tried. For example, try drawing key 5 and connecting it in a different way from that shown – that is, different from the way it was apparently used for the Chakravyuha labyrinth.

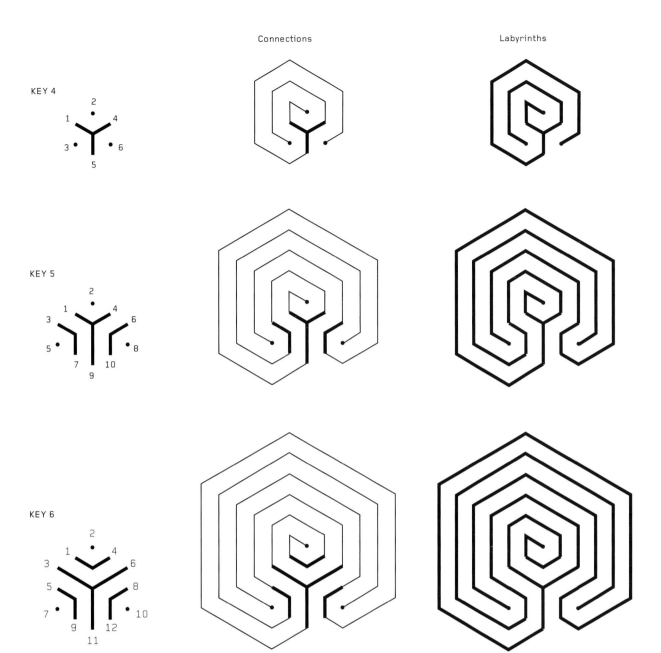

Connections

Labyrinths

KEY 4

KEY 5

KEY 6

2.33 Key logic development keys 4, 5 and 6

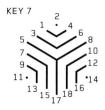

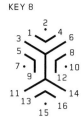

Connections

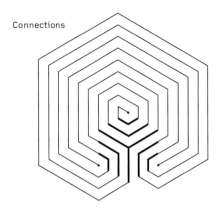

Connections

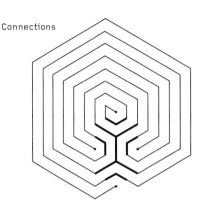

Labyrinths

Labyrinths

2.34 Key logic development key 7

2.35 Key logic development key 8

2.36 Key logic variation

The idea of keys can be extended in all sorts of ways, and the illustrations show just a few variations.

Key 7 shows a development of key 6, by adding more lines that radiate out from a central core.

Key 8 extends the central core logic of keys 4 to 7 by dividing the key into two branches, opening up the possibility of multiple branching keys.

Fig. 2.36 shows a key variation that produces a labyrinth similar to the Chakravyuha labyrinth.

Keys 9 to 14 cross the central core lines and then develop as more dots and lines are added.

Key 10 is the classical labyrinth key – with two representations. Key 10B is a prehistoric variation.

Key 11 is a variant of the Hopi Two key and breaks the symmetry of keys 9 and 10.

Key 12, and higher generations of it, will generate a number of the ancient stone labyrinths on Bolshoi Zayatsky Island (see fig. 2.10).

Key 13 is a split key but still creates a labyrinth.

Key 14 is a 24-point key.

Keys 15 to 18 add path extensions to the more standard keys, creating hybrid labyrinths and mazes, with choices of path to follow.

2.37 Petroglyph, Usgalimol, India, 8000 BCE

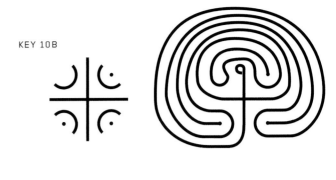

KEY 10B

2.38 Development of Usgalimol labyrinth with Key 10B

Connections

Labyrinths

KEY 9

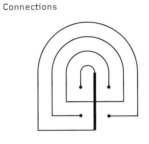

Connections

Labyrinths

KEY 10

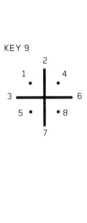

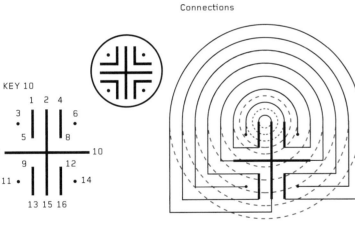

Connections

Labyrinth

KEY 11

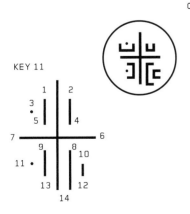

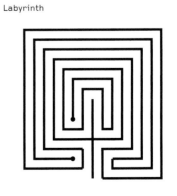

2.39 Key logic development keys 9, 10 and 11

KEY 12

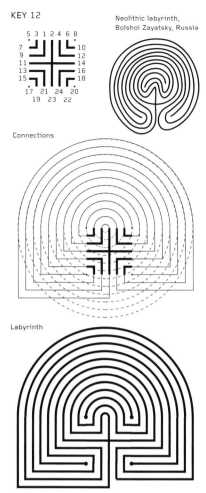

Neolithic labyrinth,
Bolshoi Zayatsky, Russia

Connections

Labyrinth

2.40 Key logic development key 12, a Bolshoi Zayatsky labyrinth

KEY 13
Split key

Connections

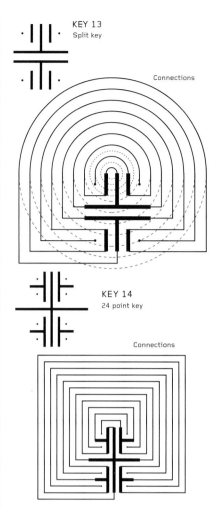

KEY 14
24 point key

Connections

2.41 Key logic development keys 13 and 14

KEY 15

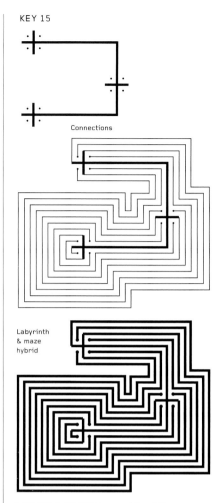

Connections

Labyrinth & maze hybrid

2.42 Key logic development key 15

Variations of key designs are almost infinite. The connecting points of the keys can be connected with straight or curved lines, or in a freehand fashion, or in a more grid-like way. To explore key logic further, the inner core structures can be changed. A greater challenge is to change the number of loops in the Chartres key development using the design devices that look like an H with a dot above and a dot below. The key itself can be changed, or more levels added.

Keys can create quite complex single-path labyrinths but some of the keys do create more than one-path hybrids of mazes and labyrinths.

Key 18A can be used to generate the Chartres labyrinth or a hybrid labyrinth and maze.

Key 18B is a variation of Key 18A to generate a true labyrinth.

Hybrid labyrinths, generated by more complex keys, indicate that the logic might be extended further to create pure mazes with paths where a person could easily get lost. There may also be other types of extension or developments of the key logic in three dimensions or in other ways.

Labyrinths have fascinated many people through time. Their logic is very simple, so the fascination must be due to their symbolic or functional applications. It is interesting to play around with the logic and to see how it can be extended and applied. The logic can reveal mindsets of the past, such as the logic used for the classical labyrinth, where the four inner chambers may have represented, perhaps, the seasons. Or the logic may be extended into the future, possibly as floor plans for futuristic buildings, or as pathways to walk, run or dance along.

The key logic may well have been the first systematic logic used to create labyrinths, and there are numerous examples of labyrinths that were probably generated by using it, including the following:

(i) the 750 BCE petroglyph in the Val Camonica, Italy;
(ii) the 300 CE mosaic in the Villa of Theseus, Paphos, Cyprus;
(iii) the 15th-century labyrinth fresco in Hesselager Church, Denmark;

KEY 16

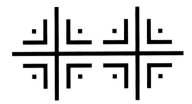

KEY 17

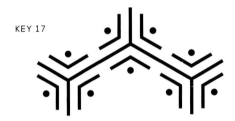

2.43 Key logic development keys 16 and 17

KEY 18A

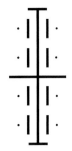

KEY 18B

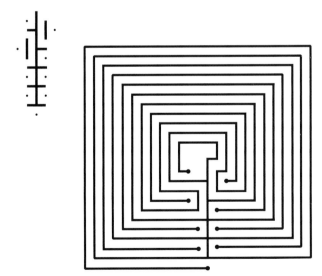

2.44 Key logic development keys 18A and 18B

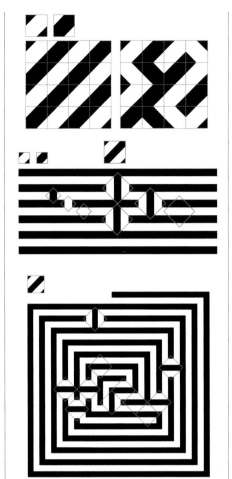

2.45 'Following the Footsteps of Daedalus'

2.46 'Following the Footsteps of Daedalus'

2.47 'Following the Footsteps of Daedalus'

(iv) the 15th-century labyrinth graffiti in Lye Church, Gotland, Sweden;

(v) the 15th-century labyrinth graffiti in Hablingbo Church, Gotland, Sweden;

(vi) the 1699 turf labyrinth on Saffron Walden Common, England;

(vii) the 1852 stone floor labyrinth in the basilica of Notre-Dame de Bon-Secours, Guingamp, France.

Many other methods for creating labyrinth designs have been used, ranging from simple doodling to grids. Examples include petroglyphs, ancient Babylonian clay tablets and Greek and Roman mosaics.

In the paper 'Following the Footsteps of Daedalus', the authors apply a cut-and-paste logic to spirals to create labyrinths and provide a methodology for describing the path structure created. In fig. 2.45, the top two sets of illustrations show how a set of diagonal 'switch' squares can be extracted from a set of parallel lines. The middle line drawings show how the switch squares can alter a basic spiral to create a labyrinth, with the switches positioned so as to change the path directions at alternating levels within the original spiral. If the switches are not positioned at alternating levels, then closed loops are generated. The 'Daedalus' paper extends the idea enough to open up possibilities that can be explored with the method, either as an art form or as a study in networks. As an algorithm, the method could be used to create an interesting maze or labyrinthine game.

Figs 2.46 and 2.47 show how a range of switch squares can be used to alter straight line grids and spirals.

Figs 2.48 and 2.49 are developments of the basic 'Daedalus' concept applied to a 45° rhombus and a square.

Another possible labyrinth design method uses concentric polygons or circles and intersecting path lines (see fig. 2.50). The octagonal labyrinth (the black lines) is the design of the labyrinth in the 13th-century Amiens Cathedral, France (see fig. 2.25).

2.48 'Daedalus' variations

2.49 'Daedalus' variations

2.50 Alternative labyrinth connection system

2.51 Extension of a 2D labyrinth into 3D

2.52 Extension of a 2D labyrinth into 3D

LABYRINTHS IN
THREE DIMENSIONS

Labyrinthine logic is really a two-dimensional path logic, although walking or dancing along the paths provides a three-dimensional experience. There is a tenuous link between labyrinthine path logic and the topology of three-dimensional space, but the topology so far considered has been strictly two-dimensional.

Labyrinthine logic can be 'extruded' into 3D simply by adding a vertical dimension to the containing lines of a labyrinth; the logic, however, stays two-dimensional.

Extending labyrinthine logic into 3D space requires a 3D grid or other 3D space-filling concept. One such extension is that of wrapping a labyrinthine path around a 3D object or allowing the path to penetrate the object (see fig. 2.53).

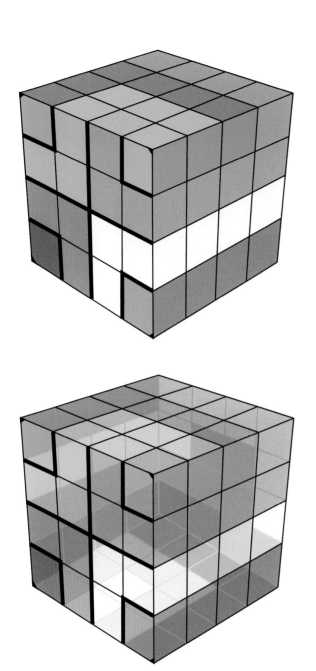

2.53 The classical labyrinth mapped onto a cube

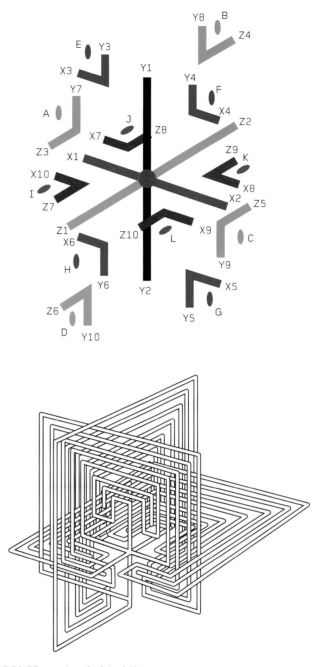

2.54 3D mapping of a labyrinth

The labyrinthine key logic can be extended into 3D in many ways where the interconnecting pathways can connect in all three dimensions, but the logic requires the addition of boundary walls that follow three-dimensional channels.

Fig. 2.54 shows an x, y, z key with basic connections that bear a curious similarity to the Chartres labyrinth. The visualization is flattened, but a true 3D model of it would show paths extending along each of the 3D axes.

The ability to visualize labyrinthine pathways in 3D might present a bit of a challenge; however, 3D modelling software should make the task easier.

2.55 Göbekli Tepe, Turkey (ancient Mesopotamia), 9000 BCE

NEOLITHIC ASTRONOMY AND TIMEKEEPING

As much as labyrinthine logic represents an early exploration into the path logic of two-dimensional space, it is only a part of the human disposition to find or create patterns. Drawing two-dimensional images of circles, spirals and zigzags is all part of the same drive.

Predicting the cycles of the seasons would have been critical for cultures whose survival depended on farming. Anyone looking at the motions of the sun, moon and stars across the sky would have noticed that the celestial bodies followed paths that moved in cyclical patterns – that appeared to match, in some way, the seasonal cycles. Imagine then the challenge of finding enough patterns in the motions to reliably predict when to plant crops, when rivers might flood and when winter might set in.

At the top of a mountain ridge in southeastern Turkey there is a perfect spot for observing the night sky. In 1994, excavations revealed a Neolithic stone circle complex on the ridge, named Göbekli Tepe (fig. 2.55). The site has been carbon-dated to around 9000 BCE, predating the famous Stonehenge site by about 6,500 years. The stone circles of Göbekli Tepe are composed of T-shaped monoliths surrounded by circular stone walls that are inset into the ground. The monoliths are positioned with an outer ring at one height and two higher monoliths in the centre. The flat tops of those of the outer ring, as well as their positioning, suggest that they supported five or six flat platforms, leaving the central T-monoliths standing proud of them, possibly supporting an even higher platform. Although the site's function has yet to be unravelled, if this is a correct assumption then the platforms might well have served an astronomical function.

Standing stones or wooden poles, positioned in an unobstructed area, provide a simple way of tracking seasonal time. The shortest shadows fall at midday and lengthen as the year progresses towards the winter solstice. The shortest shadows cast by a 6 m (20 ft) standing stone at Stonehenge, England, will extend by about 20 m (65 ft) and at the pyramids of Giza, Egypt, by about 7.5 m (25 ft) during the course of a year: the difference is a function of latitude. Placing a stone at the end point of these shortest shadows, for example one every seven days during the course of a year, will reveal a repeating annual pattern of (in our example) 26 stone positions lying along a north–south line. Recording the sun's shadows in this way will create a reliable solar-year timekeeper – and within a few years it would be easy to identify the stones that correspond with important events in the seasonal

2.56 Neolithic yearly timekeeper

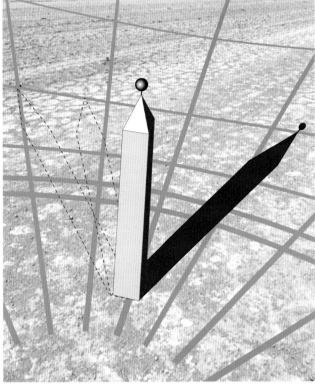

2.57 Daily and yearly shadow obelisk

calendar, such as the equinoxes, the winter and summer solstices, seasonal floods, and even optimum planting and harvesting times.

Tracing a line that follows the end points of the shadows cast by a monolith during the course of one day will reveal a curved path for the shadows of that day. Repeating the process for every day, or selected days, of the year will reveal a series of curved paths that stretch out in the same way as the solar-year stones, and the paths can be divided to create a daytime solar clock.

Daily shadow paths stretch out, one from another, the further they are from the equator. At the equator the equinox path passes directly over the shadow source and the daily paths are at their closest to each other. Shadow paths at different latitudes are shown in fig. 2.58: the paths at the latitude of Stonehenge, approximately 51°, are more stretched out than the paths at latitude 0°.

Shadow timekeepers keep solar time, for both a day and a year, but solar timekeepers are not linear, meaning that they do not measure time in equal units. The Earth follows an ellipse and speeds up a little when it is closer to the sun. Also, its 23.4° axial tilt means that positions on the Earth's surface move closer to or further from the sun over the course of an orbit. Because of this, solar timekeepers do not exactly correspond with linear timekeepers (clocks). In fact, the deviation between linear time and solar time is as much as 16 minutes. For ancient cultures the difference would probably not have been significant, but as the means to develop linear timekeepers were developed, such as water or mechanical clocks, the discrepancies would have become evident.

If we take photographs of the sun from a fixed position at exactly the same linear time of day for a whole year, we will see how the Earth's solar time, with its orbital and rotational variables, differs from linear time. The sun's positions are not in sync with a linear progression but differ from it, with the differences tracing a figure-of-eight path. A similar yearly path can be traced with shadows using a fixed linear time. This path, known as an analemma (see fig. 2.60), is significant in that it highlights the incompatibility of linear measurement (seconds, minutes and hours) with the variables of solar timekeepers and other natural cycles and dimensions. The analemma effectively demonstrates why the sun is not always on the north–south line at 12.00 linear time; in fact, owing to time zones and orbital variables, it rarely is. This does not negate the fact that the shortest shadows of any day correspond with a position of the sun on the north–south line, in accordance with solar time.

Undoubtedly we need an objective linear time basis for comparing such things as orbital paths and the motions of planetary bodies, and for navigational plots, but we also need to remember that our measuring systems are incompatible with the things we are measuring, where nothing is in fact linear or spaced in equal increments.

Another way in which ancient cultures tracked time may have been to use the moon. Besides the 29.5 day synodic (moon-phase) cycle, it is possible to predict the time of the seasons by observing the angle of the moon's crescent. The width of the moon's shadow may have been used to indicate the time of moonset, and by tracking the moon's progress across the sky it may also have served as a nighttime clock.

Possible Neolithic means to keep track of small increments of time might have included beating rhythms on a drum or the use of water clocks. The earliest-known water clock was found in ancient Egypt in the tomb of Amenhotep I and dated around 1500 BCE.

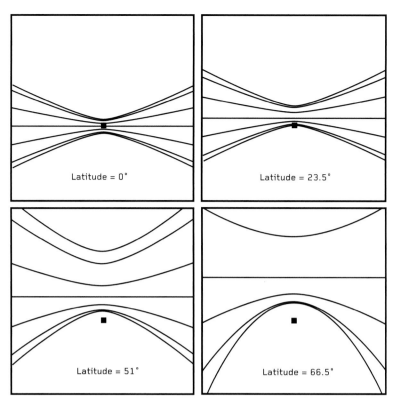

2.58 Shadow lines by latitude

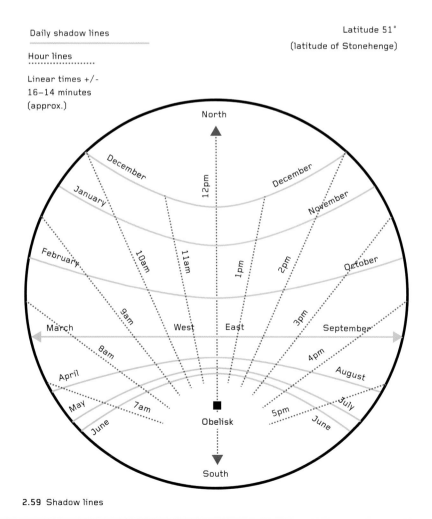

2.59 Shadow lines

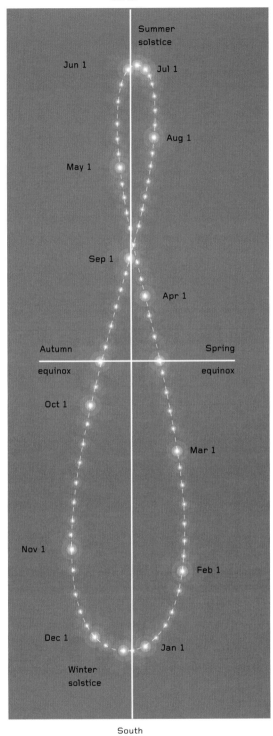

Latitude 23.5°

North

Summer
solstice

Jun 1   Jul 1

Aug 1

May 1

Sep 1

Apr 1

Autumn   Spring

equinox   equinox

Oct 1

Mar 1

Nov 1

Feb 1

Dec 1

Jan 1

Winter
solstice

South

Azimuth	4.4°	3.8°
Time variance	16 min	14 min

2.60 The analemma

Time of year by the angle of the moon's crescent at the equator. In June the horns of the crescent are horizontal. The tilt of the crescent moon varies based on latitude.

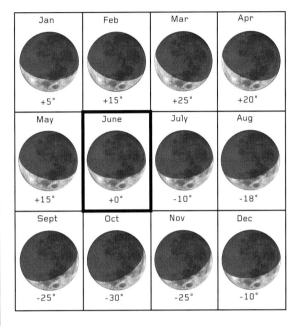

Jan	Feb	Mar	Apr
+5°	+15°	+25°	+20°
May	June	July	Aug
+15°	+0°	-10°	-18°
Sept	Oct	Nov	Dec
-25°	-30°	-25°	-10°

Moon sets about three hours after sunset

Moon sets about six hours after sunset

Moon sets about four hours after sunset

Moon sets about eight hours after sunset

2.61 The moon as a timekeeper

NEOLITHIC ARCHITECTURE

The simplicity and largely two-dimensional nature of Neolithic logic is echoed in the architectural structures of the time. Surviving Neolithic structures, conceptually, are not much more than 2D extrusions into 3D space with a few more or less accidental solids thrown in. Many Neolithic structures are round with circular rings, or mounds, ditches and platforms, and these can be found throughout Europe and the Middle East from about 9000 BCE. Other structures follow straight lines, such as the banks known as cursuses in Britain, and lines of standing stones, for example at Carnac in northern France.

Many Neolithic architectural structures are thought to have been built for ritualistic as well as for astronomical purposes, with alignments to mark the positions of the equinoxes and the solstices. The Nabta Playa stones in the Nubian Desert were erected 6,000–7,000 years ago with north–south and east–west alignments and with a pair of slabs positioned to align with the summer solstice. Stonehenge, constructed some 4,000–5,000 years ago in England (see fig. 2.62), is more impressive, and during its earliest phases had alignments similar to those of the Nabta stones. During this early period the large inner stones had not been erected and alignments were probably with stones that stood in the so-called Aubrey Holes and with the North and South Barrow stones, the Avenue and the two Station Stones (see fig. 2.63). Later construction phases added, and later moved, the bluestones and then the trilithon and outer sarsen stones (these are the big stones with horizontal lintels). Although there are various celestial alignments, considering Stonehenge as a major astronomical machine is undermined by the fact that there are much easier ways to observe the heavens without building such a large structure, such as using standing stones or simple stone alignments.

2.62 Stonehenge, England, 3000–2000 BCE

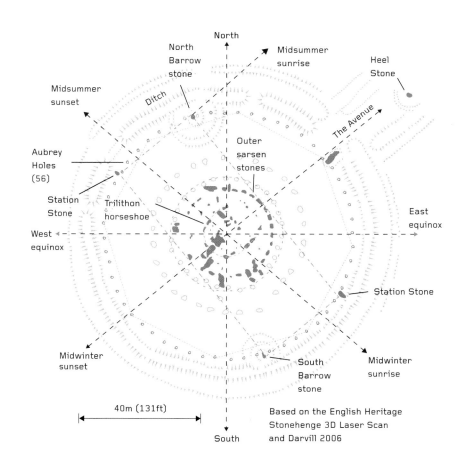

2.63 Stonehenge alignments

Silbury Hill, England (c.2400–2300 BCE), is a massive artificial mound about 40 m (130 ft) high with a diameter of approximately 167 m (550 ft) (see fig. 2.64). The hill's inner structure is made up of six concentric terraces each supported by a limestone wall. Four of the terraces were filled in with earth to create an even slope of approximately 27°, leaving one exposed terrace and a flat top about 5 m (17 ft) above the fifth terrace. The mound itself is surrounded by an inner and outer ditch that might have served as some sort of moat system. There is some evidence of celestial alignment: the 27° slope of the mound corresponds with the morning and evening paths of the sun on 19 June, close to the summer solstice; the top platform of the mound is off-centre towards the west, which is also the direction of an extension of the outer ditch, and this suggests an equinox alignment. A north–south alignment is also ideal for observing the east–west paths of the sun and the moon.

The Newgrange mound and passage tomb in County Meath, Ireland (c. 3200 BCE), is 13.5 m (45 ft) high with a diameter of 85 m (280 ft) (see fig. 2.65). A carved entrance stone (see fig. 2.3), lies across the entry to a 19 m-long (63 ft) passage chamber aligned with the rising sun at the winter solstice. Surrounding the tomb are 97 large megalithic stones, and it is possible that before the mound was constructed the position of the tomb aligned with two of the kerbstones to indicate the positions of the winter solstice sunset and the summer solstice sunrise on the horizon.

2.64 Silbury Hill, Avebury, England, c.2400–2300 BCE

2.65 Newgrange, County Meath, Ireland, 3200 BCE

03. THE RIVER CULTURES

THE INDUS, NILE, YELLOW AND EUPHRATES RIVERS

'Mathematics is the language in which the gods speak to people.'
PLATO, C.427 BCE

3.1 The pyramid complex at Giza, Egypt, c.2560–2500 BCE

The geometries of the river valley cultures were developed to measure, to survey, to build, and to predict the seasons. Driving forces were the determination of flood cycles, taxation, and the control and management of societies. In many cases logic was replaced by mystical ritual or kept secret by a privileged few.

The end of the Neolithic period between 4500 and 2000 BCE was heralded by the development of new types of metallurgy, domesticated livestock, and the use of wild and domestic crops. These new technological developments supported larger social groups that ultimately founded the 'river cultures' – all of which were dependent on water cycles and the availability of fertile land. Given the advantages of combining new agricultural methods with fairly reliable water and irrigation cycles, major river valleys became a highly desirable area to occupy – and this led to an incessant cycle of wars of occupation and, correspondingly, the rise and fall of numerous empires, dynasties, kingdoms and city-states.

Historically the most significant river cultures were those of the Indus (South Asia), the Nile (Egypt), the Euphrates–Tigris (Mesopotamia) and the Yellow River (China), and on the banks of these rivers arose the first civilizations and empires. With them came control and taxation – both of which were driving forces of early mathematics.

THE FOUR MAJOR RIVER CULTURES

The Indo-Gangetic, or Indus-Ganga, plain was home to civilizations from about 3300 BCE, more than a thousand years before civilizations arose in China. The first major civilization has been called the Harappan, after its chief city, Harappa; the second major city of the time was the citadel Mohenjo-daro. Around 1750 BCE, the Harappan civilization began to decline, possibly because nomadic Aryan invaders from Central Asia started to occupy the Indus Valley, or perhaps for climate reasons. From about 1700 BCE to 700 BCE various kingdoms occupied the land and adopted new traditions. By about the 5th century BCE Hinduism and Buddhism emerged to the southeast of the Indus-Ganga plain

and new civilizations arose, bringing a renewal of artistic and architectural achievement. The so called Golden Age starts with the Maurya Empire (322–185 BCE), and reaches its zenith in the Gupta Empire (320–520 CE).

The ancient Egyptian dynasties flourished along the river Nile from 3100 BCE to around 500 BCE, after which time the Egyptian civilization started to lose continuity, with invasions by the Persians, Alexander the Great, the Ptolemies (Greeks) and the Romans.

The Yellow and Yangtze rivers also saw many Chinese dynasties come and go from the 16th century BCE right up to the 20th century CE, including the Shang, Western Zhou, Qin, Han, Tang, Ming and Qing. In general, the nomadic tribes that periodically invaded and occupied China were assimilated into local Chinese cultures, leading to a cultural continuity.

The area known as Mesopotamia, formed by the Tigris–Euphrates river system and considered one of the cradles of civilization, was the site of many empires from around 3000 BCE to the arrival of Alexander the Great in 334 BCE, including the Akkadian, Neo-Sumerian, Babylonian, Assyrian and Achaemenid (Persian).

This summary of the rise and fall of river cultures indicates just how complicated it is to try to unravel a clear path of logical development. However, it is possible to look at some of the developments of numeracy and geometry in these cultures, to consider the differences – and similarities – between them, and to speculate about what these might mean.

All of the river cultures had to create numeric and geometric systems to predict the seasons, to navigate, to count, to survey land and crops and to build. Whereas the Indus, Euphrates and Nile cultures benefited from the exchange of concepts among one another, the Yellow and Yangtze river cultures were generally more isolated. So there are many foundational similarities between the numeric and geometric systems of the South Asian and Middle Eastern civilizations as a result of trade and communication between 3000 BCE and 1500 BCE, and major differences between them and Chinese systems.

THE RISE OF NUMERACY

Initially people kept track of things by looking for correspondences – for example, by comparing the number of fingers on a hand with a number of sheep. Problems arose when there were more than ten sheep. A solution to this problem was to count in groups where some item, or symbol, was used to represent, say, ten sheep – this might be a stone, a knot in a length of rope or an etched cross. Practicality would favour etched marks for counting and the development of words to correspond with the marks. Custom or culture would then determine the size of the groups – whether to count in groups of two (binary), five, ten (decimal), 12, 20, 60 (sexagesimal), and so on. The first evidence of counting in groups, though not necessarily number bases, can be seen in the markings on a 20,000-year-old bone found in the Ishango area of the Congo, near the headwaters of the Nile. The bone is marked in columns, with the left column appearing to perform the following addition: 19 + 17 + 13 + 11 = 60. The central column adds 7 + 5 + 5 (?) + 1 + 9 + 8 + 4 + 6 + 3 = 48, and the right column 9 + 19 + 21 + 11 = 60. As evidence for the use of number bases this is tenuous, but it is suggestive that the totals are multiples of 12.

Transition from numbers to geometry

When we count a number of objects our number sequences follow a linear progression: 1, 2, 3, 4… The correspondence is immediately apparent. Once we need to measure areas – which arose out of the need to estimate crop sizes, floor spaces and so on – then something unexpected happens: linear sequences of side lengths generate the area progression 1, 4, 9, 16, 25… The need to compare and standardize the measuring of weights and volumes generated something even more surprising, as linear sequences of side lengths generated the cubic progression 1, 8, 27, 64, 125…

It must have seemed strange, at the time of discovery, that doubling the side length of a field increased its estimated crop size by a factor of four. Similarly, the fact that doubling the side length of a cube of stone increased its weight eight times must have seemed quite

amazing. However, at least for the initiated, the sequences would have become predictable.

The need to build and to navigate led to the invention of triangles, particularly right-angled triangles, and with them new sequences were generated such as (3, 4, 5), (5, 12, 13), (7, 24, 25) and (8, 15, 17); and these too would have become predictable for those that became responsible for managing numbers – the numerologists, the geometricians, the priests. We can imagine the numeric and geometric managers of a culture being given the task of predicting the seasons, flood cycles, wet and dry periods – something essential for a civilization. Looking skyward they would most likely have expected something as predictable as weights and measures. After all, there seemed to be cycles of the moon and stars; the sun moved across the sky daily; even the seasons seemed to cycle in a regular fashion. We can further imagine their confusion when they found that the heavens did not behave in a simple numeric clockwork fashion.

Calendar development The moon follows an elliptical path as it orbits the Earth and this affects the apparent size of the full moon. The moon also speeds up a bit when its elliptical orbit brings it closer to the Earth. The situation is made more complex by the fact that the Earth's orbit around the sun is also elliptical and, as the cyclical appearance of the full moon is dependent on the position of the sun relative to the Earth, there are cycles upon cycles. At the simplest level we can approximate the time for two lunar months as 59 days, but this is only roughly accurate. Measuring the time of the moon's orbit in ancient times was done either by counting the approximately 27 days required for the moon to return to the same position against a star pattern (sidereal month) or by counting the approximately 30 days between one new moon and another (synodic month). There is an approximate concurrence of orbits between the solar and lunar cycles of 19 years: approximately 19 solar years corresponds with 235 synodic months – the Metonic cycle. The cycle was used in the Babylonian calendar, ancient Chinese calendar systems, and the

medieval computus (the calculation of the date of Easter). It still regulates the 19-year cycle of intercalary months of the Hebrew calendar.

Furthermore, the Earth's axis is tilted in relation to the plane of its orbit around the sun, and the axis wobbles. Following a 26,000-year cycle, the axial wobble changes the direction that the poles face. The North Pole currently points towards the star Polaris but thanks to the precession of the equinoxes (the wobble), the pole star in 3000 BCE was the faint star Thuban, in the constellation of Draco. In 1000 BCE the pole star was Beta Ursae Minoris, but was so faint that in 320 BCE the Greek navigator Pytheas described the celestial pole as being devoid of stars.

We know today that the Earth and its sister planets orbit the sun and that the moon orbits the Earth, but in ancient times this was not known – so the variations would have appeared quite bewildering. At least the star patterns appeared to stay in fixed positions in relation to each other, but there were some wandering stars – now known to be planets – that appeared to follow odd paths across the constellations and seemed at times to go backwards.

The river cultures needed a reliable means to predict seasonal changes, as their civilizations depended on the reliability of their forecasts. Predicting seasons probably started with observing the cycles of the moon and the recognition that roughly 12 cycles of the moon corresponded to the full cycle of seasons. Further observations would have revealed that the angular positions on the horizon of the rising and setting stars, moon and sun also cycled with the seasons. Observers would have noticed that the angle of the sun from the vertical (the zenith) also cycled from a minimum to a maximum as the seasons progressed, and the use of shadow timekeepers would have developed to create a solar-year time line (see p.53).

It is evident that initial assumptions were made about seasonal cycles based on linear and predictable number sequences. In the first case the correspondence of 12 lunar phases with a seasonal year would have been used to predict the events of a solar year, but then rejected as lunar cycles were found to be out of phase with seasonal and solar cycles. At a latitude of 37° the angle between sunrise and sunset at the summer solstice, from a fixed point looking at the horizon, totals 120°; at a latitude of 30.5° the angle is 125°. Using such knowledge, sighting stones placed in the ground in an environment where the horizon could be seen would allow observers to fairly accurately predict the solstices, and similarly the equinoxes.

Shadows from the same sighting stones would also serve as solar-year timekeepers. Keeping a day tally of the solar cycle, according to the angular positions of the sunrise and sunset, as well as with midday solar shadow positions, would have indicated the number of days in a solar year at about 365, creating a basis for mapping out the seasonal cycles.

Any calendars based only on lunar cycles – on 360 days in the year – would require an additional month to be added every six years to make the orbits roughly correspond with seasonal and solar cycles. Culturally, much would depend on the celestial events that were considered to be the most relevant to calculating time, whether the stars, sun or moon. Similarly, the number of resets to calendars to compensate for errors would have depended on cultural establishments and on those who would be given the responsibility to recalibrate calendars to correspond to star, solar and lunar positions. Once seasonal, solar or star cycles were reasonably understood then lunar cycles could have been used in conjunction with solar cycles – not to predict a full seasonal year but to provide fairly reliable time frames from solstice or equinox positions.

The 30-day lunar assumption There are many conventions regarding numbers and many began in civilizations located at or near latitude 37°, where the summer solstice sunrise–sunset angle of 120° would support concepts of harmony within the universe, in this case simple whole number ratios. The ancients would not think in terms of 120° but in terms of divisions of a circle, in this case a third; 90° was a one-quarter division. The 30-day lunar cycle was a one-twelfth division of a 360-day annual cycle. Geometrically six equal-sized circles exactly fit around one of the same size. We see the legacy of

these observations today in the 360° of a circle, in the use of base 60 in Babylonian mathematics, and in the use of 90° in right triangles.

The way in which cultures prioritized the celestial timekeepers, and then the way they managed and further explored the discrepancies of celestial events, shaped much of what was to follow – differentiating one culture from another, or, in some cases aligning them. The correspondences between linear, square, cubic and circular measurements and the divisions of 360° were a defining influence on the nature of the geometries of the later dynasties of the Egyptians and the Chinese and the development of Vedic and Pythagorean mathematics. (It may be significant that the ancient city of Antep (now Gaziantep) lies at a latitude of 37° and is close to the Euphrates, as does Jinan, on the Yellow River, occupied continuously for more than 4,000 years.)

Practicalities of the early river cultures
A group within the higher echelons of river civilizations probably protected a community's system of weights and measures and, in a sense, it also controlled time. This group most likely announced the beginning of the lunar and solar cycles and the seasons – with a few days added regularly to compensate for the yearly lack of concurrence between lunar and solar orbits. For finer divisions in time the positions of the sun rather than the moon would have been used, and maybe measured with sundials, or even types of water clock. At night, under clear skies, the stars rotating around the pole star, Thuban, would have given fairly precise nighttime increments. All of this would have required a level of social organization to ensure reliable time management. Methods of keeping records ranged from stacking or aligning stones to marking clay tablets or drawing star charts on tomb walls or on papyrus. Breaks in civilization usually resulted in rituals of some sort created to preserve knowledge, although in many cases rituals lost their meaning. The means to preserve or ritualize knowledge strongly influenced the development of geometry in the later river cultures – and consequently much that was to follow them.

'The marvellous and incredible regularity of the stars in their eternal and unvarying courses, shows that they have divine power and intelligence.'
MARCUS TULLIUS CICERO
(106–43 BCE)

3.2 Harappan clay seal stamps with script

THE INDUS-GANGA PLAIN

THE INDUS VALLEY CIVILIZATION

Archaeological finds in the Indus Valley have shown that the Harappan culture (c.3300–c.1700 BCE) was highly civilized for its time, with well-established city layouts, plumbing, bathhouses and public buildings. The Harappans developed a beautifully formalized pictographic script, which remains undeciphered (see fig. 3.2), and a formal weights and measures system. Examples of weights in the shape of cubes, hexahedra, barrels, cones and cylinders survive in weight ratios, one with another, of 1, 2, 4, 8, 16, 32, 64.

Some of the surviving Harappan city foundations indicate many buildings that were square or rectangular with evidence of ratios of 1:1; 1:2; 1:3; 2:3; and 1:3:5. The main city bath measures approximately 7.3 x 12 x 2.5 m (24 x 40 x 8 ft). Circles were used in pot decorations, in the circular foundations of the city, for wells and granaries, and for wheels (as seen on surviving toy

chariots and carts). Designs on pottery fragments have geometric patterns of various sorts, including zigzags, triangles, squares and intersecting circles. Harappan geometry appears to be primarily rectilinear and circular – and their numerology suggests the deliberate use of specific ratios and numeric bases. There is evidence of circle-drawing instruments from as early as 2500 BCE. Excavations at Harappa, Mohenjo-daro and other sites of the Indus Valley civilization have uncovered evidence of the use of 'practical mathematics' – for example bricks manufactured with dimensions in the proportion of 4:2:1, considered favourable for the stability of a brick structure.

The inhabitants of Indus Valley towns and cities also tried to standardize measurements of length to a high degree of accuracy. They designed a ruler – the Mohenjo-daro ruler – whose unit of length, approximately 3.4 cm (1 $\frac{3}{10}$ in), was divided into ten equal parts. Bricks manufactured in ancient Mohenjo-daro often had dimensions

that were integral multiples of the ruler's unit of length.

The foundations of the Harappan buildings so far excavated are only roughly rectangular, so the use of specific ratios for their proportions is questionable. The use of intersecting circle designs is suggestive of a more refined geometrical knowledge, but there is no evidence that they had anything systematic other than simple rectangular, square and, possibly, circular grids. If there were a geometric description for this early Indus Valley civilization then maybe it would be 'rectilinear with the beginnings of numerology and the use of ratios'.

For the Harappan civilization to have survived and flourished there must have been a knowledge of solar, lunar and celestial cycles, with ideas similar to those of the early Egyptians and Babylonians, thanks to trade and to the comparable circumstances of their civilizations. However, except for the remains of a few fire altars, the only evidence that we have of a true

A

B

C

D

knowledge of astronomical events comes from the much later Vedic scriptures (see p.66).

Harappan patterns Harappan rock carvings and pottery fragments have been dated to around 2500 BCE and do provide us with some sense of Harappan geometries.

Patterns A and B in fig. 3.3 are derived from Harappan rock carvings and show tessellating spiral patterns very similar to those created by other late Neolithic cultures. Patterns C and D in fig. 3.3, and patterns E, F, G and H in figs 3.4 to 3.7 (see next page), are all derived from pottery fragments and elaborated by the author. The geometry of the patterns was likely worked out prior to the patterns being copied onto clay pots. The original geometric constructions were also probably more precise than the copies, based on the shapes and symmetries used, as well as on the numeric traditions of the culture.

Fragment E (see fig. 3.4) was found in Chanhu-daro, Pakistan, and is now in the Brooklyn Museum, New York. The fragment is painted with a circular pattern, with circles arranged within a square symmetry. From the fragment it looks as if the design unit repeats six times around the pot. Designs F, G and H are of a similar age to E (c.2500 BCE). Design F appears to have been based on a 6 x 6 square grid and design G on a 15 x 15 square grid. Design H is based on an equilateral triangle and may have been constructed by dividing the side of the equilateral triangle into 17 equal parts for the verticals and by dividing the inner triangle into 5.5 segments if we count the inner triangle.

3.3 Harappan rock patterns, Indus Valley

E

F

3.4 Harappan pottery design construction, Indus Valley

3.5 Harappan pottery design construction, Indus Valley

G

H

3.6 Harappan pottery design construction, Indus Valley

3.7 Harappan pottery design construction, Indus Valley

3.8 Sri Yantra painted on paper, Rajasthan, India, 1700

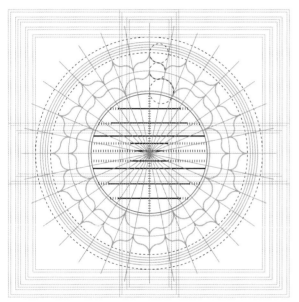

3.9 Sri Yantra Vedic construction

THE VEDIC ERA

After the decline of the Harappan civilization around 1700 BCE there were hundreds of years of tribal conflict in the region, and during this time knowledge was transmitted orally and through ritual. Harappan knowledge became the domain of priests and much was maintained only through chants and ceremonial practices. The Vedic era is characterized by the composing of the Vedas, the oldest scriptures of Hinduism, originally passed down orally. The Rigveda, the earliest of the Vedas, may have been composed as early as 1700 BCE. The earliest renderings of the Rigveda in script form (Vedic Sanskrit) were in about 1500 BCE.

The Sri Yantra The contemplative Hindu Sri Yantra mandala (spiritual and religious diagram representing the universe) may have been designed as long ago as 1700 BCE. There are many design variations; the drawing shown in fig. 3.8 was derived from a Sri Yantra painted on paper and found in Rajasthan, India, dated 1700. The corners of the two primary triangles touch 15° marks on the surrounding circle. Equilateral triangles are then drawn to align with the primary triangle intersection points, creating new intersection points that are used to shape the remaining triangles. The design has nine interlocking triangles that create 43 triangular intersections.

The reader might like to count the total number of triangles in the design.

A second method of constructing a Sri Yantra is based on whole numbers and is precise (fig. 3.9). The vertical diameter of the circle surrounding the triangles is divided into 48 parts and the horizontal lines of the triangles are spaced down this diameter 6 parts, 6 parts, 5 parts, 3 parts, 3 parts, 4 parts, 3 parts, 6 parts, 6 parts, 6 parts. The length of the horizontal lines is reduced left and right from the surrounding circle by 3, 5, 0, 16, 18, 16, 0, 4 and 3 parts. The apexes of the triangles touch the bases of the other triangles as shown. The outer three rings are spaced in 5

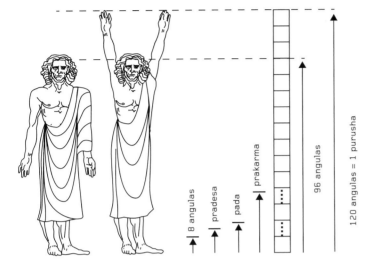

Calculating area based on
the dimensions of a particular human
1 angula = finger width = approx. 20mm (3/4in)

8 angulas

pradesa

pada

prakarma

96 angulas

120 angulas = 1 purusha

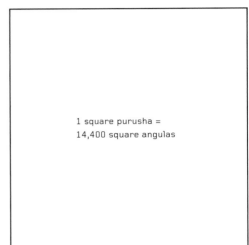

Units
1 pradesa = 12 angulas; 1 pancomi = 24 angulas
1 pada = 15 angulas; 1 prakrama = 2 padas
1 purusha = 5 aratnis = 120 angulas

1 square purusha =
14,400 square angulas

3.10 Indus Valley Vedic units of measurement

parts, and the outer wall in 5, 10 and 5 parts. Even the curvature of the petals is determined by circles that divide equally onto the 16 and 8 symmetries.

For some, perceiving the Sri Yantra is a form of worship of the goddess Tripura Sundari (she who is beautiful, she who plays, she who reveals illusion). The outer walls with four openings are said to represent the Earth; the three rings the mind, intelligence and soul; the 16 lotus petals the energies of the body; the eight lotus petals the soul or essence of the body. The triangles facing up represent masculine (heaven) drives (Shiva) and the five triangles facing down feminine (the body) drives (Shakti). There are many levels by which the Sri Yantra can be approached – symbolism, numerology, perception, logic. To the geometer there will seem to be imperfections in the ways the lines intersect, but the intersections are precise and intentional. As one begins to perceive the Sri Yantra the forms may start to become three-dimensional – and all the forms may start to interact one with another. As with many other things associated with the Vedas, the Sri Yantra is a puzzle of sorts,

or even a memory exercise, combining numbers with Sanskrit root meanings, symbolism and geometric structure.

Vedic measuring systems Featured in the Vedas are rules relating to the construction of fire altars, whose origins probably started with Harappan practices of counting stones and arranging them in patterns to keep a daily tally of the seasonal progress of the sun, moon and stars. As with many Neolithic and post-Neolithic cultures, Vedic measuring systems were based on human proportions: the width of the finger, the hand, the height of the body from the base of the foot to the middle of the forehead; the height from the base of the foot to the tips of the fingers with arms raised high (fig. 3.10; note the multiples of 8 in the measuring system and consider the association with the number 360). The creation of measurement units from the middle of the forehead might have derived from various beliefs regarding where the 'soul' or 'essence' of an individual resides and where the soul or essence perceives the world, similar to the concept of the

third eye, or inner eye. Whatever the rationale, the basemark of the middle of the forehead was also followed in Egypt and ancient Greece (as evidenced by the work of Vitruvius), and later picked up in the Renaissance, as can be seen in Leonardo's *Vitruvian Man* (see p.210).

Unlike the Greeks and Egyptians, the Vedic cultures, for ritualistic purposes, did not base their proportions on an idealized or 'absolute' man, but relatively, on any man: the individual man that was selected to provide the benchmark proportions for a specific fire altar ritual. This approach is consistent with the Vedic notion of connections between the astronomical, the terrestrial and the physiological, so that every man is seen as a reflection of the greater universe. This relative rather than absolute approach determined the nature of Vedic mathematics and geometry.

Vedic scriptures describe the dimensions of fire altars and the surrounding enclosures in terms of the units of measurement shown in fig. 3.10.

Fire altars Vedic fire altars are generally considered to provide a means for carrying prayers to the highest heavens. The altars in the Prachinavamsa (Old Hall) described in the Vedic scriptures are probably the oldest of the known Indus Valley fire altars and may well be the same as those used during the earlier Harappan civilization. There are in fact three altars in the Prachinavamsa – the altars of the Earth (circular), space (half circle and half square) and the sky (square). According to Vedic traditions the Earth altar is to be surrounded by 21 stones, the space altar by 78 stones, and the sky altar by 261 stones: the total of surrounding stones is 360 – an approximation of the lunar year. The dimensions of the Prachinavamsa altars are given in fig. 3.11. According to the Vedas, the Prachinavamsa altars are to be positioned just below an altar complex, the Mahavedi (see fig. 3.16), with an alignment towards the east, a direction that corresponds to the solar equinoxes but not to lunar cycles, although it would be relatively easy to estimate concurrent phases of the moon during successive solar years.

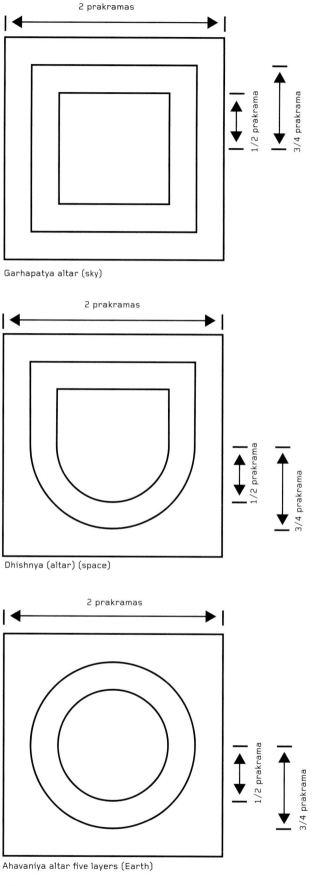

Garhapatya altar (sky)

Dhishnya (altar) (space)

Ahavaniya altar five layers (Earth)

3.11 Prachinavamsa altars

The Uttaravedi altar The Mahavedi is defined as an isosceles trapezium with dimensions that create multiple Pythagorean triples of two types: 9, 12, 15 and 3, 4, 5. Within this enclosure are the Prachinavamsa altars as well as the largest altar, the Uttaravedi (illustrated in fig. 3.16 as a falcon) – an altar that is to be built in five layers, each layer with 200 fire bricks, and a surface area of 7.5 square purushas. The Uttaravedi seems to be able to be of any shape as long as it meets the surface area limitation. If this is the case then the Prachinavamsa can be a square, a circle, a tortoise, a falcon or any other form – current practices favour the falcon. Mathematically, then, the scene is now set for matching areas, for calculating proportions, and for various types of geometrical construction. The practice of area conservation led to a development of Indian geometry that might have inspired some of the proofs described by Euclid (fl. 300 BCE). The Sulba Sutras (800 BCE) and the Dharma Sutra of Pastamba (450–350 BCE) contain many geometric proofs relating to the construction of fire altars – trigonometric constructions, approximations of irrationals including pi, and sine, tan and cosine, ratios, and many proofs relating to calculating equal areas.

As the area of the Uttaravedi is to be 7.5 square purushas, whatever its form, the author has considered various ways in which this might be made to happen, without just counting tiles. To create a square with an area equal to a rectangle of proportion 7.5 purushas x 1 purusha (see fig. 3.12), a method for 'squaring' the rectangle has been used based on a method in the Baudhayana Sulba Sutra (8th–7th centuries BCE): 'A rope stretched along the length of a diagonal (of a rectangle) produces an area which the vertical and horizontal sides make together.' No proof is given in the Baudhayana Sulba Sutra but it anticipates the theorem later credited to Pythagoras (see p.128).

In fig. 3.13 a Euclidian theorem has been applied to geometrically 'square a rectangle'. Both methods are equivalent and give exactly the same result. In the Euclidian drawing, a Vedic approximation of pi of 256/81 has also been used to geometrically 'square the circle'.

Constructing a falcon with an area of 7.5 purushas is a little more complex than 'squaring a rectangle', as we have the

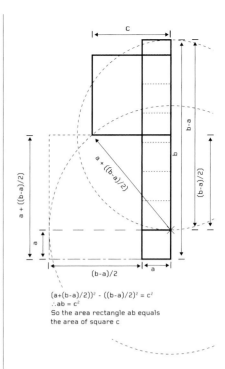

$(a+(b-a)/2))^2 - ((b-a)/2)^2 = c^2$
$\therefore ab = c^2$
So the area rectangle ab equals the area of square c

3.12 Vedic method for squaring the rectangle

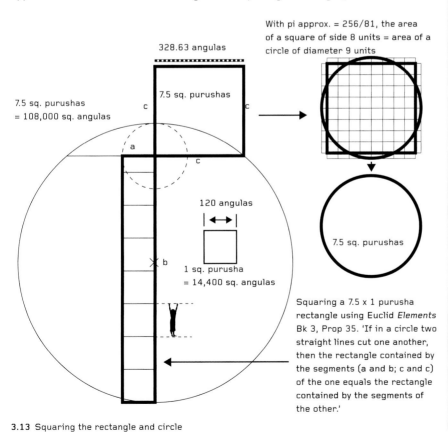

328.63 angulas

7.5 sq. purushas

7.5 sq. purushas = 108,000 sq. angulas

120 angulas

1 sq. purusha = 14,400 sq. angulas

With pi approx. = 256/81, the area of a square of side 8 units = area of a circle of diameter 9 units

7.5 sq. purushas

Squaring a 7.5 x 1 purusha rectangle using Euclid *Elements* Bk 3, Prop 35. 'If in a circle two straight lines cut one another, then the rectangle contained by the segments (a and b; c and c) of the one equals the rectangle contained by the segments of the other.'

3.13 Squaring the rectangle and circle

200-tile limit for each of its five layers. To make things a little easier, the fire bricks that are used are proportioned as whole-number fractions of a square of 2 pada, or a pancomi (see fig. 3.14).

Many variations of falcons can be constructed with the fire bricks, but all must meet the area and brick count limitation. Another limitation is that the brick arrangements must change for the five alternating layers, with both layer types fitting the same profile with the same brick count and area.

Area-preserving transformations and lengths of Vedic altars

The Vedic texts clearly indicate a long-standing tradition of area-preserving transformations of plane figures. We do know that the 'same area' shapes selected were thought to have distinct properties, whether they are circles, squares, falcons or other shapes.

In the Vedas it is stated: 'He who desires heaven is to construct a fire altar in the form of a falcon. A fire altar in the form of a tortoise is to be constructed by one desiring to win the Hindu world of "Brahman" [the Hindu creative principle underlying the world]. Those who wish to destroy existing and future enemies should construct a fire altar in the form of a rhombus.'

The origin of the practice of area conservation might have been fairly mundane and linked to the taxation practices of the Harappan civilization, for re-establishing field and crop boundaries and areas after annual flood cycles and calculating the volume of baked clay bricks where thicknesses were standardized. The basic units of field measurement may well have been proportionately linked to the shapes of the whole number ratio tiles used for the fire altars.

Although we are forced to speculate as to why the 7.5 square purusha area was selected, the number multiples of the altar complex are suggestive (see fig. 3.15). We know that later traditions used

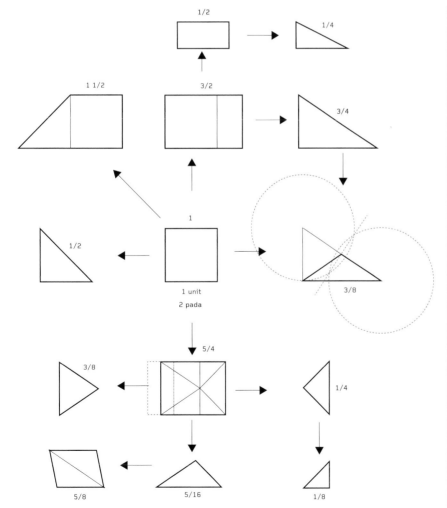

3.14 The Ultravedi sky altar tiles used in the Mahavedi altar ground

Calculations to ensure that a falcon fire altar equals 7.5 square purushas

2 padas = 30 angulas

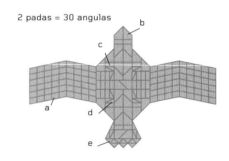

Area to equal 7.5 square purushas.
To be built in five layers each with 200 tiles.
Tile arrangements to alternate per layer.

108 x a	a = 5/8 sq. units
30 x b	b = 1 sq. units
28 x c	c = 1/2 sq. units
24 x d	d = 1/4 sq. units
10 x e	e = 1/4 sq.sq. units

So total area of falcon is
  a = 67 1/2 sq. units
+ b = 30 sq. units
+ c = 14 sq. units
+ d = 6 sq. units
+ e = 2 1/2 sq. units

Total area is 120 sq. units
Unit = 2 padas
Area = 108,000 sq. angulas = 7.5 sq. purushas
Total tiles = 200

3.15 Falcon altar construction

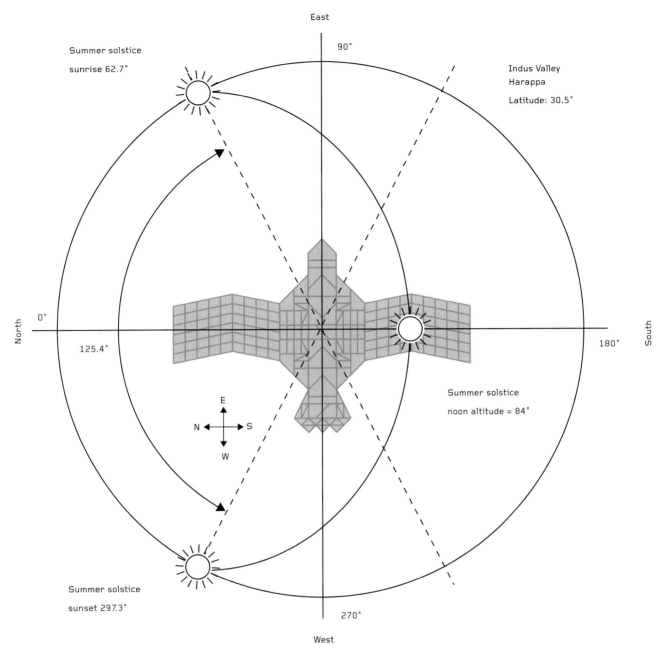

East

90°

Summer solstice

sunrise 62.7°

Indus Valley
Harappa

Latitude: 30.5°

0°

North

125.4°

E

N ←→ S

W

Summer solstice

noon altitude = 84°

South

180°

Summer solstice

sunset 297.3°

270°

West

3.16 Altar alignment

numeric values of Sanskrit letters, in
poems, to memorize number sequences.
So it is possible that the numeric values
of the areas of fire altar stones were
used in the same way (fig. 3.16). The
number 7.5 has multiples of 15, 30, 60,
120 and 360, with possible numeric
links to the lunar calendar. The two side
lengths and the height of the Mahavedi
add up to 90, the stones placed around
the Prachinavamsa altars add up to
360, both of which numbers have lunar
associations. The fact that there are
108,000 square angulas in 7.5 square
purushas may be a coincidental link to
observations of the transit of Venus in

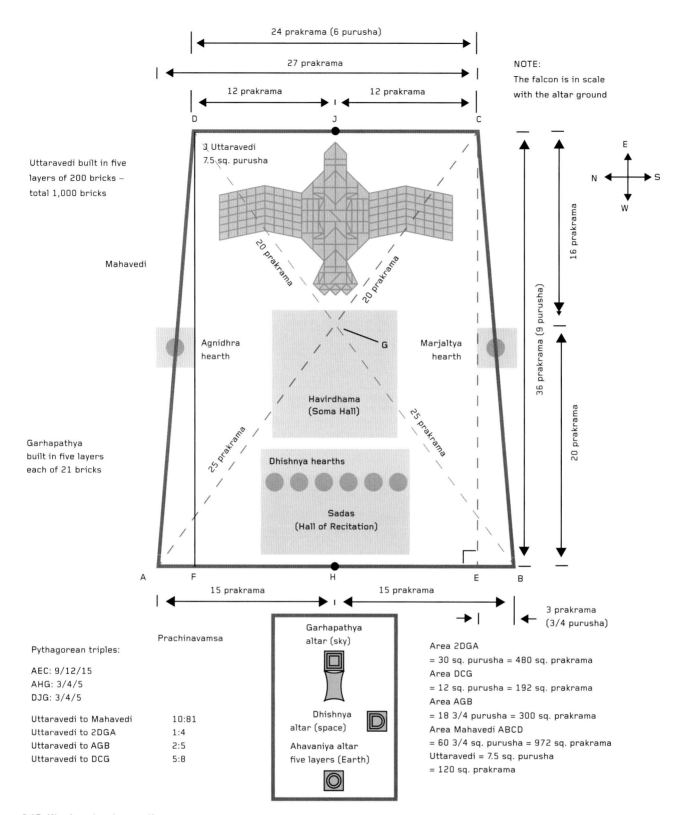

24 prakrama (6 purusha)

27 prakrama

12 prakrama   12 prakrama

D   J   C

NOTE:
The falcon is in scale
with the altar ground

Uttaravedi built in five
layers of 200 bricks –
total 1,000 bricks

J Uttaravedi
7.5 sq. purusha

Mahavedi

20 prakrama   20 prakrama

16 prakrama

36 prakrama (9 purusha)

Agnidhra
hearth

G

Marjaltya
hearth

Havirdhama
(Soma Hall)

25 prakrama   25 prakrama

20 prakrama

Garhapathya
built in five layers
each of 21 bricks

Dhishnya hearths

Sadas
(Hall of Recitation)

25 prakrama

A   F   H   E   B

15 prakrama   15 prakrama

3 prakrama
(3/4 purusha)

Prachinavamsa

Pythagorean triples:

AEC: 9/12/15
AHG: 3/4/5
DJG: 3/4/5

Uttaravedi to Mahavedi   10:81
Uttaravedi to 2DGA   1:4
Uttaravedi to AGB   2:5
Uttaravedi to DCG   5:8

Garhapathya
altar (sky)

Dhishnya
altar (space)

Ahavaniya altar
five layers (Earth)

Area 2DGA
= 30 sq. purusha = 480 sq. prakrama
Area DCG
= 12 sq. purusha = 192 sq. prakrama
Area AGB
= 18 3/4 purusha = 300 sq. prakrama
Area Mahavedi ABCD
= 60 3/4 sq. purusha = 972 sq. prakrama
Uttaravedi = 7.5 sq. purusha
= 120 sq. prakrama

3.17 Altar layout and proportions

the 18th century; and may link to an observation that the distance of the sun, from the Earth, is approximately 108 times the sun's diameter (actually closer to 107), and the sun is roughly 108 times the diameter of the Earth (actually 109). The number 108 appears many times in Hindu traditions: the number of names of God and Goddess, for example.

Therefore, the complex shown in fig. 3.17 presents a sort of number depository that is linked to Vedic scriptures and may have been a ritualized means to preserve knowledge of solar and lunar cycles as well as of calculating field and crop areas for taxation. Unit conversions, ratios and the Pythagorean triples have been added to fig. 3.17, which are precisely derived from the dimensions given in the Vedas. Preserving Pythagorean triples, lengths, areas and ratios would be a means to preserve key numbers and provide a medium for calculating.

THE GUPTA EMPIRE

The Gupta Empire (320–550 CE) covered most of the Indian subcontinent; a time of flourishing arts and sciences, it is described as the Golden Age of India. During this period the Indian numerals were devised that would evolve into Hindu–Arabic numerals and the numbers that we use today. Mathematicians of the Gupta Empire originated the concept of zero and developed the decimal system. A theory of gravity was promulgated by astronomers of the Gupta period.

Aryabhata (476–550 CE) was the first of the great mathematician-astronomers of the classical age of Indian mathematics and astronomy. He put forward the theory that the Earth is spherical in shape, and proved that the Earth revolves around its own axis every day. He believed that the motion of stars was a result of the motion caused by the rotation of the Earth, a theory that contradicted the previously held notion that it is the stars that rotate and not the Earth. He believed that the Earth's orbit was elliptical and not circular. Aryabhata scientifically elucidated the reasons for the occurrence of the solar and lunar eclipse, stating that the lunar eclipse occurs when the moon enters into the shadow of the Earth. He calculated the sidereal year and stated that it takes around 365 days for the Earth to complete one revolution around the sun.

At some point the consonants of Sanskrit were given numerical values. By around 300–400 CE the Bhutasamkhya method of recording numbers, using ordinary words having connotations of numerical values, had developed. The method was popular among Indian astronomers and mathematicians, and Sanskrit was the language used. Concepts, ideas and objects from all facets of Indian cultural life were compiled to generate number-connoting words. The system, in combination with Egyptian hieroglyphics and hieratic script, possibly inspired the abjad system that was later used in Islam (see p.175).

CONCLUSION

The development of geometry on the Indian subcontinent was strongly influenced by practices associated with estimating the seasonal cycles. Many architectural forms and their structure and orientation, including fire altars and temples, reflect this influence through to the Gupta Empire. Indian mathematics was more tailored to application than to abstract theory, distinguishing it from the deductive and axiomatic disciplines of the Greeks and Pythagoreans. The cultures and practices of the Indian subcontinent show much evidence of degradation at different times, owing to disruption from wars and invasions. These disruptions might be used to explain why intelligent astronomical practices often degenerated into ritual or magic. Yet the practice of calculating different shapes with equal areas resulted in geometric proofs that predated many commonly credited to the Greeks. Even the so-called Pythagorean theorem appears in the Baudhayana Sulba Sutra of the 8th century BCE:

(a) The diagonal of a square produces double the area [of the square].
(b) The areas [of the squares] produced separately by the lengths of the breadth of a rectangle together equal the area [of the square] produced by the diagonal.
(c) This is observed in rectangles having sides 3 and 4 [5], 5 and 12 [13], 8 and 15 [17], 7 and 24 [25], 12 and 35 [37], 15 and 36 [39].

'Om, Let me meditate on the great flame, Oh, God of fire, grant me with higher intellect, Oh let the radiant God of Fire illuminate my mind.'
MANTRA TO AGNI, HINDU GOD OF SACRIFICIAL FIRE

THE NILE

To the south of Egypt, and before a new cycle of desertification, at around 9500 BCE what is now central Sudan was a rich farming environment that supported a large population. In 6000 BCE, in the southwestern corner of Egypt, the land was still fertile enough for farmers to grow a variety of cereals, vegetables and fruits, and to herd domesticated animals. The thriving farming communities must have been organized enough to create what appears to have been the world's first celestial sighting device: a megalithic stone circle that predates Stonehenge by some 2,000 years. The circle can still be seen on the Nabta Playa, about 100 km (60 miles) west of Abu Simbel.

By 3400 BCE, owing to climate change, most of Egypt had become as dry as it is today, with scattered settlements around desert oases and little trade or commerce between them. The one major exception was the Nile Valley.

The first farming settlements along the Nile are thought to have been established around 3600 BCE, and the first kingdom of record formed in approximately 3100 BCE. So the transition from small farming communities to an established kingdom happened relatively quickly – probably owing to the narrowness of the Nile Valley corridor and the desertification of the nearby lands.

Critical to the survival of the communities living in the Nile Valley were the river cycles, with an increase in water flow occurring around the summer solstice. A key indicator of the Nile's rise was the heliacal rising of the star Sirius at about the same time (the heliacal rising of a star is the annual occasion when it first becomes visible above the eastern horizon just before sunrise). The Nile generally reached a high point in July and then remained relatively high until the beginning of September, with another high point in October, after which the water levels subsided to their lowest levels between November and May. A predynastic seasonal timekeeper for the Egyptians was the moon, and first calendars were based on lunar cycles, with the year divided into 12 months, and a calculation of 30 days in each month.

As with all the great river civilizations, predicting the river cycles was critical to survival, and in Egypt this resulted in a change from the lunar calendar to a solar one, with a calculation of 365 days in a solar year, and periodic adjustments to compensate for the slight inaccuracy. Despite intermittent periods of unrest and warfare, Egyptian culture enjoyed a remarkable overall continuity between the beginnings of its first high point in the Old Kingdom (2686 BCE) and its final decline in the Late period, ending in 332 BCE. As a result, Egyptian astronomers were able to record celestial events over a period of almost 2,500 years and thereby find patterns in the cycles of the heavens that would otherwise have remained hidden.

NUMBERS AND GEOMETRY

Egyptian number systems developed in a way similar to those of the Indus Valley. Egyptians counted in base ten, and calculated areas with squares and volumes with cubes. The fact that the Nile flooded every year meant that boundary markers between fields were swept away and had to be re-established regularly, necessitating sophisticated surveying techniques – using computations of squares and establishing right angles with Pythagorean triples. Formulas were written in prose form, and surviving evidence such as on the Moscow Mathematical Papyrus (1850 BCE) and the Rhind Mathematical Papyrus (1650 BCE) indicate that many were used, including formulas for establishing the surface areas of triangles, rectangles, circles and hemispheres – with an approximation of pi as 256/81 – and also for finding the volume of a truncated pyramid. The Rhind Papyrus is more detailed than the Moscow Papyrus, with expressions of fractions as sums of unit fractions (no decimals); formulas for various volumes, including volumes of cylinders; and calculations for the slope of a pyramid in terms of ratios for half the base length and the height.

In the Rhind Papyrus there is evidence that Egyptian mathematicians wrestled with problems that remain unsolved to this day. Rhind problem number 50 is that of 'squaring the circle', an effort to find a square of an area equal to that of a given circle. The solution given was that a circle of nine units in diameter is equal in area to a square with a side of eight units – a solution that is only correct if pi equals 256/81, which, unfortunately for the Egyptians, it does not, as pi is irrational (3.141592653589793…)

Celestial and seasonal measuring systems Surviving Egyptian monuments, sculptures and art forms clearly demonstrate high standards of craftsmanship as well as of geometrical construction and control. Similarly, Egyptians had high standards for predicting seasonal and astronomical cycles – standards that were unparalleled up to about 300 BCE.

To keep track of seasonal time the Egyptians recorded the rise and set times and positions of the sun, individual stars and groups of stars over a solar year, and, particularly, of solstice and equinox positions on the horizon. They also kept track of lunar cycles and moon rise and set positions. To confirm annual time the Egyptians were particularly interested in when a single star, such as Sirius, seasonally appeared back above the horizon. For nightly timekeeping, priests observed the stars that rotated around the pole star – stars that never set below the horizon – such as Dubhe, a very bright star that is the northernmost of the pointers in the Big Bear.

Over the millennia the pole star changed thanks to the precession of the equinoxes – the Earth's 26,000-year cyclical wobble (see p.60). Today, the star closest in alignment is Polaris, but in 3000 BCE it was Thuban. The precession is something that the Egyptians would have noticed, given their 2,500 years of observation.

The nightly rotations of the never-setting stars around Thuban would have worked as an accurate nighttime timekeeper, just like the hour hand on a clock. One means, used by the Egyptians, of observing this celestial clock, was to sit a priest on a platform and have him support some sort of measuring frame and a plumb line, with a second priest precisely positioned in relation to the first, so that his view of the first priest was vertically aligned with Thuban and his viewpoint accurately scaled. The second priest would then observe the positions of the never-setting stars as they appeared above the horizon. This method would divide the night

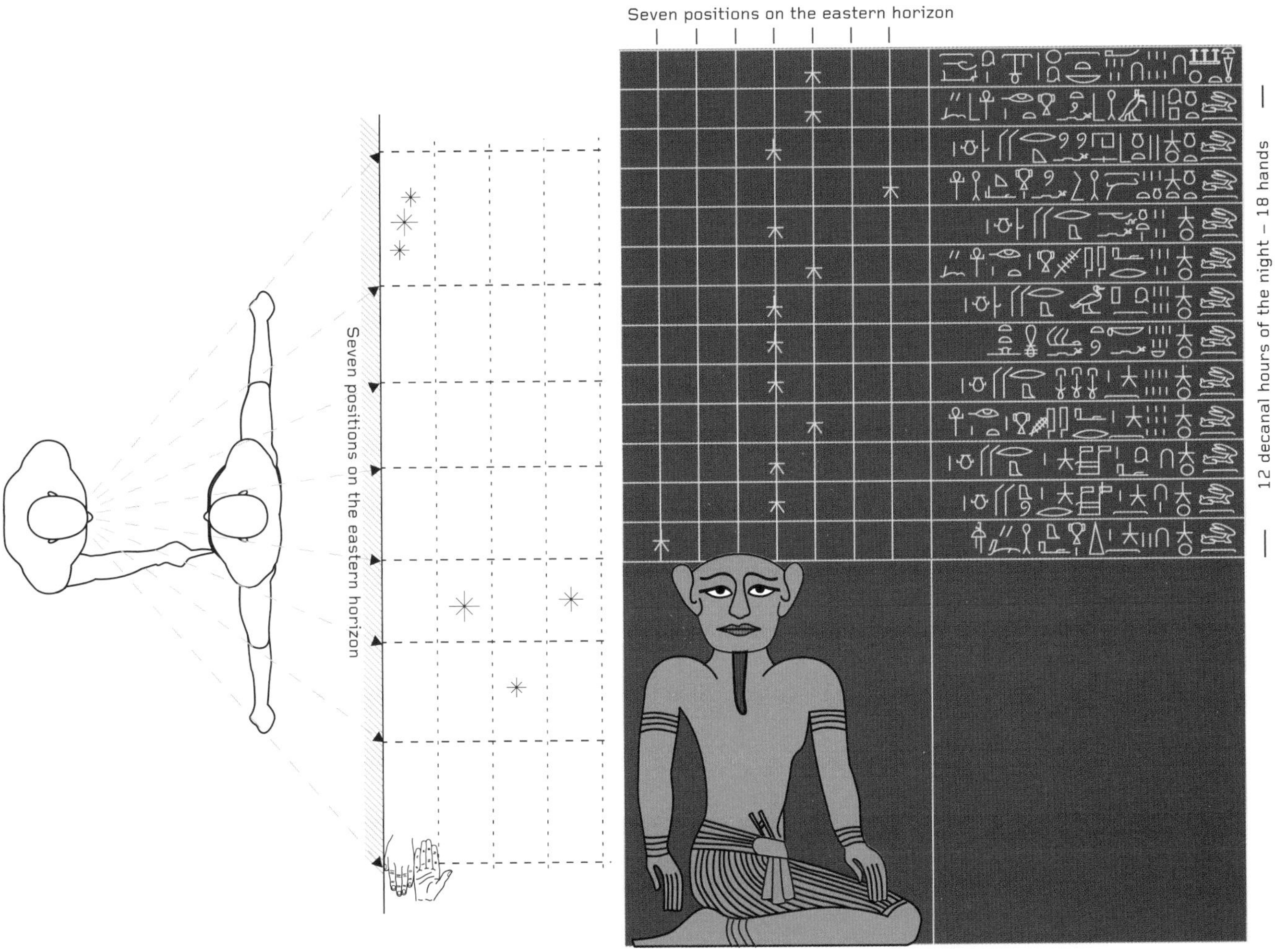

Seven positions on the eastern horizon

12 decanal hours of the night – 18 hands

3.18 Tomb of Ramses IV star grid based on a drawing by Carl Richard Lepsius, 1842 CE

into periods of time – but the times of a star's appearance would change as the Earth moved around the sun. Coordinating the measurements of the Thuban nighttime clock with other means for calculating small time increments – such as water clocks and candle clocks – would have provided a fairly accurate means to measure the nighttime annual progression of the times of a star's appearance. This type of coordination would create a dual function for the Thuban clock, that of a nighttime and an annual timekeeper.

Measuring systems Egyptians mapped nighttime star alignments on to square grids to record star positions, a method that corresponded to their use of height and base ratios of right triangles to determine slope angles, and to their use of grids to proportion 2D and 3D art and architectural forms.

Star grids have been found on ancient Egyptian tomb walls, and on the insides of coffin lids. A number of these star grids appear in the tombs of Ramses IV through IX in the Valley of the Kings dated 1100–1200 BCE. Fig. 3.18 shows a gridded sketch in the tomb of Ramses IV.

The star grid layout typically shows star positions marking the 12 hours of the night as stars rose above the eastern horizon within seven zones (the seven vertical lines of the grid). Stars appear to rotate around the pole star, moving from the eastern horizon to the west, every hour crossing the width of a hand

plus four fingers held at arm's length (about 15°). The Egyptians observed 36 individual stars or small groups of stars known as the decans, with the rising of a decan marking the beginning of a new hour. Stars always rise and set at the same two points on the horizon. But the time of rising and setting changes as the year progresses. A new decan appears above the horizon every ten days – roughly three decans a month and 36 a year. Many star grids feature a kneeling priest, with some indicating that two priests were involved in observations – one to record and the other to divide the eastern sky into seven observation zones, (see fig. 3.18).

Egyptian linear measuring systems were based on idealized human

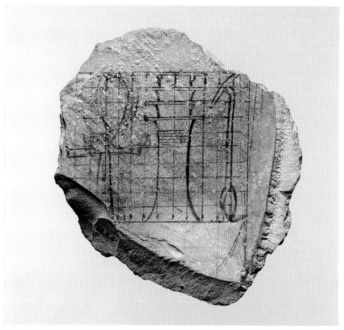

3.19 Artist's gridded sketch, New Kingdom, 18th dynasty, reign of Hatshepsut, c.1479–1458 BCE

proportions: a hand of five fingers, a fist of six fingers, three palms of 12 fingers, a short cubit of six palms, a royal cubit of seven palms, a rod of 100 cubits, and an iteru of 20,000 cubits. The use of grids in Egyptian astronomy, art and architecture based on the proportions of an idealized human body, corresponds well with the later proportionate systems of the Greeks, and as described in the works of Vitruvius.

Early evidence of designers using a proportionate grid system to scale and position images can be seen in various Egyptian artefacts, such as that shown in fig. 3.21. The design grid is that of a simple square tessellation and there is evidence of its use in wall paintings, and on stone reliefs on columns, and walls. Square grids were also used to proportion 2D front, back and side

3.20 Kagemni, vizier of the pharaohs, Saqqara, Egypt, 5th dynasty

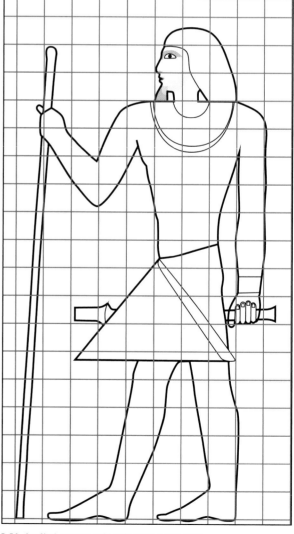

1 Royal Cubit

3.21 Applied square grid using the royal cubit

views of 3D forms. The grids created a consistency of design – a harmony of sorts.

Within square grids, Egyptian designers stylized images of natural forms in an iconographic way, with side-profiled flat views that served to integrate images with the largely pictographic hieroglyphics.

Figs 3.20 and 3.21 show the use of a grid in the construction of an image of Kagemni, vizier of the pharaohs Djedkare Isesi, Unas (5th dynasty) and Teti (6th dynasty) in the 24th century BCE.

The Egyptians were generally not concerned with realism but with simple pictographic and symbolic communication, often distorted to support the pharaonic status quo, as well as to exaggerate the success of ventures and the wealth and social structure of the nation. The fact that huge art and architectural forms were created by humans inspired awe, and their great scale implied that the rulers themselves, who commissioned the forms, were larger than life.

The image of the pharaoh shown in fig. 3.22, with a schematic in fig. 3.23, dates to around 1450 BCE, and is drawn on a flat wooden board coated with a paste made of stone flakes and fragments of broken pottery. The illustration is that of the 18th-dynasty warrior pharaoh Thutmose III and appears to be a preliminary drawing, possibly intended to be transferred to a tomb or temple wall.

Before the 18th dynasty, standing figures were generally laid out on a vertical grid of 18 squares measured to the figure's hairline, and seated figures on one of 14. The horizontal lap of the seated figure accounts for the missing four squares.

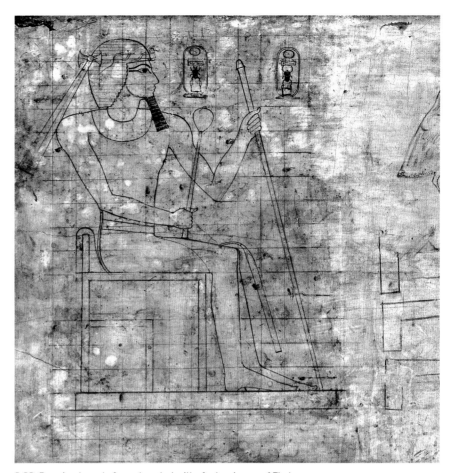

3.22 Drawing board of wood coated with plaster, image of Thutmose III, Egypt, 18th dynasty

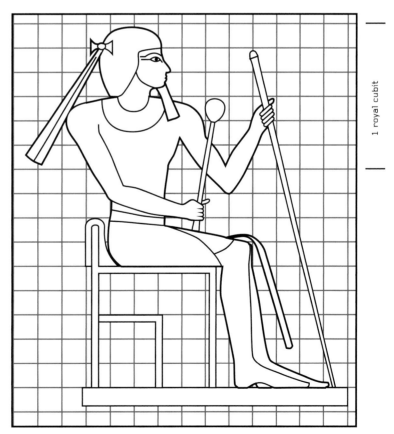

1 royal cubit

3.23 Schematic detail of the square grid using the royal cubit

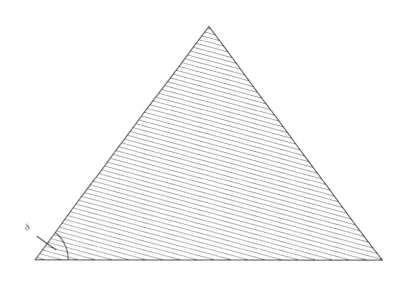

4/3 Pyramids:
Slope angle δ = 53° 7' 48"
Angle ratio 4:3 – the 3, 4, 5 Pythagorean triple
Pyramids with this angle are:
Userkaf, Neferirkare, Teti, Pepi I, Merenre,
Pepe II. (The Khafre pyramid is close to a 4:3 slope
ratio with an angle at 53° 10')

δ

14/11 – Great Pyramid:
King's and Queen's chamber
dimensions in royal cubits:
King: L = 10; W = 20; H = 11.17
Queen: L = 10; W = 11; H = 9

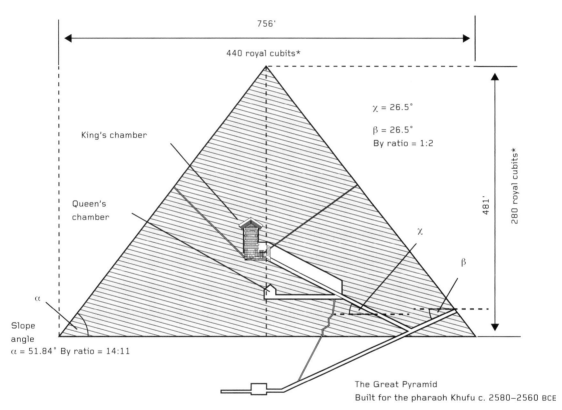

756'

440 royal cubits*

King's chamber

Queen's
chamber

χ = 26.5°

β = 26.5°
By ratio = 1:2

481'

280 royal cubits*

χ

β

α

Slope
angle
α = 51.84° By ratio = 14:11

The Great Pyramid
Built for the pharaoh Khufu c. 2580–2560 BCE

NOTE: The royal cubit = 7 palms; the cubit = 6 palms

3.24 Pyramid proportions

THE PYRAMIDS OF GIZA

The slope angles of the Pyramids of Giza may have been limited by the exterior surface treatments – if too steep, the white Tura limestone might have become unstable. This could perhaps explain the construction of the so-called Bent Pyramid (c.2600 BCE, 4th dynasty), where the slope angle started off at about 60°, was then adjusted to just under 54.27°, and then adjusted again to 43.22°.

The slope angle of the pyramid of Khufu, or the Great Pyramid (c.2580–2560 BCE, 4th dynasty), as measured from the surviving base layer casing stones, is approximately 51.84°. This is a curious angle if we are looking for circular measurements, as it does not divide equally into 360° – as does, say, 60° or 45°. Nor does it correspond to the angle of the sun to the horizon at the solstice or equinox positions, although the tip of the shadow would have corresponded to

a specific date in the Nile's flood cycle in early April or September (fig. 3.24).

An alternative rationale for determining pyramid slope angles, and more in keeping with what we know of Egyptian grid proportionate systems, would have been based on whole number ratios. Such a rationale would provide an efficient means to control the slope angle during construction, for example using a wooden right-angled triangle with vertical and horizontal sides in a whole number ratio.

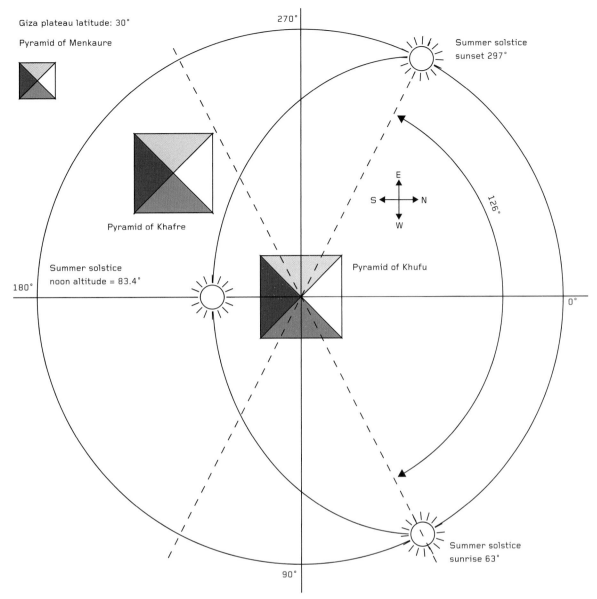

Giza plateau latitude: 30°

Pyramid of Menkaure

270°

Summer solstice
sunset 297°

E
S — N
W

126°

Pyramid of Khafre

Summer solstice
noon altitude = 83.4°

Pyramid of Khufu

180°

0°

90°

Summer solstice
sunrise 63°

3.25 Celestial alignment of the Giza Pyramids

From the Rhind Papyrus we know that the ancient Egyptians used ratios to determine slope values, an approach that parallels the use of whole number grids. The Great Pyramid's slope angle of 51.84° corresponds nicely to a whole number ratio of 14:11 – or, using ancient Egyptian measurements, 11 palms by 2 royal cubits, with 7 palms equal to 1 royal cubit. (Note the regular cubit only equals 6 palms.)

Many other pyramids are proportioned in the ratio 3:4 – corresponding to the Pythagorean triple 3:4:5 and generating the slope angle 53.13°.

Many people have made much of the fact that the cross section of the Great Pyramid appears to fall neatly within the golden ratio (see p.132) – the

corresponding 'golden' angle would be 51° – but there is nothing else in the structure to really support a link with the famous rectangle. All the evidence points to the use of whole number grids, but as to why a given whole number ratio was used to determine a slope angle rather than another can only be the subject of conjecture. Possibly ratios were the result of architectural convenience, such as using the ratio 4:3 (from the Pythagorean triple 3, 4, 5); possibly a seasonal alignment was intended and a corresponding whole number ratio selected, such as 14:11. Another possibility for the 14:11 ratio is that of a correspondence with pi – where the circumference of a circle with

a radius of 14 approximately equals the perimeter of a square with a side length of 22. It would be interesting to impose a three-dimensional royal cubit or palm grid over the Great Pyramid and look for correspondences.

In terms of celestial alignments, the northwest alignment of the Pyramids of Giza is fairly precise (see fig. 3.25), and, given their size, a number of sighting positions must have been used to calculate solstice and equinox positions – possibly from the temple of the Sphinx. The shadows of the pyramids would also have served to measure the time of day and the date of the year, but only in the same way that any other tall structure would; and obelisks would do a better job.

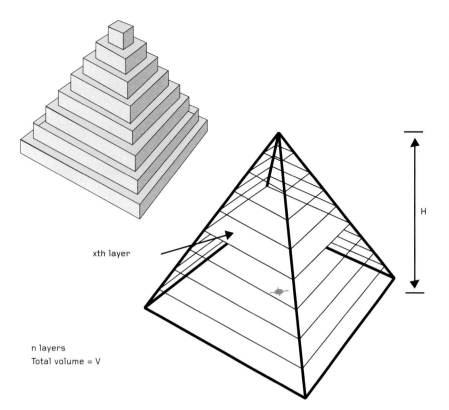

xth layer

n layers
Total volume = V

3.26 Pyramid volume

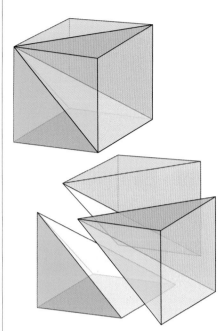

3.27 Pyramid volume

Geometry of the pyramids Geometrically, the pyramids represent a magnificent achievement. From the Rhind Papyrus we know the Egyptians were able to calculate the slope of a pyramid in terms of the ratio of its height to the side of its base. From both the Moscow and the Rhind papyruses we know the Egyptians knew how to calculate the area of a triangle as half base x height. From the Moscow Paprus we know the Egyptians had a formula equivalent to $1/3$h (a^2 + ab + b^2) and used it to calculate the volume of a truncated pyramid in terms of one third the height, times the sum of the base and upper platform areas, plus the product of the width of the base and the width of the upper platform. From this formula, if we make the upper base of the truncated pyramid zero, we can see the relationship between the truncated formula and the formula for the volume of a complete pyramid: $V = 1/3h$ (a^2).

The volume of a pyramid We know that the first Egyptian pyramids were the so-called step pyramids, built in layers of blocks. The only constructional difference between these early pyramids and the Pyramids of Giza is that the layers of the Giza pyramids were smoothly connected with white limestone triangular blocks.

So, it seems likely that a deductive method evolved for calculating the number of stone blocks required to build a pyramid of a particular slope and height – essentially the means to calculate the volume. There is a method credited to Eudoxus of Cnidus (400–355 BCE), a Greek astronomer, mathematician and student of Plato, that uses a 'layered approach' to derive a formula for the volume of a pyramid. Eudoxus spent 16 months in Egypt during the reign of Nectanebo I (380–363 BCE) studying astronomy and mathematics, so it is likely that he was at least inspired by an ancient Egyptian method:

Let us assume that the pyramid is divided into n layers of equal height, that the area of the pyramid's base is A, that the xth layer is a selected layer, and that V is the volume of the whole pyramid. By similarity the width of the x layer will be x/n multiplied by the base width.

Step1: The area of layer x will be: $a_x = (x/n)^2 A$

Step 2: From the top of the pyramid, the area of each layer will be: $(1/n)^2 A$, $(2/n)^2 A$, $(3/n)^2 A$, ... $(n/n)^2 A$

Step 3: The height of each layer will be H/n so the volume of each layer will be: $(H/n) \times (x/n)^2 A$

Step 4: So the volume of the whole pyramid can be estimated:
$V \approx (H/n) \times (1/n)^2 A + (H/n) \times (2/n)^2 A + (H/n) \times (3/n)^2 A + ...$
$+ (H/n) \times (n/n)^2 A = (AH/n^3)(1^2 + 2^2 + 3^2 + ... + n^2)$

Step 5: Add the 'sum of all squares' equation (see p.319):
$V \approx (AH/n^3)(n(n+1)(2n+1))/6) = (AH/6)(1+ 1/n)(2 + 1/n)$
If the number of layers, n, increases towards infinity then 1/n becomes insignificant: $V = AH/3$ (see fig. 3.26).

Conclusion: The volume of pyramid, then, is one third the volume of a surrounding cube or rectangular box.

A Chinese mathematician of the 3rd century CE, Liu Hui, provides three formulas for dissecting a cube. One of them (fig. 3.27) dissects a cube into three congruent 'yangma', which is a rectangular pyramid whose vertex is above one corner of its base. Liu concludes that the volume of a regular yangma is one third the volume of a cube. The concept is similar to that of Eudoxus.

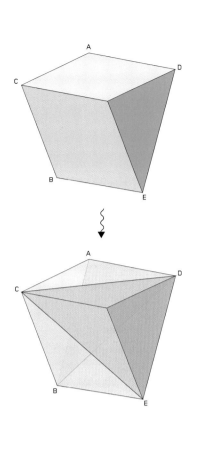

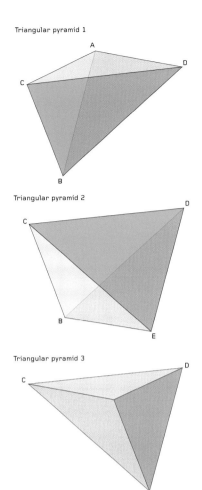

Triangular pyramid 1

Triangular pyramid 2

Triangular pyramid 3

3.28 Pyramid volume

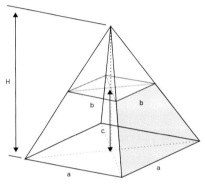

3.29 Truncated pyramid volume

Triangular pyramids The Rhind Papyrus provides us with clear evidence that the ancient Egyptians had developed the means to create equations for volumes and that they were used to express fractions as long sequences of progressively smaller, whole number fractions. So it seems clear that they had the mindset to come up with a formula for calculating the volume of a pyramid using an equation similar to that credited to Eudoxus. The Rhind Papyrus also provides us with evidence that the Egyptians had the means to create formulas for the volumes of spheres, cylinders, and various types of prism. It is not inconceivable, then, that Euclid's proposition 7, from Book 12 of the *Elements*, was picked up from Egyptian texts. Proposition 7 serves as an example of a high level of abstract reasoning where, in this case, Euclid breaks a prism down into three triangular pyramids and proves, through references to similar triangles, that the volumes of each pyramid are the same (see fig. 3.28).

It may be that the Egyptian study of volumes parallels that of the Vedic mathematicians' study of shapes with same areas, such as 'squaring the circle'. Of course, there are many other categories of Egyptian geometries, but the study of volumes and pyramids does serve to categorize at least a segment of Egyptian mathematics.

The truncated pyramid We have said that the Moscow Mathematical Papyrus contains a formula for the volume of a truncated pyramid. If we start with the Eudoxus formula for a complete pyramid, we can easily generate a formula for a truncated pyramid, by simply subtracting a smaller pyramid off the top of a bigger one. The nice thing about the formula for a truncated pyramid is that it would have provided a means to calculate the volume of stone needed for each layer of the pyramid – and the volumes (and block numbers) of layers with different block heights could be calculated (see fig. 3.29).

Pythagoras in Egypt There is no direct evidence that Pythagoras went to Egypt to study, but many of his contemporaries and successors did. So it is very possible that, one way or another, Pythagoras picked up his famous Pythagorean formula from ancient Egyptian manuscripts. Whereas we have some evidence that the Pythagorean formula was known within the Babylonian and Vedic cultures, there is no hard evidence of the knowledge in ancient Egypt, but we do know that the Egyptians were aware of Pythagorean triples.

Given the scale of the Giza pyramids, the materials used (limestone on the interior and white limestone on the exterior), the inclusion of the interior chambers, and the relative accuracy of the construction, the calculations needed would have rivalled any modern major civil engineering project and there must have been many equations in use, of which the Pythagorean theorem might have been one.

Geometrical construction for the volume of a pyramid Fig. 3.30 shows one of the ideas that resulted from the author's looking for a visual proof of how the volume formula for a Giza pyramid might have been derived using Euclid and a geometrical construction.

(i) Volume of Giza pyramid = V
(ii) Volume of prism FGBJKE = S
(iii) Volume of square-based pyramid FGKJB = T
(iii) Volume of triangular pyramid FGKB = U (note that 8U = V)
(iv) Volume of triangular pyramid FKJB = W
(v) Volume of triangular pyramid EKJB = X
(vi) Let AB = a, then FG = a/2
(vii) Let GB = H

Step 1: $S = (a/4) \, H \, (a/2) = a^2(H/8)$
Step 2: $T = V/4 = U + W$
Step 3: $U = W$ (Euclid, Book 12, proposition 5)
Step 4: $U = V/8$ (combines steps 2 and 3)
Step 5: $U = S/3$ (Euclid, Book 12, propositon 7: any prism with a triangular base can be divided into three pyramids equal to one another)
Step 6: $V = 8 \, (S/3) = 8 \, (a^2(H/8))/3 = 1/3 \, Ha^2$ (combines steps 1, 4 and 5)
Conclusion: The volume of eight FGBJKE prisms equal the volume of the Giza pyramid.

Why were Egyptian tombs shaped as pyramids? Tombs of the early dynastic period of ancient Egypt were box-like structures with sloping sides, known as mastabas. These stone-built edifices still survive and can be geometrically described as flattened truncated pyramids. The architect Imhotep (c.2650–2600 BCE) is credited with coming up with the idea of stacking mastabas on top of each other. The result was Egypt's first step pyramid, built for the pharaoh Djoser, which may have symbolized a giant stairway by which the pharaoh's soul could ascend to the heavens. The development of step pyramids into true pyramids, with smooth sides, would have been a natural progression – a development that ultimately resulted in awe-inspiring gigantic structures that dwarfed everything around them. It may be thought curious that the perfection and simplicity of the great pyramids, with their polished white limestone facing-stones, stood in such contrast to the more complex architectural forms that surrounded them. The only equivalents were the obelisks, and, possibly, the rectangular, box-like tomb structures.

'From the heights of these pyramids, 40 centuries look down on us.'
NAPOLEON BONAPARTE (1769–1821)

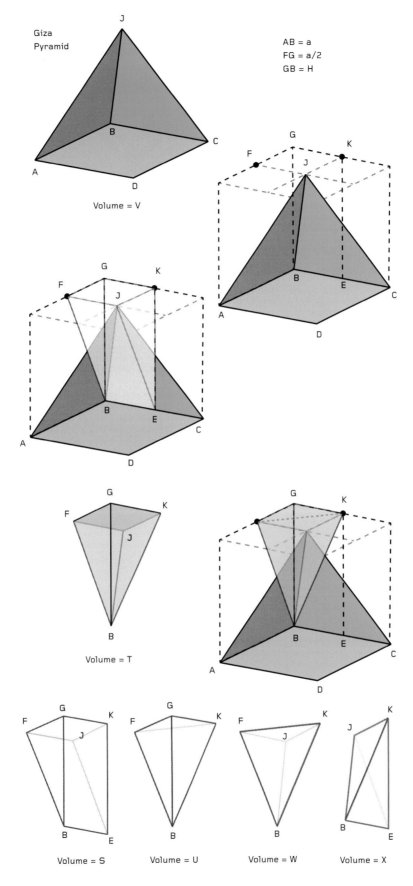

Giza
Pyramid

AB = a
FG = a/2
GB = H

Volume = V

Volume = T

Volume = S

Volume = U

Volume = W

Volume = X

Triangular prisms U, W, X are equal in volume
(Euclid Bk 12, Prop 7)

3.30 Pyramid volume visual proof

LETTERS, NUMBERS, PATTERNS

Whereas there are specific numeric symbols for the Egyptian base ten number system – symbols for units, tens, hundreds, thousands, and up to one million – this author can find no evidence for numeric values assigned to Egyptian hieroglyphic consonants. However, the phonetic values of hieroglyphic consonants can be ordered to correspond with the Semitic scripts that came afterwards, such as Hebrew and Arabic, and these are ordered in numeric sequences. Semitic scripts appear to have evolved from hieroglyphics, so it is possible that hieroglyphic consonants had a numeric interplay of meaning as much as the Semitic abjad scripts (see p.175).

There is no evidence of any sophisticated development of polygonal or cursive forms other than square grids, some use of hexagonal tessellations and occasional use of spiral designs. This is significant only in that it sets Egypt apart from the later geometrical studies of Greece and Islam.

Most of the decorative elements of ancient Egypt are figurative, taking the form of papyrus plants, palm leaves, lotus flowers, scarabs, and so on. Patterns based on abstract polygonal geometries or geometrical curves are less common. Geometric patterns are shown in figs 3.31, 3.32 and 3.33. Pattern A is a variant of a common ancient Egyptian water design. Patterns B, C, D and H appear on pottery fragments from the 13th dynasty found in Kerma, Nubia. Pattern B has the same geometrical construction as that of the Harappan pottery design shown in fig. 3.4. Pattern E can be seen in the tomb of Sennedjem in a mural showing Anubis and a mummy (19th dynasty). Pattern F is a stylization of feathers and appears on a sarcophagus of the Amarna period (18th dynasty). Pattern G is from the gilded sarcophagus of Tutankhamun (18th dynasty). Pattern I is a pattern on a ceiling in the tomb of Userhet (18th dynasty). Pattern J is a pattern on a ceiling of the tomb of Senenmut, reign of Thutmose III (18th dynasty). Pattern K appears on the ceiling of the tomb of Haremhab (19th dynasty), and L is from the tomb of Nefersekheru during the reign of Ramses I (19th dynasty).

A

B

C

D

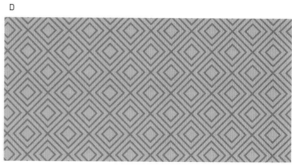

3.31 Egyptian patterns A, B, C and D

E

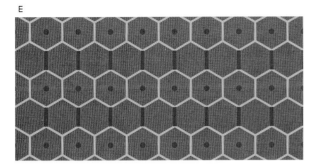

F

G

H

3.32 Egyptian patterns E, F, G and H

I

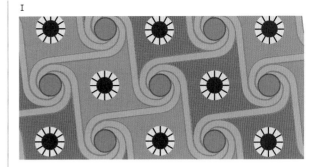

J

K

L

3.33 Egyptian patterns I, J, K and L

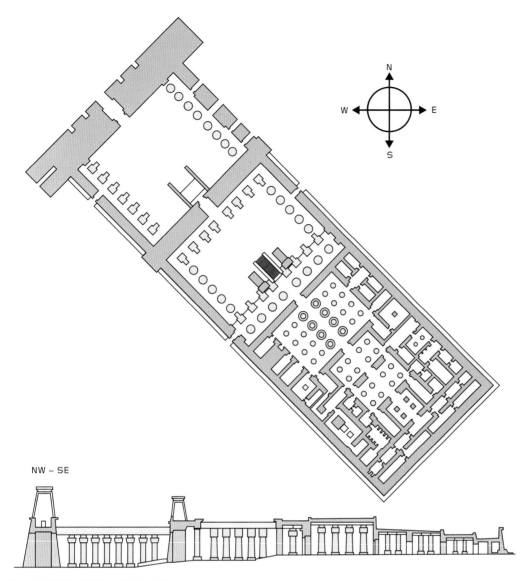

NW – SE

3.34 Mortuary temple of Ramses III

ARCHITECTURAL LAYOUTS

A comparison between Egyptian and Japanese mausoleum layouts exemplifies, in some small way, the way in which cultural differences impact architectural and geometrical forms.

Mortuary temple of Ramses III This was built for the second pharaoh of the 20th dynasty, Ramses III (reigned 1187–1156 BCE). Entry is through a fortified gatehouse in the style of an Asiatic 'migdol' fortress. Just inside the gatehouse, to the southwest, are the later chapels of Amenirdis I, Shepenwepet II and Nitoket, wives of the god Amun. To the northeast side is the chapel of Amun. On the northeast wall of the temple are reliefs depicting the victories of Ramses over the Sardinians, Cretans, Philistines and Danu. Beyond

the first massive pylon (27 m / 88 ft high) is an open courtyard, where athletic sporting events such as wrestling were held. Reliefs on the southwest wall depict Ramses' victory over the Libyans. In the northwest wall the 'Window of Appearances' connects the temple with the connected royal palace. The compass orientation of the temple is similar to that of the Great Ziggurat of Ur (see fig. 3.68).

For ancient Egyptians the mortuary temple was the house of many gods. Amun was the patron deity of Thebes; Amon Ra was the champion of the poor and troubled; the pharaoh himself was also considered a god and a protector. The practices of Egyptian religion were designed to gain the favour of the gods and thereby improve daily life or gain entry into the afterlife. Spells, study,

devotion, offerings, pilgrimages and rituals were developed to help a believer navigate through life and through the labyrinths of the afterlife. The mortuary temple of Ramses III allowed the chosen few to navigate a path through the world of the gods: only the pharaohs, priests and initiates could enter the inner sanctuaries.

Taiyuin Mausoleum The mausoleum complex (1653) in Nikko, northern Japan, was built after the death of the third Tokugawa shogun, Iemitsu. The layout of the mausoleum contrasts wonderfully with the Ramses mortuary temple. Comparing the two gives an insight into how cultures can impact geometry. Whereas the Ramses complex characterizes a controlled and autocratic religious society, the Taiyuin

Koukamon
Gate

Okunoin

Haiden,
Ainoma,
Honden

Inukimon Gate

Karamon
Gate

Yashamon Gate

Nitenmon Gate

Niomon Gate

Omizuya
(water house)

3.35 Taiyuin Mausoleum

mausoleum layout characterizes an individual's way through life. Statues of gods watch over visitors and remind them of their paths through life, of their ancestors and of their life essences. By the Niomon Gate, the main entrance, two fearsome Deva kings stand to protect the place from evil. After entering the complex visitors can wash their hands in purification at the Omizuya water house before proceeding further. By the Nitenmon Gate stand statues of the gods Jikokuten (a guardian) and Komokuten (a punisher of evil). The Yashamon Gate enshrines four female devils, with the colour of each body symbolizing east, west, south and north. To journey through the Taiyuin Mausoleum complex is to be reminded of the Buddhist journey to enlightenment.

Other layouts Interconnecting spaces, between functional spaces, can be as important to the overall harmony and emotional experience of an architectural form as the shapes and materials of the spaces themselves. For the Egyptians the approach was regimented and formal, based on status and hierarchy. The Egyptian approach can be contrasted with other cultural layouts such as those of Neolithic labyrinths, or the more organic growth of the sequences of spaces in, say, a kasbah (medina quarter). Other examples include the garden layouts and the interconnecting interior spaces of Islamic funerary complexes or the Alhambra Palace (1333) in Granada, Spain.

CONCLUSION

Egyptian geometries appear to have been driven by practical need rather than abstract speculation. Surviving evidence shows us that dynastic Egyptians were well aware of the mathematical means to measure lengths, areas, volumes and even time, with the use of precise records, fairly sophisticated measuring systems and algebraic equations. It does seem, though, that the Egyptians operated in a whole number world where whole number grids and ratios predominated. It appears that irrational numbers did not enter the mathematical vocabulary, although concepts of progressions of fractions were in use and probably led to the deduction of, for example, a formula for calculating the volume of a pyramid. Even pi was considered as a whole number ratio – even though it may have been explored as the sum of an ever smaller progression of ratios. The apparent lack of development of polygonal and cursive geometries also supports the idea that the Egyptians were not concerned with abstract concepts unless they led to an immediate, concrete result. Culturally an Egyptian 'whole number' world is in keeping with a regimented and autocratic state.

As with many other cultures contemporary with the dynastic Egyptians, arithmetical, astronomical and geometric knowledge appears to have been the domain of a privileged few, being mostly in the hands of the priestly castes. Such knowledge would have served as a means to impress and control the lay population.

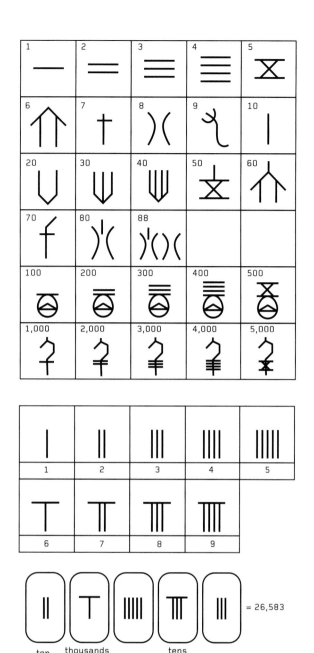

3.36 Ancient Chinese numerals

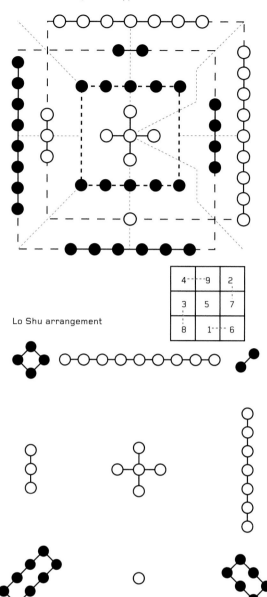

Fu Hsi's He Tu (River Map)

Lo Shu arrangement

4	9	2
3	5	7
8	1	6

3.37 He Tu and Lo Shu number arrangements

THE YELLOW RIVER

As with other ancient cultures, shadow timekeepers were used to track yearly and daily solar time – and were, in fact, developed to an extraordinary degree. Eighth-century records exist of gnomons (see p.53) placed along a north–south line stretching 3,500 km (2,200 miles) – a remarkable construction planned and organized by the Tang dynasty astronomer, mathematician and Buddhist monk Yi Xing (683–727 CE).

Lunar cycles were used with solar cycles to monitor and predict the seasons, as were the motions of constellations.

Calendars were mostly lunar, with extra months regularly added to align lunar time with solar time and therefore with seasonal time. Stars and constellations were categorized into 28 mansions, one for each day of a lunar month, cycling until the moon once again occupied the same position in relation to the stars. The elliptic of the night sky was divided into four regions, the Azure Dragon (east), the Black Tortoise (north), the White Tiger (west) and the Vermilion Bird (south): each region contained seven mansions, and served as a way to track the moon's progress across the sky.

PRE-SHANG DYNASTY

The Shang dynasty ruled from c.1600 BCE to c.1046 BCE, and was preceded by the Xia dynasty (c.2070–c.1600 BCE) – the earliest, possibly mythical, Chinese imperial dynasty.

Number system There are a number of variations in early Chinese numerals but they share similarities and all are base ten. The Chinese used place values for their number systems in multiples of ten. Weights and measures were standardized, and rudimentary means to calculate areas and volumes were developed.

Fu Hsi's He Tu (River Map)

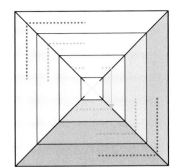

a. 5
b. 10
c1. 3 + 1 + 4 + 2 = 10
d1. 8 + 6 + 9 + 7 = 30
c2. 2 + 3 and 4 + 1 = 5
d2. 7 + 8 and 6 + 9 = 15

Luo Shu arrangement

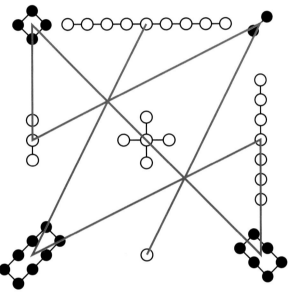

3.38 Number combinations in the He Tu River Map

4	9	2
3	5	7
8	1	6

15

16	3	2	13
5	10	11	8
9	6	7	12
4	15	14	1

34

52	61	4	13	20	29	36	45
14	3	62	51	46	35	30	19
53	60	5	12	21	28	37	44
11	6	59	54	43	38	27	22
55	58	7	10	23	26	39	42
9	8	57	56	41	40	25	24
50	63	2	15	18	31	34	47
16	1	64	49	48	33	32	17

260

3.39 Magic squares

MAGIC SQUARES

There are many magic squares other than the 3 x 3 Lo Shu square. For example, German Renaissance artist Albrecht Dürer created a 4 x 4 square in 1514. The 8 x 8 magic square was first described by Benjamin Franklin in 1769. In the diagrams above, some of the numeric symmetries are indicated in colour.

Complementary and opposite forces

A fundamental ancient Chinese philosophical belief was that the universe was subject to constant change owing to the interactions of two complementary and seemingly opposite forces, known as yin and yang. The literal meaning of yin is the north side of a hill, facing away from the sun and lying in shadow, while yang means south side of the hill. Yin is associated with passivity, reception, female energy, even numbers and the moon – and yang is the complement, being associated with the active, positive, male principle in nature, odd numbers and the sun.

The diagrammatic building blocks of yin and yang are broken lines (yin), and whole lines (yang), and the classic representative symbol is composed of the two tadpole-like shapes, which can be seen throughout Asia, yin being the black and yang the white.

The Lo Shu magic square was first described during the reign of Yu the Great in around 2200 BCE. In a magic square, each row, column and diagonal adds up to the same number, in this case 15. The Lo Shu serves as a representation of yin and yang quantities. As seen in fig. 3.37, the sums of the yin quantities (black), by row, column and

diagonal, are 6, 8, 10, 10, 12 and 14, and the sum of yang quantities (white) by central row and central column is 15.

Legend has it that in the years of the mythical emperor Fu Xi (2800 BCE) a dragon horse emerged from the Yellow River carrying the He Tu River Map. It was from this map that Fu Xi derived the eight trigrams of the I Ching and their properties (see overleaf). The He Tu arrangement (see fig 3.38) of yin and yang quantities looks in some ways similar to the Lo Shu diagram; both highlight yin and yang quantities and both inspired theories of Feng Shui (a system of laws believed to govern the

3.40 Fu Xi's I Ching trigram arrangement

location of objects in relation to qi, the flow of energy). There is correspondence between the He Tu and the Fu Xi (see fig. 3.40) in terms of even (e) and odd (o) numbers: for example, 7, 2 and 5 (o-e-o) represents 'water'. Clockwise from the top of the He Tu: o-e-o; e-e-o; o-e-e; o-o-o; e-o-o; e-e-e; e-o-e; o-o-e, where the 'Wind' and 'Earth' trigrams count to the centre (5) of the He Tu and 'Thunder' and 'Heaven' to the surrounding ring (10).

The I Ching The I Ching (Yijing), or Book of Changes, is an ancient Chinese

book of wisdom constructed in 64 parts – a book designed to communicate the idea that all things are the result of a dynamic balance between yin and yang and therefore, inevitably, subject to change. Traditionally it is believed that the principles of the I Ching were first formulated by the mythical emperor Fu Xi, although it is now thought to have been compiled sometime between the 12th and 4th centuries BCE. Each of the 64 parts of the I Ching is represented by a hexagram – six lines that are either broken (yin), or solid (yang). The 64

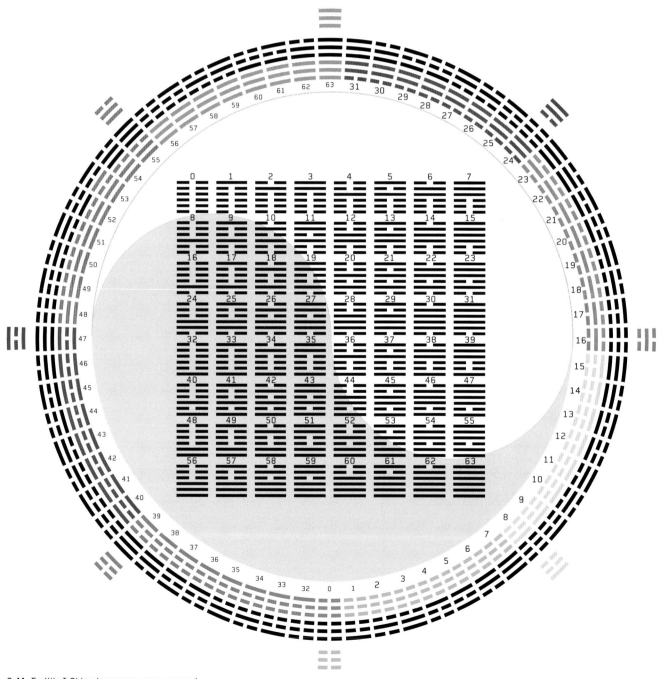

3.41 Fu Xi's I Ching hexagram arrangement

Order of hexagrams in the I Ching

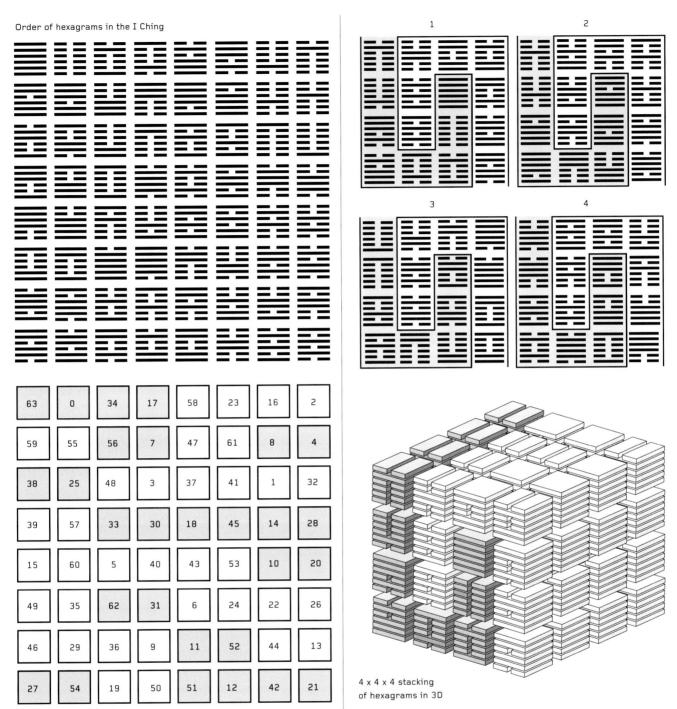

3.42 I Ching King Wen sequence of hexagrams

4 x 4 x 4 stacking
of hexagrams in 3D

3.43 I Ching hexagrams in 3D

parts are paired combinations of the primal eight trigrams, each carrying with it a core meaning, as shown in fig. 3.40. The 64 concepts of the I Ching are so structured that many believe that by reflecting upon them they will shed light on all aspects of life and the universe (see fig. 3.41).

The I Ching is commonly used as a book of divination: 50 yarrow stalks, or three coins, are cast as a question is contemplated. The belief is that a universal yin—yang force will direct the stalks or coins to conjure a particular one of the eight trigrams. A second round conjures a second trigram, and the two trigrams are combined to form a hexagram matching one of the 64 universal I Ching concepts. The hexagram is then meditated upon to reveal the answer to the user's question.

The meaning of the hexagrams derives in large part from the juxtaposition of the core concepts of the eight primal trigrams, for example Heaven over Earth. The actual order of the hexagrams in the I Ching appears in fig. 3.42, where the hexagrams are grouped in pairs of structural opposites. In the corresponding numeric grid the colours highlight pairs that combine to make 63 (green), or where one hexagram in a pair has a numeric value double that of the other (blue). Fig. 3.43 shows a 3D rendering created by the author.

From the *Zhou Bi Suan Jing* (1046–256 BCE)

朱冪 Zhu: Vermilion

朱冪 Vermilion area (D)

冪 Mih: Area

黄 Huang: Yellow

黄冪 Yellow area (E)

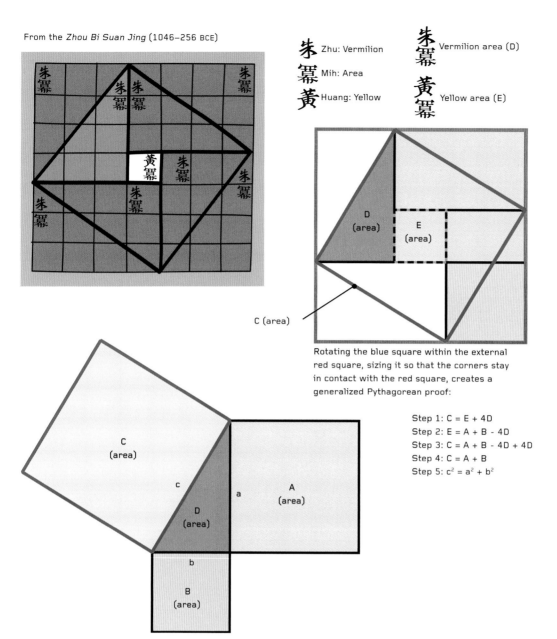

C (area)

Rotating the blue square within the external red square, sizing it so that the corners stay in contact with the red square, creates a generalized Pythagorean proof:

Step 1: C = E + 4D
Step 2: E = A + B - 4D
Step 3: C = A + B - 4D + 4D
Step 4: C = A + B
Step 5: $c^2 = a^2 + b^2$

3.44 *Zhou Bi Suan Jing* 'Pythagorean theorem' proof

ZHOU TO HAN DYNASTIES

Following the Shang, the Zhou dynasty ruled China from 1046 to 256 BCE, and was itself followed by the short-lived Qin dynasty (221–207 BCE). From 206 BCE to 220 CE the Han dynasty reigned over a golden age in Chinese culture.

Evident proofs The *Zhou Bi Suan Jing* is one of the oldest and most famous Chinese mathematical texts. The title literally means 'The Arithmetical Classic of the Gnomon and the Circular Paths of Heaven', and the volume is a collection of 246 problems encountered by the Duke of Zhou and his astronomer and mathematician, Shang Gao. The work dates from the Zhou dynasty, and includes the oldest-known representation of the Pythagorean theorem (see fig. 3.44). It is often the case that ancient Chinese mathematical statements survive without the logic that was used to derive them, leaving them to function more as self-evident 'proofs'. Given the appearance of the *Zhou Bi Suan Jing* diagram, it is possible to interpret it as presenting a generalized proof of the Pythagorean theorem and not one limited to the 3, 4, 5 triangle represented. (See also chapter 5.)

Interpretations of diagrams
in the Zhou Bi Suan Ching

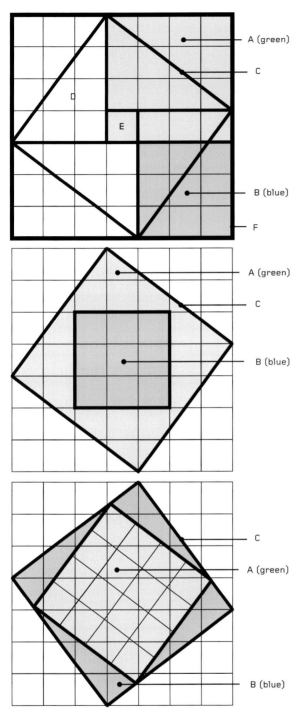

A (green)

C

D

E

B (blue)

F

A (green)

C

B (blue)

C

A (green)

B (blue)

3.45 Zhou Bi Suan Ching Pythagorean visuals

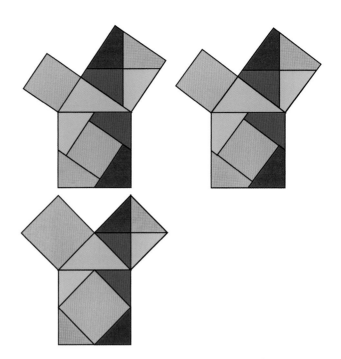

3.46 Henry Perigal's constructional proof

Three diagrams appear in the *Zhou Bi Suan Jing* that relate to the Pythagorean theorem (see fig. 3.45). The first has been shown – but not as a general case, rather as a 3, 4, 5 triangular case. The two other diagrams may show thoughts that relate to the first diagram. The second diagram brings to mind 19th-century British mathematician Henry Perigal's constructional proof of the Pythagorean theorem (see fig. 3.46). Some liberty has been taken with the third *Zhou Bi Suan Jing* drawing as the surviving diagram shows an inner square not in contact with the outer square.

In the drawings of fig. 3.45, D is a 3, 4, 5 triangle.

Areas: E = 1 square; triangle D = 6 squares; B = 9 squares; A = 16 squares; C = 25 squares; F = 49 squares

$C = A + B$; $C = E + 4D$; $E = A + B - 4D$; $F = A + B + 4D$

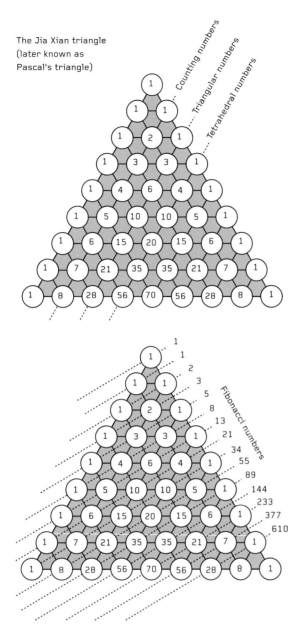

The Jia Xian triangle
(later known as
Pascal's triangle)

Counting numbers

Triangular numbers

Tetrahedral numbers

Fibonacci numbers

3.47 Jia Xian triangle

'Conditions are not invariable, terms
are not final. Thus the wise man looks
into space, and does not regard the
small as too little, nor the great as too
much, for he knows that there is no
limit to dimension.'
ZHUANG ZHOU
(4TH CENTURY BCE)

Mathematical works In 263 CE Liu Hui, one of the greatest mathematicians of ancient China, wrote a detailed commentary on the renowned Chinese book of mathematics *The Nine Chapters on the Mathematical Art* (*Jiuzhang Suanshu*), which was highly influential. His work focuses on applied mathematics in engineering and administration and includes nine distinct chapters on such things as impartial taxation, engineering works and the surveying of land. Liu's work includes simultaneous linear equations. Liu provided a diagram (now lost) of the Pythagorean theorem – 'a diagram giving the relations between the hypotenuse and the sum and difference of the other two sides whereby one can find the unknown from the known'. Liu also provided a relatively accurate value for pi derived as 3.14 using a regular polygon of 96 sides, and as 3.14159 using a polygon of 3,072 sides.

Another work, the *Mo Jing*, was inspired by Mozi (470–390 BCE), a mathematician, scientist and philosopher of the Eastern Zhou period (770–221 BCE) whose school of logic was known as Mohism. Mozi and his followers were in some ways similar to Pythagoras and the Pythagoreans, in that Mozi provided the original inspiration and then his followers continued with the idea, compiling the *Mozi*, a larger work of essays and dialogues that contained within it the *Mo Jing*. The *Mo Jing* provides definitions of points, lines and space, similar in a way to the definitions of Euclid, but not stated axiomatically. The work also includes statements about indivisibility as well as definitions of circle geometries and volumes.

The following is a comparison between the *Mo Jing* and Euclid:
(i) The *Mo Jing* describes a line separated into parts, and states that a part that has no remaining parts is a point; also that a point may stand at the end of a line or at its beginning like a head-presentation in childbirth. It also states that a point is the smallest unit,

Using the Jia Xian triangle
to create a Fibonacci triangle

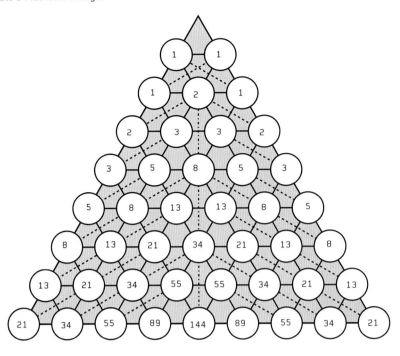

Pascal fractal

3.48 Fibonacci triangle and Pascal fractal

and cannot be cut in half, since 'nothing' cannot be halved.

(ii) Euclid provides a positioning definition of the geometric point, stating that a point has no part and serves as an indivisible location.

The definitions appear to be similar but the *Mo Jing* describes a part that cannot be divided into smaller parts, whereas Euclid describes a point that is no part, that has no dimension. So one describes something indivisible and fundamental, much like the ancient concepts of an atom, and the other defines something more abstract – something that has no existence just a position.

The *Suan shu shu* (*Writings on Reckoning*) is a c.200 BCE text on mathematical problems of the early Han period and is approximately 7,000 characters in length, written on 190 bamboo strips. The problems cover elementary arithmetic, fractions, inverse proportion, factorization of numbers, geometric progressions, interest-rate calculations, handling of errors, conversion between different units, the false position method for finding roots and the extraction of approximate square roots, calculation of the volume of various three-dimensional shapes, calculation of an unknown side of a rectangle, given area and one side, and relative dimensions of a square and its inscribed circle, with all the calculations about circumference and area of a circle being based on a value of pi equal to 3.

ELEVENTH CENTURY

Jia Xian (c.1010–70) was a Song dynasty (960–1279) mathematician who invented 'Pascal's triangle' about six centuries before Blaise Pascal's invention of it in the 17th century. Jia used his Jia Xian triangle as a tool for extracting square and cubic roots, but the numbers of the triangle have many properties that result from its additive patterns (see fig. 3.47).

Fig. 3.48 shows a construction similar to the Jia Xian triangle used to create a Fibonacci triangle and an attempt at a Pascal fractal.

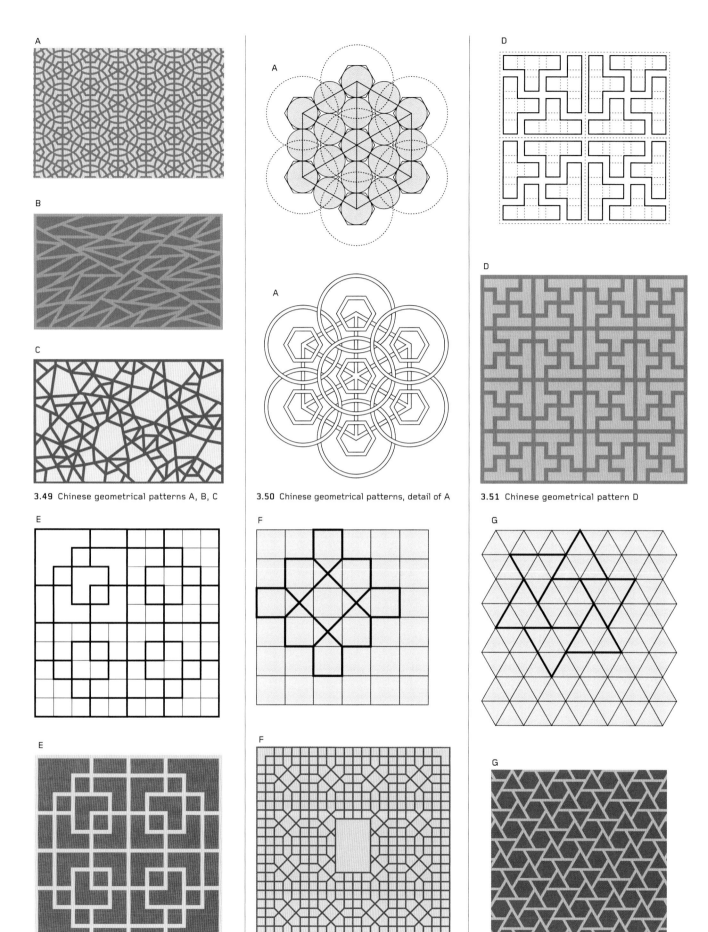

3.49 Chinese geometrical patterns A, B, C

3.50 Chinese geometrical patterns, detail of A

3.51 Chinese geometrical pattern D

3.52 Chinese geometrical pattern E

3.53 Chinese geometrical pattern F

3.54 Chinese geometrical pattern G

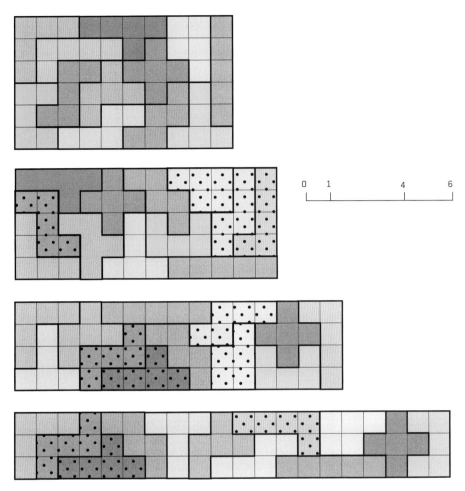

3.55 Golomb's pentominoes, with (inset) a Golomb ruler

CHINESE LATTICES

As in other cultures, Chinese 2D designs can give us an insight into the geometries explored even when written evidence is lacking. Chinese craftsmen used wooden lattice designs to divide architectural spaces. One of the oldest was found in a grave from the Zhou dynasty dating to around 1000 BCE. More evidence of Chinese lattices can be found in Han dynasty (206 BCE–220 CE) pictures on grave bricks and clay house models, and on patterns on tomb walls. From the Tang dynasty (618–907) we can see lattice designs on pottery, clay houses, paintings, prints and fabrics. From later dynasties there are surviving real wooden lattices.

Summary of lattice styles

Pre-Han dynasty: vertical line lattices.
Han dynasty: squares, circles, ovals, waves, willow leafs and thunder-scroll lattices.
Tang dynasty: equally spaced vertical lines, sometimes crossed by parallel

horizontal bars on top, in the middle and at the bottom.
Song dynasty (960–1279): complex circle and square lattices. Also, octagon and superimposed square lattices. Multiple borders and flower patterns were used in the late Song period.
Ming dynasty (1368–1644): octagon and square patterns.

Figs 3.49, 3.50, 3.51, 3.52, 3.53 and 3.54 show a range of various lattices.

Design A is based on close-packing circles and includes the equilateral triangle lattice created by the circles.

Design B is a random arrangement of triangles – but the design is pleasing to the eye. The lattice is reminiscent of willow leaves.

Design C is a random arrangement of irregular polygons, with the design suggesting many linear forms to the visual imagination.

Design D is based on a square and half-square grid.

Designs E and F are based on a square grid.

Designs D and E are reminiscent of pentominoes – geometric puzzle pieces formed by joining five equal squares edge to edge (see below).

Design G is based on an equilateral grid.

Golomb's pentominoes Some Chinese lattices resemble pentominoes. The pentomino challenge is to arrange the tiles in four rectangular configurations (see fig. 3.55). There are 12 tiles, each composed of five squares. The dotted pentominoes are reflected tiles, so tiles need to be two-sided for this game. American mathematician Solomon Golomb coined the name *pentomino* and in 1953 was the first to fully describe the idea. He is also known for the Golomb ruler – a set of marks at integer positions along an imaginary ruler such that no two pairs of marks are the same distance apart.

An 8 x 8 square can be constructed with the pentominoes if a 2 x 2 square tetromino is added.

3.56 Chinese tangram shadows

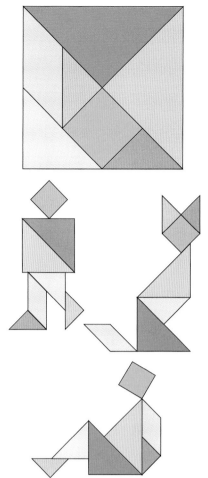

3.57 Chinese tangram solutions

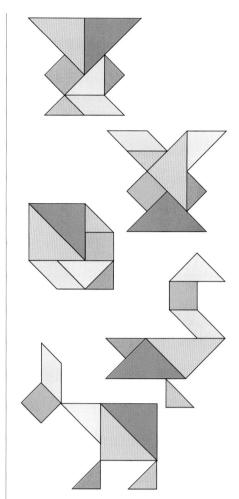

3.58 Chinese tangram solutions

THE TANGRAM

Possibly invented during the Song dynasty, the tangram ('seven boards of skill') is a dissection puzzle consisting of seven flat shapes, called tans, derived from a square. The objective of the puzzle is to form a specific image (given only an outline or silhouette of it), using all seven tans, which must not overlap (see figs 3.56, 3.57 and 3.58).

PAGODA AND PALACE ARCHITECTURE

Classic examples of ancient three-dimensional Chinese geometry include structures with multiple-tiered roofs. The origin of the tiered-roof design may well date back to the tiered-roof watchtowers of the Han dynasty or possibly before.

Whatever their structural origins, pagodas and temples with tiered roofs are mostly associated with Buddhism, where pagodas in particular had, possibly, two primary religious functions: to house religious relics or ashes, and to provide a place for the 'voice-hearers'

and 'cause-awakened ones' to attain Buddhahood. With their two functions they had two names: 'Buddha Towers' and 'Treasure Towers'.

Geometrically, pagodas have highly symmetrical floor plans, initially squares but later hexagons, octagons and dodecagons and circles. The tiers were normally in odd numbers – 3, 5, 7, 9, 11, 13, 15. According to Chinese tradition, and as seen in the numerology of the I Ching, odd numbers are yang (white) and masculine, and even numbers are yin (black) and feminine. So, symbolically the tiers ascending to heaven are masculine and the core of the structure is feminine. The Iron Pagoda (1049, fig. 3.59) has 13 tiers and an octagonal footprint; the Giant Wild Goose Pagoda (652 CE, fig. 3.62) has seven tiers and a square footprint; the Temple of Heaven (1402–24, fig. 3.63) has three tiers and a circular footprint (divided into ten parts); the Longhua Pagoda (220–265 CE, fig. 3.61) has seven tiers and an octagonal footprint.

The floorplan of the Hall of Supreme Harmony (see fig. 3.60) is almost exactly in the ratio of 2:1 – an even number – and above the throne there is an octagonal star. The building sits on three levels of a marble stone base and with its two-tiered roof conjures the number five.

Tulous are circular or rectangular buildings of rammed earth that serve as fortified villages (see fig. 3.64). The buildings of the Chuxi tulou group in Yongding county, Fujian, were built in the 15th century during the reign of the Yongle Emperor. Most tulous are occupied by a single large clan; the largest can hold up to 80 families, or nearly 800 people, in total.

3.59 Iron Pagoda, Kaifeng City

3.62 Giant Wild Goose Pagoda, Xi'an

3.60 Hall of Supreme Harmony, Beijing

3.63 Temple of Heaven, Beijing

3.61 Longhua Pagoda, Shanghai

3.64 Interior of a Chuxi tulou, Yongding, Fujian

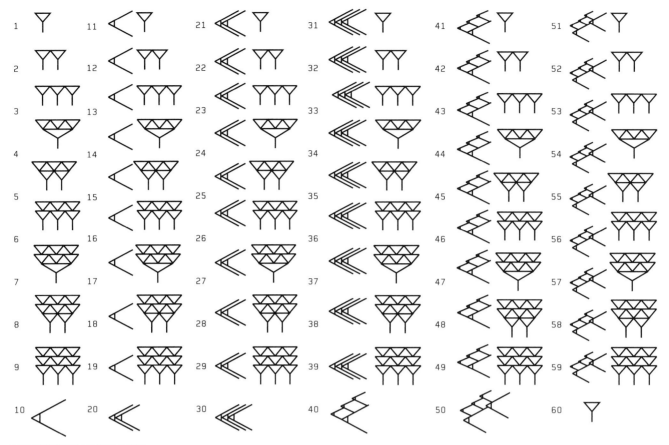

3.65 Cuneiform number system

THE TIGRIS AND THE EUPHRATES

Mesopotamia (the name derives from the ancient Greek for 'between rivers'), one of the earliest cradles of civilization, is the area between the Tigris and the Euphrates roughly corresponding to parts of present-day Iraq, Kuwait, Syria and nearby regions. The area was settled from about 8000 BCE, and in much the same way as in the other river valley cultures, societies evolved into city-states and empires. The most important include the Sumerian and Akkadian cultures, the Babylonians and the Assyrians, all of whose fortunes rose and fell as they won and lost power in the region from approximately the 3rd millennium BCE onward.

In pace with the development of local organized societies was the creation of highly bureaucratic systems of control and with it the development of a written language (cuneiform), a number system (see fig. 3.65), arithmetic, mathematics and geometry. Maths tables, meteorological data, celestial events and equations (to calculate lengths, areas and volumes), were recorded on clay tablets, many of which still survive. Not only were equations and numeric tables developed to estimate such things as field sizes and the volumes of piles of grain, but also many items were standardized, such as weights and measures and even brick sizes. From this level of control material usages could be estimated and labour time calculated. Equations were also developed to calculate the dimensions of architectural structures such as the lengths and areas of 2D and 3D polygonal and polyhedral shapes including truncated pyramids. Pi was approximated with a value of 3.

Clay tablets Many clay tablets survive, dated around 1800 BCE, from which we can read about methods of accounting and even get to know the number system – with number symbols grouped in tens with a positional base 60 system.

One clay tablet, known as the Plimpton 322 tablet, contains a list of 15 Pythagorean triples and also school exercises in the trigonometry of areas and dimensions of triangles (see p.16).

Another tablet from c.1800 BCE, now in the Yale Babylonian Collection, shows calculations of the diagonal of a square (see fig. 3.66). The diagonal displays an approximation of the square root of two in four sexagesimal (base 60) figures, $1 + 24/60 + 51/60^2 + 10/60^3 = 1.41421296$.

The tablet also gives an example where one side of the square is 30, and the resulting diagonal is 42 25/60 35/60² or 42.4263888...

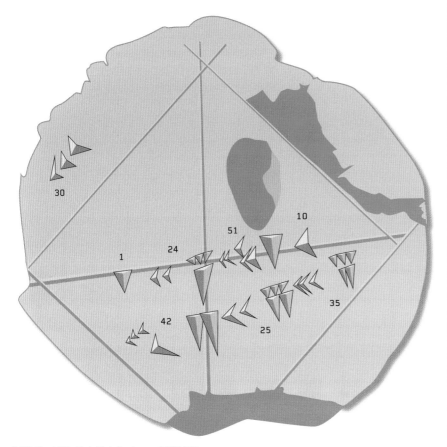

3.66 Root 2 tablet, Babylonian, c.1800 BCE

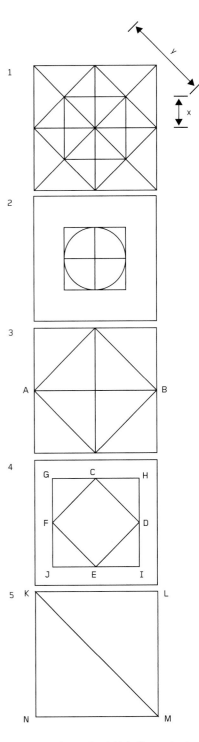

3.67 Student exercise tablet, Mesopotamian, c.1800 BCE

Many student exercise tablets survive: the drawings in fig. 3.67 are copied from a tablet written in cuneiform and dated during the 18th century BCE, found in the city of Larsa in what is now southern Iraq. All calculations would have been in base 60.

Let $x = 1$

Drawing 1: $y = 2(\sqrt{2})$

Drawing 2: Inner circle radius is x (using a Mesopotamian approximation of pi = 3)

The area of the circle is $3x^2 = 3$

Drawing 3: $AB = 4x = 4$

Drawing 4: $FC = 2x = 2$ and $GC = x\sqrt{2} = \sqrt{2}$

Drawing 5: $KL = 4x = 4$ and $KM = 4x(\sqrt{2}) = 4\sqrt{2}$

Astronomy Astronomical observations coupled with the fact that the area flooded in annual cycles resulted in the adoption of a formalized year of 12 months, each of 30 days, plus five extra days to predict the dates for planting and harvesting.

The Metonic cycle, by which the period of approximately 19 solar years corresponds with 235 synodic months (see p.60), was known to Mesopotamian cultures and used as a basis for the Babylonian calendar. The Metonic cycle created a basis for aligning solar and lunar cycles as well as calculating the occurrence of eclipses. Many traditions of the region have survived through to the present day, including grouping the stars into 12 zodiacal constellations and using multiples of 60 for angular measurement.

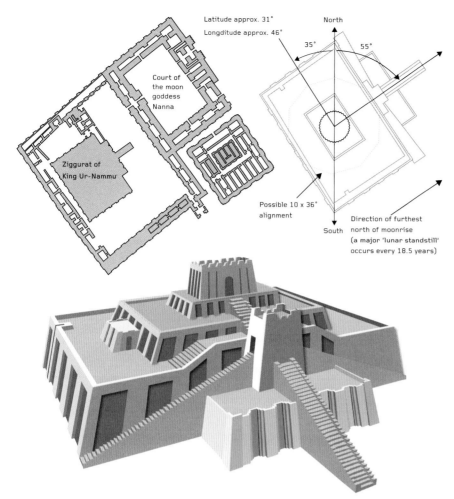

3.68 Possible reconstruction of the Great Ziggurat of Ur

ZIGGURATS

Ziggurats were built by the Sumerians, Babylonians, Elamites, Akkadians and Assyrians. As there was a very limited range of available building materials such as iron, stone or hard timber, clay was a primary medium for construction, mixed with hay and sun dried or baked. The precursors of the ziggurat were raised platforms built during the Ubaid period (c.6500–3800 BCE). The earliest ziggurat, situated in present-day Iran, dates to c.3000 BCE, while the latest Mesopotamian ziggurats date from the 6th century BCE.

Built in receding tiers on a rectangular, oval or square platform, the ziggurat was a terraced step pyramid with a flat top. Sun-baked bricks made up the core with facings of fired bricks on the outside, often glazed in different colours.

The Great Ziggurat of Ur in present-day Iraq, begun by King Ur-Nammu in around 2100 bce (see fig. 3.68), was a massive truncated-pyramid structure with a first tier base dimension of approximately 62 x 42 m (205 x 138 ft), and a first tier dimension top of approximately 57 x 38 m (187 x 127 ft). The original ziggurat is thought to have consisted of three tiers, with the first tier at a height of 20 m (70 ft). The second tier is no longer there but is thought to have been about 30 m (100 ft) from ground level. The ziggurat was surrounded by a large complex of buildings and was dedicated to the moon goddess Nanna, the divine patron of the city-state of Ur. The latitude of the site is approximately 31° north and the longitude is approximately 46° east (the Giza pyramids are at 30° and 31.13°). The main axis of the long side of the ziggurat is 35° from the north–south line but maybe this was just a slight misalignment and the angle was intended to be 36° – a 36° angle is a ten-part division of 360° and an effective division of the platform for priests to track celestial alignments. The staircase seems to align with the northernmost position of moonrise, which takes place every 18.6 years.

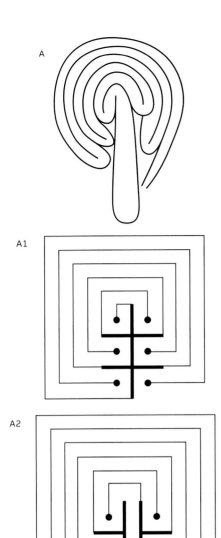

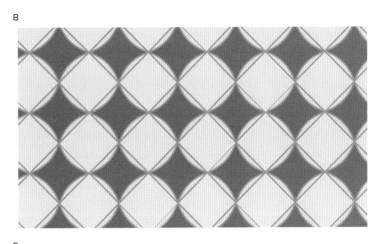

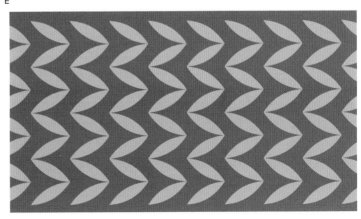

3.69 Mesopotamian labyrinth pattern A

MESOPOTAMIAN PATTERNS

Fig. 3.69 A: A number of small clay tablets from Mesopotamia dated around 1800 BCE contain labyrinth-like designs considered to show conditions of the liver used for the purpose of prophesy. Drawings A1 and A2 show possible keys for the design (see chapter 2).

Fig. 3.70 B: A 5th-millennium BCE pattern based on a Sumerian clay pot.

Fig. 3.70 C and D: Clay cone mosaic patterns from Uruk.

Fig. 3.70 E: Pattern based on a painted pot from the Ubaid period (c.6500–3800 BCE) found at the site of Tell al-Ubaid, near Ur, in present-day southern Iraq.

3.70 Mesopotamian patterns B, C, D, E

3.71 A lamassu with a human head and the body of a winged lion, 700 BCE

G

H

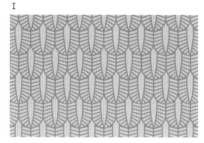
I

3.72 Mesopotamian patterns

3.73 Patterns from the palace of Nebuchadnezzar II

Fig. 3.71: A lamassu was a colossal sculpture with a human head and a winged bull's or lion's body that served as a protective deity. This statue was excavated at Nimrud (ancient Kalhu) in northern Mesopotamia.

Fig. 3.72: Pattern elements used on the lamassu in fig. 3.71.

Fig. 3.73: Pattern elements from a brilliantly coloured glazed-brick decoration from the façade shown in fig. 3.74.

Fig. 3.74: Coloured glazed-brick decoration from the façade of the throne room in the palace of Nebuchadnezzar II, Babylon, c.600 BCE.

Fig. 3.75: Royal Lion Hunt of Ashurbanipal, Nineveh, Mesopotamia, c.645–c.635 BCE: relief carvings of extraordinary finesse.

Fig. 3.76, 3.77, 3.78: Pattern elements featured on Babylonian clay tablets, c.1700 BCE.

3.74 Tiles from the palace of Nebuchadnezzar II

3.75 Royal Lion Hunt of Ashurbanipal, Nineveh, Mesopotamia, relief carving, c.645–c.635 BCE

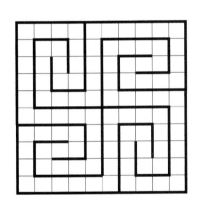

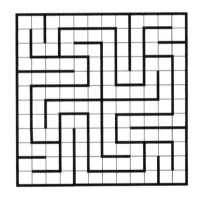

3.76 Babylonian clay tablet MS4516, 1700 BCE, and unidentified tablet of similar date

3.77 Babylonian clay tablets MS4516 and MS4515, 1700 BCE

3.78 Babylonian clay tablet MS4516, 1700 BCE

04. NATIVE AMERICAN CULTURES

THE PRE-COLUMBIAN AMERICAS

The geometries of the pre-Columbian era of the Americas were separated from the cultures of Asia, Europe and Africa by at least 15,000 years and, geographically, by the Bering Strait.

The general consensus is that the human migration into the 'New World' began towards the end of the last glacial period, around 25,000 to 20,000 years ago. Arrowheads found in Clovis, New Mexico, have been carbon dated at about 13,500 years old and there are possible Stone Age remains in Monte Verde, Chile, dated to approximately 12,800 BCE.

It is thought the first people that arrived in the Americas probably came from eastern Siberia across the Bering Land Bridge, or by small boats following the Bering Strait coastline. The diversity of Native American languages together with genetic evidence suggests that multiple migrations occurred from different parts of Asia, particularly through Alaska, with tribes initially travelling down the western shoreline of North America.

Early Native Americans moved from place to place following the migrations of animals and feeding off such things as wild fruits, berries and wild corn. There is evidence that farming began about 5,000 years ago with the development of corn crops. As agricultural methods became more productive and sustainable, seasonal and permanent settlements were established.

It appears that prehistoric Americans, up to the arrival of the Spanish in 1492, essentially remained in the technological Stone Age and did not advance into the Iron Age. This is said because there is no evidence of the use of hard metals such as iron or steel. Recent finds date the earliest use of gold and bronze to about 2100 BCE in the Andes and the earliest copper work to about 5000 BCE in the Great Lakes area of North America. Gold and copper were extracted, purified and shaped using heat and cold hammering techniques and used to make ceremonial or decorational items, tools and utensils.

NORTH AMERICA

Mound-building cultures The construction of mounds in the Americas commenced as long ago as 3400 BCE and possibly much earlier. These early mounds served either as burial sites or as ceremonial sites – and, in some cases, as astronomical observation platforms, particularly when positioned on hilltops. In certain areas, such as southern and eastern North America and Mesoamerica (Central America), mounds evolved into pyramids (200 BCE to 1500 CE), with similar functions as the earlier mounds but also to support or protect major civil buildings.

There are a number of mounds in the Mounds State Park of Anderson, Indiana. The largest is the Great Mound, believed to have been constructed around 160 BCE. The mound is circular with a diameter of 91 m (300 ft), and it is surrounded by a ditch with a south-to-southwest entrance. The mounds in the complex were constructed by the Adena people (flourished 1000 BCE to 200 BCE), a name given to the inhabitants of the region at the time, farmers and fishermen who traded their goods along the Illinois, Mississippi, Ohio and Tennessee rivers. Many Adena mounds were constructed as part of a burial ritual in which earth was piled up over a burned mortuary structure; the process would be repeated until a large earthwork had formed. From its alignments, it is likely that the Great Mound at Anderson was used for astronomical observations (see fig. 4.2).

The Adena culture was a precursor to the Hopewell tradition or culture (100 BCE–500 CE), a wide-ranging group of related populations connected by trade networks. The Portsmouth Earthworks is a large prehistoric mound complex constructed by the Ohio Hopewell culture. The three interconnected sections of the original site extended over 30 km (20 miles) in Ohio and Kentucky. The site was one of the largest earthwork ceremonial centres constructed by the Hopewell cultures. Portsmouth Group C, also known

4.1 Teotihuacán, Mexico

as the Biggs Site (see fig. 4.3), consisted of a series of concentric ditches and banks, with an Adena-era conical mound at the centre.

The Etowah Indian Mounds site is in Bartow County, Georgia, and was constructed and occupied in three phases from 1000 to 1550 by a regional variation of the Mississippian culture. There are three main platform mounds on the 22 ha (54 acre) site, which originally had log and thatch temples built on top of them. Mound C is shown in fig. 4.4.

The Mississippians were a mound-building people active between 800 and 1600. Their largest city is believed to have been Cahokia, of which only the Cahokia Mounds remain, near the modern city of St Louis, Missouri. At its peak, from the mid-10th until the mid-11th century Cahokia may have had a population of up to 20,000 people. We know from excavations that houses or ceremonial structures were built on top of the mounds and that other buildings were organized into city streets, public places and defensive structures. With a height of 30 m (100 ft) and covering 5 ha (12 acres), Cahokia's central focus, Monks Mound, is the largest prehistoric earthwork in the Americas (see fig. 4.5).

The Ocmulgee National Monument in Macon, Georgia, includes major earthworks built before 1000 by the South Appalachian Mississippian culture. The largest mound is the Great Temple Mound (see fig. 4.6), but there are also other ceremonial mounds, a burial mound and defensive trenches on the site.

The Great Serpent Mound (see fig. 4.7) in southwestern Ohio measures 411 m (1,348 ft) in length and is around 1 m (3 ft) high; it was probably constructed around 1070. The mound may have been constructed by the Fort Ancient people – a tribal or cultural name given to the Native American group that occupied the area from approximately 1000 to 1650, or perhaps by the Adena culture. The snake-like shape of the mound is markedly different from the circular and rectangular mounds common to the area. One interpretation of the form is that it is a representation of a rattlesnake about to swallow an egg – a snake with a spiral for a tail rather than a rattle. Alignments of certain parts of the snake may correspond with various celestial cycles.

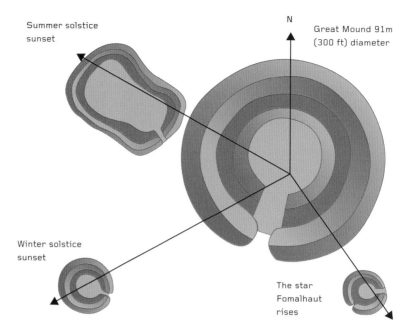

Summer solstice sunset

N

Great Mound 91m (300 ft) diameter

Winter solstice sunset

The star Fomalhaut rises

4.2 Adena Great Mound, Indiana, USA

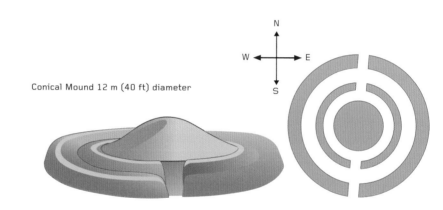

Conical Mound 12 m (40 ft) diameter

N
W — E
S

4.3 Biggs Site, Kentucky, USA (as per a drawing of the 1800s)

4.4 Mound C, Etowah Indian Mounds, Georgia, USA

4.5 Monks Mound, Cahokia Mounds, Missouri, USA

4.6 Ocmulgee National Monument, Georgia, USA

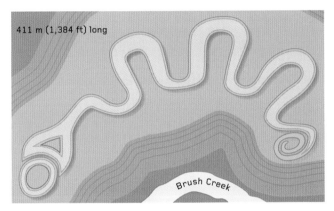

411 m (1,384 ft) long

Brush Creek

4.7 Great Serpent Mound, Ohio, USA

4.8 Mound City, Hopewell Culture National Historic Park, Ohio, USA

The Hopewell Culture National Historic Park in Chillicothe, Ohio, comprises six earthwork complexes over a large area. The Mound City site features a rectangular enclosure that accommodates at least 23 prehistoric tribal mounds. All the mounds are dome-shaped except for one that is elliptical. The largest mound is estimated to have been 5.3 m high (17.5 ft) and 27.5 m (90 ft) in diameter. Two other mounds are positioned just outside the enclosure. Carbon dating indicates that the mounds were constructed between 200 BCE and 500 CE (see fig. 4.8).

Medicine wheels and sighting stones

Hundreds of prehistoric cairns (piles or mounds of stones) are found throughout North America, some of which appear to have been in use since 2500 BCE. The cairns are often positioned on mountain or hill tops and many are in quite remote areas. It seems most likely that these early stone cairns served the same sort of purposes as the mounds – as ceremonial or astronomical sites. Some cairn sites were expanded with various types of stone arrangement. These sites are often known as 'medicine wheels' (see figs 4.9 and 4.10 overleaf). Exactly when the cairns were expanded is open for debate as there is no exact science for dating when stones are placed on the ground – stones could have been placed a hundred or a thousand years ago, or even further back in time.

It is logical to think that many of the tribes of North America observed the stars and noted how star and planet positions cycled as one year progressed into another, as well as noticing correspondences with the natural cycles of weather, plant and animal life and the seasonal migrations of animals. It therefore seems reasonable to assume that these early peoples selected special places within their territories to confirm solar and seasonal cycles – places on hill tops with clear views where sighting stones or landmarks could be used to confirm solar, lunar and star cycles; and places where ceremonies could be conducted to herald specific changes in the astronomical year.

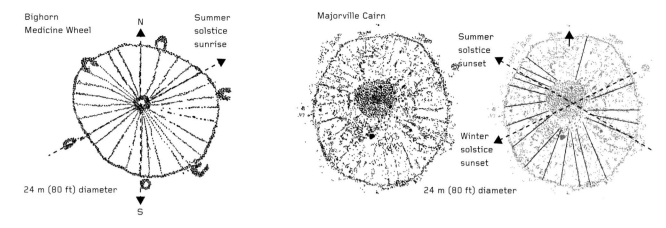

Bighorn Medicine Wheel

N

Summer solstice sunrise

Majorville Cairn

Summer solstice sunset

Winter solstice sunset

24 m (80 ft) diameter

24 m (80 ft) diameter

4.9 Bighorn Medicine Wheel, Wyoming, USA (left), and Majorville Cairn and Medicine Wheel, Alberta, Canada

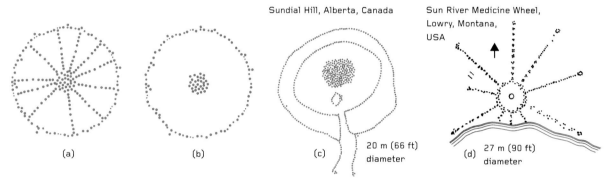

Sundial Hill, Alberta, Canada

Sun River Medicine Wheel, Lowry, Montana, USA

(a)

(b)

(c) 20 m (66 ft) diameter

(d) 27 m (90 ft) diameter

4.10 Types of medicine wheel built around cairns

Early North American dwellings

Like other prehistoric peoples, pre-Columbian Americans constructed their homes and meeting places out of the materials of their environment, using earth, clay, seashells, branches, bark, timber, bones, animal hides, sod, roughly shaped stone, rocks and even ice. Materials were combined creatively – for example mud, clay, animal dung or even snow was used to cover sticks or branches. Architectural technologies included weaving, sewing, carving, curing, coating, cutting, and sun or pit baking (mixes of clay, shell fragments and sand).

Tribes of the North American plains constructed short-term seasonal or portable habitats such as wigwams or tipis. Tribes living in areas that provided year-round resources constructed more permanent dwellings such as the plank houses of the Northwest, the longhouses of the Northeast, or the wattle-and-daub, sod and mud houses of the Southwest. The Pueblo group of American Indians constructed houses made of stone and bricks formed out of adobe clay, sand, grass and straw mixed together. Pueblo homes were built in canyons,

on top of mesas, in caves and in some cases partially underground – often accommodating communities for more than a thousand years.

Geometric shapes The geometric shapes of Native American dwellings mirror those of the ancient and classic societies of Europe, Africa and Asia, even though they are separated by at least some 10,000–15,000 years and the Bering Strait. This equivalence raises thoughts as to the nature of the primary geometric forms used in the Americas and whether or not they are structurally derived from the materials used, or the product of common human spatial abstractions, or a remnant of concepts brought over from Asia when the ancestors of the Native Americans braved the late ice-age land bridge or the post ice-age coastal waters. It is intriguing, for example, that the Pueblo peoples created rectangular block housing very similar in style and construction to structures found in the ancient Indus and Nile valleys; that the Cherokee built homes that would not have been out of place in medieval England, with their rectangular bases and triangular roofs;

that Abenaki portable wigwams almost exactly anticipate the construction of modern tents with external flexible rods supporting inner flexible coverings; and that Northwest plank houses seem to have been teleported back in time from America's Wild West (see fig. 4.11). Similarly, the Ancestral Puebloan buildings shown in figs 4.12 to 4.15 would not seem out of place in ancient Mesopotamia or Celtic Spain.

Speculations regarding the parallels in geometric forms used by the ancient societies of the Americas, Europe, Africa and Asia can run wild but, architecturally, the most likely reasons for the similarities are that the structural properties, and the possibilities of the materials used, fulfilled the same essential requirements for all the different peoples – along with the nature of human invention.

Stars and alignments Northern tribal concepts of the stars are woven into legends and stories rather than recorded as written documents.

The Pawnee of the southern Great Plains had no calendar as such but reckoned the year in moons, alternately

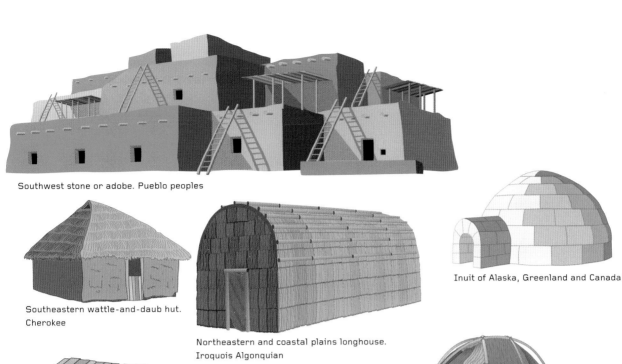

Southwest stone or adobe. Pueblo peoples

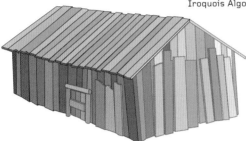

Southeastern wattle-and-daub hut. Cherokee

Northeastern and coastal plains longhouse. Iroquois Algonquian

Inuit of Alaska, Greenland and Canada

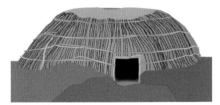

Northwest coast plank house, Salish style. Chinook and Yurok

Mat or bark wigwam. Cone and dome shapes. Algonquian and Abenaki

Tipi – tent-like house. Plains tribes, Sioux and Crow

West coast and plateau mud pit house. Navajo and Sioux

Sod or adobe hogan. Navajo

4.11 Tribal habitats

12 and 13, like the Maya (see p.115). There were three moons in each of the four seasons – spring, summer, autumn and winter – and the thirteenth moon was added at the end of the summer quarter when needed to realign lunar and solar cycles. Anthropologists believe that the seasonal moons had names that corresponded with seasonal events such as 'the moon when the caribou arrive' or 'the moon when there is no food'.

Navajo creation legends describe earlier worlds, or ages, before the Earth was formed. Like the Navajo (and the Maya and Aztecs), the Hopi believed that

there were eight worlds before this one, and that today's Earth is the last of the worlds – a world that will ultimately be destroyed.

Navajo traditions have it that the Earth was originally illuminated by four sources of light: a white light from the east, a blue light from the south, a yellow light from the west, and darkness from the north; there was no sun and no moon. It is said that the First Woman created the sun and moon from a slab of quartz to provide more light for the First People – the sun to provide heat and light and the moon to provide coolness and moisture. The

quartz story relates that there were bits of quartz left over and the First Woman tossed them into the sky to make the stars.

The Pawnee built lodges aligned east–west that also functioned as observatories, with the smoke hole aligned to enable observation of the Pleiades. Four posts were positioned at the four cardinal directions. Pawnee seasonal rituals were tied to celestial observation. The Skidi band of Pawnee were known for their Morning Star ceremony, a ritual human sacrifice that took place in spring, in which a young girl would be captured

4.12 Mesa Verde National Park, Colorado, USA

4.13 Aztec Ruins National Monument, New Mexico, USA

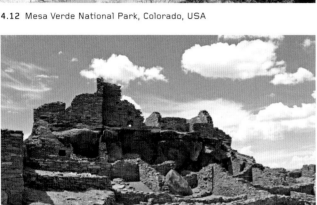

4.14 Wupatki National Monument, Arizona, USA

4.15 Pecos Pueblo, Pecos National Park, New Mexico, USA

from a neighbouring tribe and sacrificed to the Morning Star. Human sacrifice of this type is reminiscent of the practices of the Maya and the Aztecs.

Native Americans noticed how some groups of stars appeared above the horizon and then disappeared during the course of a year, and they matched these appearances and disappearances with seasonal events. To the Lakota, the constellation we know as Orion is known as the Wintermaker, as its full formation appears only in the winter. For the Pawnee, the horseshoe shape of the Corona Borealis was considered to be a circle of chiefs presided over by the Great Chief – the star we know as Polaris (see fig. 4.16).

NOTE: The stars, planets and sun appear to rotate around the Earth's axis every 24 hours – around the pole star in the north and empty space in the south. Because the rotational axis of the Earth is at a 23° angle to the plane (ecliptic) of the Earth's annual orbit around the sun the paths of the stars, planets and sun appear to move higher and lower during each calendar year.

4.16 Northern hemisphere constellations

Native American counting It has been estimated that there were in the order of one thousand Native American tribes speaking about the same number of languages, although those languages were derivatives of possibly ten core languages. Given this level of diversification, it is not surprising that many variations of mathematical skill evolved.

As might be expected, early Native American counting systems started with the human body – the number of fingers on the hands and feet – and counting in groups of 10 and 20 was common.

The Yuki tribe occupied the western coastal region (present-day California) and counted the gaps between the fingers of both hands, creating a base eight numeric system. It is interesting to speculate how a number system might have developed if fingers, toes and gaps were counted. One hand would create the number nine and, if base ten was used, two hands (counting only fingers on the second hand, with each finger representing ten) could be used to count up to 59 (5 x 10 + 9) and, using fingers and toes, 159 (15 x 10 + 9).

Another California people, the Maidu, counted just fingers and toes, no gaps, describing the number 10 as 'hand-double' and the number 20 as 'man-one'. The Pomo, also of California, counted up to the tens of thousands using long strings of clamshell beads and corresponding stick lengths with 400 to a 'big stick'.

Symbols, tallies and dots One of the largest concentrations of petroglyphs in North America is in the Boca de Potrerillos archaeological site in Mexico. Fig. 4.17 shows a petroglyph representation of, possibly, a necklace of approximately 193 beads, and rectangular arrangements of marks representing the numbers 14, 17 and 62. Carving representations of quantities on stone would take time and might indicate that a permanent record was needed – maybe a tally of items as part of a trade or treaty.

The marks on the 'count stone' of Presa de La Mula in northwestern Mexico are organized in six rows. The marks could be a pictographic representation of something that communicates quantity, possibly a record of something valuable that could be supported by two poles – maybe pelts or scalps (see fig. 4.18).

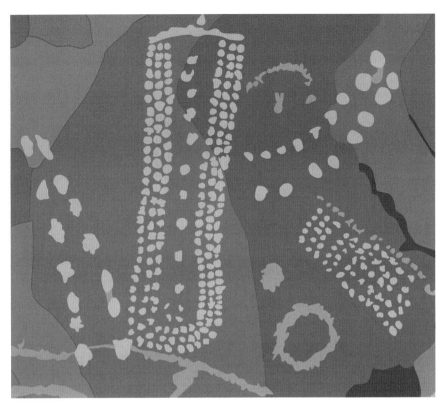

4.17 Petroglyph, Boca de Potrerillos, Nuevo Léon, Mexico

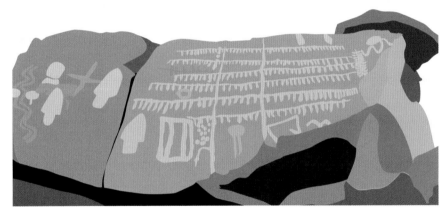

4.18 Petroglyph, count stone, Presa de La Mula, Nuevo Léon, Mexico

Patterns The patterns shown in fig. 4.19 (overleaf) are from ancient Ancestral Puebloan, Apache and Navajo tribal pots and baskets, although many tribes used similar patterns. The step patterns evoke the pyramids of Mesoamerica. The geometries are not especially sophisticated, but many are unique to the Americas and quite distinctive.

4.19 Examples of Apache, Navajo and Ancestral Puebloan patterns

MESOAMERICA

THE MAYA

The Preclassic period of Maya civilization dates from 2000 BCE to 250 CE, with the first cities established around 750 BCE. The Classic period, starting around 250 CE, is defined by the establishment of large city-states covering an area that encompasses today's Guatemala, El Salvador, Belize, Honduras and much of Mexico. The area includes the flat plains of the Yucatán Peninsula and the mountains of western Mexico, Guatemala, and El Salvador. The climate and soil fertility of the area varies from the relatively fertile valleys of western Mexico to the semi-arid brush forests of northern Yucatán and the evergreen forests of southern Yucatán and Guatemala. Overall the lack of usable land and the poor condition of the soil presented a challenge for the Maya farmers of Mesoamerica, and much depended upon predicting when the wet season would start and end – a time frame that (in terms of our Western calendar) starts in mid-April and ends in mid-November.

It seems most likely that the first settlers in the Mesoamerican region brought with them traditions associated with the seasons of the North, where climatic changes are much more severe than the more temperate temperature cycles of Central America. However, once the region had been settled and civil societies established then maximizing crop yields would have become essential, necessitating an accurate means to predict the wet season. Any northern traditions for predicting seasonal cycles probably only survived in legends or in ritualized form. Over time traditions and practices evolved in the area to become what we now know as 'Mayan' – and during that time the means to forecast seasonal and astronomical time became quite sophisticated.

Calendars The Maya developed various calendars, each with a unique logic. There were calendars based on the observed cycles of the moon, the sun and Venus (the second brightest object in the night sky).

Much like the Egyptians, the Maya used a pictographic script (known as glyphs) that combined symbolic and syllabic images, similar in function to modern Japanese script. To indicate time or quantity the Maya combined numeric symbols, including a symbol for zero, with their pictographs (see fig. 4.20). To show numbers greater than 20 they used a placement system (see figs 4.20, 4.21 and 4.22), which was, in some ways, similar to the units and multiples of ten that we use in our decimal system.

To illustrate the phases of the moon, the Maya drew glyphs with numbers drawn at the side illustrating a count of days from the last new moon (see fig. 4.21). The truncated U-like symbols at the bottom of the moon glyphs for 21 days, 28 days and 29 days show 20s as multiples of five. The Maya knew that the phases of the moon roughly cycled over a 28½-day period, but as they had no specific symbols for fractions they averaged out the lunar calendar year by alternating 28- and 29-day months – hence the 28-day and 29-day glyphs.

The Maya seasonal calendar of 365 days is known as the Haab and follows cycles that correspond, as we know today,

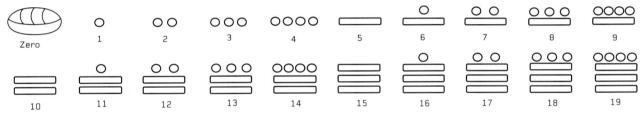

4.20 Maya numbers from 0 to 19

4.21 Maya lunar series glyphs

7,200s (20x360)			○
360s (18x20)		○	○ ─
20s	○ ○	○ ○ ○	○ ○ ○ ═
1s	○ ○ ═	○ ─	○○○○
	52	426	9629

4.22 Number placement system

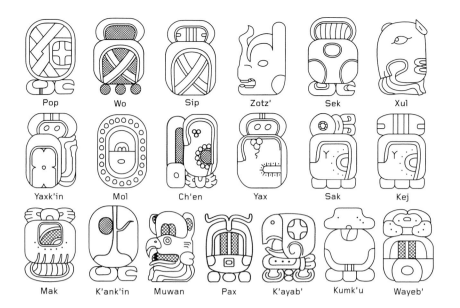

4.23 The Maya seasonal year calendar, or Haab

Pop | Wo | Sip | Zotz' | Sek | Xul
Yaxk'in | Mol | Ch'en | Yax | Sak | Kej
Mak | K'ank'in | Muwan | Pax | K'ayab' | Kumk'u | Wayeb'

4.24 The Chak Ek' (Venus) glyph

with the Earth's orbit around the sun. The Haab consisted of 19 months, made up of 18 months of 20 days and one (unlucky) month, Wayeb, of just five days (see fig. 4.23).

Venus, for the Maya, was the companion of the sun and the herald of war, and was known as Chak Ek', or the Great Star. Its reappearance in the evening sky after being absent from the morning sky for about 50 days (during a superior conjunction – that is, being hidden behind the sun) was a time to make human sacrifices and to make war (see figs 4.24, 4.25 and 4.26).

There are no indications that the Maya had a concept of planets travelling along elliptical paths around the sun, or even that they knew that the Earth is roughly a sphere that rotates around its own axis once a day. We now know that the planet Venus orbits the sun, that the orbit is roughly circular and that it takes 224.7 Earth days for Venus to complete one orbit. We also know that Venus orbits the sun almost exactly 13 times for every eight orbits of the Earth, passing the Earth five times within the eight years. In fact, from a starting position of the two planets at their closest (at their 'inferior conjunction') – Venus rapidly rotates away from the Earth, travels around the backside of the sun (at its superior conjunction), passes the starting point, and does this twice to finally catch up with the Earth after a total of 583.92 days, and then repeats the cycle every 583.92 days thereafter (see fig. 4.25).

For the Maya it was important to observe, record and understand the movements of Venus, despite not having any planetary models to help them. Even so, their observations revealed five cycles of Venus's position in the skies, ten cycles of brightness, and five star backgrounds for each cycle within an eight-year period – and they noted that

Venus at the end of the eight-year period would once again lie in front of the same star background as it did at the beginning. The Maya also observed another cycle: a slow progression of the patterns of Venus against its background of stars – a movement in a clockwise direction at a rate of about one day every 20 years.

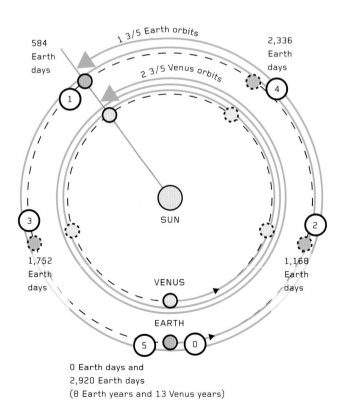

4.25 The orbits of Earth and Venus

Venus' orbit is closer to the sun than the Earth, which is why it always appears in the sky close to the sun – either before it (morning) or behind it (evening)

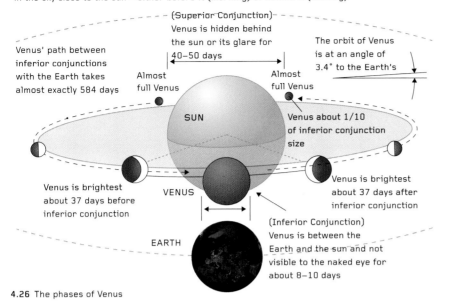

(Superior Conjunction)
Venus is hidden behind the sun or its glare for 40–50 days

The orbit of Venus is at an angle of 3.4° to the Earth's

Venus' path between inferior conjunctions with the Earth takes almost exactly 584 days

Almost full Venus

Almost full Venus

SUN

Venus about 1/10 of inferior conjunction size

Venus is brightest about 37 days before inferior conjunction

VENUS

Venus is brightest about 37 days after inferior conjunction

EARTH

(Inferior Conjunction)
Venus is between the Earth and the sun and not visible to the naked eye for about 8–10 days

4.26 The phases of Venus

Seasonal events were predicted using the Haab calendar, and the moon's cycles and variances provided a readily observable seasonal clock. However, there was another calendar known as the Tzolk'in. As to why this calendar was considered necessary is open to debate, although it was (and still is by present-day Maya communities) used to determine the timing of ceremonial events and for divination. The adoption of the calendar is odd because of its unusual means of creating day sequences – a means that does not immediately correspond with lunar or solar cycles (see fig. 4.27).

The Tzolk'in calendar combines 20 day-names with 13 day-numbers to produce 260 unique days. Each successive day is numbered from 1 up to 13 and the cycle then starts again at 1.

For the Maya a calendar date is specified by its position in both the Tzolk'in and the Haab calendars, so that each day is defined by two numbers and two symbols, combining the number and symbol of the 260 Tzolk'in days with the number and symbol of the 365 Haab days. This makes a total of 18,980 combinations for a total of 52 years, known to the Maya as the Calendar Round. Arithmetically, the duration of the Calendar Round is the lowest common multiple of 260 and 365: 18,980 is 73 × 260 Tzolk'in days and 52 × 365 Haab days.

Since the Calendar Round dates repeat every 18,980 days, approximately 52 solar years (a period thought to correspond

with a human lifetime), a more refined method of dating was needed if history was to be recorded accurately. To specify dates over periods longer than 52 years, Mesoamericans used the Long Count calendar. The Long Count calendar identifies a date by counting the number of days from the Maya creation date 4 Ahaw, 8 Kumk'u (11 August 3114 BCE) in years of 360 days. Long Count days are given using a modified base 20 placement and number base system such that the

third digit from the right (and only that digit) functions as multiples of 360 (20 × 18) with multiples of 20 thereafter (see fig. 4.22). For example: 8.5.16.9.7 days represents 8 × (20 × 20 × 20 × 18) + 5 × (20 × 20 × 18) + 16 × (20 × 18) + 9 × (20) + 7 = 1,193,929 days = 3,316 years (each of 360 days). This means that the Long Count diverges from the Haab by five days every year, making it a unique and separate cycle.

As we have seen, the numbers 13 and 20 determine the sequence of the Tzolk'in calendar and their multiple of 260 is the number of number-glyph pairs generated. Why these particular numbers were used is unknown and open to speculation.

It seems most unlikely that the use of the number 13 arises from the fact that Venus orbits the sun 13 times when the Earth rotates eight times. Without a planetary model the Maya would have to have observed 13 correspondences of Venus with stars, or star clusters, over an eight-year Earth cycle – very difficult if not impossible to see. However, the start of the Maya Long Count calendar was what they referred to as the 'birth of Venus'. A Venus Round was a period of 104 years, or two Calendar Rounds, which was the point in time when all of the sacred Maya calendars were realigned with the cycle of Venus. The number 104 is a multiple of 8 (8 × 13).

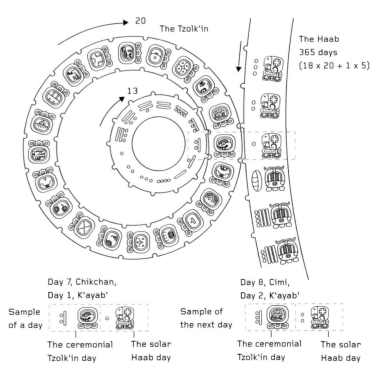

20 The Tzolk'in

13

The Haab
365 days
(18 × 20 + 1 × 5)

Day 7, Chikchan,
Day 1, K'ayab'

Sample of a day

The ceremonial Tzolk'in day

The solar Haab day

Day 8, Cimi,
Day 2, K'ayab'

Sample of the next day

The ceremonial Tzolk'in day

The solar Haab day

4.27 Maya calendar with Tzolk'in and Haab wheels

At the equator, shadows fall to the north for half a year and to the south for half a year except at the equinoxes, 22 June, and 22 December, when the sun is directly overhead at noon. At latitude 14° 47' 21" N, shadows fall for 260 days to the north and 105 days to the south, with the sun directly overhead at noon on 30 April and 13 August. Given this, it is possible that the 260-day count of the Tzolk'in calandar originated at one of the oldest Maya sites, Kaminaljuyu, latitude 14° 37' 55" N. Fig. *4.28* uses an image of Stela 31 (a carved stone shaft) from Tikal, Guatemala, to represent a sighting stone similar to one that might have been used to count days at Kaminaljuyu.

Another possible explanation for the numeric quantities used in the Tzolk'in calendar is that the Pleiades constellation appears directly overhead at midnight every 52 years in Mesoamerica, with a Venus alignment every 104 years (52 x 2). The Mayans believed that the Pleiades was the home of their ancestors.

A Tzolk'in pairing with Venus and possibly with the Pleiades, combined with Maya legends, might well explain why the numeric values of 52 and 104 were used to determine ceremonial dates and served as a sort of fortune-telling system, by which the number-glyph pairs of the Tzolk'in functioned a bit like the Chinese I Ching (see chapter 3).

Maya pyramids Mesoamerican pyramids are usually step pyramids with a temple on top – more akin to the ziggurats of Mesopotamia than to the pyramids of ancient Egypt. Early Maya pyramids were not much more than simple burial mounds but they rapidly evolved from about 1000 CE into the spectacular pyramids that we can still see today. Maya pyramids, as with Egyptian pyramids, were built as part of larger complexes and functioned as centrepieces for ceremonies, for burying powerful rulers, for conducting sacrificial rituals, and for observing the motions of the sun, moon, stars and planets, particularly Venus.

The region's largest pyramid by volume is the Great Pyramid of Cholula, in the Mexican state of Puebla. In fact the Cholula pyramid is the largest in the world by volume (see fig. 4.33 for a size comparison with other pyramids).

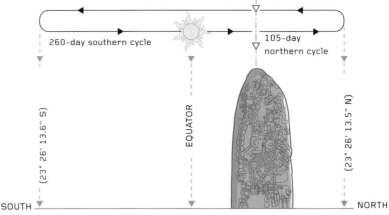

The sun appears directly overhead twice a year within the tropics, once a year at the tropics of Cancer and Capricorn during the summer solstice, and never north or south of the tropics.

14° 47' 21" N

260-day southern cycle

105-day northern cycle

(23° 26' 13.6" S)

EQUATOR

(23° 26' 13.5" N)

SOUTH

NORTH

4.28 Possible link between the Kaminaljuyu 260-day shadow cycle and the Tzolk'in calendar

4.29 El Castillo, Chichén Itzá, Mexico

4.30 Pyramid of the Magician, Uxmal, Mexico

4.31 Pyramid of the Sun, Teotihuacán, Mexico

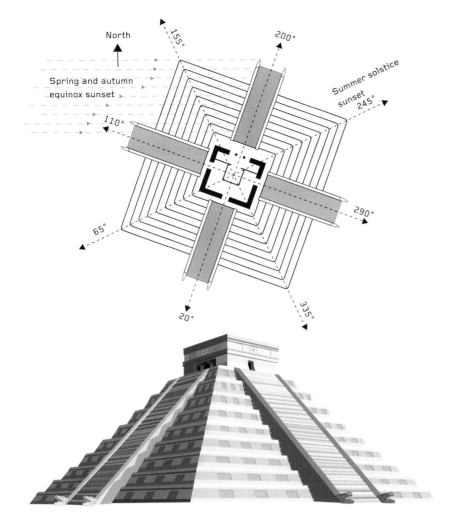

North

Spring and autumn
equinox sunset

155°

200°

Summer solstice
sunset
245°

110°

65°

290°

20°

335°

4.32 El Castillo, Chichén Itzá, Mexico

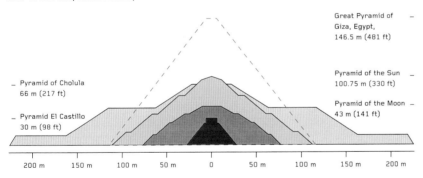

Great Pyramid of Giza, Egypt,
146.5 m (481 ft)

Pyramid of the Sun
100.75 m (330 ft)

Pyramid of the Moon
43 m (141 ft)

Pyramid of Cholula
66 m (217 ft)

Pyramid El Castillo
30 m (98 ft)

200 m   150 m   100 m   50 m   0   50 m   100 m   150 m   200 m

4.33 Maya pyramid sizes compared with the Great Pyramid at Giza, Egypt

4.34 El Caracol, Chichén Itzá, Mexico

El Castillo (the Castle; also known as Kukulcán's Pyramid) stands in the centre of Chichén Itzá on the Yucatán Peninsula of Mexico. Its diagonal alignment appears to be along the line of the summer solstice. The pyramid has four stairways each with 91 steps, making a total of 365 steps if one counts the top platform as a step – a correspondence with the number of days in a year (see figs 4.29 and 4.32).

Twice a year, during the late afternoon, and over a few days surrounding the equinoxes, an unusual shadow appears on the west-facing balustrade of the northern stairway. As the shadow slowly descends from the top of the pyramid one level at a time it has the appearance of a serpent with its head at the base of the staircase (see fig. 4.32). The pyramid's diagonal aligns with the summer solstice and its western side faces the direction of sunset on the 25 May – traditionally the date of the transition from the dry to the rainy season.

Another structure in Chichén Itzá is known as El Caracol (the Snail – named after its internal spiral staircase). It is a tower that sits high on a four-cornered, though not quite square, platform that would have given excellent unobstructed views of the skies and surrounding landscape and was likely used as an observatory (fig. 4.34). It does seem to have some alignment with the positions of Venus and other astronomical events known to the Maya. Fig. 4.35 (overleaf) uses some guesswork as to how the structure might have actually looked.

Many of the architectural structures in places such as Chichén Itzá, Uxmal, Uaxactun and Edzná appear to be aligned with celestial bodies and cycles, including solstices, equinoxes, and positions of the moon and planets, particularly Venus. However, a level of guesswork is required when interpreting Maya architectural alignments as building methods were not that precise.

Mathematics Not much survives in the way of evidence for mathematics higher than simple addition and subtraction, although basic Maya arithmetic would have benefited from the use of their symbol for zero – one of the earliest recorded uses of such a symbol. Maya numerology is easily capable of being adapted for multiplication and division,

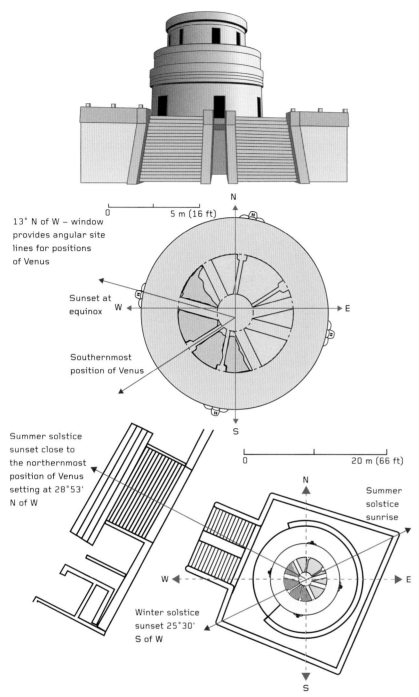

13° N of W – window provides angular site lines for positions of Venus

0   5 m (16 ft)

N

Sunset at equinox
W   E

Southernmost position of Venus

S

Summer solstice sunset close to the northernmost position of Venus setting at 28°53' N of W

0   20 m (66 ft)

N

Summer solstice sunrise

W   E

Winter solstice sunset 25°30' S of W

S

4.35 El Caracol, Chichén Itzá, Mexico

(see fig. 4.36). They clearly understood the concept of the circle, as evidenced by the many examples of circles used in Maya architecture and design. (Another Mesoamerican people constructed unique circular pyramids of Los Guachimontones near the town of Teuchitlán in the Mexican state of Jalisco.) Concepts of spheres were also well understood: a prime example is the solid rubber balls used in the ball game played by the Maya and the Aztecs (see fig. 4.37).

So why not the wheel? Various ideas have been put forward, from the difficulty of creating wheeled vehicles or constructing the wheel itself to attaching it, in a low-friction way to a wagon or a chariot. The steep, wet and muddy terrain may also have presented difficulties. The

4.36 Maya wheeled toy

4.37 Aztec ball game ring

particularly if a pure base-20 number system (units, 20s, 400s, 8000, etc.) was used rather than the calendar-adapted base 20 (see fig. 4.22). Fractions were written as simple 'parts' of a quantity: 1/4, 2/4, 4/4 parts from a new moon, or parts of a day or a period of time. There is no evidence of spatial mathematics (trigonometry, and mathematics to calculate areas and volumes), a fact perhaps reflected in the lack of regularity in architecture, with imprecise alignments, rough-cut or uncut building blocks (stone,

bricks), and no apparent use of specific ratios such as Pythagorean triples to control construction. However, given the accuracy of astronomical records it is most likely that other means besides architectural alignments were used to confirm astronomical events, such as sighting stones, shadow progressions, and alignments with objects on the horizon.

The wheel There is no doubt that the Maya understood the concept of the wheel, as wheeled toys have been found

most convincing reason, however, appears to be a lack of animals strong enough to pull loads: there were no horses and no domesticated cows or bulls.

Patterns The use of pattern elements in Maya architecture is fairly limited to simple and essentially irregular polygonal forms with more emphasis on glyphs and figurative forms for decoration or symbolism (see figs 4.38 and 4.39), where the drawing makes the patterns look more regular than they actually are.

4.38 Line drawing of decorative elements on La Iglesia, Chichén Itzá

4.39 Drawings of Maya architectural designs

THE AZTECS

Maya civilization collapsed around 900
CE, possibly owing to environmental
degradation and drought. Overlapping the
period of the collapse, and from about the
6th century, various groups of Nahuatl-
speaking people (ethnic Nahuas) began
to migrate into northern Maya territories
from what is now northwestern Mexico,
to become the dominant ethnic group
by about 1000. By the 13th century
Nahua city-states were well established,
benefiting from many of the agricultural,
cosmological and architectural practices
of the Maya. The Aztecs were a
Nahuatl-speaking people whose capital,
Tenochtitlan, was the largest city in the
pre-Conquest Americas. With their two
most powerful allies they formed the Aztec
Triple Alliance in the 14th century – a
short-lived empire that would fall at
the hands of the Spanish in 1521.

The Aztec Sun Stone The massive Aztec
Sun Stone, 3.58 m (11¾ ft) in diameter,
is a symbolic portrayal of the four

4.40 Drawing of the Aztec Sun Stone

disasters that led to the demise of the four prior universes in Aztec cosmology, surrounded by their glyphs of 20 days (see fig. 4.41) for each of their 18 months. The days correspond with Maya days but are represented by different glyphs and names.

4.41 Glyphs for the 20 Aztec days

TRIBES OF THE SOUTH

THE INCA

The vast Inca empire flourished from the early 13th century until its fall following the Spanish conquest in the mid-16th century. The empire was centred on their capital, Cuzco, in the Peruvian Andes, and at its peak ranged from Ecuador in the north to Chile in the south. The origins of the Inca are unclear but there is evidence to show that their empire was built upon earlier city-states and chiefdoms established along the western coast of South America.

Inca astronomy and measures Inca astronomy seems to have been less sophisticated than that of the Maya, but was similarly based on alignments of the sun, moon, planets and stars with sighting stones and features on the horizon. The Inca calendar matched seasonal and solar cycles with lunar cycles (average 29.5 days from full moon to full moon) by adding 11 days every winter solstice to a 12 lunar-month year. The Inca understood equinoxes, solstices, zenith passages and the Venus cycle, but they could not predict eclipses. Lunar months were celebrated with religious ceremonies and were named for seasonal tasks – for example 'the month of the potato

harvest'. Time was measured by the position of the sun and by shadow lengths. Quipus and counting boards were used to account time, space, and quantities, counting in base ten.

The quipu (fig. 4.42) was a system of knotted strings or cords used by the Inca to store information important to their culture and civilization. Inca Garcilaso de la Vega – son of a Spanish conquistador and an Inca noblewoman – described the quipu in his *Royal Commentaries*, published in 1609. As he described them, quipus are knotted arrangements of cords or strings where the colours of the materials used, the number of strings, the type of knots tied, and their arrangement and number communicated types of things to be counted and quantities. Some specific types of knot or cord would also be used symbolically. An individual quipu might be used to communicate things to do with a harvest or a military venture. Garcilaso de la Vega describes quipus that would account agricultural production starting with wheat, then rye, then peas, then beans, and so forth. In the same way, as an inventory of arms, quipus would account superior arms, such as lances, then javelins, bows and arrows, hatchets and maces, and lastly slings and any other arms that were used.

The word *quipu* literally means 'knot', and the positions of the knots were used to communicate quantities and even dates, following a positional decimal system. A knot in a row farthest from the main supporting strand represented 1, the next

farthest 10, and so on. The absence of knots on a cord implied zero.

There is debate as to whether or not quipus were also used to communicate descriptively. According to archaeologists Robert and Marcia Ascher from Cornell University, New York, about 20 per cent of surviving quipus are 'clearly non-numerical', implying that they also served as a written language. Unfortunately, at this time no 'Rosetta Stone' has been found that will help our further interpretations of the meanings of quipus.

Note: Parallels to the use of quipus include Christian prayer ropes of knots and strings of beads, and knotted lengths of rope used by Bedouins to communicate numbers and dates. The North American Pomo tribe counted up to the tens of thousands using long strings of clamshell beads.

Technology Like the Maya, the Inca did not use wheels to move heavy loads, probably for the same reasons, as they too lacked draft animals to pull wagons and ploughs. Gold and copper were often used to fashion ceremonial objects and copper, and stone tools were used to carve stone, but there is no evidence that hard metals such as iron were developed to make tools or weapons. Inca technologies were mostly those of earth and stone, and three-dimensional structures were built without binding agents such as cement or mud. Ceramics were painted with images of animals, birds, waves and cats, and

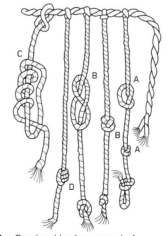

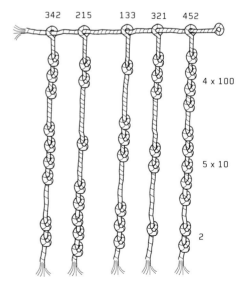

A = Overhand knot represents 1
B = Figure-eight knot represents 1
C = Long knot represents 4
D = Long knot represents 3

4.42 Quipu knots and binary numbers

with geometric patterns similar to those of the Nazca (see below).

Architecture Amazing terraces were cut into hill and mountain sides for agriculture, and stones quarried, fashioned and combined to build roads, temples, aqueducts, administrative buildings, bridges, meeting centres and homes (see fig. 4.43).

Inca carved polygonal stone work can be unique, with interlocking blocks carved out of granite or limestone (fig. 4.44). Blocks were carved with rounded edges and shaped to be roughly rectangular or in other polygonal forms. Walls were often built to slope backwards, making them particularly stable during an earthquake.

Building materials other than stone were used depending upon what was available within the environment, including sometimes fieldstone and adobe. Roofs were mostly wooden or thatched. Floor plans were mostly rectangular and buildings were often placed around a central courtyard.

THE NAZCA

The Nazca were a collection of chiefdoms that predated the Incas. The artefacts that survive them include beautifully crafted pottery, irrigation systems and the famous Nazca Lines – ancient geoglyphs constructed in the high Nazca Desert that are believed to have been constructed between 500 BCE and 500 CE (fig. 4.45). The largest figures are up to 370 m (1,200 ft) long, and there are hundreds of them, ranging from lines and geometric shapes to animal outlines, human figures, and trees and flowers.

4.43 Machu Picchu, Cuzco region, Peru

4.44 Inca polygonal stonework

4.45 Nazca Lines, Peru

05. THE PYTHAGOREANS

HIGHER LEVELS OF ABSTRACTION IN VISUAL LOGIC

The ancient Greeks recognized the perfection of their abstractions and treasured a belief that their refined geometric and numeric languages mirrored something eternal.

What is known as Greek geometry started as a synthesis of the geometries of other civilizations, such as Babylonian, Egyptian and that of the Indus Valley, and evolved into an extraordinarily high level of abstraction and deductive reasoning – into 'eternal forms' and axiomatic logic.

Ideas of length, area, volume and weight all preceded the Greeks, as did calculations for the area of a circle and knowledge of what are now called Pythagorean triples. The triples are the whole number side lengths of a right-angled triangle, where the square of one, the hypotenuse, equals the sum of the squares of the other two: for example, side lengths of 3, 4, 5 have squares with areas of 9, 16, 25 (fig. 5.2).

The Greeks beautifully refined the concepts of other civilizations and then applied a strict discipline of deductive and axiomatic reasoning to take the abstractions of geometry to a whole new level. At the same time the Greeks honoured the 'quest', so to speak, and applied it in ways never thought of before. They saw a perfection in their abstractions and treasured a belief that they were inspired by something eternal – and so they pursued the geometric forms generated by their logic and opened doors to experiences that, at least at the time, seemed outside any possible physical reality, an approach that is fundamentally different from creating geometries for immediate practical application.

It is very difficult to know who invented what during the golden days of the Greek civilization as the knowledge we have is so fragmented. There is a Greek lineage of sorts – including Thales (635–543 BCE), Pythagoras (582–496 BCE), Philolaus (470–385 BCE), Hippasus (5th century BCE), Archytas of Tarentum (428–347 BCE), Plato (427–347 BCE), Eudoxus (410–355 BCE), Aristotle

'Let no one ignorant of geometry enter here.'
PLATO (427–347 BCE)

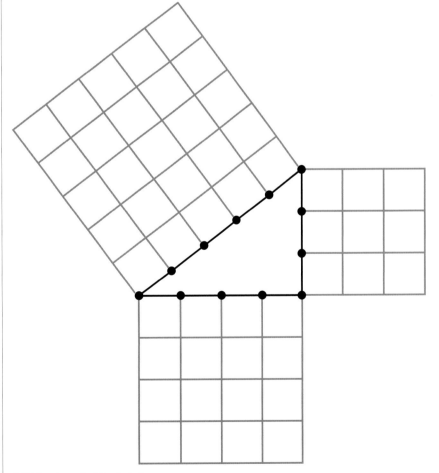

5.1 *The School of Athens*, Raphael (1509–11)

5.2 Visual proof of the 3, 4, 5 Pythagorean triple

(384–322 BCE), Euclid (325–265 BCE), Archimedes (287–212 BCE) – but what was invented by whom is difficult to tell, and many ideas, doubtless, were picked up from earlier cultures. Even the ideas in Euclid's *Elements* are not wholly original, and many of the theorems were probably just very succinct formalizations of the concepts of others.

Comparing equivalent concepts developed by different cultures is interesting as it reveals different perspectives and local influences. For example, compare the point and line axiomatic definitions of the *Mo Jing* in China with those of Euclid in Greece (see pp.95–96).

THE PYTHAGOREANS

Pythagoras (c.570–c.500/490 BCE) was a Greek mathematician and philosopher, founder of the movement known as Pythagoreanism. Little definite is known about his life and teachings, as most sources were written down long after his death. During the next centuries, the Pythagoreans were the men and women who followed, and further developed, the teachings of Pythagoras. They developed exercises, sacred music, geometries, philosophies and lifestyle practices, designed to create something in their beings that would outlast death; they believed in the transmigration of the soul.

The exploration of numbers and divine geometries was the Pythagorean means to pursue the eternal. The following is a synthesis of meanings that the Pythagoreans possibly had for the first ten numbers:

1: The ultimate point of reference; the number of reason; the simplest ratio with position but no dimension; the generator of dimensions.

2: The first division of unity, but also the first union; the first 'female' number (all even numbers were considered female); the first dimension with length but no width; the line; the number of opinion.

3: The first 'male' number (all odd numbers excluding 1 were male); the first defined area – a two-dimensional form without width; the number of harmony; the triangle.

4: Heavenly perfection; the second square number after one, and the first expression of three dimensions; the tetrahedron; the number of justice or retribution.

5: The sum of the male 3 and the female 2; harmony and balance between two opposite principles; marriage; an expression of the golden ratio (Euclid's mean and extreme ratio, see p.132) and of the pentagon.

6: Creation (possibly because it was the multiple of the first male and first female numbers, as well as the sum of 1, 2 and 3).

7: The seven heavenly bodies that had been identified: the sun, moon, Mercury, Venus, Mars, Jupiter and Saturn.

8: The second cubic number after 1; solidarity and foundation.

9: The third square number after 1 and 4; the threshold of perfection.

10: The number of the universe; Euclid's mean and extreme (golden) ratio; the sum of 1, 2, 3 and 4; the fourth triangular number after 1, 3 and 6; infinite potential.

The Pythagoreans categorized numbers into different groups (fig. 5.3), including triangular numbers (1, 3, 6, 10…), square numbers (1, 4, 9, 16…) and cubic numbers (1, 8, 27, 64…).

The triangular drawing in fig. *5.3* is the tetractys, sacred to the Pythagoreans. Consider the accumulative totals of the corners – (1) the apex, the beginning; (7) the lower left, the heavens; (10) the lower right, the infinite.

The Pythagoreans linked geometrically created spaces and harmonious sounds with numeric ratios. Just as sounds could resonate, so, they believed, could geometrical forms, although in a different sense; and so could the planets and the human body. The discovery that musical tones could be expressed as whole number ratios became a foundational part of Pythagorean belief and was consistent with their understanding of the universe, the cyclical nature of the seasons, and the motions of the stars and planets.

Legend has it that Pythagoras discovered the harmony of tones after listening to the sounds of four blacksmith's hammers striking an anvil, producing sounds in consonance and in dissonance. Pythagoras worked out that the sounds were due to the ratios of the weights of the hammers – ratios of 6:8:9:12, where 6:12 simplifies

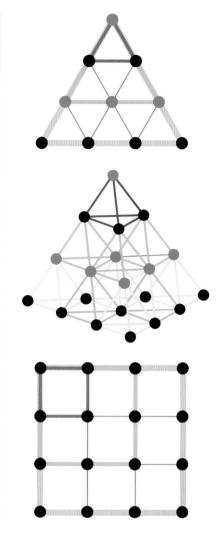

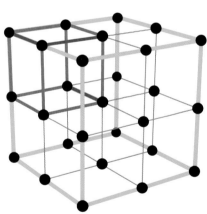

5.3 Pythagorean numbers

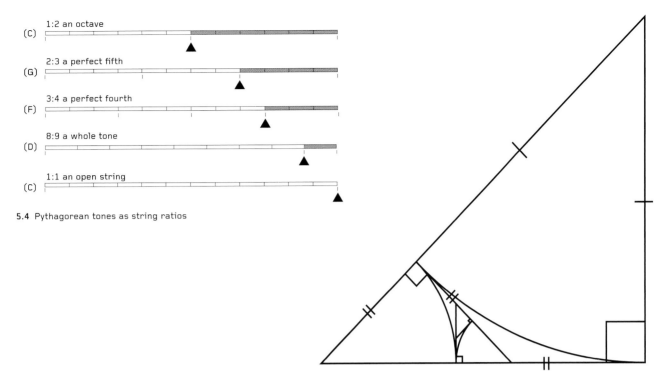

5.4 Pythagorean tones as string ratios

5.5 Proof that the ratio of the side of a square to its diagonal is irrational

to 1:2 (an octave), 8:12 simplifies to 2:3 (a perfect fifth), 9:12 simplifies to 3:4 (a perfect fourth), and 8:9 is a musical whole tone. The legend, at least with respect to hammers, is most likely false, but the ratios are relevant to a one-stringed instrument - and then with tensions adjusted to points of resonance of a multi-stringed instrument. In fig. 5.4 the letters C, D, F, G and C are the notes that we are familiar with and represent the tones of a string tuned to C and divided as in the ratios shown. Plato, in his *Timaeus*, later extended the four-note 'tetrachord' octave of Pythagoras with a further three numeric ratios to generate the seven notes of an octave known as the Pythagorean diatonic scale: 64:81 (E), 16:27 (A); 128:243 (B).

Whole and irrational numbers There are many descriptions of Pythagorean ideas regarding the mechanics of the universe and the fact that they could only be explained in terms of whole number (positive integer) ratios: the positions and orbits of the planets; the music of the spheres; the cycles of life and death. Similar beliefs were found in many cultures that preceded ancient Greece, particularly ancient Egypt. Even so, it was evident to the Pythagoreans that

representing each ratio of measured quantities was not always possible – leading to concepts of magnitude, irrationals and incommensurables that avoided the problem.

One famous problem that occupied the minds of the ancient Greeks was a legend that the Oracle of Delphi once told the people of Delphi that, to be freed from a plague, they should build to the god Apollo an altar twice the volume of the existing one – which basically involves determining the value of the cube root of 2, which is an irrational number. Another classical challenge was that of finding the ratio of the length of the side of a square to its diagonal. Fig. 5.5 is a visual representation showing that the ratio is irrational, where the length of the hypotenuse always equals the side length of its square plus the side length of a proportionately smaller square.

In Plato's *Theaetetus* dialogue there is a general proof that the square root of all prime numbers, except for 1, can be proven to be irrational (see fig. 5.5). Plato is generally considered to have been heavily influenced by Pythagorean ideas.

Even the Pythagorean foundational concept of the 'music of the spheres' does not survive irrational numbers. At the time of Pythagoras a common belief was that the Earth, moon, sun and

planets revolved around a 'central fire' on crystal spheres, separated by a 'void' and spaced in whole number musical ratios. The crystal spheres were thought to vibrate according to the speed of their rotation, creating tones that resonated with Pythagorean musical scales – although generally outside the realm of human perception. The problem was that this perfect whole number model was not fully predictive: planets appeared to travel at different speeds, go backwards, and get bigger and smaller; the sun and moon disappeared during eclipses. The fall of the whole number rational model can be traced as follows, with the concept of the crystal spheres beginning to fracture with Kepler: Philolaus (480–405 BCE) proposed a 'central fire'-centred model; Aristarchus (310–230 BCE) proposed a sun-centred model at odds with his contemporaries; Ptolemy (100–170 CE), in an attempt to explain the retrograde motion of the planets, proposed an offset Earth-centric model with the planets rotating around a point between the Earth and another point called the Equant; Copernicus (1473–1543) put forward a model of a circular sun-centred system; Johannes Kepler (1571–1630) proposed a sun-centred model with elliptical orbits, which evolved

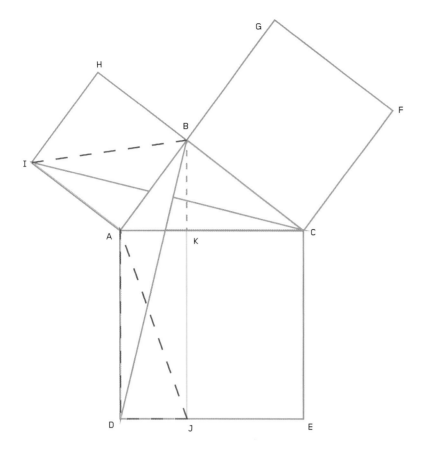

5.6 Euclid's Pythagorean proof

Clearly the Pythagoreans, at some point between the times of Eudoxus and Euclid, accepted both rational and irrational geometries and from that time we can assume that the veil lifted a little, allowing us to speculate more freely about what they might have discovered. After all, the Pythagoreans, and certainly the mathematicians of that era, were quite brilliant; and maybe, if we extend this speculative line of thinking, we can find fragments of these deduced lost discoveries in the mathematics and architectures of later times. In this new light we can start by looking at Pythagorean geometry with a broader mindset and not just in terms of rationals but of infinite series and irrationals expressed perfectly in geometric two- and three-dimensional forms. We can also speculate about possible applications of geometry by the Pythagoreans, overcoming the fact that Euclid's *Elements* is devoid of such applications.

The Pythagorean theorem The Pythagorean theorem is probably the foundational theorem of trigonometry: it states that for a right-angled triangle, the square of the hypotenuse equals the sum of the squares of the other two sides. A visual proof is given by Euclid in the *Elements* (Book 1, Proposition 47), but it is not very elegant (fig. 5.6).

< represents 'angle'.
Δ represents 'triangle'.
Step 1: Area ΔABD = Area ΔADJ (same base AD and height AK)
Step 2: ΔABD = ΔIAC (AB = AI; AD = AC; <BAD = <IAC)
Step 3: Area ΔIAB = Area ΔIAC (same base IA and height AB)
Conclusion:
Area IABH = Area ADJK and similarly
Area BCFG =Area KCEJ
Area ACED = Area IABH + Area BCFG
For something simpler see the 'self-evident' Chinese proof in chapter 3 (fig. 3.45), which predates Euclid.
A visual proof similar to the Chinese proof is shown here in fig. 5.7. Here, the square a² is the square on the hypotenuse of the right-angled triangle a, b, c, and the squares c² and b² are the squares of the other two sides. This visual proof can be interpreted in a number of ways.

into today's models with Newton's law of universal gravitation and later relativistic modifications.

Proportions that could not be expressed as whole number ratios were really not numbers in the classical sense yet they clearly existed, for example as the side length of a square with an area of five units. There are many stories about the controversy caused by irrationals among the Pythagoreans but that they existed was undeniable – and they existed everywhere in the simplest of geometrical forms to the more complex: in the ratio of a square's side to its diagonal, and in the ratio of the circumference of a circle to its diameter. It was also evident that a dimension could be divided infinitely – divide a unit in half, divide the half in half, and so on. So irrationals, infinite progressions and incommensurables had to be accommodated, and they were by Eudoxus of Cnidus, with concepts of magnitude. The accommodation was critical to the further development of geometry.

The separation of concepts of magnitude from concepts of number and whole number ratios allowed

classical numbers to remain rational and magnitude to encompass rational, irrational and incommensurable ratios and proportions. With such a division geometry could remain pure, where structures could be perfectly visualized and defined, but numerically only measurable with the knowledge that some numeric values lay at the end of an infinite progression. So pi and phi (the golden ratio; see p.132) could have perfect expression, be beautifully visualized, and yet be numerically definable with rational approximations or in terms of irrational magnitude.

(Note that the classical Greek number system changed in the 4th century BCE, from the Attic system to an alphabet number system, sometimes called the Ionic, where each letter of the alphabet was given a numerical value similar to the Arabic abjad system (see p.175), with which it shares many correspondences. The base ten system used the traditional 24 letters plus three archaic letters, with the highest letter value of 900.)

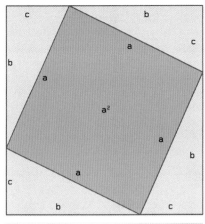

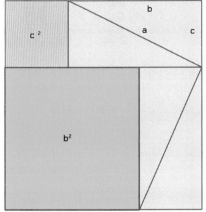

5.7 Simpler Pythagorean proof

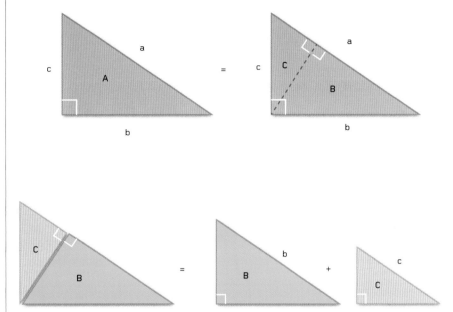

5.8 Similar right-angled triangles

For example, the second of the two figures in fig. 5.7 has an area equal to two rectangles with side lengths b and c plus the areas of the squares b^2 and c^2. Comparing the two drawings of fig. 5.7 we can see that $a^2 = b^2 + c^2$.

Many people are familiar with the Pythagorean theorem but not so many know that it can be understood as an expression of ratios linking linear dimensions with squares of dimensions (i.e. areas). As much as the square of the hypotenuse equals the sum of the squares of the other two sides, so does the area of any polygon (or indeed any shape) that is in proportion to the length of the hypotenuse equal the sum of the areas of similar shapes proportional to the lengths of the other two sides. A different way to visualize the theorem is shown in fig. 5.8, where a right-angled triangle is divided into two similar right-angled triangles. From this arrangement we can state that Area A = Area B + Area C, and proportionately $a^2 = b^2 + c^2$. From this it follows that a right-angled triangle with a height of, say, 5 units, has an area equal to the sum of two similar right-angled triangles of height 3 and 4 units.

In fig. 5.9, we have three elephants on the three sides of the triangle; suppose that the area of each elephant is $4/(3\pi)$ h^2, where h is the height. We can then calculate the height of an elephant shape whose surface area equals the sum of the surface areas of two smaller elephants – as proportional constants $4/(3\pi)$ cancel out from $4/(3\pi)$ $a^2 = 4/(3\pi)b^2 + 4/(3\pi)c^2$. So an elephant of height 17 units has the same surface area as the sum of the surface areas of two similar elephants of height 15 and 8 units (fig. 5.9).

The Pythagorean theorem, then, is an expression of ratios, linking linear dimensions with area dimensions.

The theorem can be applied to many things, from the surface areas of spheres to the complex plane (see chapter 10). The theorem can also be extended, for example $b^2 + c^2 + d^2 + f^2 = g^2$, or as a Pythagorean spiral built on the successive hypotenuse of right-angled triangles (see fig. 5.10. The upper figure is known as the spiral of Theodorus. The lower figure shows a spiral of successive hypotenuse $b^2 + c^2 + d^2 + f^2 = g^2$).

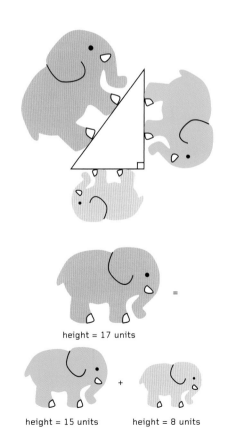

height = 17 units

=

height = 15 units + height = 8 units

5.9 Pythagorean elephants

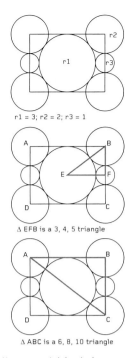

r1 = 3; r2 = 2; r3 = 1

Δ EFB is a 3, 4, 5 triangle

Δ ABC is a 6, 8, 10 triangle

5.12 Pythagorean triple circles

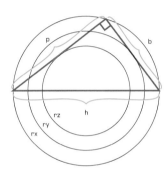

5.14 Pythagorean theorem in circular form

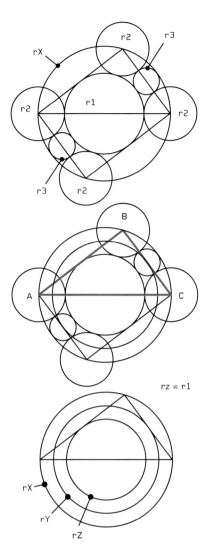

rz = r1

5.13 Pythagorean triple circles as generalized Pythagorean theorem

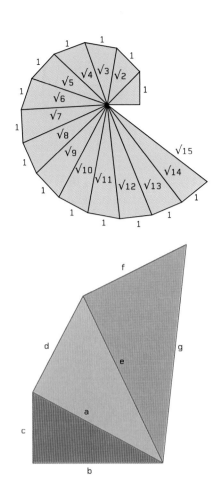

5.10 The spiral of Theodorus (top) and the successive hypotenuse

5.11 Pythagorean trees

Combining right-angled triangles can create many other interesting progressions. Fig. 5.11 shows a fractal-like progression of right-angled triangles with side ratios 3:4:5. The formation is known as a Pythagorean tree.

Pythagorean triangles and circles The dynamic close-packing sphere geometry developed by the author in the early 1970s generates a 3, 4, 5 Pythagorean triple as a close-packing circle arrangement of circles sized 1, 2 and 3 units, packing within a rectangular cell that tessellates infinitely across a two-dimensional plane, and also perfectly, as spheres of the same dimensions, nests within a three-dimensional sphere (fig. 5.12). For the 2D and 3D extension of fig. 5.12 see chapter 12.

The 3, 4, 5 triangular packing can be developed to create a more general case that dynamically shows the Pythagorean formula in terms of inscribed and concentric circles (fig. 5.13).

The Pythagorean theorem circles were first generated as part of the dynamic close-packing sphere geometry discussed in chapter 12. The bridge between the two geometries is shown in fig. 5.14.

Circles rx, ry and rz also have radii of x, y and z.

$2rx = h$; $2ry = p$; $2rz = b$

Step 1: $h^2 = p^2 + b^2$

Step 2: $(2rx)^2 = (2ry)^2 + (2rz)^2$

Step 3: $(rx)^2 = (ry)^2 + (rz)^2$

Step 4: $\pi(rx)^2 = \pi(ry)^2 + \pi(rz)^2$

Conclusion:

Area of circle rx = area of circle ry + area of circle rz.

If we consider the logic shown in fig. 5.14 then the Pythagorean theorem can be animated as a series of cells (fig. 5.15), where ry follows a progression

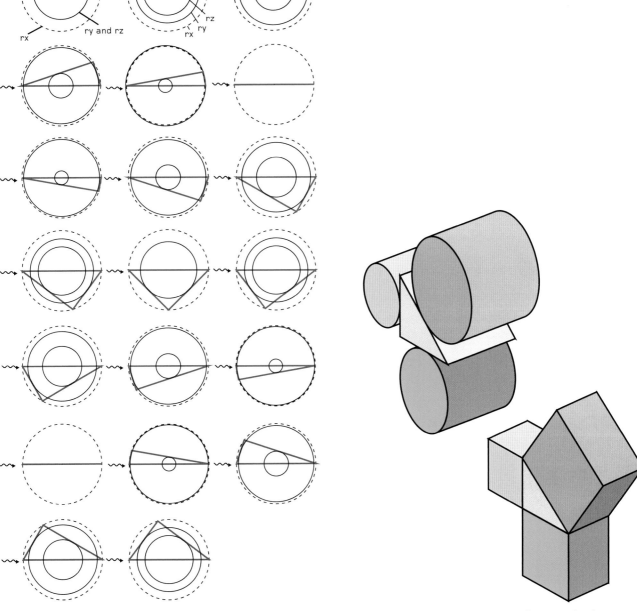

5.15 Pythagorean theorem as animated circle cells

5.16 Pythagorean theorem extensions

of expanding and contracting radii as rz correspondingly contracts and expands, given the proviso that the sum of the areas of the two smaller circles equal that of the larger circle. A right-angled triangle created as tangents to circles rz and ry, plus the common diameter, will rotate 360° within rx describing all possible right-angled triangles. The concept can be extended to cylinders and the surface areas of spheres.

The Pythagorean logic extends in all sorts of ways, including to cylinders, to prisms (fig. 5.16) provided they are of the same depth, to the surface area of spheres, and even to right tetrahedrons (see fig. 5.17).

Fig. 5.17: For the right-angled triangle a, b, c

$$a^2 + b^2 = c^2$$

For the right tetrahedron A, B, C, D

$$(area\ A)^2 + (area\ B)^2 + (area\ C)^2 = (area\ D)^2$$

EUCLID

Euclid was a Greek mathematician now famous for his treatise on geometry, the *Elements*. Not much is known of his life

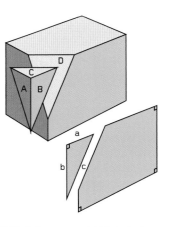

5.17 Pythagorean right tetrahedron

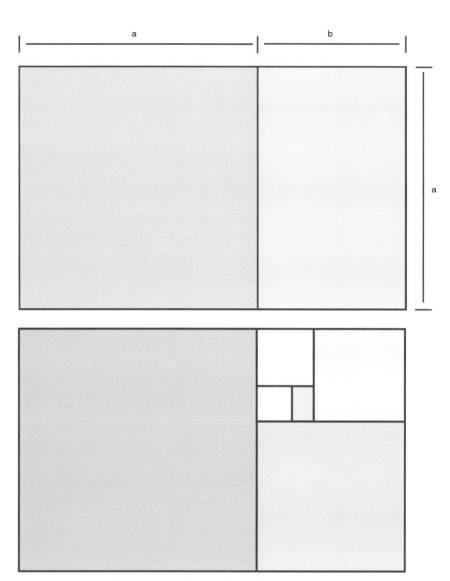

5.18 Euclid's mean and extreme ratio

other than that he flourished around 300 BCE and he spent a significant amount of time in Alexandria, Egypt. Although he is best known for the *Elements*, other works of his survive, including on optics and catoptrics (reflected light and mirrors). The *Elements* presents a foundational system of rigorous and axiomatic mathematical proofs that form the basis of Euclidian geometry and elementary number theory. The work is purely theoretical and full of definitions, postulates and propositions, with no mention of application.

Fig. 5.6 shows Euclid's proof of the Pythagorean theorem, but what is less well known is Euclid's generalized theorem (*Elements*, Book 6, Proposition 31). Euclid shows that any similarly described figures on the sides of a right-angled triangle will be in accord with the Pythagorean theorem (see fig. 5.9).

When considering proportions Euclid defines means and extremes: when A is to B as C is to D then B and C are said to be the 'means' and A and D are said to be the 'extremes'. The *Elements* contains a number of references to side lengths that are in mean proportion, for example Book 6, Proposition 13. The proposition is similar to that shown in fig. 5.30, where the ratio AF:BF = BF:FC and where BF is in mean proportion to AF and FC (the extremes). This equation can be written as $BF^2 = AF \times FC$, making BF a sort of average value, sometimes called the geometric mean.

5.19 Euclid's mean and extreme ratio shown as 'golden' rectangles

The golden ratio Book 6 of the *Elements* starts with three definitions, the second of which describes an 'extreme and mean' ratio as follows: 'A straight line is said to have been cut in extreme and mean ratio when, as the whole is to the greater segment, so the greater (segment is) to the lesser.' This can be written as (a + b)/a = a/b where (a + b) is the whole straight line, a is the greater segment and b the lesser. The ratio combines mean and extreme values (see fig. 5.18).

From the ratio we can derive the 'mean and extreme' ratio (phi, ϕ).

Step 1: a + b is to a as a is to b
Step 2: a/b = (a + b)/a then a/b = 1 + b/a
Step 3: If we let ϕ = a/b then ϕ = 1 + 1/ϕ
Step 4: $(\phi)^2 = \phi + 1$ (multiplying both sides by ϕ)
Step 5: $\phi = (1 \pm \sqrt{(1 + 4)})/2 = (\sqrt{5} + 1)/2$
 (where step 5 uses the formula for solving quadratics:
 $(-b \pm \sqrt{(b^2 - 4ac)})/(2a)$

Euclid's description of this ratio could not be less inspiring and one might wonder why the ratio was included in the *Elements*. However, our calculation has revealed a rather special numeric ratio:

$(\sqrt{5} + 1)/2$. The ratio was dubbed the 'golden ratio' by German mathematician Martin Ohm (1792–1872) and given the symbol phi (ϕ) by British-American physicist and inventor Mark Barr (1870–1950). The golden ratio turns out to be a door to many things that were known or might have been known to the Pythagoreans. Fig. 5.19 shows a golden ratio progression in terms of squares and rectangles.

Pentagons (see fig. 5.20), pentagrams, decagons and dodecahedrons contain golden ratio proportions (a + b)/a = a/b = $(\sqrt{5} + 1)/2 = \phi$, and all are featured

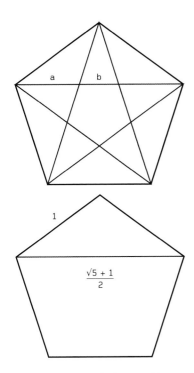

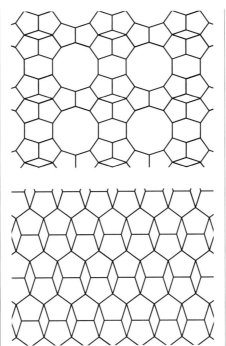

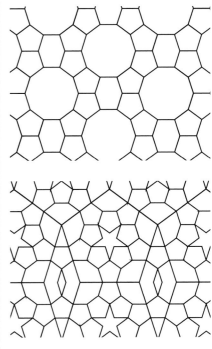

5.20 Euclid's mean and extreme ratio appears in pentagons

5.21A Tessellating pentagons, 36° rhombi, decagons and irregular hexagons with four angles at 108° and two at 144°

5.21B Tessellating pentagons, 36° rhombi, decagons, 108°/144° irregular hexagons, and pentagrams

prominently in Pythagorean legends as well as in Euclid's *Elements* (for example Book 13, Proposition 8).

Pentagons and decagons will not tile as regular or semi-regular tessellations, but they will tessellate with irregular polygons (see figs 5.21A and 5.21B). Tessellations with repeating translational patterns (the pattern looks the same when its elements are moved, or translated, in a given direction) are called periodic tilings. Non-periodic tilings are tessellations that lack translational repeats, although they can be symmetrical (see fig. 5.22).

British mathematical physicist Roger Penrose has defined a number of sets of prototiles (shapes) that combine into non-periodic tilings. The Penrose prototiles kite and dart ('a' and 'b' shapes in fig. 5.23) can combine in ways similar to the nesting pentagrams of fig. 5.24 with patterns repeating at smaller and smaller scales. The Penrose reduction ratios follow that of the inverse of the golden ratio. Penrose tiles share some features with Islamic girih tiles (see pp.196–97).

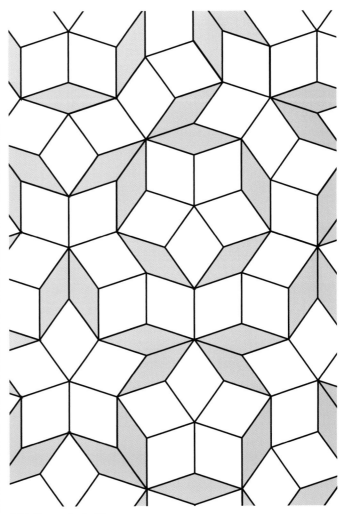

5.22 Non-periodic tilings

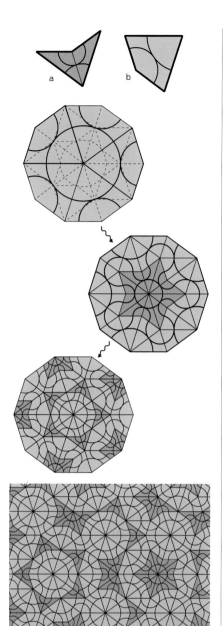

5.24 Nesting pentagrams

5.25 Nesting pentagrams

5.23 Penrose non-periodic tiling of type P2

Decagons and pentagons can also 'nest' to form infinite progressions with scaled repeats following the golden ratio. Fig. 5.25 shows a basic nesting arrangement with a scaled repeat. A coloured representation with some development is shown in fig. 5.24 and, as before, the reductions in size follow the golden ratio.

The golden rectangle The golden ratio can also be expressed as a rectangle – the 'golden rectangle' – a beautifully proportioned rectangle, which, to some, appears to have been used in many classic and ancient works of art and architecture. However, in most or all cases, the use of the rectangle in these works is, at best, approximate – suggesting either an intuitive feeling for the proportions, or a complete lack of understanding of the ratio. Renaissance artist Leonardo da Vinci is often cited as someone who used the golden rectangle but, as far as this author can find out, there is no constructional method,

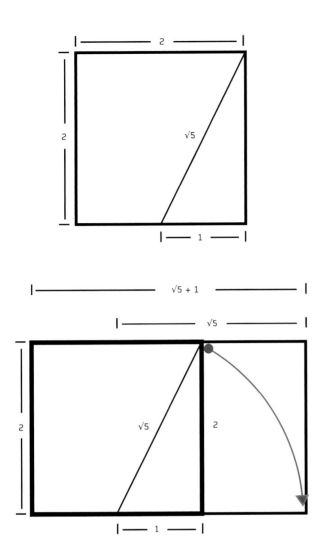

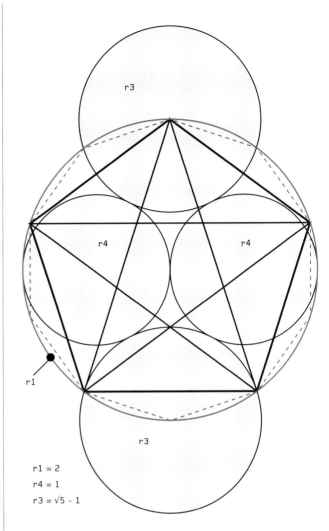

r1 = 2
r4 = 1
r3 = √5 - 1

5.26 Construction of a golden rectangle

5.27 A means to construct a pentagon and a decagon

or constructional hint, that Leonardo applied the mathematics, even though he worked with the mathematician Luca Pacioli, and even illustrated Pacioli's book *De divina proportione* (*On the Divine Proportion*), which features the mean and extreme (golden) ratio.

It was not until the 19th century that the golden ratio was specifically and precisely used, for example by the German psychologist and mathematician Adolf Zeising. In 1854 Zeising observed that the arrangement of branches along the stem of plants, and of veins in leaves, appeared to be in accord with the Fibonacci sequence and the golden ratio. He extended his researches to the skeletons of animals and the branching of their veins and nerves, to the proportions of chemical compounds and the geometry of crystals, and finally to human and artistic proportions. Zeising defined a new morphological law that he believed

permeated the whole of nature – that there was a universal law of proportions and that it was based on the golden ratio. It must be said that the correspondence of natural proportions to the golden ratio has been shown to be ambiguous at best (for reference see the work of astrophysicist Mario Livio).

Later, in the 20th century, Swiss-born French architect Le Corbusier based his Modulor system on the golden ratio as well as on proportions of the human body. It was also used in the construction of the Nancy Stetson House in Boulder, Colorado, by this author (see pp.286–87).

There are many ways in which the golden rectangle can be constructed, as in fig. 5.26, for example.

Golden circles The pentagon, pentagram and decagon can be constructed precisely using the circular arrangement shown in fig. 5.27:

Draw circle r1 and then two circles r4 of half the diameter so that the r4 circles touch each other and both sides of the circumference of r1, and are aligned along a diameter of r1. Then draw r3 with its centre on the circumference of r1 and such that it exactly touches the circumferences of the two r4 circles. The circle r3 exactly divides the circle r1 into five and ten parts (see fig. 5.27).

The dynamic sphere geometry discussed in chapter 12 generates a golden close-packing circle and sphere packing that corresponds with the pentagon and decagon construction of fig. 5.27 – where the circumference of the circle r3 exactly divides the circumference of r1 into five equal parts. The centre of r3 lies on the circumference of r1, and the arc from the centre of r3 to the point that its circumference intersects with the circumference of r1 is exactly one tenth

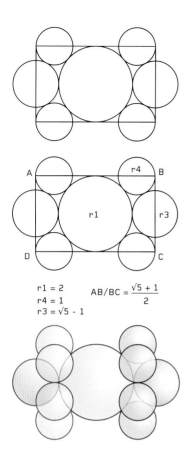

$r1 = 2$
$r4 = 1$
$r3 = \sqrt{5} - 1$

$AB/BC = \dfrac{\sqrt{5} + 1}{2}$

5.28 Close-packing circles and spheres

of the circumference of r1. The unit
cell and unit clusters of the packing are
contained within golden rectangles on
three planes and within hexagons on
two planes. The cells and clusters repeat
infinitely in three-dimensional space.

Fig. 5.28 shows the close-packing
circle cell and sphere cluster that
corresponds with the pentagon and
decagon construction shown in fig.
5.27. Chapter 12 shows how the cluster
expands in three dimensions (see p.278,
cluster HP1.3). The relative dimensions
of the circles are shown in fig. 5.28. The
lower drawing shows that six spheres
with the radius of r4 (green) exactly
encircle the sphere r1 (yellow) and the
sphere r3 (purple) to create a ring of six.

Interestingly, if a square is drawn
on the diameter AC (see fig. 5.29), so
that the top two corners of the square
touch the circumference of the circle that
circumscribes the golden rectangle, then
a derivation for the golden ratio can be
obtained (see fig. 5.30).

To make the circle and square φ
construction shown in fig. 5.30, draw a
circle and place a square on its diameter
so that its top two corners touch the top

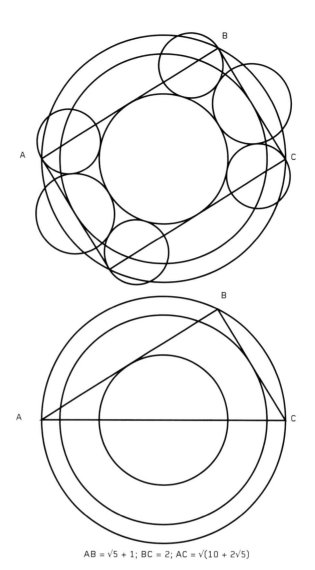

$AB = \sqrt{5} + 1;\ BC = 2;\ AC = \sqrt{(10 + 2\sqrt{5})}$

5.29 Close-packing circles link to the Pythagorean theorem

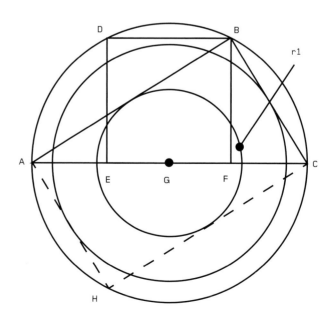

5.30 Concurrent square and circle golden rectangle

of the circle. Then connecting either top corner of the square to the ends of the diameter will create one half of a golden rectangle.

Step 1: If DBEF is a square let FB = 2
Step 2: Then GF = 1 and GB = √5 (theorem of Pythagoras)
Step 3: Then FC = √5 - 1
Step 4: Then BF/FC = 2 / (√5 - 1)
= (2(√5 + 1)) / (√5 - 1) (√5 + 1) =
(2(√5 + 1)) / (5 - 1) = (√5 + 1)/2 = φ
Step 5: Triangle ABC is similar to triangles BFC and AFB. Therefore ABCH is the golden rectangle.

Note that there is no correspondence between the size ratio of square DBEF and circle r1 and Leonardo's *Vitruvian Man* (see fig. 5.31), just as there is no link between Leonardo's *Vitruvian Man* and the golden section. In fact, as the centre of rotation of the arms of *Vitruvian Man* is not defined, the ratio between Leonardo's square and circle is unknown (see also chapter 8).

A second 'golden' circle packing can be arranged to give the 'in-circle' arrangement shown in fig. 5.32.

r1 = 2; r3 = √5 - 1; r4 = 1; ry = √5 + 1
r6 = 4 φ +2; rx = √(10 + 2√5); r7 = √5 + 3
r3's rotational angle about r1 is about 44.911.

The golden sphere packing generated by the dynamic close-packing sphere geometry in fig. 5.28 has many unique properties, which will be shown in chapter 12. Whether the Pythagoreans also discovered this packing is unknown. However, it does seem possible that they did, given the circle constructions shown in Euclid's *Elements* and the description of the mean ratio.

Another possible discovery of the Pythagoreans, although there is no evidence, could have been that of the Fibonacci sequence, named after medieval Italian mathematician Leonardo of Pisa (c.1175–c.1250), known as Fibonacci. (See following pages.)

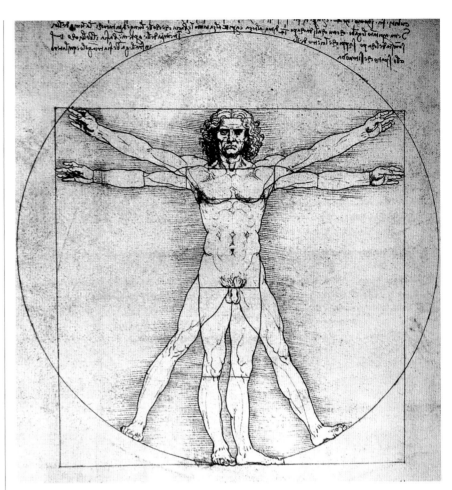

5.31 Leonardo da Vinci, *Vitruvian Man*, c.1490

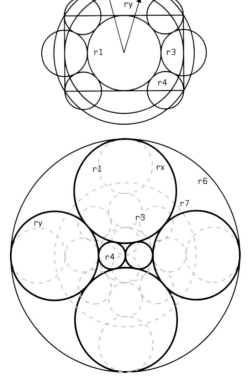

5.32 Second golden circle packing

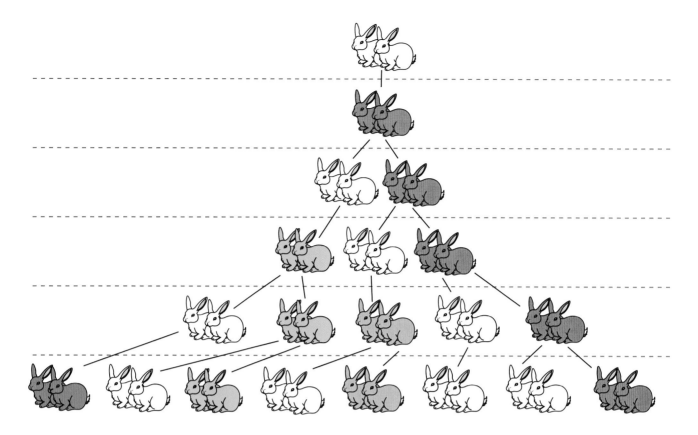

5.33 Fibonacci rabbit population growth pattern

THE FIBONACCI SEQUENCE

The Fibonacci sequence is a sequence of numbers generated to represent the growth of an idealized rabbit population. The premise is that a population begins with a newly born pair of rabbits, one male and one female. The pair will mature and will mate after one month. A new pair of rabbits, one male and one female, will be born at the end of the second month, and it is assumed that this rate of maturation, conception and birth will continue without any rabbits dying (see fig. 5.33). The numbers increase following the pattern of adding two successive numbers beginning with 0 and 1, a sequence that progresses infinitely: 0, 1, 1, 2, 3, 5, 8, 13, 21, 34, 55, 89, 144, 233, 377, 610, 987, 1597, 2584, 4181, 6765, 10946, 17711, 28657, 46368, 75025, 121393, 196418, 317811, 514229... The ratio of adjacent number pairs converges to the golden (mean) ratio as the sequence extends out towards infinity. The sequence can be represented as shown in fig. 5.34, where the sides of the squares are Fibonacci numbers. The Pythagoreans might well have discovered the sequence

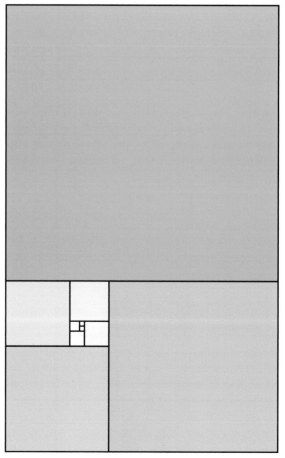

5.34 Fibonacci rabbit population growth pattern

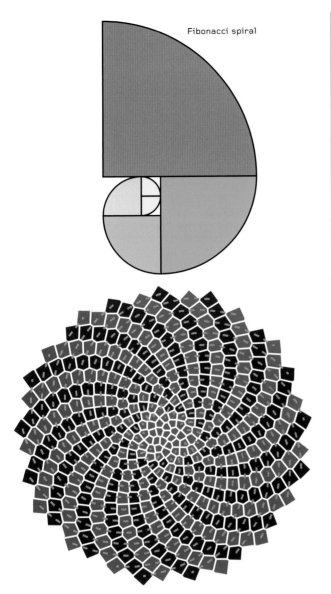

5.35 Fibonacci sunflower ratios: spiral ratios outer 21:34, inner 8:13

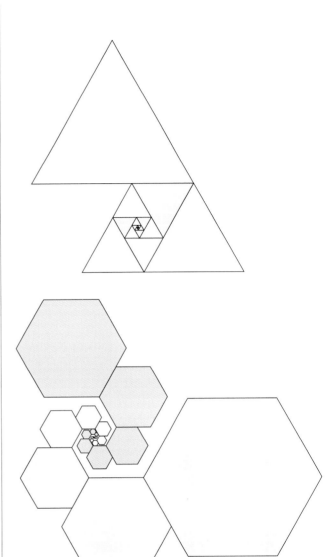

5.36 Fibonacci hexagons and equilateral triangles

and represented it as shown in fig. 5.34. Each square can be represented by a quarter circle that extends into a spiral: in fig. 5.35 the spiral in the top diagram is generated by quarter circles in this way and can be extended infinitely – but it is not a logarithmic spiral as it is often misrepresented.

The logic of the quarter circle spiral can be extended in many ways: see the hexagonal and equilateral triangle developments in fig. 5.36.

The sunflower design in fig. 5.35 shows how the ratio of the spirals in a sunflower can change as the flower grows – in this case from 8:13 to 21:34, both being ratios within the Fibonacci sequence. The illustration is a variation of a design seen in the National Museum of Mathematics (MoMath), New York.

'Geometry has two great treasures: one is the Theorem of Pythagoras; the other, the division of a line into extreme and mean ratio. The first we may compare to a measure of gold; the second we may name a precious jewel.'
JOHANNES KEPLER (1571–1630)

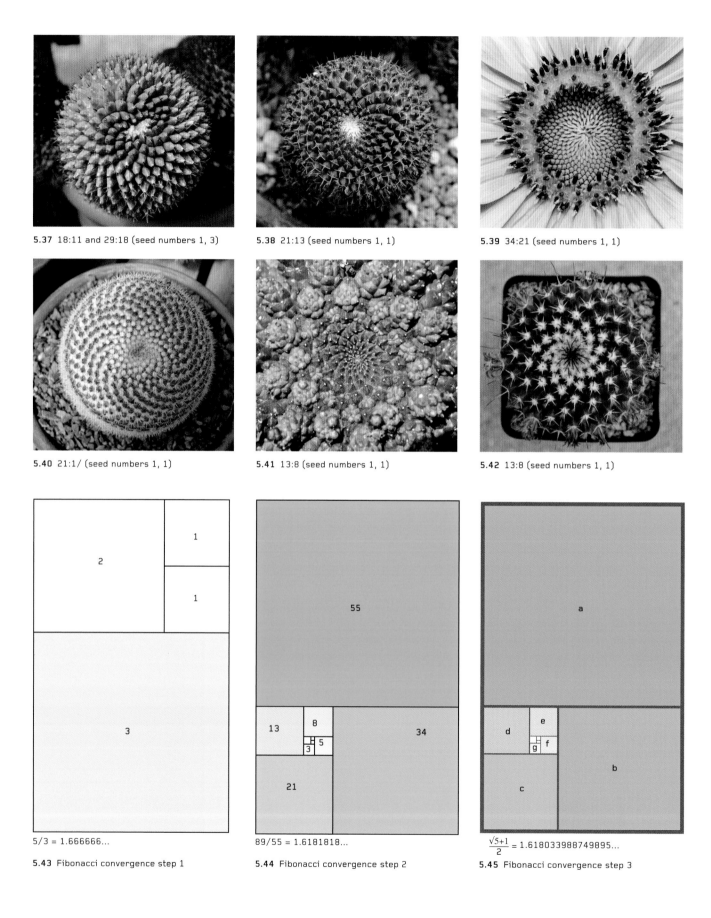

5.37 18:11 and 29:18 (seed numbers 1, 3)

5.38 21:13 (seed numbers 1, 1)

5.39 34:21 (seed numbers 1, 1)

5.40 21:1/ (seed numbers 1, 1)

5.41 13:8 (seed numbers 1, 1)

5.42 13:8 (seed numbers 1, 1)

5/3 = 1.666666...

5.43 Fibonacci convergence step 1

89/55 = 1.6181818...

5.44 Fibonacci convergence step 2

$\frac{\sqrt{5}+1}{2}$ = 1.618033988749895...

5.45 Fibonacci convergence step 3

Fibonacci in nature One of the fascinating things about the Fibonacci sequence is that it provides us with a possible link between geometric and natural growth patterns, in plants and other natural forms. In the plant examples opposite, the number of spirals in each direction (clockwise and anticlockwise) corresponds with successive numbers in the Fibonacci sequence (see figs 5.37 to 5.42). Fig. 5.37 is different from the others as the inner ratio is 18:11 and the outer is 29:18, and seemingly forms part of a generalized Fibonacci sequence with 'seed', or start, numbers 1 and 3 (1, 3, 4, 7, 11, 18, 29...) (see the paragraph on generalized Fibonacci numbers below).

Cactus growers in Tucson, Arizona, have noted that the number pairs in each pair of cactus tubercle spirals can change as the plants mature – for example a 21:13 pair can change to a 34:21 pair. This suggests that the Fibonacci process is a function of how new tubercles insert themselves between old ones.

Fibonacci and golden ratio convergence
If we look at successive ratios of adjacent numbers within the Fibonacci sequence we will notice that the ratios oscillate around the golden ratio, eventually converging as the numbers extend to infinity. For example: 55:34 = 1.617647...; 89:55 = 1.618181...; 144:89 = 1.617977...; and 233:144 = 1.618055... converge on the golden ratio = 1.618033... Similarly, figs 5.43, 5.44 and 5.45 show graphically how the Fibonacci ratios appear to converge on the golden ratio.

Convergence proof We can prove that successive ratios converge on the golden ratio by a method of induction as follows:

Step 1: The third number in any sequence of three numbers in the Fibonacci sequence equals the sum of the previous two and can be written as follows, where 'n' represents the placement of the first number in the three-number sequence:
$F_{n+2} = F_{n+1} + F_n$

Step 2: If we divide both sides of the Step 1 equation by F_{n+1} we get:
$(F_{n+2})/(F_{n+1}) = (F_{n+1})/(F_{n+1}) + F_n/(F_{n+1})$

Step 3: Simplifying Step 2 we get:
$(F_{n+2})/(F_{n+1}) = 1 + F_n/(F_{n+1})$

Step 4: As n approaches infinity we know that the ratios $(F_{n+2}):(F_{n+1})$ and $(F_{n+1}):F_n$ approach the same value – let us call this X. Substituting X for the ratios we find Euclid's expression for his mean and extreme ratio:
$X = 1 + 1/X$

Step 5: Multiplying both sides of the equation by X we get:
$X^2 = X + 1$

Step 6: Rearranging the equation:
$X^2 - X - 1 = 0$

Step 7: Solving this quadratic equation we can use $X = (-b \pm \sqrt{(b^2 - 4ac)})/(2a)$ where a = 1, b = 1, c = 1, and we find that there are two roots:
$X = (1 + \sqrt{5})/2$ and $X = (1 - \sqrt{5})/2$ where we want just the positive root – which is ϕ, so $X = \phi$.

There are many proofs and formulas relating to the Fibonacci sequence. The French mathematician François Lucas (1842–91) developed a generalized proof. Whereas the Fibonacci sequence starts with the seed numbers 1 and 1, Lucas proved that starting a similar additive sequence with any two whole numbers (seed numbers) will generate a sequence that converges on the golden ratio. For example, seed numbers 1 and 3 generate the sequence 1, 3, 4, 7, 11, 18, 29, 47, 76, 123, 199, 322..., where the ratios converge on the golden ratio: 123:76 = 1.618421...; 199:123 = 1.617886...; 322:199 = 1.618090...

Alfred Binet (1857–1911), famous for inventing the IQ test, developed a formula for calculating what the nth number of the Fibonacci sequence is:
$F_n = 1/\sqrt{5}(\phi^n - (-1/\phi)^n)$

The convergence of ratios wonderfully lays the groundwork for calculus.

The mysteries of the golden ratio
The golden and Fibonacci ratios are fascinating ratios that can be represented as spirals, as rectangles, as number sequences and as 3D forms. There are many books that make a lot of the correspondences of Fibonacci numbers and golden ratios with the Great Pyramid at Giza, with the Parthenon, with sunflowers and with paintings by Leonardo, but there needs to be more than just a rough correspondence for such associations to have any real scientific or historical value. In other words, we need to look for more evidence – for example, that of a golden ratio construction method or more exact correspondences.

The fact that the dynamic close-packing sphere geometry discussed in chapter 12 generates a close-packing cluster of spheres that has three golden ratio planes that repeat infinitely in space, and which has many rotational and interfacing properties, is quite remarkable, but so far nothing is seen in the structures formed that gives a hint as to why, say, sunflower spirals roughly follow more than just a few ratios in the Fibonacci sequence.

For reference Examples of phi (ϕ) equations (phi being the symbol for the golden ratio):

(i) $\phi = 1 + 1/\phi$
(ii) $\phi^2 - \phi - 1 = 0$
(iii) $\phi^4 - \phi - 3 = \sqrt{5}$
(iv) $\phi^4 - \phi^2 - 2\phi - 1 = 0$

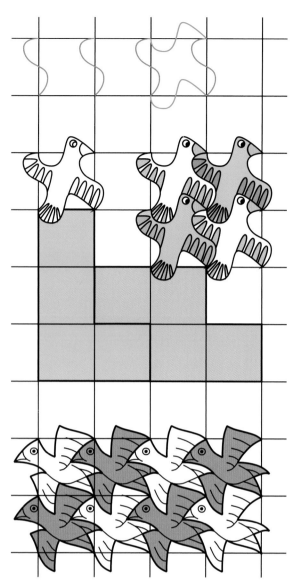

5.46 Tessellations can be perceived in many ways

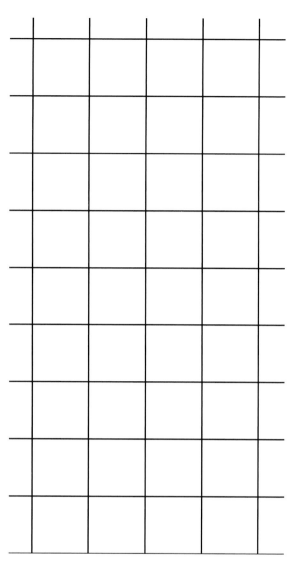

5.47 Regular tessellation: squares, interior angle 90°. At vertex: 4, 4, 4, 4

PYTHAGOREAN SURFACE DESIGNS

There are many geometrical surface designs that are associated with the Pythagoreans. Some have their origins in earlier cultures but many new ones were developed by those associated with the Pythagoreans, Archimedes in particular. Among the many types of surface design are designs created with regular polygons, where the polygons tessellate, meaning that they connect edge-to-edge and repeat infinitely across a 2D plane. Only three regular polygons can form the so-called regular tessellations: squares, equilateral triangles and hexagons. Semi-regular tessellations consist of more than one regular polygon and are known as Archimedean tessellations.

It is important to remember that the lattices of regular and semi-regular tessellations simply represent a convention. They are not sacrosanct in that they have to be viewed in just one manner, such as squares fitting edge-to-edge. Lurking within each tessellation numerous other tessellating forms can be found, including L shapes, weaving forms, spirals and even faces of animals and images of plants. Stretching the sides of the tessellating lattices, in the manner of the Dutch graphic artist M. C. Escher, transforms the lattices into starting points for free-form designs (the tessellating birds at the bottom of fig. *5.46* are copied from Escher's work). Pushing the lattices up into 3D space creates such things as shape-changing polyhedra (see chapter 11).

Fig. 5.46 shows two examples of the infinite ways in which a tessellation can be perceived. Whereas we are disposed to see squares, it is possible to see tangram shapes or even birds. A methodology for creating Escher-like patterns is to duplicate shapes on opposite sides of the squares such as with the green and blue lines.

The regular and semi-regular tessellations fall into four basic symmetries: square, hexagonal, rectangular and rhombic, as can be seen in figs 5.48–5.65 on the following pages. In these diagrams, the 'at vertex' numbers refer to the number of sides of the tessellating polygons and the number of times they meet at a vertex.

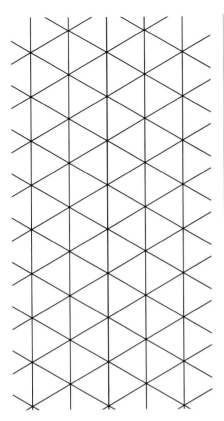

5.48 Regular tessellation: equilateral triangles, interior angle 60°. At vertex: 3, 3, 3, 3, 3, 3

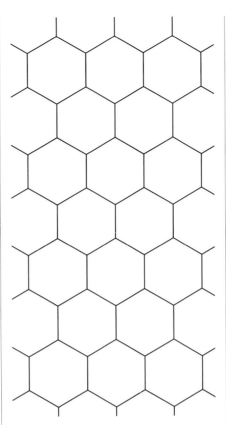

5.49 Regular tessellation: hexagons, interior angle 120°. At vertex: 6, 6, 6

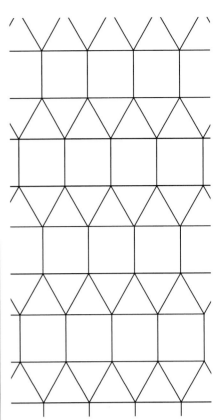

5.50 Semi-regular tessellation: squares and equilateral triangles, interior angles 90° and 60°. At vertex: 3, 3, 3, 4, 4

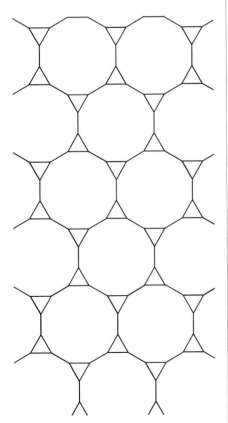

5.51 Semi-regular tessellation: equilateral triangles and regular dodecagons, interior angles 60° and 150°. At vertex: 12, 12, 3

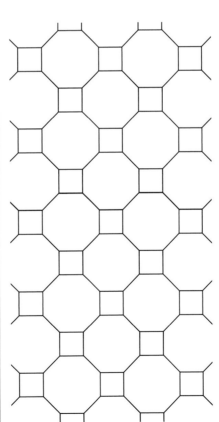

5.52 Semi-regular tessellation: squares and regular octagons, interior angles 90° and 135°. At vertex: 8, 8, 4

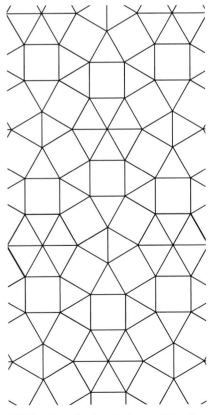

5.53 Semi-regular tessellation: equilateral triangles and squares, interior angles 60° and 90°. At vertex: 3, 3, 4, 3, 4 and 3, 3, 3, 3, 3, 3

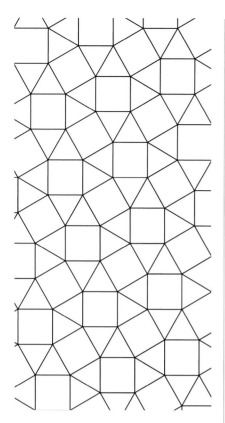

5.54 Semi-regular tessellation: equilateral triangles and squares, interior angles 60° and 90°. At vertex: 3, 3, 4, 3, 4

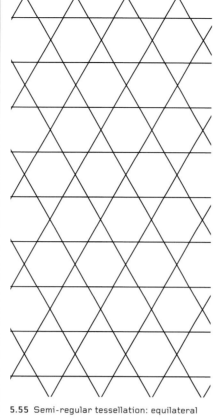

5.55 Semi-regular tessellation: equilateral triangles and hexagons, interior angles 60° and 120°. At vertex: 3, 6, 3, 6

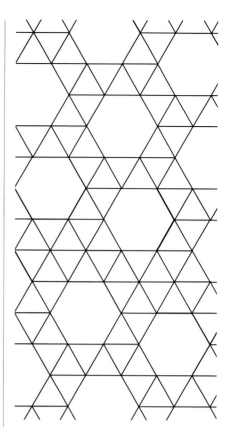

5.56 Semi-regular tessellation: equilateral triangles and hexagons, interior angles 60° and 120°. At vertex: 3, 3, 3, 3, 6

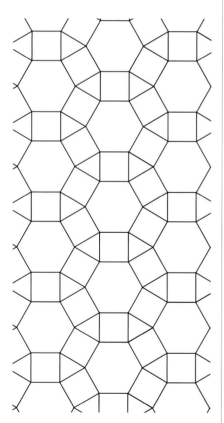

5.57 Semi-regular tessellation: equilateral triangles, hexagons and squares, interior angles 60°, 90° and 120°. At vertex: 3, 4, 6, 4

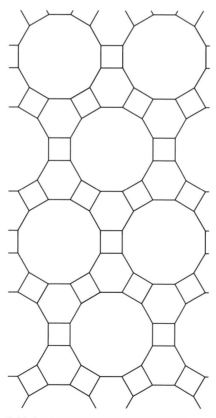

5.58 Semi-regular tessellation: hexagons, squares and dodecagons, interior angles 90°, 120° and 150°. At vertex: 12, 6, 4

5.59 Semi-regular tessellation: squares and equilateral triangles, interior angles 60° and 90°. At vertex: 3, 3, 3, 4, 4; 3, 4, 3, 3, 4; and 3, 3, 3, 3, 3, 3

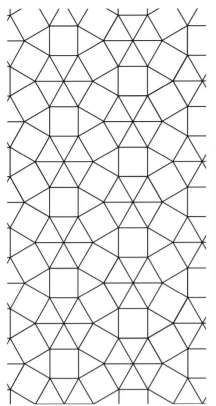

5.60 Semi-regular tessellation: squares and equilateral triangles, interior angles 60° and 90°. At vertex: 3, 3, 4, 3, 4

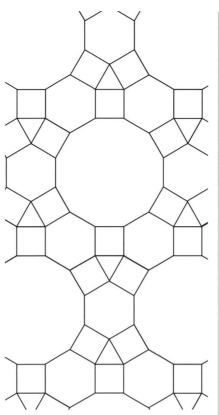

5.61 Semi-regular tessellation: squares, equilateral triangles, hexagons and dodecagons, interior angles 60°, 90°, 120 and 150°. At vertex: 12, 4, 6 and 6, 4, 3, 4

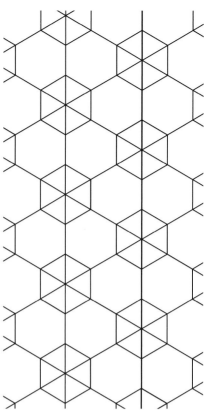

5.62 Semi-regular tessellation: equilateral triangles and hexagons, interior angles 60° and 120°. At vertex: 6, 6, 3, 3 and 3, 3, 3, 3, 3, 3

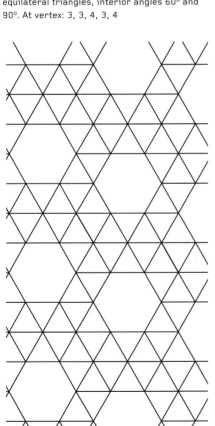

5.63 Semi-regular tessellation: equilateral triangles and hexagons, interior angles 60° and 120. At vertex: 6, 3, 3, 3 and 3, 3, 3, 3, 3, 3

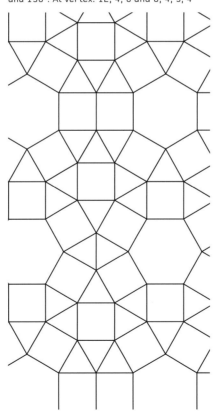

5.64 Semi-regular tessellation: equilateral triangles, hexagons and squares, interior angles 60°, 90° and 120°. At vertex: 4, 3, 3, 4, 3 and 3, 4, 6, 4

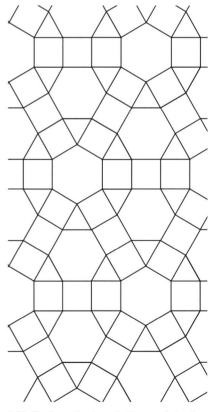

5.65 Semi-regular tessellation: equilateral triangles, hexagons and squares, interior angles 60°, 90° and 120°. At vertex: 4, 4, 3, 6 and 3, 4, 6, 4

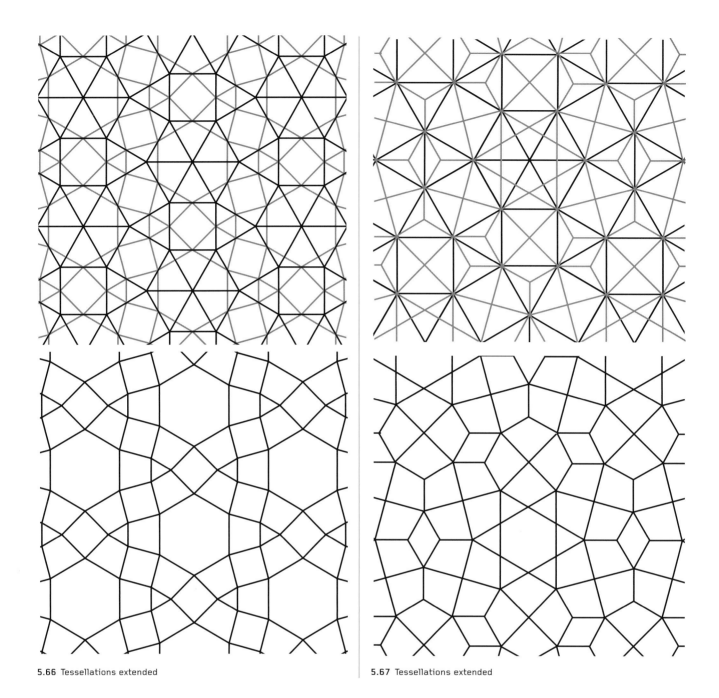

5.66 Tessellations extended

5.67 Tessellations extended

Semi-regular tessellations can be further extended by subdividing regular polygons. Variations can include replacing regular polygons with stars and radii to centres, and so on (see figs 5.66 and 5.67).

POLYHEDRA

Platonic solids Platonic solids (see fig. 5.68) are described as regular polyhedra composed of one repeating, regular polygon that can be inscribed within a sphere such that all corners touch the surface. There are five Platonic solids: the tetrahedron (four faces) the cube (six faces), the octahedron (eight faces),

the dodecahedron (12 faces) and the icosahedron (20 faces). Symmetrical equivalents of the five solids can be found naturally, for example in crystals of iron pyrite, fluorite and sodium chloride (salt); and we now know that icosahedronal forms are extremely common among viruses.

It has been shown that the symmetries associated with the five Platonic solids were known in Neolithic times, as represented by some of the hundreds of carved stone balls found in Scotland (fig. 5.69). The balls show an appreciation of symmetry, balance and logic, but there is nothing to support the idea that the various symmetries were derived from any sort of axiomatic logic. The stones have been dated as early as 3200 BCE.

The cube appears to have been the first regular convex polyhedron created by humans. Cubes in the form of dice, dated around 3000 BCE, have been found in Iran.

Pythagoreans in 3D Even though the symmetries of regular solids were known thousands of years before Pythagoras, we should nonetheless probably still credit the Pythagoreans with the development of regular convex polygonal solids – with their invention of strict rule sets similar to those that generated 2D tessellations. These rule sets specified limits of spherical boundaries and regular polygons. Given the limitations it should not be surprising that the solids ended up having many characteristics in common with regular tessellations. For example, stacked cubes have two-dimensional planes of squares and √2 rectangles as well as hexagonal and triangular cross-sections – and there are many other such correspondences between all of the regular polygonal solids. So there is a type of unexpected 3D harmony, a type of resonance or, conceptually, a 'folding of space', between the solids – something not missed by the Pythagoreans. We now know that these 3D correspondences are merely a product of the rule sets applied, but without this knowledge the correspondences would have been quite beguiling.

There is much evidence that the Greeks studied the Platonic solids extensively. Theaetetus (417–369 BCE) and Euclid both described the five regular convex solids and Plato wrote about them in his dialogue *Timaeus* (360 BCE). Proclus (412–485 BCE) credits Pythagoras with their discovery. Theaetetus may have been responsible for the first known proof that there are no convex regular polyhedra other than the five Platonic solids, although Euclid also argues the same thing in Book 13,

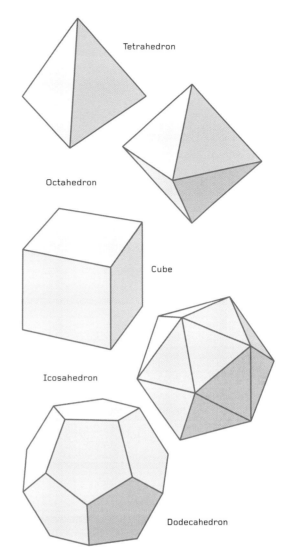

Tetrahedron

Octahedron

Cube

Icosahedron

Dodecahedron

5.68 The five Platonic solids

5.69 Neolithic carved stone balls, Scotland, 3200 BCE

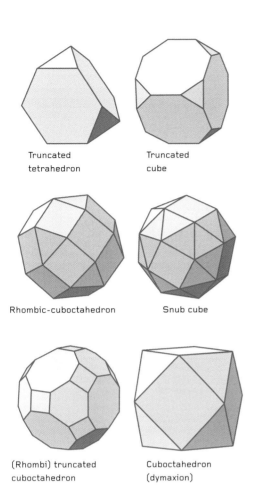

Truncated
tetrahedron

Truncated
cube

Rhombic-cuboctahedron

Snub cube

(Rhombi) truncated
cuboctahedron

Cuboctahedron
(dymaxion)

5.70 Archimedean solids

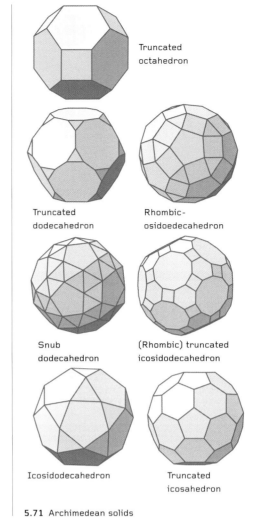

Truncated
octahedron

Truncated
dodecahedron

Rhombic-
osidoedecahedron

Snub
dodecahedron

(Rhombic) truncated
icosidodecahedron

Icosidodecahedron

Truncated
icosahedron

5.71 Archimedean solids

Proposition 18. In the *Timaeus*, Plato associated the four classical elements (earth, air, water, fire) with these solids: earth with the cube, air with the octahedron, water with the icosahedron and fire with the tetrahedron. Plato said that the dodecahedron was a form that 'the gods used for arranging the constellations on the whole heaven'.

In the *Elements* Euclid gives a complete mathematical description of the Platonic solids, and Book 12 is devoted to their properties. Propositions 13–17 in Book 13 describe the construction of the tetrahedron, cube, octahedron, dodecahedron and icosahedron. For each solid Euclid gives the ratio of the diameter of the circumscribed sphere to the edge length.

Archimedean solids Archimedean solids are defined as semi-regular convex polyhedra composed of more than one regular polygon that connect edge-to-edge. As with the Platonic solids, the

Archimedean solids can be inscribed within a sphere such that their corners touch the inner surface. There are 13 Archimedean solids.

Quantitative elements of polyhedra
Polyhedra have many characteristics; for example, each polyhedron has its specific dual, by which the faces of one polyhedron correspond with the vertices of another, and vice versa. Polyhedra can be transformed in a number of ways. They can, for example, be truncated, stellated or bevelled. A truncated polyhedron is a polyhedron with symmetrical slices cut away from its corners (vertices) to create a new polyhedron, typically a new semi-regular polyhedron (for example, look at the tetrahedron in fig. 5.68 and then at the truncated polyhedron in fig. 5.70). Stellation is a process by which the edges or faces of a polyhedron are extended. For example, imagine triangular pyramids added to the faces of a

tetrahedron. Bevelled, or cantellated, polyhedra, are polyhedra with cut-away edges. This cut-away can be progressive, where, for example, the edges of a cube can be cut away to transform the cube into a rhombic-cuboctahedron (see fig. 5.80), and then, with more cut away, into an octahedron (see fig. 5.68).

Each of the regular (Platonic) and semi-regular (Archimedean) polyhedra has a set number of surfaces, edges, and vertices, as well as planes that symmetrically cut through the polyhedra. The numeric and planar correspondences of one polyhedron with another means that there will be some sort of coincidence in 3D space. For example, an octahedron has six vertices and will fit inside a cube so that each vertex exactly touches the centre of each of the six square surfaces of a cube. An icosahedron has 30 edges and 15 symmetrical planes cutting through the centre. The 15 planes can be divided into five sets of three perpendicular planes.

5.72 Quantitive elements of polyhedra

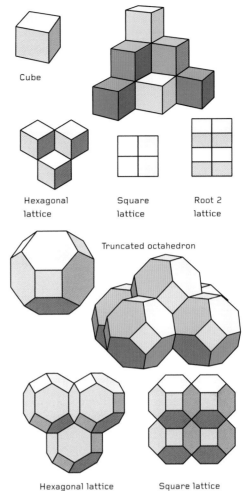

Cube

Hexagonal lattice   Square lattice   Root 2 lattice

Truncated octahedron

Hexagonal lattice   Square lattice

5.73 Space-filling polyhedra: cubes and octahedra

These planes divide the icosahedron into rectangles – in fact the golden rectangle, a/b, where a = √5 + 1 and b = 2. So the six edges, 'b', of a 3D-plane set will each exactly touch the centre of each of the six faces of a cube. Another way of looking at it is that five concentric cubes surround an icosahedron so that all edges of the icosahedron will touch all the faces of the cubes (see fig. 5.72).

Space-filling properties of polyhedra
Just as spheres, hemispheres and domes of different curvatures and facets can be precisely constructed to control space, so too can polyhedra of all sorts, ranging from regular polygons to rhombi and irregular polygons. Spheres have many properties and will also close-pack in three-dimensional space (see pp.278–88). Polyhedra, too, will close-pack in three-dimensional space, and this is often called a three-dimensional tessellation or, depending upon the configuration, a honeycomb.

Only one Platonic solid, the cube, tessellates on its own in three-dimensional space; and only one Archimedean solid tessellates – the truncated octahedron. Another polyhedron (but not an Archimedean solid) that tessellates in three-dimensional space is the rhombic dodecahedron. The long diagonal of each face of the rhombic dodecahedron (see fig. 5.75) is exactly √2 times the length of the short diagonal, so that the acute face angles are approximately 70.53°. The rhombic dodecahedron is a dual of an Archimedean solid, the cuboctahedron.

Regular prisms and certain combinations of polyhedra also tessellate in 3D space – and there is an almost infinite number of combinations of same and different polyhedra that do not tessellate but that form interesting 3D structures. Sections within tessellating polyhedra can be found that reveal two-dimensional polygonal lattices, as shown in fig. 5.73, where cubes have hexagonal

and √2 rectangular lattices, and where truncated octahedrons have square and hexagonal lattices. On the following pages some of the tessellating polyhedra lattices are shown (see figs 5.74–5.89).

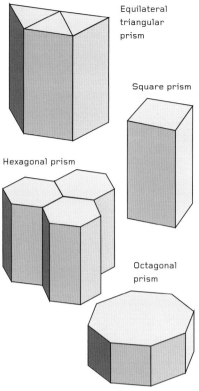

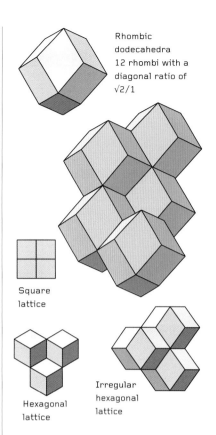

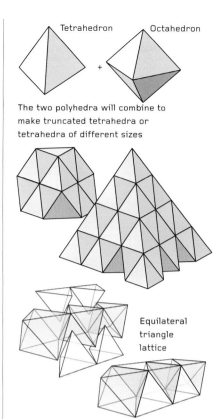

The two polyhedra will combine to make truncated tetrahedra or tetrahedra of different sizes

Tetrahedron + Octahedron

Equilateral triangle lattice

5.74 Space-filling polyhedra: triangular, hexagonal and octagonal prisms

5.75 Space-filling polyhedra: rhombic dodecahedra and cubes

5.76 Space-filling polyhedra: tetrahedra and octahedra

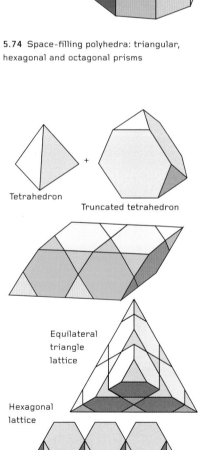

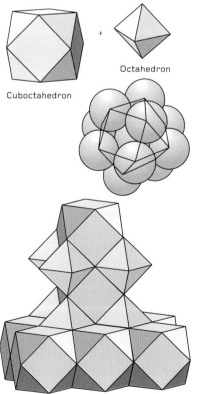

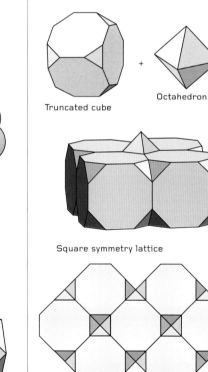

5.77 Space-filling polyhedra: tetrahedra and truncated tetrahedra

5.78 Space-filling polyhedra: cuboctahedra and octahedra

5.79 Space-filling polyhedra: truncated cubes and octahedra

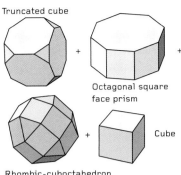

Truncated cube

+

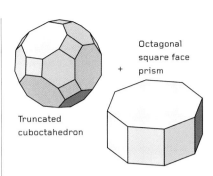

Octagonal square
face prism

+

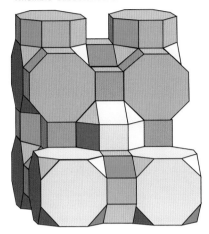

+

Cube

Rhombic-cuboctahedron

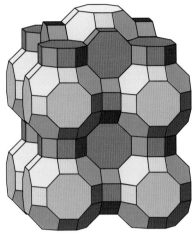

Truncated
cuboctahedron

+

Octagonal
square face
prism

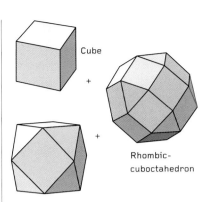

Cube

+

+

Rhombic-
cuboctahedron

Cuboctahedron

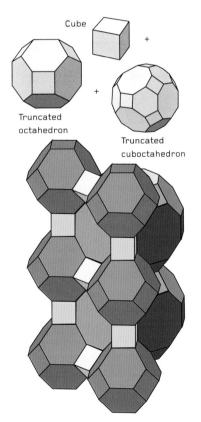

5.80 Space-filling polyhedra: truncated
cubes, octagonal prisms, rhombic-
cuboctahedra and cubes

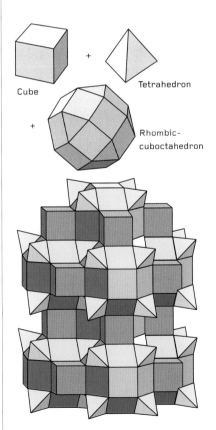

5.81 Space-filling polyhedra: truncated
cuboctahedra and octagonal prisms

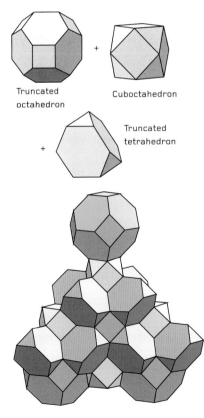

5.82 Space-filling polyhedra: cuboctahedra,
rhombic octahedra and cubes

Cube

+

Truncated
octahedron

+

Truncated
cuboctahedron

5.83 Space-filling polyhedra: truncated
cuboctahedra, truncated octahedra and cubes

Cube

+

Tetrahedron

Cube

+

Rhombic-
cuboctahedron

5.84 Space-filling polyhedra: tetrahedra,
rhombic octahedra and cubes

Truncated
octahedron

+

Cuboctahedron

Truncated
tetrahedron

+

5.85 Space-filling polyhedra: truncated
octahedra, cuboctahedra and truncated
tetrahedra

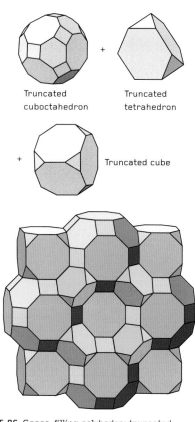

Truncated
cuboctahedron

+

Truncated
tetrahedron

+

Truncated cube

5.86 | Space-filling polyhedra: truncated cuboctahedra, truncated tetrahedra and truncated cubes

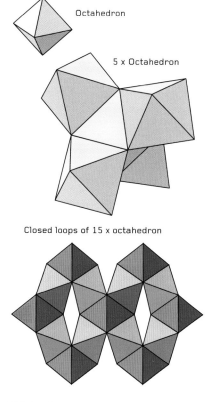

Octahedron

5 x Octahedron

Closed loops of 15 x octahedron

5.87 Semi-space-filling polyhedra: octahedra

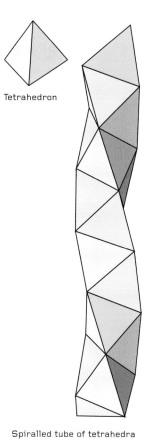

Tetrahedron

Spiralled tube of tetrahedra

5.88 Semi-space-filling polyhedra: tetrahedra

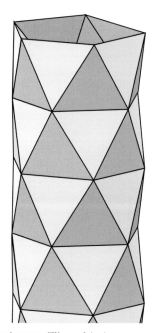

Pentagonal
anti-prism

5.89 Semi-space-filling polyhedra: pentagonal anti-prisms

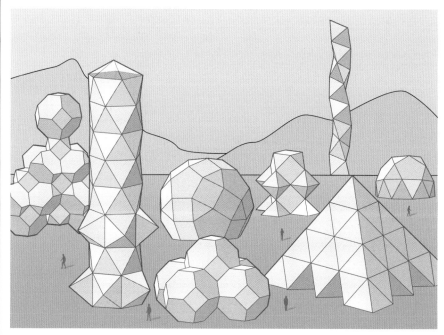

5.90 Hypothetical Pythagorean test centre

PYTHAGOREAN ARCHITECTURAL STRUCTURES

It is difficult to imagine that the Pythagoreans did not build human-sized architectural structures to investigate sound, light, emotional and symbolic properties of their 3D geometrical solids – particularly given the sort of 'harmonic' properties of their 2D planes. However, surviving stone temples do not appear to apply any rigid mathematical or scientific properties; and even numerical proportions rarely match established whole number ratios (but see p.157). The amazing perspective distortions added to façades and columns to make temples appear bigger and grander, as well as the intricately carved stonework, suggest that precision would have been possible had it been wanted. Moreover, structures built to investigate sensory properties would more than likely have been built of materials that could be more easily fashioned than stone. Such structures could have been built using timber, mud-brick (mud or clay mixed with straw or dried grass), adobe (sun-dried brick), terracotta (baked clay), ceramics or glass. A negative to this possibility is that no supportive evidence has yet been found.

Structures that might have been investigated would have included spheres, hemispheres, domes, Platonic solids, prisms and Archimedean solids. Surfaces, too, might have been coloured in many ways and decorated with symbolic images or perceptually challenging designs. Surfaces might also have been constructed to reflect light and sound in unique ways, perhaps using various material types such as granite particles mixed in with mud, and incorporating various polygonal surfaces, where polygons might have been connected to add three-dimensional details. Within the internal spaces sounds and music would have been played, and as later traditions suggest, sacred exercises, dances and poetry would have been performed, possibly similar to those of the Whirling Dervishes, circle dances and Confucian temple dances.

If the Pythagoreans did construct 3D geometrical forms for sensory testing then it would be most likely that they would have been, as noted, of many types, sizes and materials (see fig. 5.90). Domes would have been of varying curvatures and some would be raised up, possibly on an octagonal base and similar to the Nancy Stetson art studio in Boulder, Colorado (see pp.286–87).

Geodesic domes The circular and spherical characteristics of regular polygons and polyhedra were known to ancient Greek geometricians, and it is possible that they created geodesic domes, although no evidence remains. A geodesic dome is a polyhedron with edges and vertices that are aligned with the surface of a sphere, or part of a sphere. Any of the Platonic or Archimedean polyhedrons can be made into geodesic domes but typically only regular or semi-regular polyhedra with more than 12 faces are used.

More complex geodesic domes are produced by subdividing the faces of simpler geodesic domes while maintaining the alignment of the edges and vertices of the polygons produced with the surface

5.91 Geodesic dome: the Montreal Biosphere, 1967

of a sphere. The number of times the polygonal face is subdivided is called the 'frequency' of a geodesic dome (see figs 5.92, 5.93, 5.94 and 5.96). The lattices of most geodesic domes are triangular, hexagonal or pentagonal. It is possible that ancient Greek geometricians subdivided the polygonal spaces of polyhedra but, as there is no evidence, the credit must go to German engineer Walther Bauersfeld, who designed the first geodesic dome in the 1920s. Geodesic domes were popularized by American architect and inventor R. Buckminster Fuller from about 1948.

To create geodesic domes Platonic and Archimedean solids are typically used as a starting point, although other polyhedra, or even random 3D forms, can be used. Figs 5.92, 5.93 and 5.94 show a projection from a polyhedral lattice onto a sphere, with 0, 1, 2 and 3 frequency subdivisions of the polyhedron's polygonal face. Geodesics can be generated as complete spherical forms but also as partial domes. Variations can be of all sorts from projections of irregular polyhedra onto spheres to projections onto various types of curved surface.

Fig. 5.95 is a drawing of a geodesic radome, manufactured by AFC (Antennas for Communications), used for weather protection of radar and radio-astronomy installations. It uses an irregular tessellation method, as the geometry of an individual radome panel could cause radio-scattering errors and a radome constructed of repeated regular panels would compound the errors.

Fig. 5.96 shows three different polyhedron types: a geodesic dome variation of an icosahedron, a truncated-icosahedron dome with radii, and a geodesic projection on a sphere with a shifted icosohedron grid.

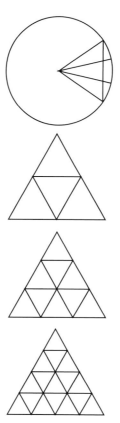

5.92 Geodesic construction – projection and 2, 3, 4 frequency

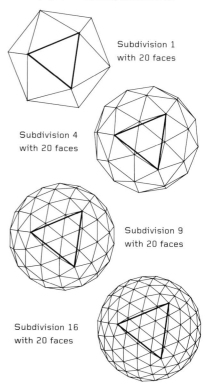

n = 0, 1, 2, 3 frequency icosahedron

Subdivision 1 with 20 faces

Subdivision 4 with 20 faces

Subdivision 9 with 20 faces

Subdivision 16 with 20 faces

5.93 Geodesic construction

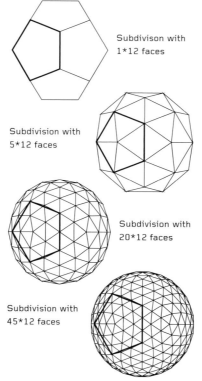

n = 0, 1, 2, 3 frequency dodecahedron

Subdivison with 1*12 faces

Subdivision with 5*12 faces

Subdivision with 20*12 faces

Subdivision with 45*12 faces

5.94 Geodesic construction

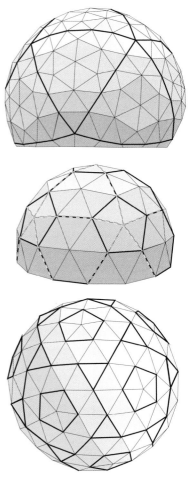

5.96 Geodesic construction

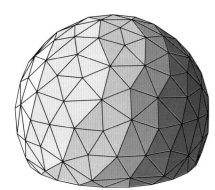

5.95 Irregular geodesic

GREEK ARCHITECTURE

If we accept that the Pythagoreans were as influential as the works of Plato would suggest, then we would expect to see architectural structures that include the sort of spaces and numerical values associated with the Pythagorean schools.

The Roman architect and engineer Vitruvius (c.70/80–c.15 BCE) is known for his ten-volume treatise on architecture, *De architectura* (*On Architecture*). At the beginning of Book 3 he specifically mentions Pythagoras and the Pythagorean schools. Book 3 describes a proportionate system, based on whole numbers, that is derived from the human body – proportions that are most famously applied by Leonardo in his *Vitruvian Man* (see fig. 5.31 and pp.210–11). Vitruvius credits the system to the Greeks and describes how the proportions were applied in their architecture. For example, the rectangular floor plan of a forum should be proportioned in the ratio of 2:3 and the rectangular floor plan of a basilica should, ideally, not be elongated more than 1:3 or shortened less than 1:2.

After describing proportions Vitruvius goes on to discuss the use of colour, acoustics and harmonics. He also recommended the positioning of resonant bronze vessels or vases in theatres to amplify sounds of specific frequencies. The books are fascinating and in many aspects follow the notions attributed to the Pythagoreans. The ten books are as rich in concepts as Leonardo's notebooks and they most definitely inspired Leonardo in art, architecture and engineering.

Vitruvius does not mention the golden ratio, although he does describe the number ten as the perfect number. There is also no real evidence that the golden ratio was used architecturally by the Greeks. It is possible to find some rough correspondences in the Parthenon but the proportions more accurately are in whole number ratios: 3:7, for example.

It seems feasible that temporary structures were built by the Pythagoreans to explore the sensory impact of architectural spaces on people, the sound-reflective properties of dimensions and surfaces, the reflection and diffusion of light, and the use of colour. The work of Vitruvius supports

5.97 Tholos at Delphi, 380–360 BCE

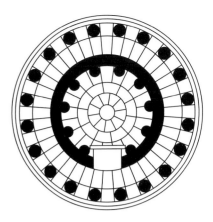

5.98 Plan view of tholos at Delphi

5.99 Tower of the Winds, Athens, c.50 BCE

the idea that this was a possibility. We may speculate that such structures might have been based on various whole number ratios; irrationals such as the golden ratio; spheres and domes; and Archimedean and Platonic polyhedra.

Figures 5.97 to 5.102 show a number of surviving ancient Greek architectural structures, including examples of the standard rectangular temple design, circular designs in sanctuaries and amphitheatres, and an octagonal design.

It is interesting to see that the *tholos* (circular building) at the centre of the sanctuary of Athena Pronaia at Delphi (380–360 BCE; figs 5.97 and 5.98), credited by Vitruvius to the sculptor and

architect Theodorus of Samos, contains the numbers 20 (columns) and 10 (inner columns) and 40, 20, and 10 paving stones; all contained in circles. The timing is right too for a structure linked to the Pythagoreans.

The Tower of the Winds in Athens (c.50 BCE; fig. 5.99) is an octagonal marble tower, attributed to the Macedonian astronomer Andronicus of Cyrrhus. Each of its eight sides faces a compass point and bears a relief representing one of the eight principal winds. At one time the tower is known to have contained eight or nine sundials, a water clock and a weather vane. The tower is about 12 m (40 ft) tall, a height

5.100 Treasury of Atreus, Mycenae, c.1250 BCE

5.102 Theatre of Epidaurus, 4th century BCE

5.103 The Parthenon, Athens, 447–432 BCE

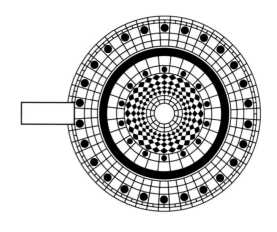

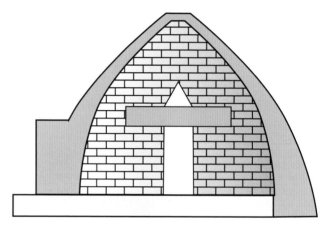

5.101 Treasury of Atreus, Mycenae, c.1250 BCE

that would have made a sundial positioned on the roof as visible as a clock tower.

The Treasury of Atreus (c.1250 BCE) dates from a much earlier period – the Mycenaean civilization (figs 5.100 and 5.101). Its interior space has been preserved and the acoustical properties can still be experienced. The dome itself is not a true dome, being composed of horizontal layers that are corbelled towards the centre.

The Theatre of Epidaurus (4th century BCE) (fig. 5.102) is a prime example of acoustical architecture, in this case, within a semicircular bowl.

The proportions of the Parthenon

Vitruvius states that the architects of the Parthenon (447–432 BCE; fig. 5.103), were Ictinus and Callicrates. He also notes that Ictinus co-authored a treatise explaining the proportions of the building, but unfortunately this has been lost, leaving us with the remains of the stone structure as our primary means to understand its proportions.

Measurements of the Parthenon either follow the perspective-compensating curves of the structure (the horizontals curve upwards and inwards and the columns tilt upwards) or follow straight lines from corners, but determining the

intended proportions is not so easy. The Pythagoreans believed that musical ratios such as 1:1, 1:2, 2:3 or 3:4 resonated with the universe, but these proportions are not immediately evident in the Parthenon. Some people see the golden rectangle in the proportions, even though there is no evidence that Euclid's mean and extreme ratio was used, plus some licence has to be taken to perceive the ratio by selecting almost random points from which the proportions are measured.

Given that Vitruvius explained how, in the Doric order of architecture, all temple parts depend on the size of a module, we might consider proportional ratios based on something that can easily be perceived, modules that might have been selected by the Parthenon's builders – counts of stone blocks. The first set of proportions shown in fig. 5.104 is based on the architrave stones that bridge the eight end pillars. The counts given seem to be the most obvious ones, i.e. the overall height and width, the height of the roof's triangular structure, and the proportions of the front façade. There are seven architrave stones running along the top of the front façade, and, if the length of each stone is treated as a module, the width of the façade is seven modules, the height from the top of the stylobate (top step) to the top of the 15 triglyphs (the blocks with three vertical channels above the architrave) appears to be three modules, and from the top of the stylobate to the projected apex of the roof is approximately four modules. The long side of the Parthenon had 16 architrave stones – i.e. it was 16 modules long. So the enclosed cuboid volume would be precisely 7 x 3 x 16 = 336 (= 6 x 7 x 8).

If we consider, as an alternative, that a module is equal to the width of a triglyph, then we find that the metopes (the 14 blocks next to the triglyphs) are one and a half modules wide, except for four that are one and a quarter triglyphs wide, making the overall width, corresponding to the front seven architrave stones, equal to 35 modules. In this scenario the height from the top step to the top edge of the triglyphs is equal to 15 modules (see fig. 5.105).

Interestingly, the Leonardo 'Vitruvian man' will fit neatly on the front steps of the Parthenon with his grid of 16 squares, corresponding nicely with the positions of the architrave stones and the pillars, as well as with the rectangular and triangular heights (see fig. 5.105). If nothing else this coincidence shows a correspondence of possible whole number ratios – 1:3, 3:3, 3:7 and 4:7, or proportionately 7, 9, 12 and 21.

Proportional ratios can be communicated numerically as well as in the visual balance of a design and it may be that both types of ratio were intentionally used in the design of the Parthenon: (i) in whole number rectangular ratios used to proportion the front, side, back and plan views of the

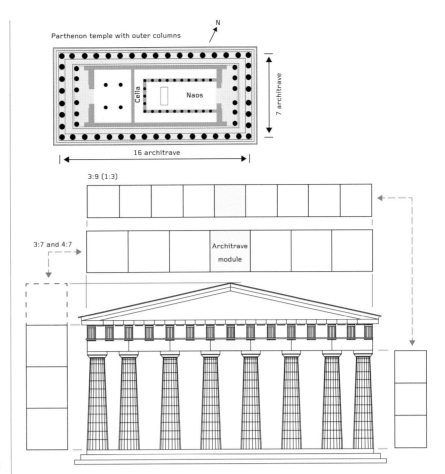

5.104 The Parthenon, Athens, 447–432 BCE

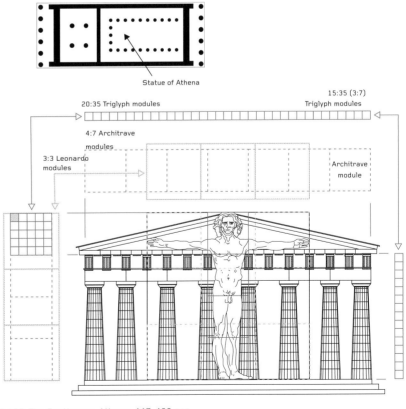

5.105 The Parthenon, Athens, 447–432 BCE

Parthenon; and (ii) in the numeric values used on the front façade with the seven (architrave stones), the eight (columns), and the 15 (triglyphs), with 15 being the fifth triangular number. However, there seems to be no clear evidence of an integrated proportional methodology, making any conclusions speculative.

Probably coincidentally, the numbers 7, 8 and 15 fall into a generalized Fibonacci sequence with 1 and 7 as the seed numbers: 1, 7, 8, 15, 23...

GEOMETRY AND DANCE

There are legends of Pythagorean dances, although no reliable descriptions have survived. Over the centuries from Neolithic times, dances, meditations, breathing exercises, rites of passage and gymnastics have all been associated with geometry, and have used labyrinthine structures, followed specific angles, or positioned themselves within circles, cubes, polygons, icosahedrons and domes. Some dances have even followed geometric paths through spaces and structures.

Linked to dances are movements associated with the seasons and the passing of time in general. Many rituals follow geometric sequences that are linked to the passage of the sun and stars, or the coming of spring, summer, autumn and winter. Legends describe circular movements around henges and barrows, and across plains towards sacred sites. Examples include the circular movement around the Kaaba in Mecca; the dances within Platonic solids and other spatial patterns and pathways identified and developed by the 20th-century Hungarian dance artist Rudolf Laban; classical ballet's facing-directions, alignments and angles; early 20th-century Armenian mystic and philosopher George Gurdjieff's line and enneagram dances; traditional circular and line folk dances; Confucius temple dances within circles and rectangular grids; Whirling Dervish dances within circles, pentagons and decagons; in Indian classical dance, Bharatanatyam dances within triangles; and the slowly whirling and unwinding Cham dances of the Tibetan Buddhists.

The treatises of the Ming dynasty prince Zhu Zaiyu (1536–1611) on dance, movement and ritual include mathematics, calendar studies, music

and dance because they are all closely linked to essential aspects of ritual. Mathematical sciences, for example, are essential to the ritualization of time (the calendar) and to the harmonization of sound (music), while dance concerns the ritualization of space, or the geometry of ritual.

Dance is an extraordinary thing beginning, as it seems, with semi-conscious movements to basic rhythms, the mimicking of the motions and movements of natural things and animals, and then progressing to semi-coordinated group movements, all the way to dances and posture sequences designed to build consciousness and awareness. In a similar way that air can be considered a food, music and movement can be considered an integral part of life's rhythms – as much as breathing, the beat of our hearts and the cycle of the seasons.

Although there are no reliable descriptions of Pythagorean geometrical dances there are more than 4,000 traditional Greek dances, many of which follow geometrical patterns and sequences – and some might owe their lineage to the Pythagoreans. The *geranos* (crane dance) was said to have been performed on the South Aegean island of Delos from as early as the time of Plutarch (46–120 CE). Theseus, the mythical founder king of the Attic state under Athens and slayer of the Minotaur, was said to have danced the *geranos* on his return from Crete. The dance was performed with various turnings and windings, and was said to be an imitation of the windings of the Cretan labyrinth.

Dances and exercises really intermix when it comes to dancing within geometric shapes. In many cases body posture aligns with the geometrical forms in 3D, as in the case of dancing within a polyhedron, or directionally, as is the case when dances are within polygons. Breathing and music too come into play. In the case of labyrinths we know that chanting was accompanied by movement. Of course these are all dances and exercises that have developed over the centuries and cannot be directly traced back to the Pythagoreans, but such characteristics of personal and physical control could well have been used by the secretive group. We do know that music

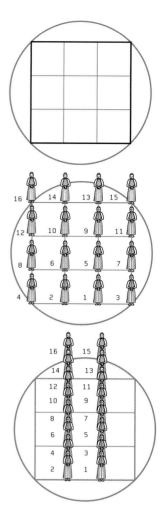

5.106 Zhu Zaiyu dance positions, 16th century

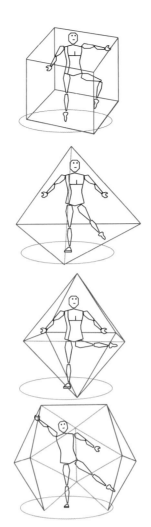

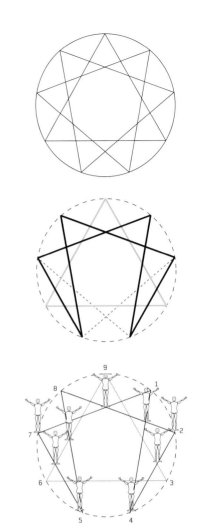

5.107 Circle dance; Whirling Dervishes; Laban dancers

5.108 Laban dancers

5.109 Gurdjieff dancers

played its part with the Pythagoreans, as well as logic, philosophy and mathematics, and all of this may well give us a glimpse as to the activities of the Pythagorean schools.

THE PYTHAGOREANS AND THE I CHING

It is interesting to compare how the Pythagoreans linked number and shape to something eternal, through whole number ratios and geometric axiomatic forms, with the ancient Chinese classic text the I Ching (see pp.90–91).

The I Ching appears to have been connected with the 'eternal' by associating a binary number system and related graphics (trigrams) with archetypal symbols such as mountains, lakes and fire, and then pairing the trigrams into hexagrams through a meditative process. A user would somehow tune into the 'eternal' and cast coins or sticks that the eternal guides to

select trigrams and their combinations. The process might be viewed as chance, but the users of the I Ching would probably describe it as something else – something about tuning into the fabric of the universe so that the coins or sticks, as they fall, inevitably follow patterns. In this way a pairing of trigrams, with its associated meanings, is somehow selected for the user to interpret, as part of a dynamic process that follows what users call the 'laws of change'.

The Chinese approach as expressed in the I Ching is profoundly different from Pythagorean beliefs about the eternal. For the Pythagoreans the mathematical nature of the universe exists and their quest appears to be that they should strive to experience its manifestations. This is in accord with their belief in the transmigration of the soul, whereby the human soul is just part of that same mathematical universe – being cycled by the machine, transformed into different

life forms, and thereby witnessing, from different perspectives, the machine. The Chinese, as represented by the I Ching, are not part of a mathematical machine but rather part of something much more dynamic and much more subject to change, yet that still accords to universal patterns. The difference is almost like comparing mechanical theories of the universe to quantum effects and the temporary appearance of energetic quantum particles.

RE-EMERGENT VISUAL LOGIC

After the fall of the Roman Empire in the 4th–5th centuries, European Celtic artists re-established their own visual identity with cursive, circular and interwoven designs, interpreting and adapting older geometries.

POST-ROMAN EUROPEAN TRIBES

The Book of Kells is a lavishly illuminated manuscript containing the four Gospels of the New Testament and written on vellum (calfskin). It was produced from the 8th to the 9th centuries by Columban monks, perhaps at the Columban abbey on the island of Iona, Scotland, perhaps at the Abbey of Kells in County Meath, Ireland, where it was kept until the 17th century. The illustrations, in a style known as 'Insular' that was particular to post-Roman Britain and Ireland, include many European tribal designs, such as geometrical circle arrangements and woven or interlaced structures.

The Chi Rho page from the Book of Kells is shown here (see fig. 6.2). This page introduces St Matthew's account of the Nativity. Chi and rho, the first two letters of the Greek form of the word 'Christ' (XP), were traditionally used as a religious symbol; here they include the third letter, I, and are elaborately decorated.

While knowledge of Greek geometry and mathematics is fragmented, knowledge of European tribal geometry following the collapse of the Roman Empire is practically nonexistent, with the exception of a few stone carvings, artefacts and books such as the Book of Kells. However,

as there is a significant chapter in this book on the new 'dynamic sphere geometry' (see chapter 12), it may be useful here to look at some of the designs that are based on circles and regular tessellations. There is also a possible tie-in with the previous chapter on Greek mathematics, particularly as there is evidence that isolated Irish and Scottish monasteries managed to preserve copies of Greek and Roman masterpieces in the same way that such works were preserved by Islamic scholars after the fall of Rome.

The pages in this chapter present Celtic art as something essentially two-dimensional, with designs based on circles and simple tessellations. Applications are largely decorative – from designs in the Book of Kells and the 7th-century Book of Durrow to ornamental designs on shields, Pictish stones and crosses.

PROTO-CELTIC AND CELTIC ART

Celtic art has its origins in Neolithic times and appears in petroglyphs of spirals, labyrinths and simple circle designs. One of the carved stone balls found in Towie, Aberdeenshire (2500 BCE) (see fig. 6.3), has a similar symmetry to one of the Platonic solids, the tetrahedron. The Towie Stone ball also has spiral designs carved into the faces that were common in pre-Celtic and Celtic designs.

Created within the same time frame as that of the Towie Stone was the Newgrange entrance stone, in County Meath, Ireland (see fig. 6.4). Newgrange

6.1 (opposite) Battersea Shield, 350 BCE

6.2 Book of Kells, Folio 34r, 8th–9th century

6.3 Neolithic carved stone ball, Scotland, 2500 BCE

6.4 Newgrange entrance stone, County Meath, Ireland, 3200 BCE

6.5 2nd-century Roman-era bowl, England, known as the Staffordshire Moorlands Pan

6.6 Celtic triskelion symbol

is a large circular mound with a stone passageway and interior chambers. In keeping with many Neolithic architectural structures of the time, the inner chamber is aligned to catch the sun during the winter solstice (see p.57).

The ancient people that carved the Towie Stone spoke any one of a group of languages now called Proto-Celtic, with their origins in Indo-European languages. Certainly, spiral and labyrinth designs occur over a wide area from India to Europe – and covering a great span of time. Proto-Celtic art is found, for example, in Neolithic mounds at Boyne in Ireland, dated 3200 BCE, and across Europe in the Bronze and Iron Ages. It seems fair to say that Proto-Celtic art was integrated over time into the areas visited by the early Celts.

However, the refinements of art that has now been characterized as 'Celtic' took place in areas that 'survived' the Roman Empire: parts of northern Spain, France and Germany, Scandinavia, and the northern and far western parts of the British Isles. The high point and most characteristic period of Celtic art is that of the early medieval period, but this is probably because a fair amount of artwork survived or was re-created in isolated monasteries in northern England and Ireland from about 600 CE. Other works do survive but are rare, such as a bronze enamelled 2nd-century CE bowl found in Staffordshire, England, and known as the Staffordshire Moorlands Pan (see fig. 6.5). The bowl has a common design element, the triskelion

(see below), frequently found in monastic 'Celtic' Bibles such as the books of Kells and Durrow. Also surviving are such items as a Celtic bronze mirror (50 BCE), the Battersea Shield (350–50 BCE; see fig. 6.1) and the Wandsworth Shield (2nd century BCE).

Illuminated manuscripts The best-known surviving illuminated manuscripts from early medieval times are the Book of Durrow (c.670 CE), the Gospels of Lindisfarne (c.690 CE) and the Book of Kells (c.800 CE). Their creation coincided with a period when monastic life in the area was becoming less isolated and more open to the transmission of knowledge from the Eastern Roman Empire (330–1453) and the Islamic Umayyad Caliphate (661–1031).

The geometrical systems used for some Celtic monastic illustrations are clear and obvious, but in many other cases, designs seem to be based on crude interpretations of classical systems. The assumption that the scribes had access to copies of the works of Euclid and other Pythagoreans would explain why many designs were apparently inspired by classical geometric constructions – but the imprecision of the monastic designs suggests that, if this was the case, the principles of the geometries were not correctly understood.

The surviving illuminated manuscripts are small: for example, the Book of Kells is only 24 x 33 cm (10 x 13 in), making details almost microscopic, suggesting that the designs were worked out at a

larger scale and then scaled down. On some pages in the Book of Kells there is evidence of the use of guidelines as well as a compass, but their minute size suggests the illustrations were mostly drawn freehand. The designs were typically rendered in layers of colour.

As stated, in monastic Celtic design there is little evidence of a precise understanding of the mathematics of the Greeks, nor of that of the refined geometries of early Islamic designers. As Celtic design evolved into early Gothic design we find that the wonderful deductive logic of the Greeks, which is often featured and elaborated upon in the designs of Islam, is mostly absent. In fact, Celtic – and early Gothic – monastic art and associated architectural forms are mostly based on simple geometries, with architectural designs based more on symbolism and numerology than on elaborate and precise geometrical systems, although in later Gothic art we do see a resurgence of more elaborate and precise geometries.

The triskelion A design that appears on the Staffordshire Moorlands Pan resembles a three-way yin-yang symbol. Known as a triskelion, this is based on three circles of the same size packed within a larger circle (see fig. 6.6). This close-packing arrangement appears throughout the Book of Kells. Connecting the circle centres creates an equilateral triangle, and the close-packed circles will repeat infinitely across a two-dimensional plane. Connected centres also create

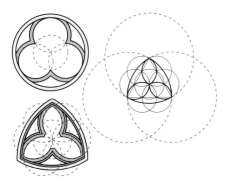

6.7 Trefoil designs

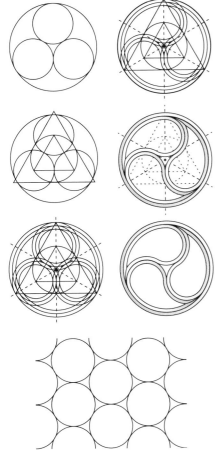

6.8 Development of triskelion

6.9 Matthias Church, Budapest, Hungary, 13th–15th century

6.10 Minden Cathedral, Germany, 13th century, and the Royal Abbey of Santa Maria de Poblet, Spain, 12th century

hexagons and equilateral triangles – a lattice that has been developed around the world to create all sorts of designs, from China to Europe. The packing also forms one plane of a three-dimensional spherical packing from which such 3D forms such as a tetrahedron can be constructed (see chapter 12).

In Christianity the triskelion is a feature of many medieval church and cathedral windows. The symbol was probably used to represent the Trinity – the Father, Son and Holy Ghost. The design is typically contained within a circle, representing the oneness of the Christian Trilogy, and is similar in construction to the Gothic trefoil, although in the trefoil the three circles overlap and connect at the centre of an escribed circle (see fig. 6.7).

The construction of the three-way triskelion design (see fig. 6.8) starts with the Celtic base of three touching circles within an escribed circle. A new circle is then drawn to connect the centres of the three circles, with the connecting

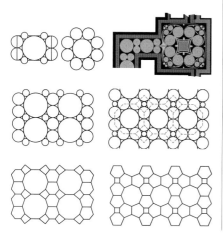

6.11 Book of Kells, St Matthew, Folio 28r, close-packing circle design

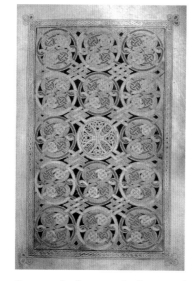

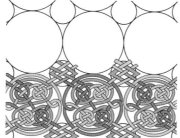

6.12 Book of Durrow, Folio 85v, close-packing circle design

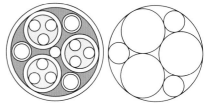

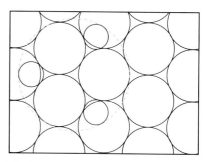

6.13 Book of Kells, detail Folio 34r, close-packing derivative

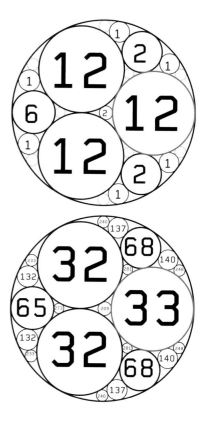

6.14 Book of Kells, close-packing derivative of fig. 6.13

circle having a larger diameter than the three original circles. The connecting circle is then escribed with an equilateral triangle that extends outside the outer circle; if making a window, the height of the extension determines the width of the stonework frames.

Triskelions appear in a circular window above one of the entrance doors to the Gothic-style Matthias Church in Budapest, Hungary (see fig. 6.9).' Trefoil designs appear as small windows in the 12th-century Cistercian monastery the Royal Abbey of Santa Maria de Poblet in Catalonia, Spain, and at Minden Cathedral, Germany (see fig. 6.10).

Circle packing An illustration in the Book of Kells (see fig. 6.11) includes two types of circle packing. The first circle arrangement close-packs if extended across a two-dimensional plane. If the circle centres of the 2D plane are connected then a classic semi-regular tessellation of octagons and squares will be generated, with the symbolic numbers 8 and 4. Drawing tangents at the circle contact points creates a lattice of eight-, six- and four-sided polygons,

representing the symbolic numbers 8, 6 and 4. In early Christianity the number 4 represented the four corners of the world and the number of the gospels, the number 6 represented perfection – the six-petalled lily was the emblem for the Virgin Mary – and the number 8 represented the transition from Earth to Heaven – the number of resurrection. In the Book of Kells design, the circle packing is limited to that enclosed within a square, with other circles roughly placed to pack within the outer areas that would roughly close-pack if other circles were added. The second close-packing arrangement is not fully completed but it still appears to define a close-packing that can be seen if four circles are added. The packing creates a cell that will repeat infinitely across a 2D plane. If polygons are created around each circle, by drawing tangents at contact points, the polygons created will have four, six and ten sides, which would probably have had a numerological significance.

An illustration in the Book of Durrow shows a knowledge of a close-packing within a square symmetry (see fig. 6.12).

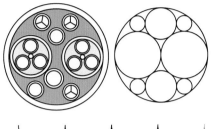

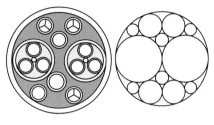

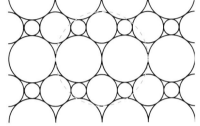

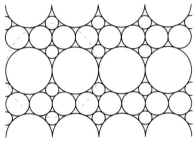

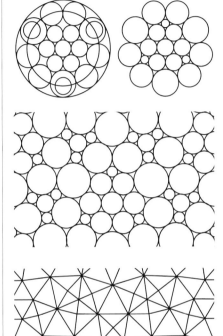

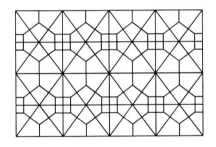

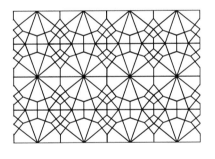

6.15 Book of Kells, Folio 34R, 1, 2, 3 circle ratios

6.16 Book of Kells, Folio 34r, 10, 6, 4 polygons

6.17 Book of Durrow, Folio 192v, centred circles

If circles are drawn to fill the gaps between the large circles, a classic close-packing will be generated. Adding the extra circle also creates a triangulation making the geometry structurally stable. Drawing tangents at the circle contact points creates a semi-regular tessellation of octagons and squares – symbolic numbers 8 and 4. Connecting circle centres creates a lattice of squares and quarter-squares.

Fig. 6.13 shows an extract from another design in the Book of Kells. The three-circle core of the design appears similar to that used in the triskelion design, but the additional three outer circles suggest something more. It is possible that the

designer was aware of something like the 'kissing circles' of Descartes, in which three mutually tangent circles can be used to calculate a fourth tangent circle. In ancient Greece, the 3rd-century BCE geometer and astronomer Apollonius of Perga devoted an entire book to the subject, *On Tangencies*. Fig. 6.14 shows a kissing circle arrangement that could be considered a development of the fig. 6.13 design. The arrangement is known as an Apollonian gasket, with curvatures 32, 33, 65, 68, 132... – where the curvature of a circle is defined as the inverse of its radius. From the gasket we can see that the Kells circles are close to the ratios of 2:3:6:12.

As the Celtic designers considered circle packing, it is possible that they were aware of close-packing arrangements other than those illustrated: for example a design in the Book of Kells could have an associated packing with ratios 1:2:3 (see fig. 6.15).

Rather than the 1:2:3 packing, another might have been considered (see fig. 6.16), although perhaps it is unlikely. A design in the Book of Durrow can be interpreted as shown in fig. 6.17. While the close-packing extension over a two-dimensional plane looks perfect, in fact it is not, although without a knowledge of the mathematics involved this would be difficult to prove.

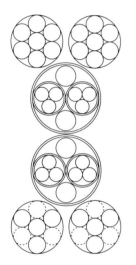

6.18 Book of Durrow, Folio 3v

6.19 Triskelion development

6.20 Detail from the Book of Durrow, Folio 3v

Circles arranged to close-pack within a circle appear in another Book of Durrow design (see fig. 6.18). The central circle arrangements extend into the 1:2:3 ratio packing interpretation of the earlier Book of Kells design (see fig. 6.15).

Spirals and knots A development of the triskelion arrangement into a classic Celtic spiral design is shown in fig. 6.19. The use of the spiral is in accord with ancient traditions extending back to Neolithic times but, in this case, the spiral centres are left open, creating a labyrinth or maze-like function.

The spiral in Celtic art and in many early Neolithic traditions may well have been associated with the energy of spiralling winds or water. In ancient

Greece the traditions surrounding the labyrinth suggest an association with a portal to the spiritual world or to a life beyond, into eternity.

Fig. 6.21 shows a logic different from that of packing circles: that of knots – a common Celtic design form. The illustration shows two possible construction methods for a knot design, though of course the design could just be a stylization of something drawn freehand, or even a copy of an actual piece of rope arranged in the form shown.

Fig. 6.22 shows a design that might have started with a more formal grid of either six or 12 circles or at least six lines of symmetry. Other possible methods for constructing spiral designs can only be guessed at. It might have

6.21 Possible design systems for knot design development

6.22 Possible circular knot design development

6.23 Circular knot design development

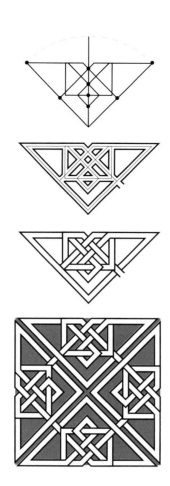

6.24 Circular knot design development

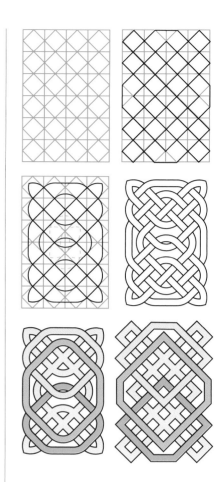

6.25 Possible systems for knot design development

been, as mentioned, that the designers started with actual ropes or threads, worked out a weave on some sort of peg board, and then rendered the spiral design with a stylized geometrical construction. There seem to be too many accidental design elements in the designs shown in figs 6.23, 6.24 and 6.25 for the methods of construction to have been much different from those shown; they are logical but not always precise.

Greek and Roman circle designs share design methodologies with Celtic designs. For example, a 6th-century mosaic floor in the remains of a Byzantine monastery (see fig. 6.26) is similar to classic Celtic designs. The monastery was discovered near the village of Hura in the northern part of the Negev Desert region of Israel. The 9th-century Hilton of Cadboll Stone

6.26 Negev circular knot design development

6.27 The Hilton of Cadboll Stone, Scotland, c.800 CE

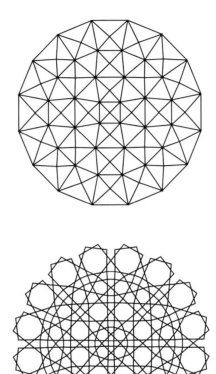

6.28 Possible circular design developments

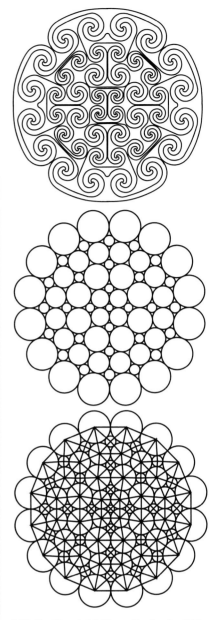

6.29 The Shandwick Stone, Scotland, c.800 CE, and possible circular design developments

(see fig. 6.27) on the Tarbat Peninsula in northeastern Scotland shares a similar geometry to the Negev mosaic design. The stone is a 2.43 m-high (7½ ft) Pictish monumental slab with Christian and secular carvings of both figurative and geometric designs. The Picts were the ethnolinguistically Celtic tribal peoples who lived in northern and eastern Scotland from late antiquity to the early Middle Ages. Another Pictish stone situated in the same area is the Shandwick Stone (c.800 CE), and figs 6.28 and 6.29 show a drawing of a design found on the stone as well as possible developments.

'If I be worthy, I live for my God to teach the heathen, even though they may despise me.'
SAINT PATRICK (385–461)

CELTIC 3D DESIGN

In 1850, on the island of Orkney off the northeastern coast of Scotland, a violent storm disturbed the sand dunes and revealed four Neolithic houses; further excavations in the 20th century uncovered more structures. Skara Brae is a 5,000-year-old village of one-roomed houses constructed of circular stone walls, which would probably have been topped with timber lean-tos, woven branches and grass. Internally there are beds, hearths, dressers and storage units, all carefully crafted in stone. In Galicia, northwestern Spain, there are the remains of a pre-Roman Celtic settlement with buildings constructed in a way similar to those at Skara Brae (see fig. 6.30). Conceptually, Celtic architectural concepts and those of associated tribes appear to be simple extensions of earlier Neolithic concepts – often circular and topped with simple cones or thatched domes, or rectangular with A-frames. The most innovative Celtic and Norse three-dimensional designs can be seen in the designs of surviving Viking longships (see fig. 6.33).

Fig. 6.30 shows Celtic ruins in the ancient village of Castro de Santa Tegra in Galicia, Spain. A *castro* was a fortified settlement usually consisting of round or oval constructions. The building on the right in the photograph is a reconstruction, showing what a dwelling might have looked like.

Fig. 6.31 shows a reconstructed Viking farm in Ale, near Gothenburg, Sweden.

Fig. 6.32 shows the Grianan of Aileach – a group of ancient structures atop a 244 m (800 ft) hill in County Donegal, Ireland. The main structure is a stone ring fort (fortifed farmhouse), thought to have been built by the Northern Uí Néill dynasty in the 6th or 7th century. The wall is about 4.5 m (15 ft) thick and 5 m (16 ft) high. It has three terraces, which are linked by steps, and two long passages within it.

Fig. 6.33 shows the prow of the 9th-century Viking longship that was uncovered in a burial mound at Gokstad in the Vestfold county of southern Norway. The longship showcases the remarkable construction and design practices of the time – beautifully streamlined and efficient. The Gokstad ship is approximately 5 m (17 ft) wide and nearly 24 m (78 ft) long with a hull constructed of 16 tapered planks on either side. The planks overlap and are progressively wider from keel to topside, making the sides of the ship light and flexible. The stern and keel are cut from single pieces of oak. Under sail the ship could reach speeds estimated at 12 knots (22 km/h; 14 mph) or even higher. In shallow waters or calm seas the ship could be propelled by 32 oarsmen.

6.30 Castro de Santa Tegra, Galicia, Spain, c.1st century BCE

6.31 Reconstructed Viking house, Viking Centre, Fyrkat, Hobro, Denmark

6.32 Grianan of Aileach, Donegal, Ireland, 6th–7th century

'In this year terrible portents appeared over Northumbria, and miserably frightened the inhabitants: these were exceptional flashes of lightning, and fiery dragons were seen flying in the air. A great famine soon followed these signs; and a little after that in the same year on 8 [June] the harrying of the heathen miserably destroyed God's church in Lindisfarne by rapine and slaughter.'
THE ANGLO-SAXON CHRONICLES
(9TH CENTURY)

6.33 Prow of Gokstad Viking longship, Norway, 9th century

07. GEOMETRIES OF THE EARLY ISLAMIC PERIOD

A CULTURALLY INTEGRATED GEOMETRY

Scholars in the early Islamic period saved many ancient Greek and Roman geometric manuscripts, studied them and then developed their own geometries influenced by the numerous cultures newly encompassed by Islam.

Islamic architecture and design became stylistically recognizable from the late 7th century, as exemplified by the Dome of the Rock in Jerusalem. Its Corinthian columns, plant-like mosaics and Roman arches set a precedent for a patchwork of styles that were to become a feature of later mosques. The simple geometries of the upper façade (685–91 CE) may have set the path towards the complex geometrical patterns that followed. The pointed dome may also have been the inspiration for the diverse range of Islamic dome shapes of later ages, quite different from the hemispherical domes of Byzantium (see fig. 7.2 and pp.200–01).

From the 7th century to the 15th century, Islamic two- and three-dimensional design systems evolved and diversified, and studying them provides a treasure trove of ideas for the present and the future. Many Islamic geometrical systems are derivations of Greek systems, while others follow the traditions of earlier cultures. At a time when many Christian scholars were destroying the works of the Greeks and Romans, deeming them unholy and pagan, Islamic scholars preserved them, studied them and saved them for the future. Islam became the conduit for knowledge when Europe was in disarray – and it is likely that the European Renaissance would not have happened without it.

The cultural roots of Islamic geometric design have their origins in nomadic and tribal lifestyles. Symbolism and numerology are pervasive, together with an active interest in such things as knots, astronomy, garden images of trees, vines, rosettes and birds, and transcendental images of water (linked to self-reflection). Dominant in Islamic art is the tradition of not trying to directly represent God, or 'that which should not be named'. The closest definition of God, in Islam, is the characteristics of God, said to number 99. The numeric value of alif, the Arabic letter A, is 1, and Allah is 'the One', epitomized by the fundamental creed *la ilaha illa'llah*, which may be translated as 'Allah is Allah' or 'One is One'.

The Qur'an prohibits idolatry and the worshipping of statues or pictures.

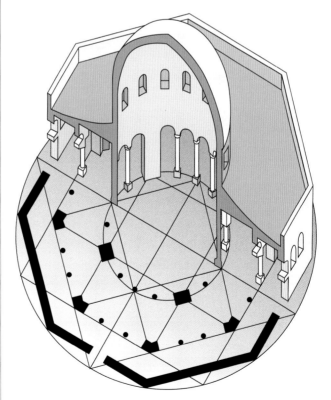

7.1 Imam Mosque muqarnas, Isfahan, Iran, 1611

7.2 The Dome of the Rock, Jerusalem, 691 CE

Although it does not explicitly forbid the representation of living beings – whether human or animal – as Islamic art developed, such depictions came to be seen as idolatrous and were prohibited by numerous official commentaries, or *hadith*. Therefore, Islamic art shows a clear disposition towards using abstractions rather than realistic representations. Many Islamic surface designs show abstracted and patterned representations of plants and trees, often picked up from earlier cultures including Egyptian, Roman, Byzantine, Mesopotamian and Persian. (Islamic architectural structures and layouts show similar influences.) Persian and central Asian Islamic designs allowed more realistic depictions of certain animals, particularly birds, and even people, possibly because of the closer proximity to India and the historical regard for poetry and its allegorical illustrations.

The predilection for abstract art provided a wonderful setting for the development of geometry. There is no better way to describe the uniqueness of Islamic architecture, art and design than to use the term 'geometric'.

The primary design elements of Islam are based on the script of the Qur'an, communal prayer, numerology, geometry and symbolism. In some sects of Islam, particularly certain schools of Sufism, the basis is broader and includes the sensory and intellectual impact of architectural spaces, perceptual designs, dances, exercises, chants, music, poems and literature; Sufism draws heavily on the structure of the Arabic language as much as on earlier esoteric traditions in Egypt, Greece, Tibet, India and China.

There are three main types of 'geometric' Islamic surface design. The first is that of Arabic script, often citing verses from the Qur'an. The second is that of what may be called perceptual geometric designs. The third are designs that transition the two-dimensional surface into three dimensions, such as in the muqarnas (honeycomb-style architectural features, see fig. 7.1 and p.197).

Qur'anic script The script is often created within a geometric square grid, but that is as close as it gets to geometry

as such and so it does not fall within the scope of this book. Islamic illustrative calligraphy is quite beautiful and brilliant. On two-dimensional surfaces, such as mosque walls, Islamic script serves to orient visitors, to remind them of why they are in a certain place. The script can also (possibly) communicate by means of the abjad system (see p.175) and so combine the rhythm of a stanza with the multiple symbolic meanings derived from the abjad. The *Islanders* illustrative calligraphy in fig 7.3 by 'Mohamed, son of Shafiq' of the Mevlevi order of Sufis roughly translates as: 'I take refuge in Allah from Satan the stoned one. In the name of Allah the Beneficent, the Merciful. Oh Allah who opens the doors, open for us the best door.' ('Door' in Arabic is '*dar*', and relates to the word 'dervish'.)

Perceptual 2D designs Perceptual designs are designs that visually 'change before your eyes' – sort of visual-logic puzzles, such as the typical geometric rosetted designs associated with Islam. Two-dimensional perceptual designs provide by far the most 'geometry' in Islamic art, even more than three-dimensional architecture. Five primary two-dimensional geometrical systems were used, with each system having the potential of generating an almost infinite number of variations. Why one design was chosen rather than another for a given space, such as in a mosque, might have been purely for its decorational merit. But if we consider the importance of numerology and symbolism, as well as the perceptual values of the architect, then there may have been a further logic to positioning a design. If this was the case, then of particular interest would be designs that appear on doors and rugs, near entrances, in specific rooms and in the vicinity of mihrabs (prayer niches). If a design was meant to communicate then it was by the structural numbers within the design, the symmetry, the construction method, the colours and, in some cases, the symbolic forms woven into the design. An intended communication would make sense within the context in which it was placed.

Numbers In Islam the use of numbers falls into two categories: the symbolic, by which a specific number has a specific

No God but Allah, Muhammad is His Messenger

The Bismillah

The Islanders by Mohamed, son of Shafiq (1291)

7.3 Examples of stylized Arabic script

symbolic meaning, and the abjad system, by which letters have a corresponding numerological value (see below). There is also a possible legacy of Pythagorean and other ancient cultural uses of number.

Symbolism can be ambiguous, but there are accepted correspondences between certain numbers, images and concepts. In some cases symbols have different meanings to different groups of people: the swastika, for example, was a sacred and auspicious symbol in Hinduism, Buddhism and Jainism before being co-opted by the Nazis. In Islam the number 5 has several symbolic meanings. There are five Pillars of Islam – the declaration of faith (*shahada*), the prayer (*salat*), fasting, giving alms (*zakat*), and the pilgrimage to Mecca (*hajj*). Prayers are said five times every day. There are five categories of Islamic law and five

Hamza	ء	0
Alif	١	1
Ba	ب	2
Jim	ج	3
Dal	د	4
Ha / Ta	ة ه	5
Waw	و	6
Zay	ز	7
Ha	ح	8
Ta	ط	9
Yah	ي	10
Kaf	ك	20
Lam	ل	30
Mim	م	40
Nun	ن	50
Sin	س	60
Ayn	ع	70
Fa	ف	80
Sad	ص	90
Qaf	ق	100
Ra	ر	200
Shin	ش	300
Ta	ت	400
Tha	ث	500
Kha	خ	600
Dhal	ذ	700
Dad	ض	800
Za	ظ	900
Ghayn	غ	1000

7.4 The abjad numeral system

7.5 Seljuk period door, Ince Minareli Medrese (school), Konya, Turkey, 13th century

law-giving prophets (Noah, Abraham, Moses, Jesus and Muhammad). With regard to the number 8, the Dome of the Rock has an octagonal footprint, whereby the dome rests on an octagon and the octagon on the earth. So one might use the octagon to symbolize the faith of Islam, and also to symbolize the bridge between Earth and Heaven. Structurally the octagon shape was generally used in early Islamic architecture as the transitional form between a dome and the rest of a building.

Abjad numerology An abjad is a type of alphabet that features only consonants, not vowels, such as the early Arabic and Hebrew writing systems. Vowels are represented by the squiggles and dots (diacritics) that appear above and below the main consonantal script. An Arabic consonantal word is called its root, and words with different meanings are formed by adding different diacritics. An abjad is also a system of notation by which each letter in the Arabic alphabet is assigned a number (see fig. 7.4). Using this methodology, numbers can be translated into words and vice versa. The system was used to great effect in classical Arabic and Persian literature, as well as in Islamic designs. Each Arabic consonant has a specific numeric value so, if three numbers appeared in any form, then each number could represent a letter, and the three letters a word (known as a triliteral root). The system is such that numbers can be rearranged and multiples of 10 substituted to create a word with a suitable meaning. For example, 5, 6, 9 can represent letters with numerical values of 5, 6 and 9, but also of, say, 50,

60 and 90; and they can also be rearranged, for example as 6, 9, 5.

The Seljuk period door in fig. 7.5 dating from 13th-century Anatolia shows an example of a possible use of numeric values to communicate a message. The design of the door is based on a close-packing arrangement of circles positioned within a pentagon and 36° rhombus tessellation. Polygons are positioned within the circles as shown in fig. 7.6, and then pentagrams and decagrams are placed within the polygons. The lines of the pentagrams and decagrams are used to create rosettes (see fig. 7.7).

The numbers associated with the rosettes in a design would, if a communication were intended, be the principal numbers of a communication. In the case of this door the numbers 5

7.6 Construction for the Seljuk door design
(see fig. 7.5)

and 10 are the principal numbers, but,
using the abjad system, so are multiples
of 5 and 10. Fig. 7.8 shows the abjad
translation of the door's numerology.

Looking at the Arabic calligraphy at the
top of the door, the top right panel reads
'and performs prayers' and the top left
panel reads 'and pays the alms'. The whole
sentence appears in the Qur'an, in the
Surat (chapter) Al-Baqarah, 'The Cow',
in Verse 2:177. The verse defines
righteousness in terms of belief in Allah,
the Last Day, the angels, the Book and the
prophets, and in terms of giving away one's
wealth, in spite of one's love for it, to
relatives, orphans, the needy, travellers
and those who ask [for help], and to
free slaves.

7.7 Construction for the Seljuk door design (see fig. 7.5)

10	5	Astronomy, cry for calling
ي	ه	camels for water.
		To prepare, to arrange, thing agreed upon.

50	5	10	To loose the mind.
ن	ه	ي	Receive a blessing, on the right side, the right hand.

100	5	Cry to excite horses, they
ق	ه	thronged at the water.
		Three stars in Orion, fifth mansion of the moon.

5	100	Top of the head.
ه	ق	Summit of the body.

7.8 Abjad interpretation of the Seljuk door (see fig. 7.5)

7.9 Design and detail of the Seljuk door
(see fig. 7.5)

Whirling Dervishes It seems likely that the Seljuk door was a door to a school where the Whirling Dervishes practised and performed their dance. Konya, the capital of the Anatolian Seljuk sultanate, was the location of the Mevlevi, a Sufi order also known as the Whirling Dervishes (see below). A description of the Whirling Dervish dance follows and is in accord with the abjad meanings given in fig. 7.8.

They are called to dance.
They meet as arranged.
They turn in circles.
Their right hand faces up
and their left hand faces down.
They wear tall hats on top of their heads.
They whirl like stars in the night sky.
They gather together to dance.
They are like thirsty travellers looking
for water.

During the 13th century a group of people concerned with elevating human perception of the world created a dance to complement their other rituals and practices. The group was headed by the Sufi mystic Jalal ad-Din Muhammad Rumi and the dance was the dance of the Whirling Dervishes. Imagine, then, a builder receiving a commission to design a building within which the dance was to take place. He would certainly wish to weave into the architecture as much of the accumulated knowledge of the group as he could. The builder designed the door in fig. 7.5 of the *tekke* (Sufi school) with a close-packing circle arrangement that evokes the whirling circles of the Dervishes. Carved into the door are symbols and script, so the door communicates on multiple levels. The lower image in fig 7.9 shows a detail carved into some of the spaces in the rosettes – note the Celtic-like interlinking. The pentagon that dominates the overall design conjures associations with the Pythagorean pentagram and the music of the spheres (see p.127).

7.10 Whirling Dervishes

7.11 Bukhara prayer rug, 19th century

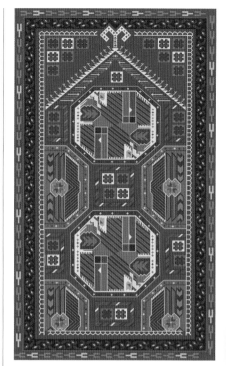

7.12 Graphic of the Bukhara prayer rug

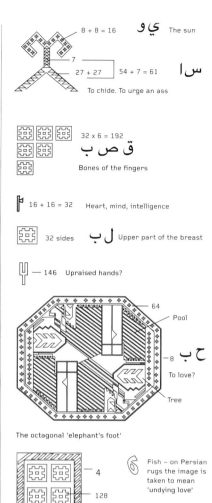

The octagonal 'elephant's foot'

7.13 Detail of Bukhara prayer rug, with abjad translations

The c.1820s Bukhara prayer rug shown in figs 7.11 and 7.12 appears to show a walled garden, or 'paradise' – derived from the Persian 'pairidaeza', meaning a walled garden. Surrounding the wall are images of interlocking fish and around them are symbols that could represent upraised hands. Within the walls there is a garden with two octagonal inner areas with images of minarets, trees and possibly two minbars (mosque pulpits). Other areas contain half-octagonal and square gardens. It is not easy to be completely certain, but the images and the numbers in the prayer rug do seem to add up to a story. Through the abjad system, the numbers appear to communicate things that are quite mundane – for example, where to put your head, hands and chest. Maybe the 61 triangles in the hornlike symbol at the top of the garden are intended to 'urge' the one who is praying to be devout (see fig. 7.13).

Bukhara was traditionally a carpet trading town and was known for trading prayer rugs from areas of central Asia such as northeast Persia, Uzbekistan and northern Afghanistan. The rugs almost always have a red field and are mostly of medium size and highly individualized. Many patterns and colours are used, but

the traditional and most typical is that of the octagonal 'elephant's foot'.

Many common elements appear in the rug shown here – for example, the horn shape at the top of the mihrab and the trees – but there are many unusual design elements too. Fig. 7.12 shows a line drawing of the same rug and is an attempt to be as accurate in its rendition as possible. The colours of the rendition are picked up from the back of the carpet as much as from the front. The following are some numbers in the Bukhara rug together with their associated meanings.

32

To stop in (a place)
To be prepared
Upper part of the breast
Heart /mind / intelligence

192

To cut off. To abstain (from drinking)
Reeds: any plant with a jointed stem
Bones of the fingers. Bone of the nose
Musical reeds. The bronchia. Ducts of the lungs
Channel. Wind pipe. Player of the pipe
Twisted curled hair

61

To chide. To urge an ass

The possible abjad communication in the rug seems to be as follows. Hands and fingers are placed in the spaces indicated by 'Bones of the fingers' – abjad 192. The head touches the 'sun' at the top of the mihrab design – abjad 16. The neck and upper part of the chest are positioned, in prayer, over the 'upper part of the breast' – abjad 32.

Physically, if you were to pray on this prayer rug, your heart would, in a sense, reflect in a pool within a walled garden; your heart would reflect from the water to the sky. There might be numerous meanings associated with the images woven into the rug, meanings that might change as a life passes by.

To translate numbers in Islamic designs, to see if the abjad system has been applied, an old Arabic root dictionary is required, organized by roots and then by vowels. Our interest is primarily in the geometry of Islam and not the possible use of the abjad system, or symbology for that matter. However, the abjad system does add a possible level of interest as to why one geometrical design was chosen over another and, for the purposes of this book, serves to add meaning to the design systems and resulting design variations. For interest, a few abjad values have been added to some of the Islamic design examples that appear later in this chapter. Symbolism might also explain the use and position of a particular geometrical design.

2D ISLAMIC DESIGN SYSTEMS

There appear to have been six primary 2D Islamic design systems.

1. The Grid System
The simplest is that of designs based on the parallel line grids of equilateral triangles and squares – where the lines of a design follow the lines of the grid or simple interconnections across a grid.

2. Polygonal Systems
A little more complicated is a system based on regular and semi-regular tessellations of regular polygons other than squares and equilateral triangles.

3. The Ray System
The ray system generates lines at angles corresponding to specific polygons and then builds designs based on the intersections of the rays.

4. Circle Packing
Circle systems were based on circle packings of various types – overlapping, centred and close-packing.

5. Nesting Polygons
Another system is based on what might be called nesting polygons, where combinations of polygons are repeated successively, and infinitely, within larger polygons.

6. Modular Design System
Regular and irregular polygonal tiles that will tessellate in more than one way.

Ray, circle and polygonal systems generate designs mostly within square, equilateral triangle, hexagonal and rectangular symmetries (repeating tiles),

as well as centred progressions. Also, the systems are often combined.

The design systems generate many types of design variation; the most popular were rosette, knot, abstract linear and cursive. Often the design systems were used to generate grids from which an almost infinite number of images was derived.

1. The grid system As said, this is a design-generating system based on simple square and equilateral triangular grid lattices, where design developments from the grid benefit from a broad knowledge of tessellations, symmetries, knots and symbols.

The system starts with a regular tessellation that is to be used as the base grid. Tessellating design units are then abstracted from the grid – units that will tessellate and repeat infinitely across the 2D plane. The system then applies internal line constructions to the tessellating design units.

In the first example, fig. 7.14, the base grid is that of equilateral triangles. From this grid an almost infinite number of tessellating design units can be extracted. In fig. 7.14 a tessellating equilateral triangle unit is selected from the grid with internal line constructions that create an arrow-like repeating design when repeated across the grid (see figs 7.15 and 7.16). Other extracted designs are shown in figs 7.17–7.21.

One useful rule to follow when creating internal line constructions, is to make sure that line ends at the edge of the tessellating design units match symmetrically – so that line ends will connect when the design units tessellate. If this basic rule is followed then many repeating pattern units can be generated. In Islam designs were generated for hundreds of years by thousands of craftsmen, so the pattern generation and the variations that can be found in mosques, for example, are as diverse as musical variations are today.

All sorts of design variations were generated from grids. Designs were generated that repeated infinitely, tile-like, but also from a centre point. Grids were used as guidelines for adding circles or other shapes. In fig. 7.22, circles are used to create a curved triangular shape. In this particular case the design can be

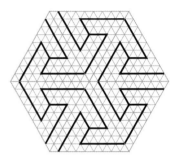

7.14 Equilateral triangular grid and design units

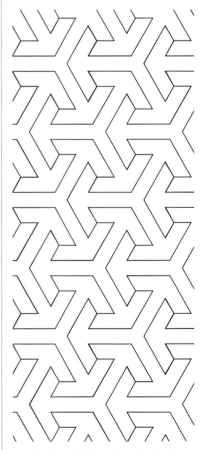

7.15 Equilateral triangular grid design

7.16 Equilateral triangular grid design

7.17 Equilateral triangular grid design

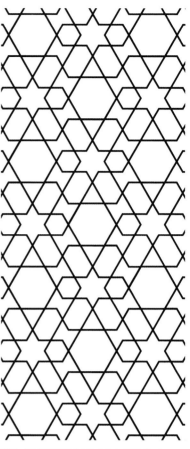

7.18 Equilateral triangular grid design

7.19 Equilateral triangular grid design

7.20 Equilateral triangular grid design

7.21 Equilateral triangular grid design

seen in the Alhambra Palace in Granada, Spain (see fig. 7.23), and might have symbolic and numeric value using the abjad system, for example 3 and 6. Fig. 7.24 shows the completed design.

2. Polygonal systems The design shown in fig. 7.25 is generated using a hexagonal regular tessellation. The lines of the hexagons are used to size and position squares, so that the diagonals of the squares align with the sides of the hexagon. In this case the designer extended the sides of the hexagons to create six-sided, non-regular polygons that when interlocked with one another map onto a hexagonal regular tessellation (see figs 7.25, 7.26 and 7.27).

7.23 Tiles in the Court of the Myrtles, Alhambra Palace, Spain

7.24 Recreated Alhambra Palace design

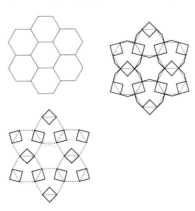

7.25 Hexagonal grid design development

7.26 Hexagonal grid design

7.27 Hexagonal grid design development

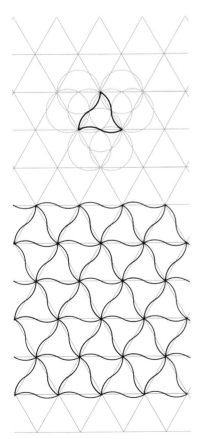

7.22 Grid construction of Alhambra Palace design

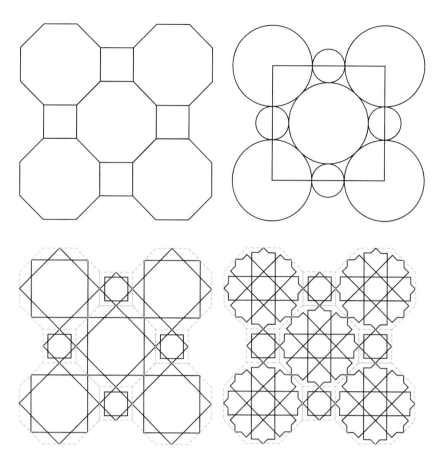

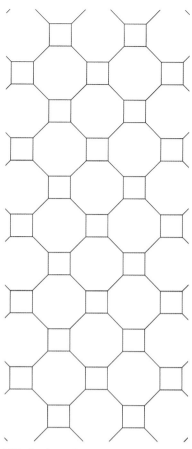

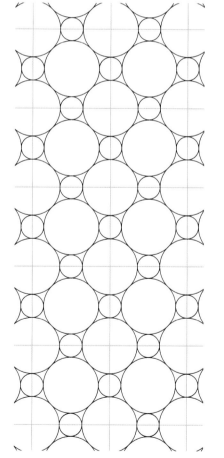

7.28 Semi-regular tessellation grid design

7.29 Semi-regular tessellation grid

7.30 Semi-regular close-packing circles

7.31 Semi-regular tessellation grid design

7.32 Semi-regular tessellation grid design

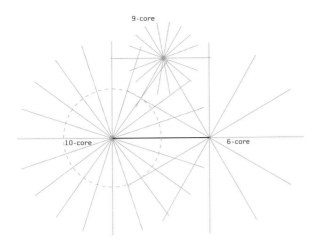

7.33 Ray system for 10-, 6- and 9-core design

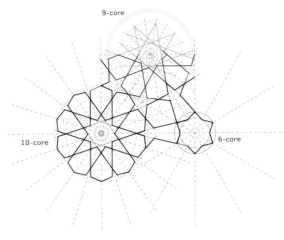

7.34 Ray system for 10-, 6- and 9-core development

7.35 Ray system for 10-, 6- and 9-core design

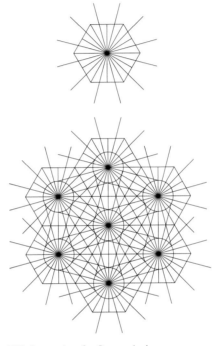

7.36 Ray system for 6-core design

Figs 7.28 to 7.32 show simple cases of designs based on a semi-regular tessellation of octagons and squares. This tessellation can also be rendered as a close-packing arrangement of circles (see chapter 12, RTR 1.1). A common means of generating a design using the polygonal system was to draw stellated polygons (stars) within regular or irregular polygons. Islamic designers also looked for ways of aligning lines within a repeating tile, or directing lines to create some larger design feature. In fig. 7.28 the design generation is very simple and linear.

3. The ray system The ray system was the system used to generate designs based on number sequences. Rays are lines drawn from a centre point that follow the angles that generate regular polygons: call this a 'ray core'. The basis of the ray system starts with aligning ray lines from two ray cores: call these the 'primary ray lines'. Once the primary ray lines align then the angles of intersection of other rays are analysed and used to generate a new ray core, which will have an angular correspondence (even if only approximate) with another regular polygon. For example, we can start with a ray core that has lines angled at 18°, the angles of a decagon, and then we

can add a second ray core on one of the 10-core rays with lines angled at 30°, the angles of a hexagon (see fig. 7.33). Looking at the angles of the intersection points between the rays of the 10-core and the 6-core, we find that a 9-core, with angles of approximately 20°, can be added. The intersection of a 9-core, a 10-core and a 6-core ray accommodates the approximate angles and determines the size of the 10-core and 9-core rosettes. The end result is a design of regular polygonal rosettes of 10, 9 and 6 sides (see figs 7.34 and 7.35).

The design seen in fig. 7.36 starts with a hexagonal grid within which 6-core rays, with angles of 30° and 60°, are

7.37 Ray system for 6-core design variation

7.38 Ray system for 6-core design variation

7.39 Ray system for 6-core design variation

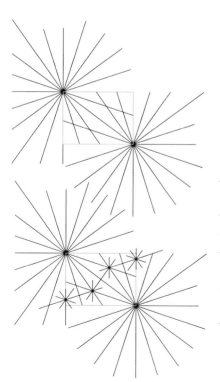

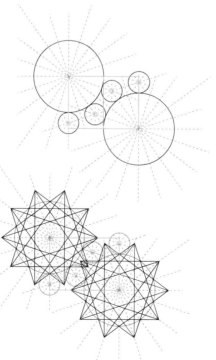

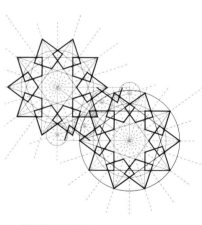

7.40 Ray system for 10- + 4- x 5-core design

7.41 Ray system for 10- + 4- x 5-core design development

7.42 Ray system for 10- + 4- x 5-core design

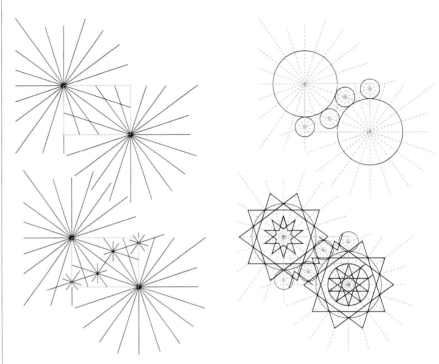

7.43 Ray system for 10- + 4- x 5-core design variation

7.44 Ray system for 10- + 4- x 5-core design development

7.45 Ray system for 10- + 4- x 5-core design variation

positioned. Here, only 6-core rays are used and the primary ray lines intersect at 120° to create a repeating hexagonal tile. The intersections of the non-primary lines are used to generate a 12-sided dodecagon and the shapes within it. Other shapes could have been generated from the lines and their points of intersection (see figs 7.37, 7.38 and 7.39).

Fig. 7.40 shows a ray design that starts with two 10-core rays and then adds in four 5-core rays. Figs 7.41 and 7.42 show how designs are then developed. Fig. 7.43 shows a variation with design developments shown in figs 7.44, 7.45 and 7.46.

7.46 Ray system for 10- + 4- x 5-core design variation

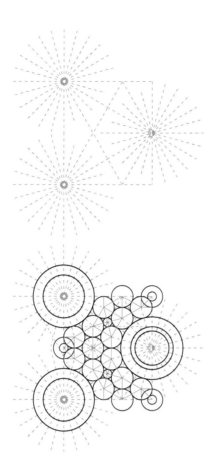

7.47 Ray and close-packing circle convergence

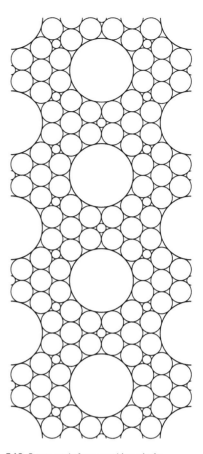

7.48 6-ray and close-packing circle convergence

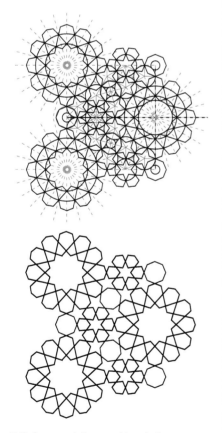

7.49 6-ray and close-packing circle convergence design development cell

7.50 6-ray and close-packing circle convergence design development

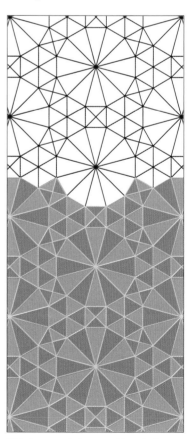

7.51 6-ray and close-packing circle convergence circle centres connected

7.52 6-ray and close-packing circle convergence with rosettes in circles

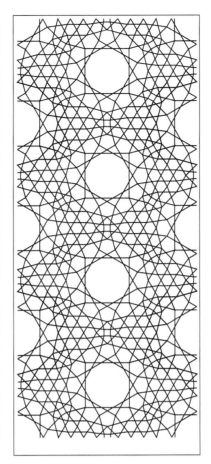

7.53 6-ray and close-packing circle convergence with stars in circles

7.54 Sarghatmish Mosque-Madrasa, Cairo, Egypt, 1356

'The mosques of Cairo are amongst the most beautiful buildings in the world. They are remarkable at the same for the grandeur and simplicity of their general forms, and for the refinement and elegance which the decoration of these forms displays.'

OWEN JONES, 1809–1874

4. Close-packing circle system Close-packing circles are circles that exactly touch each other and triangulate. Such arrangements are unique and if one circle is slightly smaller, or larger, then gaps appear and close-packing is not possible. Close-packing is a very stable and economical spatial arrangement. Many circle close-packing arrangements have a 3D sphere close-packing equivalent, where the sphere packings can correspond to molecular arrangements.

Islamic design systems often converge where one design system corresponds with another. In the following example (see figs 7.47 to 7.53) the ray system converges with the close-packing circle system. This type of convergence happens when the angles of the rays are such that a close-packing circle arrangement can be drawn that corresponds with the node points of the rays. In the example shown the design also overlaps a polygonal arrangement of regularly tessellating hexagons. If you

look at the lines connecting the circle centres, plus tangents, in fig. 7.51 you will find a tessellation of dodecagons, squares and hexagons.

The sequence followed for generating the twelve-sided rosette design shown in figs 7.47 to 7.53 might have started with the ray system or with the close-packing system. If it was the ray system then the designer used line intersections to generate and arrange twelve-sided rosettes. If you study the design structure you will see that every line is in a specific place. If a close-packing arrangement was used then it was of that shown corresponding to a hexagonal regular and semi-tessellation.

Close-packing circle arrangements can be used to generate many design variations – by connecting circle centres, by drawing internal or external polygons, by drawing stars within the circles, and so on. Variations are shown in figs 7.57 to 7.60.

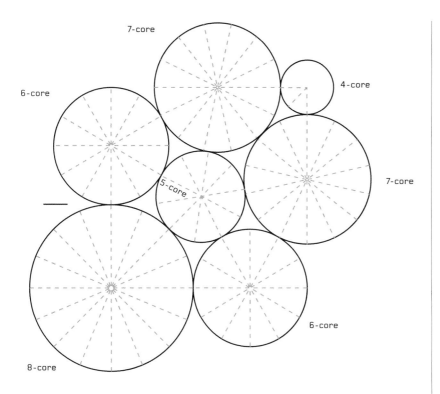

7.55 Ray and close-packing circle convergence 4, 5, 6, 7, 8

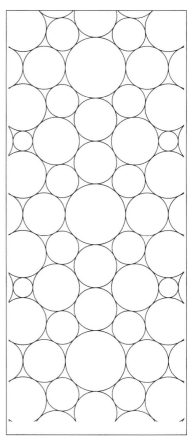

7.57 Close-packing circles 4, 5, 6, 7, 8

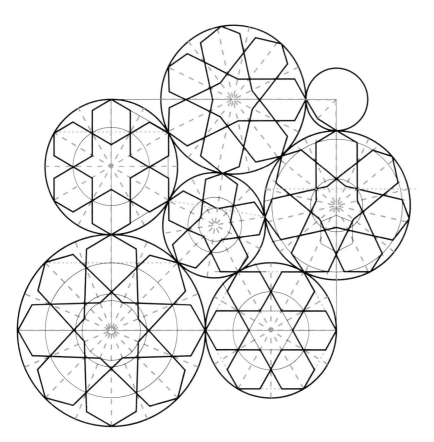

7.56 Close-packing 4, 5, 6, 7, 8 circles with rosettes

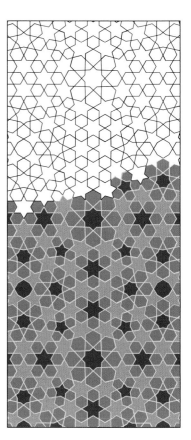

7.58 Close-packing circles 4, 5, 6, 7, 8 with stars positioned by circles

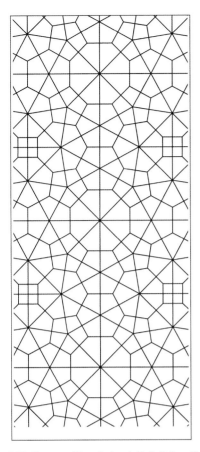

7.59 Close-packing circles 4, 5, 6, 7, 8 radii and tangents

7.60 Close-packing circles 4, 5, 6, 7, 8 polygon radii and polygons

The design shown in fig. 7.55, with developments through to fig. 7.60, appears in a window grille of the Mamluk-period Sarghatmish Mosque-Madrasa (1356) in Cairo (see fig. 7.54). The design is primarily based on the close-packing circle system, with that system taking precedence over the ray system that appears to have been used in parallel.

The arrangement is unusual in that it features regular octagons and squares and almost regular hexagons, heptagons and pentagons: 4, 5, 6, 7, 8. The close-packing circle arrangement was used to generate the series of design variations known as the Altair Designs, originally developed by Ensor Holiday. The designs in Altair Designs, Book 1, are constructed by connecting circle centres, tangents at circle contact points, star polygons, and internal and external radii to polygons (see figs 7.54 to 7.60).

To apply a close-packing arrangement of circles to generate an Islamic 2D design would have involved choosing an arrangement from a library of pre-discovered 'close-packing' arrangements, much as other Islamic designs were derived from a library of tessellations. Unlike the ray system, close-packing circles cannot, in most cases, be generated with pre-defined angles, as close-packing requires a very different approach – that of successive approximation, where some circles are reduced in size and others expanded until a unique close-packing arrangement is derived. Such an arrangement, then, has to be proved to actually triangulate and close-pack, as there are packings that appear to close-pack but mathematically do not (see also chapter 12).

5. Nesting polygons The fifth two-dimensional Islamic design system used can be described as the 'nesting' polygon system. These are arrangements of regular polygons created by connecting duplicates of a regular polygon at vertices or at edges to create a symmetrical arrangement that can be contained within a larger version of the same regular polygon. In a way the idea of nesting polygons anticipates fractals (see chapter 10).

The development is that of connecting duplicates of the larger escribed polygon, each with the inscribed polygonal arrangement, in the same way that the smaller polygons are arranged. This process can be continued infinitely and has a fractal-like quality. A development might be drawn to four or five levels to create a grid that can then be used to generate designs.

In the first example (see fig. 7.61), the regular polygon is the octagon and the first nesting stage surrounds a regular octagon with eight octagons – where the surrounding octagons each connect to the centre octagon at every other vertex. The arrangement is then circumscribed by a containing regular octagon that is then duplicated and combined to create a second stage of the design hierarchy. The process then continues, in the example, to a fourth level.

The octagonal nesting progressions shown in figs 7.62 and 7.64 follow a scale ratio of $1/(\sqrt{2}+1)$.

The sizes of the octagons reduce according to the stage of the progression 'n' where the basic octagon has an n value of zero, the first stage with eight octagons surrounding one octagon (see fig. 7.61) has an n value of 1, and the most complex progression (see fig. 7.65) has an n value of $4:(1/(\sqrt{2}+1))$ n.

This octagonal nesting arrangement is interesting in a number of ways:

(i) Every octagon in the nesting octagon sequence can be replaced with stellated octagons of various types – an example is shown in fig. 7.68.
(ii) Shapes extracted from a stage will repeat and scale in the same scale ratios as the octagons, as shown in fig. 7.66.

(iii) As the stages progress the concentrations of octagons begin to produce 'echoes' – optical effects that highlight symmetries and high and low line-density areas. These echoes, fractal-like, introduce new types of symmetrical pattern and can best be seen in fig. 7.64 – try blurring your eyes to see the lines and patterns of high and low density or try looking at the stages from different angles and rotating your field of view.
(iv) The nesting progressions can also generate patterns of polygonal

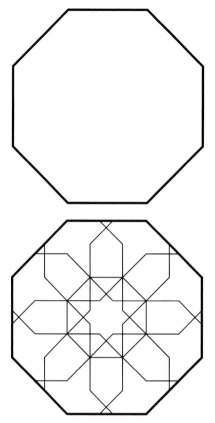

7.61 Basic octagon plus first nesting stage

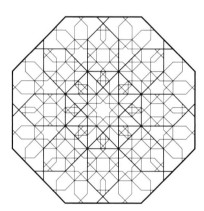

7.62 Nesting octagons second stage

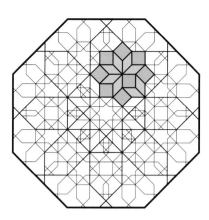

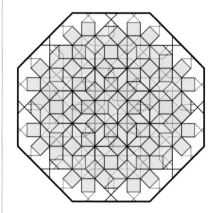

7.63 Nesting octagons second stage with squares and 45° rhombi

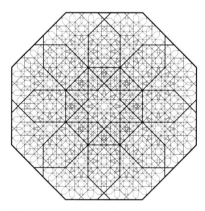

7.64 Nesting octagons third stage

tessellations. Fig. 7.63 shows how fig. 7.62 can generate a tessellation of non-periodic 45° rhombi and squares (see p.133). These two shapes appear again and again in geometrical designs; we will also see them transformed into shape-changing three-dimensional forms (see chapter 11).

Figs 7.64 and 7.65 show the third and fourth stages of the nesting octagons. In the fourth stage the lines have not been scaled according to the stage

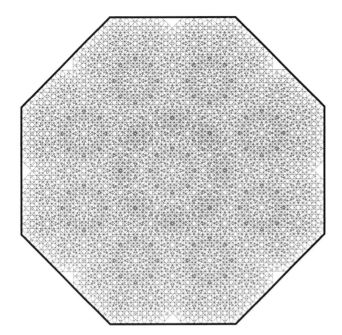

7.65 Nesting octagons fourth stage

7.66 Nesting octagons used as a grid

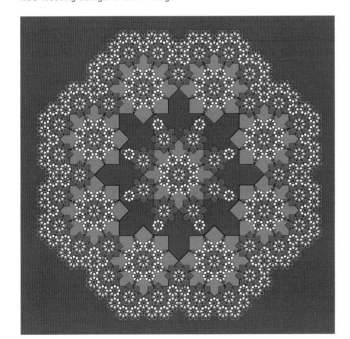

7.67 Stars drawn within nesting octagon grid

7.68 Nesting octagons used as a grid

but have been made uniform to show emerging 'echoes' of the original nesting arrangement, caused, in this case, by the linear outlines of the octagons. The two illustrations show how the two design progressions begin to generate equivalent 'echoes'.

Fig. 7.68 shows examples of designs extracted from the nesting octagon progressions. Extracted designs follow the same reduction ratio $1/(\sqrt{2} + 1)$. Numerologically the top-left design is interesting in that, in a way, 8 becomes 9. The top two progressions follow multiples

of 9, although octagons do start to progressively overlap; if we eliminate overlap then, for example, stage 2 has 61 octagons instead of 81. The top-right illustration shows the next stage in the progression. The bottom two illustrations show shapes picked out from the lattices created by the progressions.

Design elements extracted from the progressions shown in figs 7.61, 7.62, 7.64 and 7.65 will follow the same $\sqrt{2}$ progressions as the grids from which they are derived (see fig. 7.66).

The derived designs shown in fig. 7.66 will repeat just as much as the octagon progressions will.

The star progression in fig. 7.67 was first created in about 1968 after an idea of Dr Ensor Holiday – and was inspired by a Moroccan brass plate. As it happens, the progression will exactly overlay the first octagonal sequences shown in figs 7.61, 7.62, 7.64 and 7.65. The fractal-like subdivisions will continue infinitely and fill all the spaces, though the drawing shown here is selective with the subdivisions. The core structure of

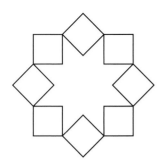

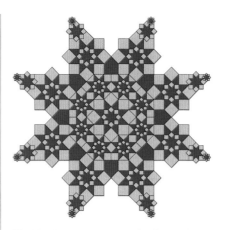

7.70 Nesting octagonal star development

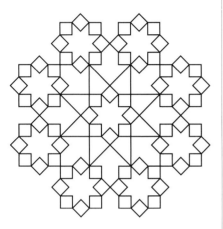

7.69 Nesting octagonal stars first stage

7.71 Nesting squares within a dodecagon

this progression can be seen in figs 7.69 and 7.70 (overleaf) – where the arrow-type shapes rapidly appear. As with many of these geometric designs, an indefinite number of variations can be explored: for example, the arrow shapes can be replaced, Escher-like, with images of birds.

There are many other potential nesting-polygonal grids. Figs 7.69 to 7.72 show a few hexagonal, pentagonal, octagonal and dodecagonal developments. As before, once a grid has been created then many designs can be derived from it. The sequences shown here are each based on just one polygon, but combinations of polygons can be tried. Variations can also be developed where irregular polygons can be sequenced to create Fibonacci-like sunflower patterns (see p.139). The hexagon progression (fig. 7.72) follows a scale progression of 1/3 and the stages scale according to $(1/3)^n$.

The nesting square progression (fig. 7.71) follows a scale progression of $1/\sqrt{2}$. The higher stages scale according to $(1/\sqrt{2})^n$.

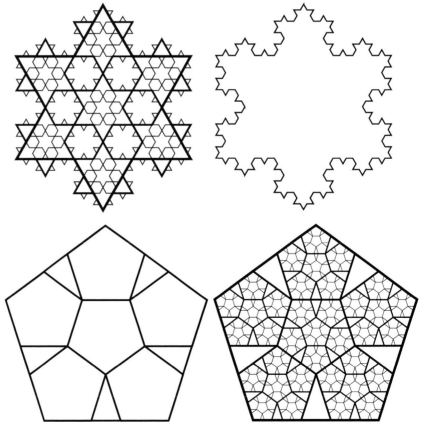

7.72 Nesting hexagons and pentagons

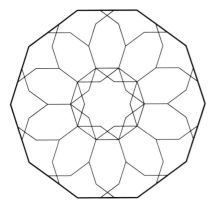

7.73 Nesting decagons type A first stage

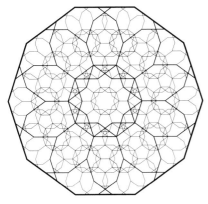

7.74 Nesting decagons type A second stage

Figs 7.73 and 7.74 show two stages of a progression of nesting decagons. The ratio of sizes of the decagons follow $(2/(\sqrt{5} + 1))^2$ proportions. This ratio can be expressed as the square of the inverse of the golden ratio.

Any regular polygons can follow infinite nesting progressions and, once grids have been created by the progression, designs can be derived from them. The reader might like to try similar progressions with pentagons, hexagons, nonagons, and so on. Fig. 7.75 shows another decagon arrangement.

The Darb-i Imam shrine in Isfahan, Iran (1453 onward), includes a variation of a nesting decagon design (figs 7.76 and 7.77). The design structure might have been developed in a number of ways, for example:

(a) Ten decagons are rotated around one decagon to create a first-generation nesting structure. A second-generation nesting structure is generated by scaling the first nesting structure to fit into each decagon of the first nesting structure – a process that can repeat infinitely – so that a few generations of scaled repeats will generate the highlighted ten-pentagon design. The ten-pentagon design, as a unit, is then repeated and interlocked as shown in the second illustration – where the overall nested design creates grid lines for the smaller pentagonal layouts (see fig 7.76).

(b) Alternatively, the design might have started with the highlighted ten-pentagon core structure and developed with combinations at that scale and also with scaled combinations to create the inner pentagonal design.

There are also variations, in the Darb-i Imam shrine design, of the smaller pentagonal designs that lie within the pentagons of the containing first-generation nesting structure. This might have been a mistake or a deliberate variation.

Figs 7.78 and 7.79 show a nesting decagon arrangement that appears on tiles surrounding a fountain in Rabat, Morocco.

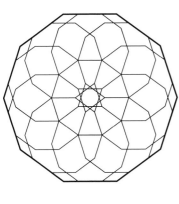

7.75 Nesting decagons type B first and second stages

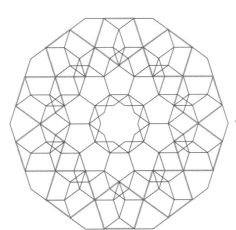

7.76 Nesting decagons type A extended

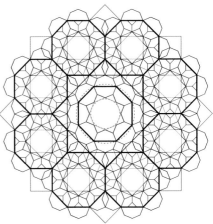

7.78 Nesting decagon development

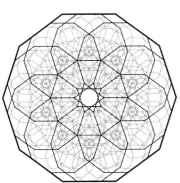

7.77 Darb-i Imam shrine, Isfahan, Iran, begun 1453

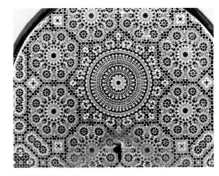

7.79 Nesting decagon development, fountain, Rabat, Morocco

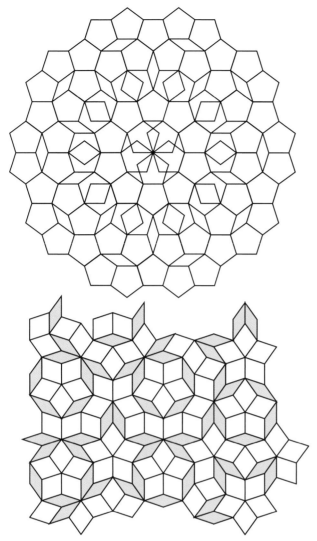

New polygons can be generated by the overlaps of nesting arrangements and these polygons can be extracted to tessellate in new and interesting ways. Fig. 7.80 shows polygons extracted from a nesting pentagon and decagon arrangement and then combined as a non-periodic tiling (see p.133). The rhombi have acute angles of 72° and 36°. In this way the system of nesting converges with the sixth Islamic system, modular design. Fig. 7.81 shows yet another nesting pentagon and decagon arrangement.

6. The modular design system A common Islamic design technique was to combine regular and irregular polygons. In figs 7.82 to 7.86, squares, half-squares, 45° rhombi and half-rhombi combine in an indefinite number of ways, creating all sorts of patterns. The same polygons also feature in a number of murqanas (see pp.197–200) and in the shape-changing polyhedral geometry shown in chapter 11. In many cases geometric line designs were placed within tessellating polygonal tiles such that, when the tiles were combined, they would generate a multiplicity of composite line designs, as seen in the girih tiles shown overleaf.

The 15th-century Persian Topkapi Scroll is a collection of geometric patterns, including designs generated

7.80 Nesting pentagons and decagons with extracted polygons in non-periodic arrangement

7.81 Nesting pentagon development

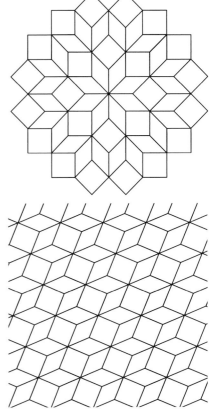

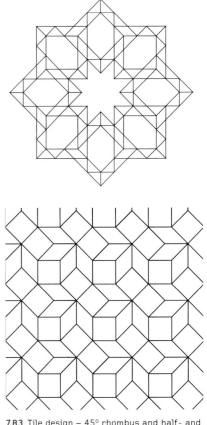

7.82 Tile design – 45° rhombus and half-square

7.83 Tile design – 45° rhombus and half- and whole square

7.84 Tile design – half 45° rhombus and half-square

7.85 Tile design – half 45° rhombus and half-square

7.86 Tile design – 45° rhombus and square

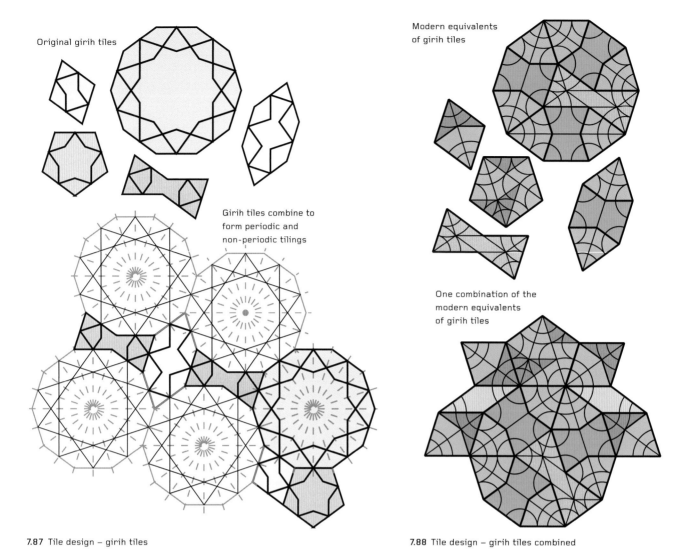

Original girih tiles

Girih tiles combine to
form periodic and
non-periodic tilings

Modern equivalents
of girih tiles

One combination of the
modern equivalents
of girih tiles

7.87 Tile design – girih tiles

7.88 Tile design – girih tiles combined

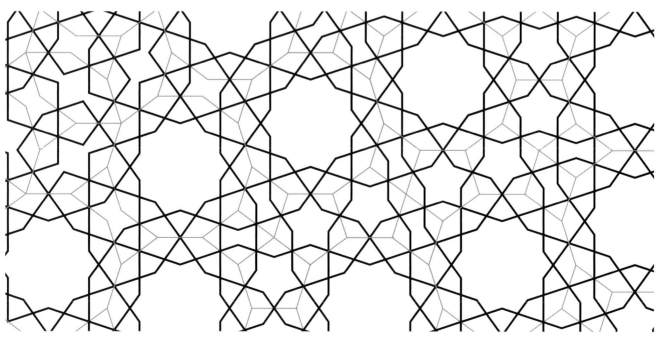

7.89 Tile design – girih tiles assembled into a classic Islamic design

by the modular design system, where five different polygons are each given an internal design structure that creates complex pattern variations when the polygons are combined (see figs 7.87 and 7.89). The polygons and their internal designs are generated by a variation of the ray method, but the combination methodology really falls within the modular design system. The tiles, known as girih tiles, can be combined in an indefinite number of ways to create quasicrystal tilings (tiles that can be combined to create a pattern that has no regular repeats and no translational symmetry: patterns look disorganized even though they fill space). Fig. 7.88 shows a modern variation of the girih tiles and one possible combination.

The scroll consists of 114 geometric patterns drawn in ink and dye. It displays decorative ornaments found on the walls and domes of structures built between the 10th and 16th centuries. It was a guidebook for architectural designs: for complex muqarnas, mosaic panels and colourful tile patterns. The scroll does not mention how the patterns were physically constructed, and has no date or signature.

MUQARNAS: EXTENSIONS INTO THREE DIMENSIONS

Muqarnas is a style of architectural vaulting common in Islamic architecture, which developed in the 10th century in Persia and northern Africa (see fig. 7.1 on p.172). Sometimes called a honeycomb vault, it features a corbelled, cellular effect, and has three possible functions. The first function appears to be that of a transitional form-filling space, where one structural form transitions into another – from a rectangular space into a corner or an arch, for example, or where a dome transitions into an octagonal space, or where the square top of a column transitions into a cylindrical or octagonal prism support. A second function was most likely to reflect, diffuse or focus sound. The third use appears to be purely decorative.

Muqarnas are constructed in layers of 2D planes each composed of polygonal tiles. The combined plan view of the planes is formed from polygonal tilings that conform to a numerical symmetry, most often eights, fives and tens. The planes connect to another with circular curves and angled surfaces. The curved 3D connecting shapes have been traditionally called cells. Muqarnas may be constructed of wood, tile, plaster or stone.

The 15th-century Persian astronomer and mathematician Jamshid al-Kashi (1380–1429) defines muqarnas, in Book 4 of his *Key to Arithmetic*, as follows: 'The muqarnas is a roofed vault (*madraj*) like a staircase with facets and a flat roof (*sath*). Every facet intersects the adjacent one at either a right angle, or half a right angle, or their sum, or another combination of these two. The two facets can be thought of as standing on a plane parallel to the horizon. Above them is built either a flat surface, not parallel to the horizon, or two surfaces, either flat or curved, that constitute their roof. Both facets, together with their roof, are called one cell (*bayt*). Adjacent cells, which have their bases on one and the same surface parallel to the horizon, are called one tier (*tabaqa*). The measure of the base is called the module (*miqyas*).'

The plane projection of muqarnas is that of a tiling of polygons. The earliest family of plane-projected polygons known to al-Kashi consists of the same polygons that appear again and again through the development of geometry and also within the pages of this book: of square, half-square (cut along the diagonal), 45° rhombus, half 45° rhombus (across the shorter diagonal), octagons, and other octagon derived shapes. A later family consists of decagons, pentagons, 36° and 72° rhombi, half-rhombi and other associated shapes. There are other combinations too, such as those that include five, six and seven-sided polygons and stars, where the polygons tessellate on the projected plane.

The elements of muqarnas are constructed according to the same unit of measure, so they fit together in a wide variety of combinations. Al-Kashi uses muqarnas, in his computations, as a basis for all proportions (see fig. 7.90 overleaf).

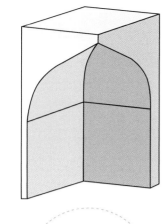

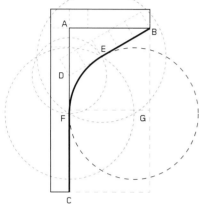

7.90 Muqarnas cell construction

7.91 Masjid-e Jameh muqarnas, Isfahan

7.93 Masjid-e Jameh muqarnas, Isfahan

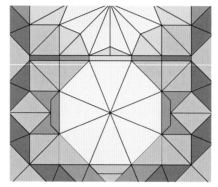

7.92 Masjid-e Jameh muqarnas, Isfahan

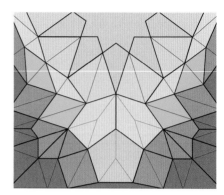

7.94 Masjid-e Jameh muqarnas, Isfahan

Muqarnas construction Al-Kashı's
Key of Arithmetic included calculations
regarding the surface of muqarnas (fig.
7.90). His definition of the curvature is
roughly translated as follows:

1. Draw a horizontal line AB
2. Construct AC perpendicular to AB with
   length twice the length of AB
3. Find point D on AC such that angle
   ABD = 30°
4. Divide line BD into five equal parts
5. Find E on BD such that BE = 3/5BD
6. Draw the circle c1 with middle point D
   and radius DE intersecting DC in point F
7. Draw two circles with radius EF, circle
   c2 with middle point E and circle c3
   with middle point F
8. Define G as the intersection of c2
   and c3 below line AB
9. Draw the arch curved side, this is
   part of the circle with middle point G
   through points E and F

The FE curve appears to be more
decorational than functional, although it

7.95 Masjid-e Jameh muqarnas, Isfahan

7.96 Takht-e Soleyman, Iran

7.97 Takht-e Soleyman muqarnas design tablet, 13th century

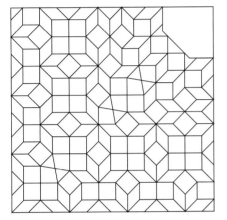

7.98 Takht-e Soleyman muqarnas design

7.99 Takht-e Soleyman muqarnas design extended

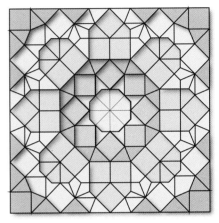

7.100 Ulrich Harb muqarnas design

could be that combinations of the curves in the cells of a muqarnas had some acoustical effects.

Muqarnas are used in large domes, in smaller cupolas, in niches, on arches and as an almost flat decorative frieze. In each instance the module as well as the depth of the composition is different and adapts to the size of the area involved or to the required transitional purpose.

Figs 7.91 and 7.92, and 7.93 and 7.94 show two muqarnas in the Masjid-e Jameh (Great Mosque) of Isfahan, Iran. The first muqarnas consists of squares, half-squares, 45° rhombi and related shapes. The second muqarnas (see figs 7.93, 7.94, and 7.95) combines a stellated decagon with a 72° rhombus, a pentagon and related polygons.

The façade of the Masjid-e Jameh shows how muqarnas can be integrated into the main entrance of a mosque.

Fig. 7.96 shows the Takht-e Soleyman (Throne of Solomon), the archaeological site of an ancient palace and Zoroastrian temple complex located in northwestern Iran. The site contains a deep water-filled crater known as the Prison of Solomon, which according to folk legend was used by King Solomon to imprison monsters. The site includes the remains of an important Zoroastrian fire temple built during the Sasanian dynasty (224–651 CE), which housed one of the three Great Fires. Nearby were a royal sanctuary and a temple dedicated to Anahita (the goddess of the waters).

After the Islamic conquest the site remained important as a Zoroastrian temple until the 9th century. In the 13th century the Mongol Ilkhanid ruler Abaqa

constructed a summer palace on the southern part of the ruins, partly based on the same layout. As the Mongol court was used to living in tents the new site was abandoned and soon fell into ruin.

In the ruins of the western part of the palace a stone tablet was found and recognized as a possible construction plan for a muqarnas vault (see fig. 7.97). The photograph shown here was taken by Dr Ulrich Harb of Heidelberg University, Germany, who was part of the team that discovered the tablet in 1968.

If the tablet does indeed show a plan for a muqarnas then it may be a complete composite design or just one quarter of a design. If the tablet just shows one quarter (see fig. 7.98), then the whole design would look as shown in fig. 7.99, except that the central octagonal design is pure guesswork and a rhombus and square detail has been substituted for a

7.101 Dome of the Rock, Jerusalem, Israel, 7th century

feature that seems out of place. Obviously no transitions are shown but one can assume that they are of standard cell construction.

In a 2006 PhD thesis by Silvia Harmesen, of Heidelberg University, a means to use computer algorithms is proposed to generate reconstructions of muqarnas. Her thesis includes a drawing of Dr Harb's proposed plan to reconstruct a much simpler octagon vault for the Takht—e Soleyman muqarnas design. Fig 7.100 shows a redrawn version of this image.

If many of the polygons used for muqarnas are flexibly connected then they will create shape-changing polyhedral surfaces. This may or may not have been known by early Islamic architects but looking at murqarnas was one of the inspirations for the geometry of shape-changing polyhedra that is featured in chapter 11 of this book.

Using the muqarnas polygons to create shape-changing polyhedral surfaces would have made sense as the surfaces could be shape-changed for optimum sound reflection and then 'frozen' by plaster – but there is no record of such knowledge being applied to the construction of muqarnas.

ISLAMIC 3D DESIGNS

Muqarnas show transitions from 2D into 3D space and are, across 2D planes, conceptually similar to Pythagorean tessellations but with regular and irregular polygons. Otherwise, Islamic 3D designs generally follow earlier traditions with extruded polygons or circles capped with polygons, circles, cones or domes. Primary innovation appears to be in the use of muqarnas and in dome design, and also in the use and form of connecting spaces.

The Dome of the Rock The Dome of the Rock on the Temple Mount in Jerusalem was built around 691 at the beginning of the rise of the Islamic empire (see fig. 7.101). The structure is built around a rocky outcrop thought by many Jews and Christians to be the Foundation Stone, the site where Abraham intended to sacrifice Isaac. For Orthodox Jews the rock represents the junction between Heaven and Earth – the conduit for their prayers. In Islamic tradition the rocky outcrop is thought to be where the Prophet Muhammad landed on his way to Heaven.

The interior and exterior mosaics of the Dome of the Rock were replaced in the 16th century, possibly with copies of the originals. However original the surface designs, they do fall into different categories in that the simple geometric patterns appear to have been derived from tribal woven designs, while the

7.102 Dome of the Rock, façade designs

7.103 Süleymaniye Mosque, Istanbul, Turkey, 1557

cursive and floral patterns are clearly from Byzantium. The octagonal structure itself fits perfectly within later Islamic traditions and represents, like the Foundation Stone, the transition between Earth and Heaven. The dome is built of wood and has been rebuilt many times over the centuries so the original shape is impossible to determine. Originally, it may have been a hemispherical dome rather than the pointed dome that it is today (see fig. 7.109).

The exterior tiles of the Dome of the Rock were added by the sultan Suleyman the Magnificent in the 16th century. The lower tile designs (see fig. 7.102) are significantly different from the upper tiles in terms of scale, simplicity and colour. The three west-facing sides of the building have designs composed of squares, squares combined with 45° rhombi, and octagons, whereas the other sides are decorated with, mostly,

empty octagonal and rectangular frames proportioned 1:2 and 2:3. The lower designs and rectangles of the south-facing wall are less regular except for octagons and octagonal stars within two of the rectangular frames. The building itself is rotated 10° anti-clockwise from north, possibly so that the west entrance faces a sunset position towards the end of February; the south face does not point towards Mecca.

Mosque design A mosque (*masjid* in Arabic) is a structure that has certain common features wherever it is in the world. It usually has one or more domes and a minaret, or tower to call the faithful to prayer. Internally the design contains a qibla wall, which shows worshippers the direction of prayer, a rectangular interior space that accommodates the community, a mihrab (prayer niche), and a minbar (pulpit). In Islam group prayer

is conducted with rows of worshippers facing towards Mecca. A mosque also incorporates places for ritual cleansing and to leave shoes, and often has an external courtyard.

The dome, as a symbolic representation of heaven, is usually lavishly decorated with geometric or vegetal designs. The qibla wall, mihrab and minbar are other areas of rich decoration, reflecting their importance in the mosque layout, often incorporating tiles in intricate geometric patterns. The prohibition against the portrayal of human or animal figures means that Islamic calligraphy has been elevated to an art form and is found curling around numerous architectural features, often citing verses from the Qur'an.

One of the most influential architectural innovations of Islam was the further development of the pointed arch and vault – which, unlike the traditional semi-circular Roman arch, channelled weight in more of a downward direction, thereby reducing the tendency to push out horizontally. This meant that the walls that supported a pointed dome, arch or ceiling vault could be thinner and the structures taller and less encumbered.

The grand Süleymaniye Mosque in Istanbul was built at the peak of the Ottoman Empire by the great architect Mimar Sinan for Suleyman the Magnificent. Showing both Byzantine and Islamic influences, it has all the classic features of a mosque and is made up of circles, rectangles and arches – moving vertically from the square geometry of the ground level to the soaring circular dome. Its four tall, slender minarets are situated at the corners of the huge external courtyard, at the centre of which is a fountain for ablutions (see fig. 7.103); its large main central dome is flanked by two half-domes, smaller domes and a series of arches. Muqarnas form the capitals of the marble and granite columns. Inside, decoration is restrained, and the walls are pierced by numerous windows, allowing light to pervade the building and the architecture to speak for itself.

7.104 Mausoleum of Inal, Cairo, 1450–56

Egyptian mausoleums and mosques

The funerary complex of Sultan al-Ashraf Inal in Cairo was built between 1450 and 1456 (see fig. 7.104). As well as his mausoleum the complex incorporates several other structures, including a *khanqah* (Sufi meeting place), a mosque, a madrasa and a minaret. The dome, in common with many others constructed in the 14th and 15th centuries during the Mamluk caliphate (1250–1517), looks a little like a cactus and stands on an octagonal structure. To the south is a later funerary complex, that of the grand amir Qurqumas (built 1506–07).

The building shown in fig. 7.105 is the dome of the funerary complex of Sultan al-Ashraf Qaytbay, completed in 1474, which stands, like Inal's mausoleum, in the Northern Cemetery of Cairo, also known as the City of the Dead. The surface design of the mausoleum's dome contains eight nine-sided and eight ten-sided rosettes (only half of each ten-sided rosette appears) and one 16-sided rosette, and also stands on the typical Mamluk-style octagonal base. The exterior circular design is characteristic of the period, sometimes with one circle, other times with six, or with three, as shown here (see fig. 7.107).

It is possible that the rosettes on the surface of the al-Ashraf Qaytbay dome were selected to have a meaning. The meaning might have been symbolic, but the numbers might also have been selected to communicate words through the abjad system. The rosettes have 16, nine and ten sides.

7.105 Sultan al-Ashraf Qaytbay mausoleum, Cairo, 1470–74

7.106 Qaytbay mausoleum dome – close-up

7.107 Sultan al-Ashraf Qaytbay mausoleum, Cairo, 1470–74

Applying the abjad system, the first level of letters corresponding to 16, 9 and 10 are: (ya (10) + waw (6)) and ta (9) – reading left to right. So the words with ya + waw + ta, in different combinations, should first be considered:

ط و ي

but there are no words that correspond with this combination.

The next order is (qaf (100) + waw (6)) and ta (9):

ط و ق

Reading right to left, the meanings from Edward Lane's 1876 root dictionary are as follows:

(i)   a ring around the neck, or a difficult burden like a ring around the neck;
(ii) a badge of favour conferred;
(iii) God strengthened me to handle the burden.

Al-Ashraf Sayf ad-Din Qaytbay (c.1416–96) was originally a slave, who was taken to Cairo and purchased by the sultan: a classic image of a slave is one with a ring around the neck. Al-Ashraf became a member of the palace guard, was later freed, and was then promoted through the Mamluk military hierarchy to become a field marshal – and eventually the sultan. He amassed a fortune during his time with the military that enabled him, when sultan, to exercise many acts of beneficence without draining the royal treasury. If a meaning was intended through the numbers, then the above fits perfectly.

The surface design method may have been that of the ray system or of close-packing circles, possibly designed using a clay model of the dome.

The surface design of the dome of Shah Ni'matullah Wali's shrine (see fig. 7.108, overleaf), is more complex than that of the Qaytbay tomb. The shrine is in the city of Mahan, Iran. The rosettes featured on the dome, starting at the top, have sides 16, 7, 9, 12, 11, 9, 10, and 8. The dome is shaped like an upside-down heart and rests on an octagonal prism.

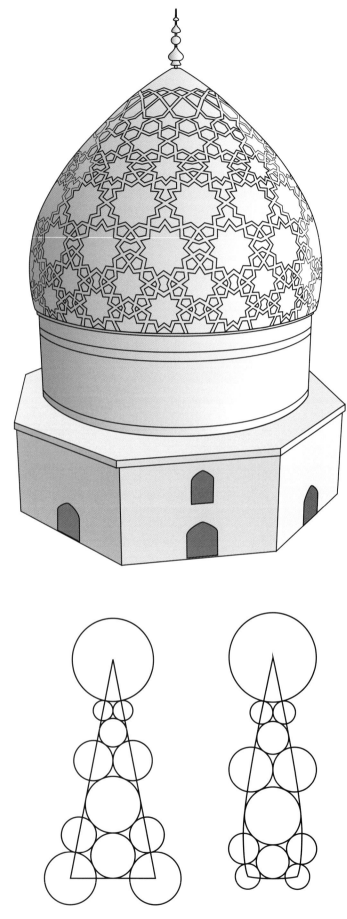

If the abjad system has any relevance here then there needs to be some way of grouping the numbers to find words with valid meanings.

Ni'matullah (1330–1431) was a Sufi mystic and poet who founded the Ni'matullah Sufi order; he lived to be 104 years old. The fact that the dome is shaped like an upside-down heart is in accord with images that occur in his poetry, while the fact that the dome rests on an octagon is probably intended to have the traditional meaning – that of the juncture between Heaven and Earth. There is nothing obvious in the poems or stories associated with Ni'matullah that directly supports the numbers that appear on the dome's surface, so the only choice is to try combinations and see if they correspond with Ni'matullah – with his music, his dancing, his poems, his teaching or his life. As he was a Sufi it might be expected that the numerology of the dome has both simple meanings and more thought-provoking secondary meanings.

Looking at the numbers from an abjad point of view, an objective would be to isolate triliteral roots (consonants in groups of three). One way to do this is to treat the 16- and eight-sided rosettes as end-pieces on the basis that they are in a harmonic relationship of sorts and do appear at the two opposite ends (top and bottom) of the dome. Between the end-pieces are six numbers: 7, 9, 12 and 11, 9, 10. These translate through the abjad system to 7, 9, 3, and 2, 9, 10 (because there are no direct letters corresponding with 12 and 11). So for primary meanings, 7, 9, 3, and 2, 9, 10 should first be explored. No words correspond with 7, 9, 3, but abjad allows a secondary meaning – 70, 90, 30 – and that translates to 'twisted tooth as is the case of advanced age'. This translation shows a correspondence with Ni'matullah's 104 years of age. The reader might like to explore the other possible numeric combinations to see if there is a valid abjad communication in the dome's design.

7.108 Tomb of Shah Ni'matullah Wali, Mahan, Iran

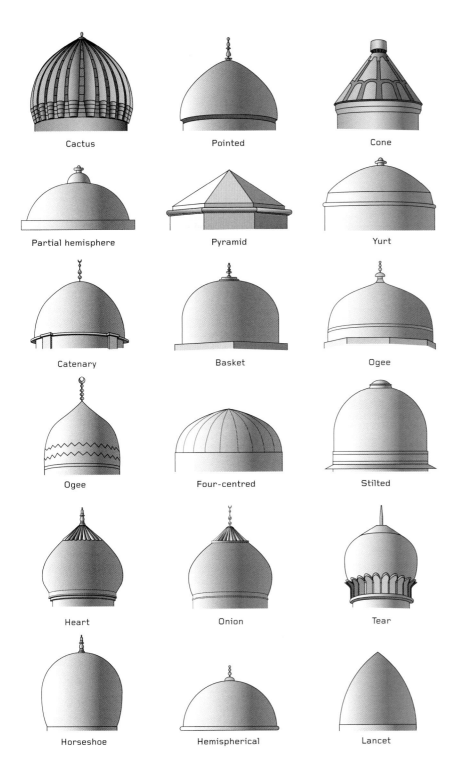

Cactus

Pointed

Cone

Partial hemisphere

Pyramid

Yurt

Catenary

Basket

Ogee

Ogee

Four-centred

Stilted

Heart

Onion

Tear

Horseshoe

Hemispherical

Lancet

7.109 Dome shapes

Dome shapes and acoustics Dome shapes and construction methods evolved during the 'golden age' of Islamic architecture (610–1258) (see fig. 7.109). The earliest dome is that of the Dome of the Rock, built with a timber frame, and currently in the shape of a pointed dome. The Mamluk domes in Cairo (1250–1517) are built of stone or brick and plaster, in ogee, onion, lancet and pointed forms. In Iran (633–1501) there are numerous heart-shaped, pointed and yurt-like domes, many of which are covered with glazed ceramic tiles.

As to whether the domes were shaped to have specific acoustic properties, this is unknown without entering them and assessing their characteristics. Given the use of sound resonators, and the use of muqarnas to focus sound in prayer niches, it seems that the knowledge existed to design architecture for its acoustic properties. The designs of some *tekkes* (Sufi halls) suggest acoustic considerations but it seems that, in general, acoustic dampening was more of a concern than acoustic enhancement. So it is possible that most dome shapes were symbolic rather than acoustically functional.

Because the inner surface of a hemispherical dome is concave it focuses and reinforces sound-creating echoes. Half-domes can help to project a sound but may make it less intelligible. Cavity resonators in the form of jars built into the inner surface of a dome were often used to compensate for this interference by absorbing sound-reducing echoes. The technique was written about by Vitruvius in his *De architectura* (see p.155).

08. THE RENAISSANCE

THE BRIDGE BETWEEN MEDIEVAL EUROPE AND THE PRESENT

'Proportion is that agreeable harmony between the several parts of a building and the result of a just and regular agreement of them with each other; the height to the width, this to the length, and each of these to the whole.'
VITRUVIUS (C.80/70–C.15 BCE)

After the fall of Rome in the 5th century, there was a tribal resurgence in Europe as new peoples and ethnic groups moved into the gap left by the collapse of centralized government. Knowledge, too, became more fragmented, with a decline in scholarship and artistic achievements. This period was followed by a cultural and economic revival around the 12th century that would lead to the Renaissance.

The European Renaissance, which lasted from around the 14th to the 17th century, owes its beginnings to numerous factors that evolved in the Late Middle Ages, including an expansion of trade, consolidations of political boundaries, the growth of city-states and the decline of feudalism, an increase in wealth, and the rediscovery of the classical texts of antiquity. In Italy, the so-called cradle of the Renaissance, humanist views informed the rebirth of art, science, writing and moral philosophy, placing secular rather than religious concerns at the centre of art and thought and thereby marking a decisive break with medieval practice. Scholars went back to the works of ancient Greek and Roman authors, tracking down originals that had survived in remote monasteries or private collections. The works of Vitruvius were discovered as well as those of many Pythagoreans – and all such works became more readily available after the invention of movable type for printing presses around 1439 by Johannes Gutenberg, together with a new scholarly propensity to write in vernacular Italian rather than Latin.

With the Renaissance came an approach to logic that was a little more objective than that of the Middle Ages. Many of the best of classical, Islamic and medieval geometries were combined into a much broader palette than had ever existed before. As religious restrictions were relaxed, individuals and universities had more freedom to explore new types of geometry, science and mathematics, and also the opportunity to integrate the philosophies of the past and the present.

Renaissance architecture may have followed on chronologically from the Gothic, but it was a world away in its conception. Consciously looking back to classical antiquity, Renaissance architects developed a style using typically Roman elements of symmetry, order and proportion – inspired, at least in Italy, by the ancient Roman remains still in existence. Similarly, developments in science, engineering and mathematics owed much to the surviving works of classical scholars, as well as to Islamic inventions, all in the new spirit of enquiry.

TOWARDS 3D THINKING

With the resurgence of interest in Greek and Roman art and architecture, European interests turned towards the recreating of classical grandeur. Renaissance artists, architects and

8.1 Filippo Brunelleschi's dome, Florence Cathedral, Italy, 1436

8.2 Villa of the Mysteries, Pompeii, 60–50 BCE

8.3 Albrecht Dürer, engraving showing a method for generating images in perspective, 1525

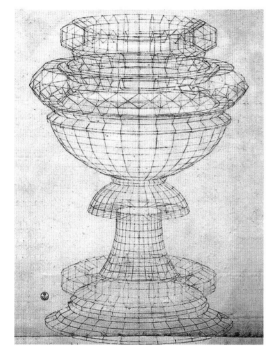

8.4 Paolo Uccello, perspective study of a vase, 15th century

8.5 Masaccio, *Holy Trinity*, c.1427 — one-point perspective is used to evoke a convincingly realistic depiction of 3D space

engineers studied the mathematical and engineering works of Vitruvius, the works of the Pythagoreans, classical ruins, Euclid's work on optics, and much more.

Perspective Starting from the 11th century, we can trace the development of a scientific method to explore three-dimensional space, from the studies of optics by Ibn al-Haytham (c.965–c.1040), through the work on perspective by Luca Pacioli (1445–1517), to Albrecht Dürer's *Four Books on Measurement* (1525). The study of optics ultimately led to the development of perspective grids — and the concept of perspective promotes visual thinking within an x, y, z matrix.

Artists working in 2D are faced with the difficulty of making their figures

appear three-dimensional on a flat plane. Early artists got round this in various ways; the Egyptians, for example, depicted figures simultaneously from the side and the front — head, legs and feet in profile and shoulders and eye in frontal view — while many ancient cultures positioned figures according to their status rather than their relative location.

The idea of drawing in perspective arose out of studying optics and from the observation that images appear to get smaller the further away they are from the eye, and parallel lines or planes appear to converge. In Western art, 14th-century Italian painters Giotto and Duccio addressed the problem of leading the viewer's eye into the picture, but it was Filippo Brunelleschi who first

demonstrated mathematical perspective in 1413 and Leon Battista Alberti who described the technique in his treatise *Della pittura* (*On Painting*) in 1436.

One-point perspective involves identifying a vanishing point on a horizon line (the x axis). Lines converging on this point act as guides for the artist to create the impression of three-dimensional space. Distant elements are made to appear smaller than nearer objects, and an effect of foreshortening is produced, important for a convincingly three-dimensional representation. More complex spaces can be rendered in two- or three-point perspective, using two or three vanishing points.

Although we can appreciate the illusion of depth in a perspective painting, we might also consider, first, that it does not accurately convey what we see in terms of the 3D images seen by our two eyes; and, second, that we do not really see in the way portrayed by a painting drawn in perspective, since our eyes wander panoramically across our field of vision, and our minds compensate for visual distortions to create the illusion of a complete image out of the individual visual elements focused upon.

Some palaeolithic rock paintings, including some of those at Lascaux, France (c.15,000 BCE, see fig. 8.8), are drawn so that their subjects appear to move or change, an effect that would have been particularly evident when viewed in flickering firelight. At the other end of the artistic timeline, Futurists in the early 20th century used sequential images and curves to show movement (see fig. 8.9). Cubists countered perspective by trying to show multiple facets of an image and distortions to communicate emotion. All such artists make the point that there is more to what we perceive, and visualize, than just a static perspective image.

Perspective does create the illusion of depth, but it has become such a

8.7 Pietro Perugino, *The Delivery of the Keys*, 1481–82

8.8 Dun horse, Lascaux Cave, France, 15,000 BCE

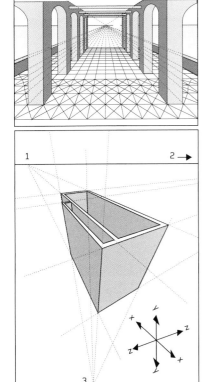

8.6 Two- and three-point perspective

8.9 Umberto Boccioni, *The Charge of the Lancers*, 1915

standardized way of considering 3D space that in some ways it has tended to handicap our spatial thinking processes – how we humanly react to proportion and to 3D forms, spaces and sequences of spaces, and perhaps even forcing us to think in terms of an x, y, z universe.

LEONARDO, VITRUVIUS AND HARMONY

With the resurgence of ancient ideas that occurred during the Renaissance came the concept of creating art and architecture in proportions that were considered to be 'divine', an idea that was strongly influenced by the discovery of the lost works of Vitruvius.

The Roman author, architect and engineer Marcus Vitruvius Pollio (c.70/80–c.15 BCE) described ideal architectural proportions in his ten-volume treatise *De architectura* (*On Architecture*; see also p.155). In Book 3, Vitruvius states that architecture should imitate nature: 'As birds and bees build their nests, so humans construct houses from natural materials, that give them shelter against the elements.' According to Vitruvius, the Greeks, in their Golden Age – the times of Pythagoras, Aristotle and Plato – applied idealized proportions of the human body to architecture. He describes an ideal man whose proportions are contained within a square and a circle and where parts of the body have proportions in whole number relationships to the whole. These proportions were followed by Leonardo in drawing his famous *Vitruvian Man* (see p.137, fig. 5.31) as the benchmark for all architectural proportions (see figs 8.10 and 8.11).

In the Leonardo head and torso drawing shown in fig. 8.11, the scaled drawings are the proportions stated by Vitruvius and repeated by Leonardo and are in relation to the overall height of the human body. The small facial proportions appear to be Leonardo's own addition to Vitruvius's system, and the best estimates of these are shown above the head. It is interesting to see that Leonardo made the front to back dimensions of the head either one ninth or one tenth of the body height.

Leonardo's *Vitruvian Man* is proportioned according to the descriptions of Vitruvius, as follows:

The ratio of the Leonardo circle to the square is dependent upon Leonardo's point of rotation between the two arm positions. Vitruvius does not give a method for determining the point of rotation – so the Greek ratio is unknown.

Leonardo added to the descriptions of Vitruvius: 'If you open your legs so much as to decrease your height 1/14 and spread and raise your arms till your middle fingers touch the level of the top of your head you must know that the centre of the outspread limbs (feet/fingers) will be in the navel and the space between the legs will be an equilateral triangle.'

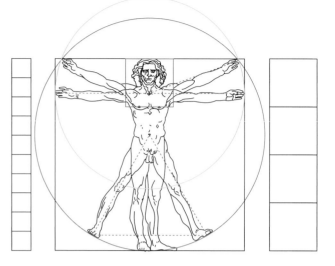

8.10 Leonardo da Vinci, *Vitruvian Man*, 1492, with correspondences of square proportions

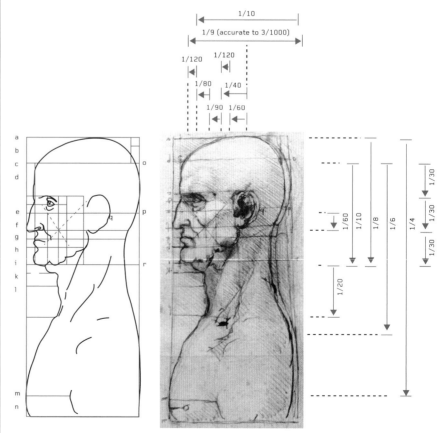

8.11 Leonardo da Vinci, male head in profile with proportions, 1487

'For the human body is so designed by nature that the face, from the chin to the top of the forehead and the lowest roots of the hair, is a tenth part of the whole height; the open hand from the wrist to the tip of the middle finger is just the same; the head from the chin to the crown is an eighth, and with the neck and shoulder from the top of the breast to the lowest roots of the hair is a sixth; from the middle of the breast to the summit of the crown is a fourth. If we take the height of the face itself, the distance from the bottom of the chin to the under side of the nostrils is one third of it; the nose from the under side of the nostrils to a line between the eyebrows is the same; from there to the lowest roots of the hair is also a third, comprising the forehead. The length of the foot is one sixth of the height of the body; of the forearm, one fourth; and the breadth of the breast is also one fourth. The other members, too, have their own symmetrical proportions, and it was by employing them that the famous painters and sculptors of antiquity attained to great and endless renown. Similarly, in the members of a temple there ought to be the greatest harmony in the symmetrical relations of the different parts to the general magnitude of the whole. Then again, in the human body the central point is naturally the navel. For if a man be placed flat on his back, with his hands and feet extended, and a pair of compasses centred at his navel, the fingers and toes of his two hands and feet will touch the circumference of a circle described therefrom. And just as the human body yields a circular outline, so too a square figure may be found from it. For if we measure the distance from the soles of the feet to the top of the head, and then apply that measure to the outstretched arms, the breadth will be found to be the same as the height, as in the case of plane surfaces which are perfectly square.'

Vitruvius, and therefore Leonardo, uses measurements from the hairline, in the same way as the Egyptians when using their royal cubit grid (see p.76). For Vitruvius, as for the Pythagoreans, the number 10 is the perfect number, though he says that the mathematicians of his time preferred the number 6.

The Vitruvian use of the hairline suggests that the Egyptian grids possibly served as a starting point to create the more intricate proportionate system developed by the Greeks. A key difference is that the Greek/Vitruvian system derives a geometric grid from a human body rather than deriving the shape of a human body from a geometric grid. These ideas link the Vitruvian system to the Pythagoreans and Vedic geometricians and support the concept that humans and geometry follow some sort of eternal design system.

The works of Vitruvius inspired many artists and engineers of the Renaissance, such as Mariano di Jacopo, known as Taccola (1382–1453), Francesco di Giorgio (1439–1502), Luca Pacioli and Leonardo, to reintroduce concepts of harmony into the art and architectural forms of the Renaissance. The readoption of proportionate grids added a consistency and a balance to a design and made it appear more harmonious than more accidental structures. Whereas Leonardo followed the proportionate system of Vitruvius very closely in his *Vitruvian Man*, some of his contemporaries did not. Drawings based on a sketch by Francesco di Giorgio, for example (see figs 8.12 and 8.13), show odd variations, as does di Giorgio's own *Vitruvian Man*, which appears in his book *Trattato di architettura*.

Vitruvian proportionate systems laid the ground for design concepts linked to natural dynamics such as fluid flow, waves and forms that follow the curves of rolling hills or a human body. Natural forms are, arguably, more harmonious than artificial grid structures that

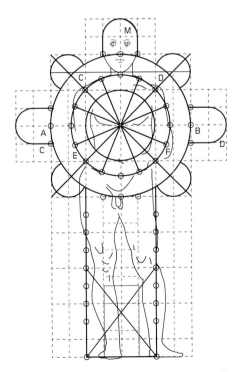

8.12 Drawing after Francesco di Giorgio, idealized proportions of a man applied to the floor plan of a basilica

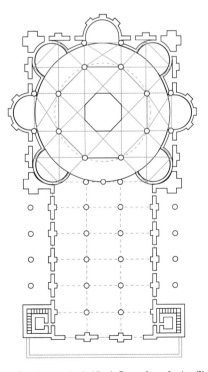

8.13 Drawing after Leonardo da Vinci, floor plan of a basilica 'teatro da predicare' (preaching theatre)

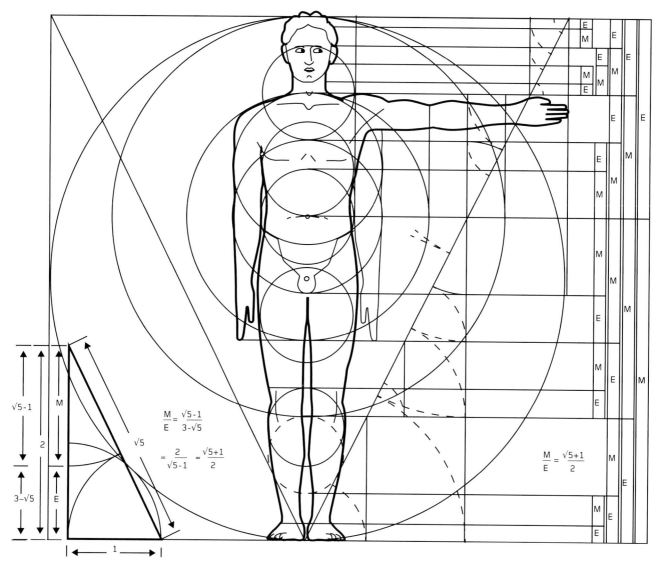

$$\frac{M}{E} = \frac{\sqrt{5}-1}{3-\sqrt{5}}$$

$$= \frac{2}{\sqrt{5}-1} = \frac{\sqrt{5}+1}{2}$$

$$\frac{M}{E} = \frac{\sqrt{5}+1}{2}$$

8.14 Ernst Neufert, divine proportions

may or may not be derived from the
proportions of a human body or some
other geometrical system. Many of the
works of the Renaissance reflect a sense
of the natural dynamics of nature, well
represented by, for example, the works
of Michelangelo and Titian.

The point is that 'harmony' and
'essence' were resurrected as important
concepts in Renaissance Europe – laying
down the challenge for later ages to find
architectural forms that enhance life in
more than a functional, decorative and
stylistic way.

The idea of 'divine proportion' stems
from the mathematician Luca Pacioli
and his three-volume treatise *De divina
proportione* (1509), which was
illustrated by Leonardo. The divine

proportion was the golden ratio,
or golden section (*sectio aurea*) as
Leonardo called it. It was the 'mean
and extreme' ratio of Euclid, where 'a
straight line is said to have been cut in
extreme and mean ratio, when the whole
line is to the greater segment, so is the
greater to the less' (see p.132). For
Pacioli, this ratio was an expression of
the divine, since the ratio of the parts,
whether large or small, is always the
same – 'as God is in all and every part
of the universe'. The association of the
ratio with the divine seems to have been
unique to Pacioli, although he may well
have been inspired by Plato's *Timaeus*
(c.360 BCE) where the dodecahedron,
with the divine proportion in its
pentagonal sides, is described as

sustaining heaven. Pacioli's ideas
regarding proportion certainly influenced
Renaissance artists, including Leonardo,
but the *De divina proportione* itself is
short of any new mathematical insights
and construction methods, leaving
readers in the dark as to how to develop
the ratio in art and architecture.

It is therefore highly debatable
whether such artists actually used
the golden ratio in any mathematically
precise sense, but as an aesthetically
satisfying visual proportion it is found
in innumerable Renaissance works
of art. In Raphael's masterpiece *The
School of Athens* (1509–11; see fig.
5.1), for example, golden ratios seem
to define many key elements of the
composition. Recent research has

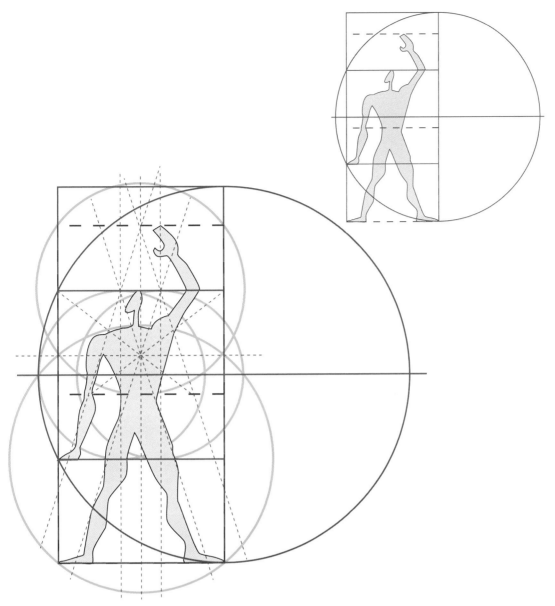

8.15 Le Corbusier's Modulor man based on Leonardo's *Vitruvian Man*

suggested that Michelangelo used the golden ratio to construct his monumental painting scheme on the ceiling of the Sistine Chapel (1508–12). Piero della Francesca's *Baptism of Christ* (c.1448–50) has a strongly geometric composition in which the golden section is evident. The list is endless, and yet in most cases it is likely that the 'divine proportion' was applied subconsciously, simply because of its uniquely pleasing visual balance.

More recently, the 20th-century German architect Ernst Neufert proposed the golden ratio as the architectural principle of proportion in the human body (see fig. 8.14). For Neufert, the golden ratio provided the primary link between all harmonies in architecture.

There is also a 20th-century system of proportions known as the Modulor, proposed by the Swiss-French architect Le Corbusier, in which the human body was placed at the centre of architectural proportion, along with the golden ratio and the Fibonacci sequence. In his manifesto *Vers une architecture* (*Towards a New Architcture*, 1923) Le Corbusier presents the golden ratio as a natural rhythm, inborn to every human organism. A comparison of Le Corbusier's Vitruvianesque man (see fig. 8.15) with that of Neufert shows some key correspondences.

The top drawing in fig. 8.15 shows a standard golden rectangle construction where the side length of the squares is 2 units and the half square diagonal,

and containing circle radius, is √5 units. So head to toe is (√5 + 1) units and the containing rectangle to the top of the head is (√5 + 1)/2. The tips of the fingers of the raised hand are 4 units above the bottoms of the feet.

8.16 Saint-Pierre de Xhignesse, Belgium, 11th century

8.17 Durham Cathedral, England, 1093

8.18 Canterbury Cathedral, England, 1077

PRE-RENAISSANCE EUROPE

The Middle Ages was not as dark as many teachers of European history would have us believe. The period was dubbed the 'Dark Ages' by the 14th-century Tuscan scholar Petrarch, who contrasted the intellectual 'darkness' that persisted after the decline of the Roman Empire with the greatness of classical antiquity. Although much was lost or deliberately destroyed, some pockets of knowledge nonetheless survived or even thrived. Many of the ideas that did survive did so through ritual alone, with little or no real understanding.

The fabric of the Middle Ages was held together by trade, farming, the Church, and the tribal chiefs and feudal despots who were later to become local royalty and aristocrats.

After the fall of Rome around the 5th century CE, buildings sometimes still vaguely looked like something from Roman or Greek times, but the techniques, the constructional and proportionate methods and the knowledge of materials were lost. It took almost 400 years before there was enough wealth and civil control to attempt anything that might truly rival the buildings of Rome.

Romanesque By around the 10th century, the Romanesque architectural style had developed in Europe, characterized by round arches, semicircular vaults, thick walls with few, small openings, and massive columns. The small 11th-century church of Saint-Pierre de Xhignesse in Belgium has many typical Romanesque architectural features (see fig. 8.16).

Up to about the 11th century many churches were either repaired and adapted Roman temples, or new Romanesque stone buildings heavily reliant on the rounded Roman arch, or extensions to Saxon or other defensive towers. Castles too were mostly built on old Roman sites and owed much of their design to Roman fort architectures.

Gothic The 12th century saw the introduction of the pointed arch, and with it Romanesque styles began to be transformed into something very different. Structurally, the pointed arch transfers weight vertically downward – unlike the Roman arch, which pushes outwards – with the result that stone buildings no longer needed the thick walls necessary to oppose the lateral forces of the round arch. Combined with the use of stone ribs to transfer weight onto columns and piers and away from walls, this meant that walls could be much thinner and have large windows. Another key development was the flying buttress, which helped to direct forces from the weight of the roof onto external buttresses, allowing building heights to be increased to extraordinary levels for stone structures.

The new style combined Romanesque with tribal and Byzantine stylistic elements. The concept of the pointed arch itself had appeared in late Roman architectural styles and was also a prominent feature in Islamic architecture. In true Romanesque and Byzantine fashion spaces were filled with statues, stone reliefs and intricately carved and painted stonework. This highly decorated mishmash of tribal, Romanesque, Byzantine and even Islamic styles was given the name 'Gothic' by scornful Renaissance architects. A derogatory term after the barbarian invaders of the Roman Empire, the Goths, this was meant to indicate the supposed chaos of the combined design elements in contrast to the ordered classical style of the Renaissance. Durham Cathedral (see fig. 8.17) provides a good example of the transition from Romanesque to Gothic, demonstrating as it does the less ornate classical influence of rectangular forms, Romanesque round arches, and also the pointed arches and ribbed vaults that were to become a distinguishing feature of the Gothic style. Canterbury Cathedral (see fig. 8.18) is another great mixture of styles, with its Romanesque core remodelled and added to over the centuries in the Perpendicular (English Gothic) style.

8.19 Gothic stylistic features

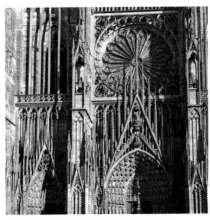

8.21 Strasbourg Cathedral, France, 1439

8.22 Regensburg Cathedral, Germany, 1520

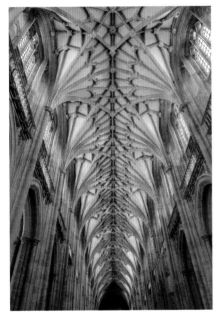

8.20 Winchester Cathedral, England, 14th century

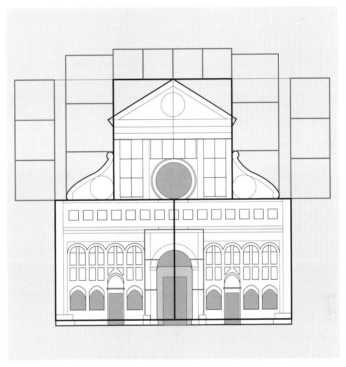

8.23 Leon Battista Alberti, Santa Maria Novella church, Florence, Italy, 1470

Gothic and Renaissance geometries

Renaissance architects replaced many of the elements of Gothic design with those of ancient Rome and Greece. In terms of basic geometric shapes, Renaissance style is characterized by the use of simpler geometric solids such as cylinders (columns), semicircles (arches), circles (windows, domes and drums), and rectangles and squares; the main Renaissance innovations appear to be in the domes, drums, pendentives and barrel vaults.

RENAISSANCE ARCHITECTURE

Geometrically speaking, styles alternated between simple and visually complicated variations of basic geometric shapes. We see the constant use of semicircular arches, triangles, circles, squares, rectangles, hemispheres, cuboids and cylinders. However, the core geometric design elements remained essentially the same. The Renaissance interest in reviving classical harmony and proportion resulted in clear, simple spaces and shapes that were stylistically far removed from the Gothic.

Leon Battista Alberti Alberti (1404–72) was an Italian architect, artist, poet,

philosopher and humanist polymath. With regard to architectural proportions he stated: 'We shall therefore borrow all our Rules for the Finishing our Proportions, from the Musicians, who are the greatest Masters of this Sort of Numbers, and from those Things wherein Nature shows herself most excellent and complete.' In his magnum opus *The Ten Books of Architecture*, Alberti's content is similar to the ten volumes of Vitruvius, though more philosophical in tone.

Alberti applies musical and mathematical principles to achieve his type of perfection of proportion in architectural design and favoured ratios: 1:1; 2:3; 3:4; 2:4; 4:9; 9:16; 1:3; 3:8; 1:4.

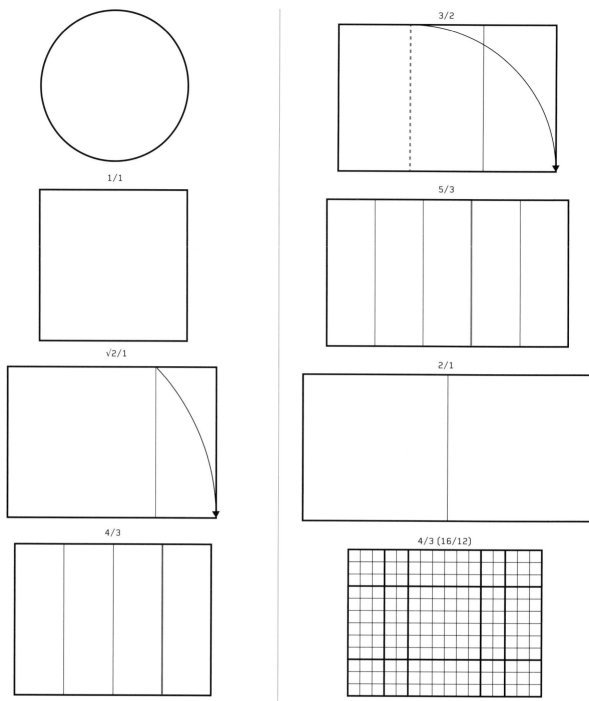

8.24 Andrea Palladio, proportions

8.25 Andrea Palladio, proportions

His Santa Maria Novella church in Florence exhibits his basic numeric proportions with a few small variations (see fig. 8.23).

Andrea Palladio The work of Venetian architect Palladio (1508–80), *I quattro libri dell'architettura* (*The Four Books of Architecture*, 1570), was one of the most influential architectural works of the Renaissance, and indeed Palladio is often seen as one of the most influential architects ever. The book itself shows the influence of Vitruvius, as do so many of the works of Renaissance artists and architects. Palladio was also greatly influenced by Alberti. *I quattro libri* present the symmetries, simple shapes, design elements and building techniques associated with ancient Roman architecture, together with Palladio's own elaborations and variations.

Palladio proposes seven sets of harmonious proportions for rooms (see figs 8.24 and 8.25), as follows:

1. Circular
2. Square (1/1)
3. Diagonal of square (√2/1)
4. A square plus a third (4/3)
5. A square plus a half (3/2)
6. A square plus 2/3 (5/3)
7. A double square (2/1)

This is a proportionate system that links the Renaissance with the Pythagoreans, the ancient Egyptians, the Babylonians and the architects of the Indus Valley.

Palladio believed in maintaining consistent ratios of all parts of a building,

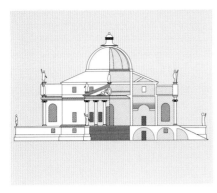

8.26 Andrea Palladio, Villa La Rotonda, Vicenza, Italy, 1566–90s

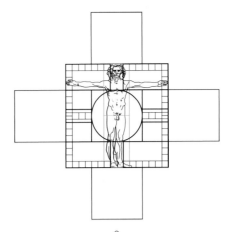

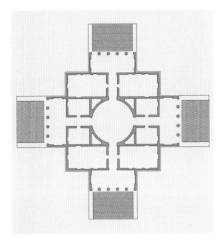

8.27 Villa La Rotonda plan view

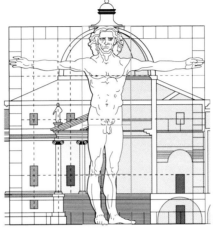

8.28 Villa La Rotonda with *Vitruvian Man* proportions

one to the other and from each part to the whole in height, width and depth. Palladio, like Alberti, especially favoured harmonic proportion, in which the parts of a building stood in arithmetical ratios that mirrored those of musical harmony.

Villa La Rotonda is a villa designed by Palladio (1566), located just outside Vicenza, northern Italy. The building is completely symmetrical – the intersection of a square with a cross. The design is illustrated in *I quattro libri*. In order for each room to have some sun, the design was rotated 45° from each cardinal point of the compass. Each of the four porticos had pediments bearing statues of classical deities (see fig. 8.26).

Fig. 8.27 shows the villa's floor plan with the circle, square and cross design elements described in his treatise. In the drawing we can see the use of whole number ratios in the rooms: 8:8, 3:4, and, apparently, 7:4, though this is not one of Palladio's seven proportions. There is an apparent concurrence with Vitruvius and with Leonardo's *Vitruvian Man* proportions that can be seen by

overlaying Leonardo's drawing over the Villa La Rotonda floorplan (see fig. 8.28).

Palladio's proportionate system extended to three dimensions – although it is clear that he did not strictly adhere to his own rules. If a room is vaulted, its height should be the geometric, arithmetic or harmonic mean of the height and width; if the room is square and vaulted, its height should be 4/3 of the width; and if the ceiling is flat, the height should equal the width of the room. In *I quattro libri* Palladio's requirement is that rooms in the same row should have equal heights and that consequently their proportions must be carefully coordinated. The aesthetics of Palladio's proportions seem to be based on symmetry and patterns of rectangular divisions – more on numbers than physics.

From Palladio's drawings for La Rotonda, it is difficult to see how the room heights obey the three-dimensional 'mean' parameters that he set. In fact, his drawings suggest the heights fall more within the 16 x 16 grid of the floorplan.

Palladio's mean ratios state that if the floor plan is vaulted then the height should be the geometric, or harmonic, mean of the width and length. If a and c are the length and width and b is the height, then the geometric mean height falls into the mean ratio $a:b = b:c$, so if $a = 7$ and $c = 4$ then $b^2 = 28$ and $b = 2*\sqrt{7} = 5.29$. The harmonic mean height falls into the harmonic mean ratio $(b-a)/a = (c-b)/c$, so $b = (2ac)/(a+c)$ and $b = 56/11 = 5.09$. The arithmetic mean falls into the arithmetic mean ratio for two numbers $(a+c)/2$ so $b = 11/2 = 5.5$.

CONCLUSION

It is interesting to see how Renaissance artists and architects explored proportion – on the one hand with perspective drawings and on the other with simple numeric systems. Visually Renaissance structures, and many styles that followed them, exhibit a discipline of symmetry and the use of grids of rectangles, with some small variations. As time passed the 'mean' proportions of Alberti, Palladio and Leonardo were

8.29 Temple of Hephaestus, Athens, Greece, 415 BCE

8.30 Basilica of Maxentius and Constantine, Rome, Italy, 313 CE

8.31 Gellone Abbey, Saint-Guilhem-le-Désert, France, 11th century

8.32 Reims Cathedral, France, 1211–75

8.33 Florence Cathedral, Italy, 1296

8.34 Cathedral Santiago de Compostela, Spain, façade completed 1740

complemented by the use of golden mean proportions, but most applications are limited to two-dimensional planes and show no exploration of space using sciences of behaviour, sound and light.

SUMMARY OF TRANSITIONS

On these pages we have a visual summary of a small part of the story of the development of architectural styles that predate and follow the Renaissance.

Fig. 8.29   Greece: Temple of Hephaestus, Athens. Simple geometric floor plan – rectangles and squares – with characteristic entabulature and fluted columns.

Fig. 8.30   Rome: Basilica of Maxentius and Constantine, Forum, Italy. Evolving from the Greek but larger and characterized by semicircular arches.

Fig. 8.31   Romanesque: Abbey of Gellone, Saint-Guilhem-le-Désert, France. Imitation of the Roman without the structural, material and geometrical knowledge.

Fig. 8.32   Gothic: Reims Cathedral, France. A huge stylistic and structural step from the Romanesque, with pointed arches and ribbed vaulting.

Fig. 8.33   Renaissance: Florence Cathedral, Italy. An application of the reinvented knowledge of classical Rome with new ideas and technologies.

Fig. 8.34   Baroque: Santiago de Compostela Cathedral, Spain. An ornate, theatrical evolution of Renaissance architecture.

Fig. 8.35   Rococo: Archbishop's Palace, Prague, Czech Republic. Still ornate, but lighter and more graceful, with fewer stylistic flourishes.

Fig. 8.36   Neoclassicism: Vilnius Cathedral, Lithuania. Reverts to the classical look of Roman architecture.

Fig. 8.37   Art Nouveaux: Hôtel Hannon, Brussels, Belgium. A move into fantasy but also to a beautiful cursive look.

Fig. 8.38   Art Deco: Chrysler Building, New York, USA. A more simple, more geometrical style.

Fig. 8.39   Modernism: Apartment complex by Mies van der Rohe, Weissenhof, Germany. Even simpler and part of a move to pure functionalism.

Fig. 8.40   Deconstructivism: Vanke Pavilion by Daniel Libeskind, Milan, Italy. A reaction against modernism, featuring non-Euclidean geometry, distorted effects and asymmetrical lines.

8.35 Archbishop's Palace, Prague, Czech Republic, rebuilt 18th century

8.36 Vilnius Cathedral, Uthania, Lithuania, 1783

8.37 Hôtel Hannon, Brussels, Belgium, 1903–04

8.38 Chrysler Building, New York, USA, 1930

8.39 Apartment complex, Weissenhof, Germany, 1926

8.40 Vanke Pavilion, Expo 2015, Milan, Italy, 2015

OUT OF THE PAST – INTO THE FUTURE

The past in geometry was dominated by fixed structures, whole numbers and static grids, particularly cubic lattices. The primary 3D space module has been a cuboid – a rectangular box. Moving into the future, we have the technologies and materials to explore 3D space in a whole new way – to investigate the properties of many types of curved and angled surfaces, scale, sequence, proportion, resonance, reflection, absorption, light and sound. We have the means to do this; we just need the will and the imagination to find out how spaces can impact our well-being, our creativity and our productivity. Twentieth-century mathematics includes dynamic geometries: in the next chapters we examine some of these, but we also look at new 21st-century geometries that are distinctive in that they are geometries of change. In this, they explore 3D space dynamically and may well be the forerunners of other dynamic geometries that will help us analyse the properties of 3D form from a diverse range of aspects, including physical and psychological.

The following chapters will explore geometries of mathematical curves, fractals, shape-changers and dynamic spheres. They intend to challenge the imagination and encourage us to step away from the strictly linear and regular. The final chapter is speculative and aims to start the process of true 3D thinking.

09. MODELLING WITH EQUATIONS

THINKING IN 3D GRIDS — AN APPROACH STARTED IN ANCIENT EGYPT

One way to model or even manufacture radically new architectural forms is to generate them by using equations, and thereby take advantage of today's manufacturing technologies and computer-aided design systems (CAD). To create the equations we need to render the forms in three-dimensional space using mathematical means to identify every surface and position of the form. One of the ways to do this is to adopt a way of thinking formalized by the 17th-century French philosopher and mathematician René Descartes, who provided us with a powerful way of positioning points, shapes and objects in three-dimensional (Euclidian) space, using what we might call x, y, z rectangular thinking.

THINKING IN GRIDS

Thinking within three-dimensional rectangular (x, y, z) grids is not new, and has its origins in ancient Egypt, where statues and architectural spaces were proportioned within cubic lattices. In Renaissance Europe scientists and artists resurrected the ancient Greek study of optics and formalized the logic of perspective, which organizes 2D space with a 3D modelling system of grids aligned with vanishing points, with the grid used to proportion 2D images in such a way that they have the appearance of 3D objects (see pp.208–09).

The Cartesian coordinate system, as developed by Descartes in 1637, continued the logic of dividing space into 2D and 3D grids. It corresponds with the Egyptian cubic grid system but is much more versatile and provides us with a means to organize space in three directions, called the three axes, each at right angles to the other: x, y and z (see fig. 9.3). The directions are divided

initially into whole number divisions and then into subdivisions. The three axes meet at a point, called the origin, with the numeric value of (0, 0, 0). Movement along any of the three axis directions is defined as positive in one direction from the zero point and negative in the opposite direction. Two- and three-dimensional forms can be plotted in Cartesian space using (x, y, z) values generated from a logical sequence, or set of operations, called mathematical equations or algorithms.

Another common way of navigating two- and three-dimensional space uses a distance, 'r', from a fixed point and an angle theta, of rotation around the vertical axis and an angle phi away from the vertical axis. Polar coordinates (r and θ) can be converted to Cartesian coordinates by using the trigonometric functions sine and cosine (see fig. 9.4).

Modelling forms Natural forms that appear to follow some sort of sequential or symmetrical logic can often be approximated with equations and can, as algorithmic steps, be inserted into software or strings of code to generate 2D and 3D images or 3D physical objects. A 2D or 3D equation is a means to concisely communicate a set of instructions that will generate plots in 2D or 3D space using a step-by-step logic. The logic can also be written out as a step-by-step set of operations, known as an algorithm. For example, we could start by using an equation to generate the image of a circle on a horizontal base and then give step-by-step instructions to stretch it vertically to create an image of a cylinder. An equation is really a shorthand representation of an algorithm and may be formed using Cartesian or polar coordinates. A computer program

9.1 30 St Mary Axe (the Gherkin), London, UK, 2004

9.2 M51, Whirlpool galaxy

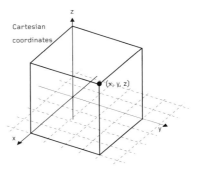

9.3 Cartesian coordinates

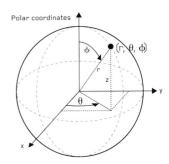

9.4 Polar coordinates

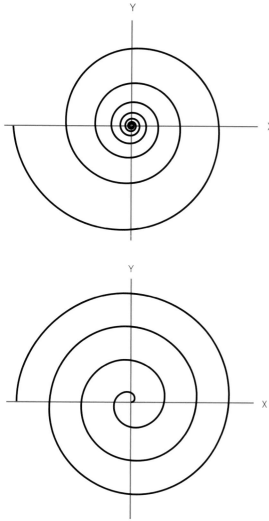

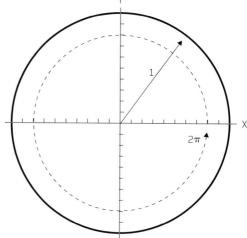

9.5 Logarithmic (upper) and Archimedean (lower) spirals

9.6 Fermat spiral and circle

follows the same step-by-step logical process used to create an equation.

Creating an equation to generate a natural-looking form necessitates a level of simplification. For example, using polar coordinates, if we assume that the distance (r) of any point on an arm of a spiral galaxy (fig. 9.2) from the galaxy's centre is an exponential function of its angle (θ) from a fixed direction, we can plot the spiral of the galaxy with the equation $r = b^θ$ – where the numerical value of b determines how quickly r increases, and where θ represents the angle of any point on the spiral's arm from a fixed starting direction. For simplicity, we can use radians as a measure of the angle rather than degrees, where one radian = $180°/π$ and $1° = π/180$ (where π is the ratio of the circumference of a circle to its diameter: 3.14159…). If we multiply the value of r with a number 'a', we will increase or

decrease the distance of any point on the spiral's arm, effectively rotating the plotted spiral. With a added our equation now looks like $r = ab^θ$. To plot the spiral we will need to incrementally increase the value of θ, for example we can calculate the value of r with θ values of 0, $π/180$, $2π/180$, $3π/180$, $4π/180$, etc (see fig. 9.5). This type of spiral, where the distance from the centre increases exponentially from a centre point in terms of its angle of rotation, is called a logarithmic spiral. The same equation with different values of a and b can be used to plot, for example, the curve of a nautilus shell or Romanesco broccoli (see fig. 10.1).

In an Archimedean spiral (see fig. 9.5) the distance between the arms does not exponentially increase with distance from the centre (the distance stays the same). The Archimedean spiral can be generated using polar coordinates and the equation

$r = a + bθ$, where r is the distance of a point on the arm of the spiral from a fixed central point, where θ is the angle of the point from the direction of the x axis, where bθ determines a linear increase in distance according to the amount of rotation, and the numerical value of a serves to rotate the spiral.

The polar coordinate equation for a Fermat spiral (the upper spiral in fig. 9.6, also known as a parabolic spiral) is $r = a \sqrt{θ}$. The doubling of the spiral is due to the fact that a square root can have a plus or minus value.

Types of mathematical equation Many types of mathematical equation are used to generate forms in two- and three-dimensional space. An equation of a circle in a rectangular form, using Cartesian coordinates, looks like $x^2 + y^2 = r^2$, which means that all values of x and y must satisfy this equation. So, if

Sphere (parametric equation)
x = rcos(t) cos(u)
y = rsin(t) cos(u)
z = rsin(u)
radius (r) = 1, t = 0 to 2π, u = -π/2 to π/2

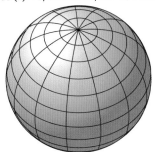

Ellipsoid (parametric equation)
x = (1 cos(t)) sin(v)
y = (1 sin(t)) sin(v)
z = 2 cos(v)
radius (x, y) = 1
radius (z) = 2
t = 0 to 2π
v = 0 to π

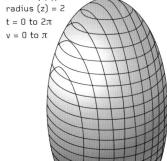

9.7 Sphere and ellipsoid

Cylinder (parametric equation)
x = rsin(t)
y = rcos(t)
z = u

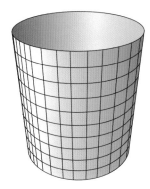

Elliptic paraboloid (parametric equation)
x = (3 √[t]) cos(v)
y = (3 √[t]) sin(v)
z = 3t
v = 0 to 2π, t = 0 to 2π

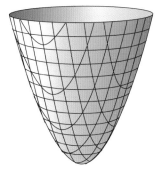

9.8 Cylinder and elliptic paraboloid

Hyperboloid (parametric equation)
x = (3 √[1+t²]) cos(v)
y = (3 √[1+t²]) sin(v)
z = 3t
v = 0 to 2π
t = -2π to 2π

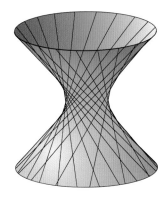

9.9 Hyperboloid

Torus (parametric equation)
x = cos(t) (3+cos(u))
y = sin(t) (3+cos(u))
z = sin(u)
t = 0 to 2π, u = 0 to 2π

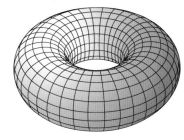

9.10 Torus

Toroid (parametric equation)
x= (3 + sin(t) + cos(u))cos(2t)
y = (3 + sin(t) + cos(u))sin(2t)
z = sin(u) + 2cos(t)
t = 0 to 2π, u = 0 to 2π

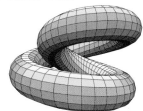

Twisted Klein bottle (parametric equation)
x = [3+cos(t/2)sin(v)-sin(t/2)sin(2v)]cos(t)
y = [3+cos(t/2)sin(v)-sin(t/2)sin(2v)]sin(t)
z = sin(t/2)sin(v)+cos(t/2)sin(2v)
t = 0 to 2π, v = 0 to 2π)

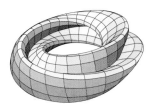

9.11 Toroid and immersion of a Klein bottle

we want to plot a circle with a radius of 2, then an x value of 1 must be matched with a y value of √3. If we use polar coordinates, the equation of a circle looks like c = √((ccosθ)² + (csinθ)²) for values of θ greater than or equal to 0 or less than or equal to 2π, where c is the circle radius. In parametric form the equation for a circle is written as x = ccosθ; y = csinθ (fig. 9.6). As our two- and three-dimensional models become more complex, equations written in the parametric form become more concise to use than rectangular equations.

Moving into three dimensions A sphere can be generated with an equation that will basically plot every point on a sphere's circumference in terms of Cartesian (x, y, z) values in a linear fashion, or, alternatively, in an angular fashion with polar coordinates that dynamically move one point equidistant

around a fixed point, the sphere's centre. Depending upon how an output is controlled, for example the head of a 3D printer, the equations can be formatted for angular or linear motion or both. Using Cartesian coordinates the equation of a sphere can look like x² + y² + z² = r². Using polar coordinates the equation, in parametric form, can look like x = rcos(t) cos(u); y = rsin(t)cos(u); z = rsin(u) where r is the radius, t is the angle θ (the azimuth angle), and u is the angle ϕ (the polar angle). The angle θ is the polar angle from 0 to 2π and the angle ϕ is the azimuthal angle from 0 to π (see fig. 9.7).

A slight modification to the sphere equation generates an ellipsoid, where the values of r in the sphere equation are stretched in the z direction to stretch out the sphere (see fig. 9.7).

The equation of the cylinder is also similar to that of a sphere, but the z value varies from 0 to 2 (see fig. 9.8).

Hyperboloids A hyperboloid (see fig. 9.9) is a doubly ruled surface that can be built with straight steel beams, producing a strong structure at low cost. Examples include the cooling towers of power stations, the James S. McDonnell Planetarium building at the St Louis Science Center, and the Kobe Port Tower in Japan (see fig 9.20).

Toroids and Klein bottles An example of distorting a plane to create a 3D form can be seen in the forms of toroids, and similarities can be seen between the parametric equations for the toroid (see fig. 9.10) and the sphere. The equation for the flattened-8 toroid is also expressed in parametric form, with polar coordinates and a z value for the extra dimension. The difference between the torus and the twisted immersion Klein bottle (see fig. 9.11) is really just that of the surface: the surface twists on the latter, so the inside surface becomes the outer. Famous toroids in architecture include the Joint European Torus in Oxfordshire, England, which is the world's largest plasma physics experiment, and the Stanford University, California, torus designed as a possible space habitat. A Klein bottle house with flat surfaces rather than curves has been built in Melbourne, Australia, by architects McBride Charles Ryan.

Boy's surface The Boy's surface (see fig. 9.12) has a three-fold symmetry and can be cut into three equal pieces. The equation shown was discovered by American mathematician Robert Bryant, where g is a function of a complex number with a magnitude of less than or equal to 1.

Hyperbolic paraboloids The Cartesian equation of the hyperbolic paraboloid (see figs 9.13 and 9.14) is similar to that of the elliptic paraboloid (see fig. 9.8), but the x value is negative and thereby creates an opposing curvature to the y value. The saddle-like form is the result of the opposing curvatures. The second hyperbolic paraboloid in fig. 9.13 is known as the 'monkey saddle' because the saddle form has a third depression that could supposedly accommodate a monkey's tail. Adding an x value to the y curvature creates the additional space;

Boy's surface
Shows the triple point
where the surface self-intersects

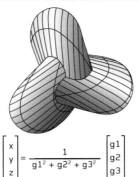

$$\begin{bmatrix} x \\ y \\ z \end{bmatrix} = \frac{1}{g1^2 + g2^2 + g3^2} \begin{bmatrix} g1 \\ g2 \\ g3 \end{bmatrix}$$

Where x, y, z are the desired
Cartesian coordinates of a
point on the Boy's surface

Boy's surface from near the top.

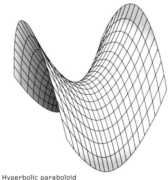

9.12 Two variations of a Boy's surface

Hyperbolic paraboloid
Plot 3D [0.3Re[(x+iy)²], (x,-5,5), (y,-5,-5)]

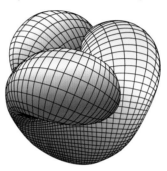

Hyperbolic paraboloid
(monkey saddle)
Plot 3D [0.02Re[(x+iy)³], (x,-5,5), (y,-5,-5)]

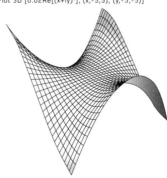

9.13 Hyperbolic paraboloids

Hyperbolic paraboloid
Five-arch monkey saddle
Plot 3D [.005Re[(0.8x+0.8iy)⁵], {x,-5,5}, {y,-5,5}]
i = imaginary unit

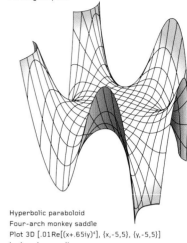

Hyperbolic paraboloid
Four-arch monkey saddle
Plot 3D [.01Re[(x+.65iy)⁴], {x,-5,5}, {y,-5,5}]
i = imaginary unit

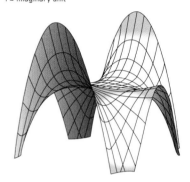

9.14 Hyperbolic paraboloid and cyclical function

3D Conchoid
Parametric plot 3D[kᵛ [(1+cos[v])cos[u],
(1+cos[v])sin[u],sin[v]-a],
(u, 0, 6π), (v, 0, 2π)],
k = 1.2; a = 1.5
Plot range (-60, 60), (-60, 60), (-40, 0)

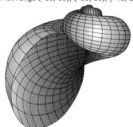

9.15 Conchoid

Kuen's surface
Parametric plot 3D [{(2(cos[s]+ssin[s])sin[t])/(1+s²(sin[t])²),
(2 (sin[s] + s cos[s]) sin[t])/(1+s² (sin[t])²),
Log[tan[t/2]]+(2cos[t])/(1+s²(sin[t])²)},
{s, -4.5, 4.5}, {t, 0, π), boxed->false, axes->false]

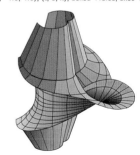

9.16 Kuen's surface

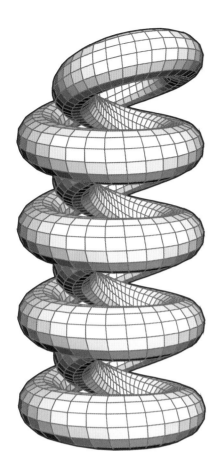

9.17 Toroid assembly

reducing the x value to 0.333...will eliminate the space for the monkey's tail and generate a simple arch.

Conchoid and Kuen's surface As equations get more complex so too can the forms that they generate. The parametric equation (see fig. 9.15) generates a seashell-like conchoid. The forms that equations can generate are probably infinite. The Kuen's surface (see fig. 9.16) has a constant negative curvature and is a special case of a whole family of three-dimensional surfaces known as Enneper's negative curvature surfaces. The surface has the same Gaussian curvature as a sphere and pseudosphere. Equations of 3D forms can easily be modified to change the curvatures and the number of saddles and arches. Once generated, the forms can be interconnected in a modular fashion, or stacked on top of themselves. Fig 9.17 shows a possible combination of an equation-generated toroid.

NEW METHODS AND MATERIALS

We are entering a new era of structural design made possible by adding internal cellular structures to materials, where we can use mathematical equations to generate cellular structures that maintain or increase the internal structural integrity of materials while reducing the overall weight of the material and therefore reducing the need for external structural support such as triangulated frameworks, cantilevered frameworks or suspension cables.

Cellular-structured materials can be manufactured out of resin; by sintering metal particles into solids with heat and pressure; out of fused ceramic particles; and even, possibly, out of organic-based materials. Cellular materials can be combined with new types of coating such as electrically conductive coatings, electrical circuits, electroluminescent materials, solar cells and even variants of OLEDs. 3D-printed assemblies of cellular-structured materials can create formed material structures that can be fixed and/or flexible – so that, for example, parts of a structure can freely bend or otherwise change

9.18 Guggenheim Museum, Bilbao, Spain, 1997

9.19 Munich Olympic Stadium (variation of a hyperbolic paraboloid)

shape, vibrate or resonate – or be fixed and inflexible. The possibilities seem endless: architectural structures with capacitance circuits, heat-generating circuits, structures that change shape and position, transparent and opaque structures, fluid-carrying structures, and so on. Cells can be macro- (one tenth of a metre or more), micro- (in the order of one millionth of a metre) or nano-sized (in the order of one billionth of a metre).

The use of new-generation 3D printers, combined with cellular materials and new-technology coatings, creates the opportunity to design radically different architectural forms, vehicles and household appliances. The external structural architecture can be of many types, such as fixed polyhedral forms, shape-changing polyhedral forms, spherical forms or clusters, bubble structures, and forms that follow mathematical or natural 3D cursive forms. This would fundamentally change the nature of the 3D structures that we might see in cities, in the air, on the roads, under the sea and outside the Earth's atmosphere.

9.20 Kobe Port Tower, Japan (hyperboloid)

9.21 Neboticnik skyscraper, Ljubljana, Slovenia (spiral)

Generating 3D forms without equations

As technology develops, the need to render the mathematical equations of 3D forms in a programming language will probably disappear as even higher-level languages and computer interfaces evolve. 3D modelling software has been available for many years and an almost infinite number of forms can be generated without using equations

of any sort. There are many types of 3D software available, for example to direct cutter tools, to create animations, construct aircraft, create simulations, or model and compute flight paths and orbits. The Guggenheim Museum in Bilbao, Spain (see fig. 9.18), designed by Frank Gehry, features complex, apparently random curves generated using the CATIA (computer-aided three-dimensional interactive application) software. The software was used to digitize points on the edges, surfaces and intersections of Gehry's hand-built models to construct on-screen models that could then be manipulated from different perspectives.

We have also seen the use of 3D scanners that can render an existing 3D form digitally such that the digital form can be used to replicate a given object, or create any sort of variation, or combination, of an existing 3D form. The Leica terrestrial light detection and ranging scanner (TLS), seen in fig. 9.22, may be used to scan buildings, rock formations and so on to produce a 3D model. The TLS can aim its laser beam in a wide range: its head rotates horizontally and a mirror flips vertically. The laser beam is used to measure the distance to the first object on its path.

An example of a scanned image is the computer rendering made from a 3D scan of Michelangelo's *David* by Henrik Wann Jensen (see fig. 9.23). The 3D image was digitally constructed by scanning the statue using a laser triangulation range finder and assembling the resulting range images to form a seamless polygon mesh. The mesh contains 8 million polygons, each about 2 mm ($^4/_{50}$ in) in size. The raw data from which the mesh was built contains 2 billion polygons, representing range samples spaced 0.25 mm ($^1/_{100}$ in) apart on the statue surface. Although the colour is also digitized, the veining and reflectance shown here is artificial. Once digitized the image could be transformed into a 3D model by way of a 3D printer.

The 3D-printed revolution Almost any shape should be 3D printable whether it is printed as component parts or in one piece (see fig. 9.24). The accuracy of 3D printers is such that connecting parts should align precisely, provided shrinkage is taken into account during forming. Materials can be any sort of particulate resin or heat-fusible material, such as particulate marble, metallic (particle) resins, silicone and clays. The 3D printing of nano-materials and organics is also under development, as is 3D-printed food — the possibilities seem endless. New generations of 3D printers include 'continuous liquid interface production' technology, or CLIP, where a pool of resin

9.22 Leica HDS-3000 3D scanner

9.23 Henrik Wann Jensen, scanned image of Michelangelo's *David*

9.24 Concept of 3D-printed house

is placed over a digital light projection system. To create an object, CLIP projects bursts of light and oxygen: light hardens the resin, oxygen prevents it hardening.

The following list gives an idea of the vast range of actual and potential 3D-printed products.

1. Ground transport: vehicle bodies, chassis, engine parts, engine prototypes, tyres
2. Air transport: bodies, shape-changing wings, engine parts, engine prototypes
3. Fashion accessories: shoes, jewelry

4. Consumer products: prototypes, housings, musical instruments, toys, clothes, and facsimiles of animals, structures and people
5. Space exploration: component parts of rocket engines, habitats, food, space cameras
6. Architecture: component parts or entire structures
7. Medical: organ printing (uses human cells), prosthetics
8. Military and consumer: body and vehicle armour, robotic parts, guns, projectiles, radar dishes

10. FRACTALS

SUBDIVISIONS OF FORM WITH ORIGINS IN ISLAMIC GEOMETRIES

The concept of using a defined set of transformations to infinitely subdivide a space can be seen in the nesting polygons of early Islam and also in the logic of fractals. An equivalent process seems to appear in nature, for example in the process that forms spiral galaxies and tornadoes.

The notion of infinite subdivisions of space can be well considered with a counterintuitive concept put forward by British mathematician Lewis Fry Richardson (1881–1953), describing the notion that a coastline's measured length changes with the length of the measuring stick used to measure it. To explain the idea a little further: when measuring the length of a coastline we make approximations using linear dimensions – effectively we segment the perimeter so that we can measure it with straight-line units. The smaller the segments the more measurements will correspond with the perimeter. An island's coastline can be measured by segmenting it into just six parts, but if the island is then segmented such that the segments touch key features of its shoreline, the measured length will greatly increase. The smaller the segments the greater the measured length – from the tips of peninsulas to particular rocks and stones and ultimately to atoms whose positions are not constant (see fig. 10.3).

Islamic nesting patterns encompass the concepts of infinite subdivisions and of scaled repeats in that they apply a repeating sequence of operations, including a scaling function, that generates a composite form (see chapter 7). A similar process is generated by the so-called Koch curve sequence of operations, which infinitely breaks down a line into equilateral triangular segments in a self-similar repeating pattern way. The Koch snowflake (see fig. 10.2) begins with a hexagram and then infinitely replaces the middle third of every line segment with a pair of line segments that form an equilateral 'bump'.

10.1 Romanesco broccoli

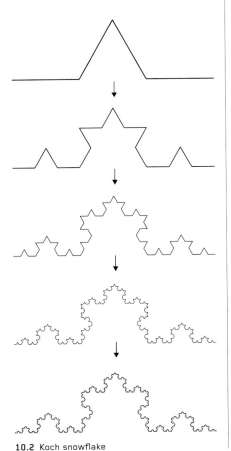

10.2 Koch snowflake

10.3 Richardson fractal

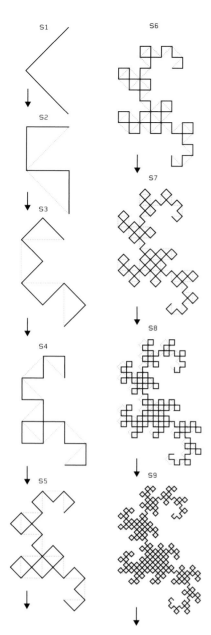

S1

S2

S3

S4

S5

S6

S7

S8

S9

10.4 Dragon fractal

Defining fractals Fractals are defined as mathematical forms that are generated using a defined set of transformations that include a scaling function whereby the set will generate a form and then infinitely break it down into scaled repeats of itself or into, more generally, self-similar patterns of many types. The Koch curve (or snowflake) and Islamic nesting polygons fall under this definition.

To generate non-symmetrical two- and three-dimensional fractal forms, a non-symmetrical sequence of operations or a dynamic element of some sort needs to be added to the operational process. An easy example of this is the generation of fractals using path sequences. Such sequences might allow incremental changes to movement directions across a two-dimensional plane, or through a three-dimensional space, rotationally and linearly – but must include some sort of staged scaling function. (For early path logic see chapter 2.)

The dragon fractal (see fig. 10.4) is drawn with a repeating process that starts with two lines, of equal length, connected at 90° to each other. This construction forms a 'seed' arrangement (s1). The seed arrangement is then reduced in size by $1/(\sqrt{2})$ and duplicated so that the duplicate lies exactly on the original. The duplicate is then rotated at 90° about one line end and then the two overlapping line ends are joined. This process creates a scaled repeat of the first seed arrangement (s2). The process can repeat through an infinite set of iterations of seed generations: s1, s2, s3, s4, s5... sn.

The Mandelbrot set Named after the mathematician Benoît Mandelbrot, the Mandelbrot set is a set of numbers generated by a similar iteration (repetitive process) to that of the dragon fractal. Although, like the dragon fractal, the Mandelbrot set is self-similar at magnified scales, the small-scale details are not identical to the whole. The operational process for generating the Mandelbrot set is based on an extremely simple equation involving complex numbers, $z_{n+1} = z_n^2 + c$, where c can be a real number, or a complex number that is composed of a real number plus a real number multiplied by the 'imaginary number'.

The square root of a positive number is a positive real number; for example, the square root of 9 is 3. Because there is no square root of a negative number the number 'i' was invented to represent the square root of -1. This means that i squared is equal to -1. So, when you square a value of i you get a negative number. For example, $(4i)^2$ is -16.

A complex number is a combination of a value of i with two real numbers, a + bi, where the real number a is an ordinary number, for example -7, and the other real number, b, is also an ordinary number, for example 2. The combination bi is called an 'imaginary number', for example 2i. An example of a complex number is -7 + 2i.

Whereas real numbers can be represented on a one-dimensional line called the real number line, where numbers like -2 are plotted to the left of zero and positive numbers like 2 are plotted to the right (see fig. 10.5), complex numbers have two parts, a real part and an imaginary part, so a second dimension is needed to graph them. A vertical dimension is added to the real number line for the imaginary part, transforming the graph into a two-dimensional plane known as the complex number plane. We can now graph any complex number onto this plane: for example, the complex number (-0.4 + -0.5i) has coordinates (-0.4, -0.5) (see fig. 10.5).

As said, the Mandelbrot set can be explained with the equation $z_{n+1} = z_n^2 + c$, where c can be a complex or a real number and the value of n starts at zero and then has values 1, 2, 3, 4,...n. The Mandelbrot set are values of c such that the value of z_n never extends to infinity – from the origin (0, 0i) on the complex number plane. In fact, it can be proved that if the distance (the orbit) of the plot of c on the complex number plane from the origin (0, 0i) ever gets bigger than 2, or if any of the z_ns have norms exceeding 2, then the value of z_n will always extend to infinity. So, any value of c equal to or exceeding 2 will produce a z_n value outside of the Mandelbrot set.

As a first example, if we start with n = 0 and a c complex number value = (-0.4 + -0.5i) then:
the first value $z_1 = (0)^2 + (-0.4 - 0.5i) = -0.4 - 0.5i$
the second value $z_2 = (-0.4 - 0.5i)^2 +$

$(-0.4 - 0.5i) = (0.16 + 0.4i - 0.25) +$
$(-0.4 - 0.5i) = -0.49 - 0.01i$
the third value $z_3 = (-0.49 - 0.01i)^2$
$+ (-0.4 - 0.5i) = (0.2401 + 0.0098i -$
$0.0001) + (-0.4 - 0.5i) = -0.16 - 49i$
Continuing these iterations we find
that after computing 256 terms in
the sequence, all of the values in the
sequence, up to and including the last
one, z_{255}, have norms that are less
than 2.0, so $(-0.4 - 0.5i)$ belongs in the
Mandelbrot set. Fig. 10.6 shows how
the values of z_n progress from z_1 to z_5.

As a second example, if we start with
$n = 0$ and a c complex number value =
$(0 + 1i)$ then:
the first value $z_1 = (0)^2 + i = i$
the second value $z_2 = (i)^2 + i = (\sqrt{-1})^2 + i$
$= -1 + i$
the third value $z_3 = (-1 + i)^2 + i = (1 - 2i +$
$-1) + i = -i$
$z_4 = -1 + i$
$z_5 = -i$
with oscillating values of z_n thereafter
of $(-i)$ and $(-1 + i)$, and we can see the
value never extends to infinity, so $0 + 1i$
belongs in the Mandelbrot set.

As a third example, if we start with $n = 0$
and a c real number value = 1:
the first value $z_1 = 0^2 + 1 = 1$
the second value $z_2 = 1^2 + 1 = 2$
the third value $z_3 = 2^2 + 1 = 5$
We can see that the value of z_n is rapidly
expanding past 2 and outside of the set.

As we test many complex numbers
we can graph those that are part of the
Mandelbrot set on the complex number
plane and colour them black. If we plot
thousands of points, an image of the set
appears (see fig. 10.7). We can also add
colour to the points that are not inside
the set according to how many iterations
were required before the magnitude
of z_n surpassed 2. Not only do colours
enhance the image aesthetically, they
help to highlight parts of the Mandelbrot
set that are too small to show up in the
graph. An example of a c value marginally
outside the Mandelbrot set is c = (-0.4
- 0.6i). Up to z_{24} all the z_n values have
norms that are less than 2.0. But z_{25}
has a norm that is just slightly larger
than 2.0, so the c value (-0.4, -0.6) is
outside the Mandelbrot set and coloured
according to how close it is to the set.

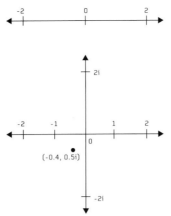

10.5 Real number line (top) and the complex
number plane (bottom)

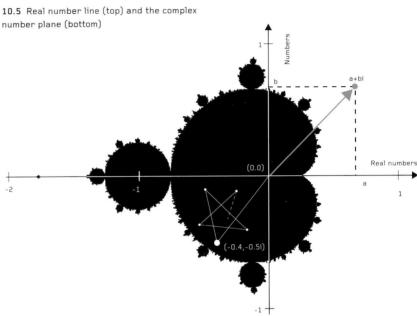

10.6 Graphic form of the Mandelbrot set

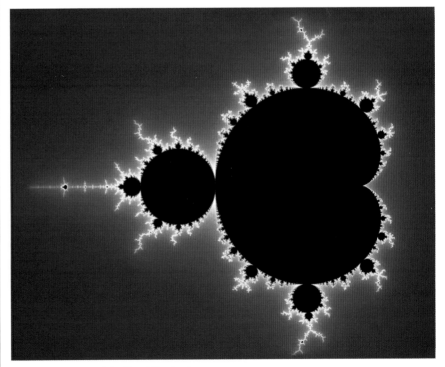

10.7 Graphic form of the Mandelbrot set

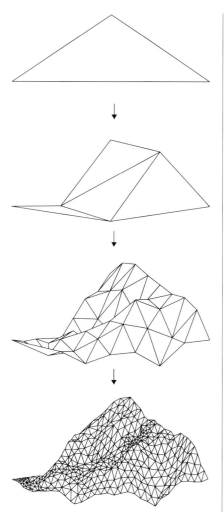

10.8 Fractal surfaces

10.9 Computer-generated landscape

10.10 Fractal-like lightning branching

Fractals in 3D To create a computer model of a natural-looking landscape we can use fractal logic. For example, we can start with a triangle in three-dimensional space and then on a logical basis add three distortion points to the seed triangle and then move these points, together with the triangle vertices, in three dimensions according to the same logical set of operations. Then add distortion points scaled to each of the new triangles generated, moving the triangle's vertices and the distortion points in three-dimensional space as before. The process can repeat to very fine details (see fig. 10.8).

In nature, many branching patterns have fractal-like features, to some extent, such as a tree that has a similar pattern in the largest branches and in the smallest leaves. Branching patterns are common in nature because there

is a need to distribute or discharge something efficiently throughout a uniform medium, such as electrical impulses in a nervous system, or rain water in a river system. However, not all branching patterns are fractal-like in their nature, as the self-similar patterning usually only extends to two or three different scales, and there is no true mathematical consistency to the forms when the scaled variations are compared. Also, in nature, there are too many variables that determine a branching pattern, particularly when one compares the mediums within which they occur – the veins in the body with the roots of a tree. However, they are nonetheless fractal-like.

Branching path patterns follow simple logical sequences. Some branching patterns follow a fractal-like scale and repeat process, others do not scale.

In fig. 10.12, image 1 follows a cell-like division path. Image 2 is a copy of a phylogenetic tree drawn by Charles Darwin to show the distance between evolutionary branches – some closer than others. Image 3 is a schematic representation of a fractal-like mammalian bronchial tree. The branching patterns shown in fig. 10.13 are based on scaled repeats; the second is a Pythagorean tree with repeats scaled on the squares of the sides of a 1, 2, 3 triangle. The branching arrangement shown in fig. 10.14 is more random and is a concept drawing designed to show how fractal logic could be applied to an architectural form.

A path logic is shown in fig. 10.15 where the letters l and r represent turn options following the line lattices. So, if you are moving forward along either one of the line lattices shown in the illustration and meet a three-way junction your option is to turn left or right. In the upper drawing of fig. 10.15 the polygonal lattice has no scaled repeats so paths generated by left (l) and right (r) sequences have no fractal-like properties. The lower lattice grid is different in that it can be naturally subdivided, infinitely, to create scaled versions of itself, and directional sequences of left and right turns can be applied to each scaled version to create a fractal-like self-similarity.

Fractals in architecture Architects through time have sought to create a sense of harmony in their designs, variously through the use of grids, human proportions, rectangles, circles, polygons, cylinders and hemispherical domes. In more recent times various types of geometrical progression have been used to generate architectural forms based on logarithmic spirals, paraboloids, parabolic curves and toroids. It can be argued that what creates a sense of harmony in these forms is the regularity of the mathematical progressions used.

In a chaotic sort of way we can see, almost everywhere, a type of fractal logic in the use of rectangles where they repeat in scale from large street plans to floor plans of buildings to rectangular picture frames, floor tiles and even to rectangular pieces of chocolate stored in a rectangular cupboard or drawer. However, there is generally no regularity to the arrangements or to the scaled repeats of rectangular architecture. The exceptions are rectangular structures that follow a proportionate system or a strict regiment of repeats of proportion and size.

Perhaps the Spanish architect Antoni Gaudí (1852–1926) has come closest to applying a fractal logic to architecture, though only accidentally, by using tree-like branching forms that scale from large features such as internal columns and external structural supports to small sculpted details. Perhaps Gaudí's more accidental application of fractals is best, as an overly regular application departs from the variations of nature.

10.11 Fractal-like tree branching

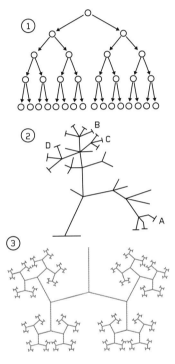

10.12 Path logics

10.13 Fractal path logic

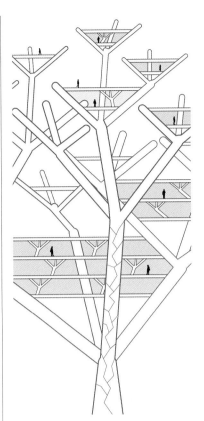

10.14 Fractal path logic

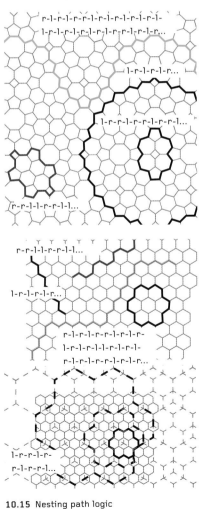

10.15 Nesting path logic

11. SHAPE-CHANGERS

MOVING FROM STATIC TO DYNAMIC

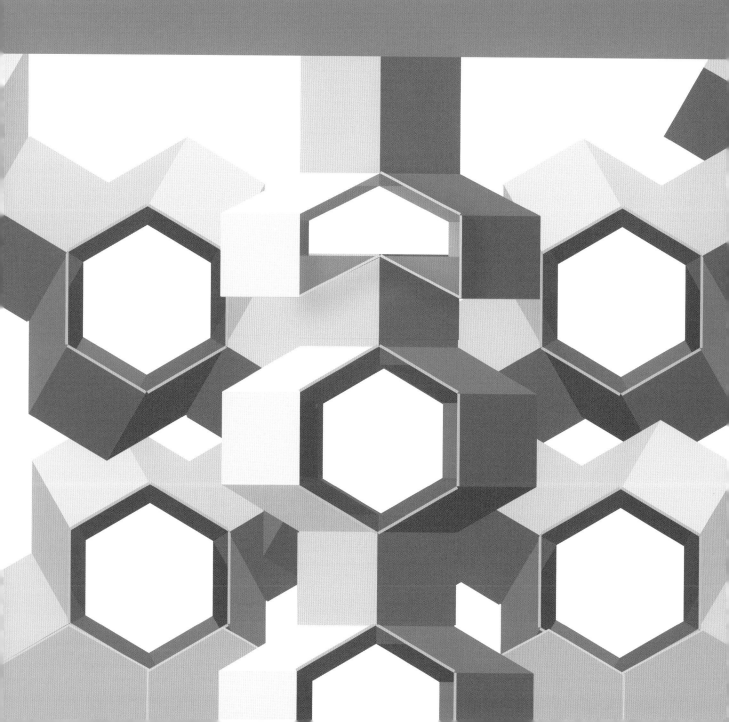

Shape-changing polyhedra – which originated in the ancient past as fixed polygonal structures – are two- and three-dimensional structures constructed with flexibly connected polygons. They can infinitely connect in 3D space and adopt multiple positions of stability. These dynamic new structures herald great changes in architecture and 3D design, allowing static structures to be transformed into dynamic structures that change both shape and size.

Before shape-changers In chapter 1 we considered the moment when polygons were first conceptualized. Greek geometricians defined geometric solids based on regular polygons with equal sides and equal angles. Islamic architects made use of regular and irregular polygons when developing the honeycomb-like muqarnas (see fig. 11.3) to focus sounds. The author's inspiration for shape-changing polyhedra came from studying the Greek and Islamic geometries but also from looking at such things as children's building blocks and wondering why they were so limited in the ways that they could be combined.

When exploring how basic polygonal shapes connect in three-dimensional space it became evident that the means of connecting one with another has mostly been with fixed hinges. This is true of Platonic and Archimedean solids, of early Islamic muqarnas and of geodesic domes. What if we simply substitute flexible hinges for fixed hinges? This is such an obvious thought but one that has apparently been only marginally explored, with the exception of origami. Before proceeding to explore the possibilities of shape-changing polyhedra, the lineage of their forms should be considered as possible sources of inspiration.

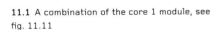

11.1 A combination of the core 1 module, see fig. 11.11

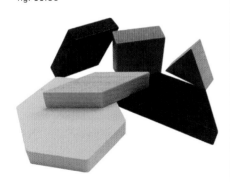

11.2 Children's building blocks

11.3 Muqarnas in the gateway of the Sultan Han caravanserai, Sultanhani, Turkey, 13th century

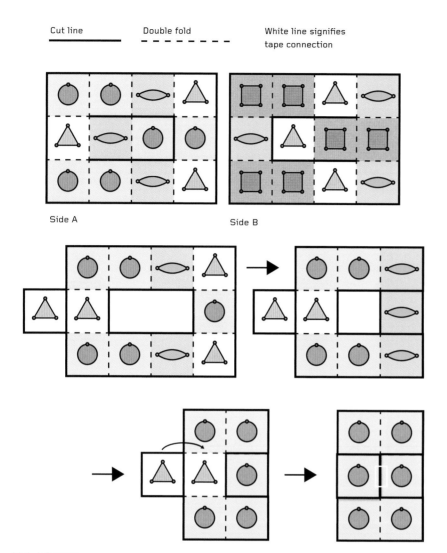

Cut line ——— Double fold - - - - - - White line signifies tape connection

Side A   Side B

11.4 A flexagon

Known shape-changing polygonal structures Flexagons are constructed by folding strips of paper into assemblies that can be flexed in certain ways to move images from front to back faces (see fig. 11.4). Flexagons are usually square, rectangular or hexagonal. Their invention is credited to British student Arthur Stone while he was at Princeton University in 1939.

Origami is mostly limited to folding single sheets of paper to create three-dimensional forms, of which some will shape-change. Origami-like folds have found applications in robotics, packaging and furniture design. Any flat-sheet fold geometry can be called an origami fold, for example (see figs 11.38, 11.43, 11.54 and 11.55). The art of paper folding probably goes back to the 1st century in China. Today it is a popular recreational activity in Japan and around the world.

Shape-changing lattices are in some ways similar to shape-changing polyhedra and can provide inspiration when developing new types of shape-changing polyhedra. A recent example of a shape-changing lattice is the Hoberman Sphere, invented by Chuck Hoberman in the 1980s. The sphere is composed of hundreds of strips connected in a scissor-like way and arranged in six great circles corresponding to an icosidodecahedron. The sphere will fold down to one fifth of its fully extended size, although the toy version will only fold down to about one-third of its full size.

Fixed polyhedra include the Platonic and Archimedean solids, stellated polyhedra and geodesics. All can provide inspiration for shape-changers.

Tessellations (see fig. 11.5) are generally considered as two-dimensional arrangements but they do provide a basis for thinking about flexibly connected three-dimensional structures. Regular tessellations consist of regular polygons that tile without leaving spaces and where adjoining polygons all meet at a common corner (vertex). Semi-regular tessellations combine more than one regular polygon to tessellate (see pp.142–46). Equilateral quadrilaterals also tessellate, as do many other types of polygon, including irregular polgons.

SHAPE-CHANGING POLYHEDRA

Polygons can be flexibly combined three-dimensionally in an indefinite number of ways, making a logical combination methodology necessary. We therefore begin with a rule set that will evolve as new possibilities reveal themselves.

1. Start with a minimum number of polygons that will create a 3D tessellating module (see note below). Call this minimum configuration a 'core'.
2. Avoid triangulation (see below) where three polygons meet at a vertex (corner) to create a rigid geometry and explore shape-changing polyhedra where more than three polygons meet at a vertex.
3. Establish and maintain symmetry.

Notes

(i) The term 'tessellating module' is used here as a 3D modular structure that will infinitely combine in a repeating pattern across one or more geometric planes.

(ii) The term 'triangulation' in this chapter is used to describe a join between polygons that is fixed and that cannot shape-change. The use is similar to that in navigation where a triangulation determines a fixed point.

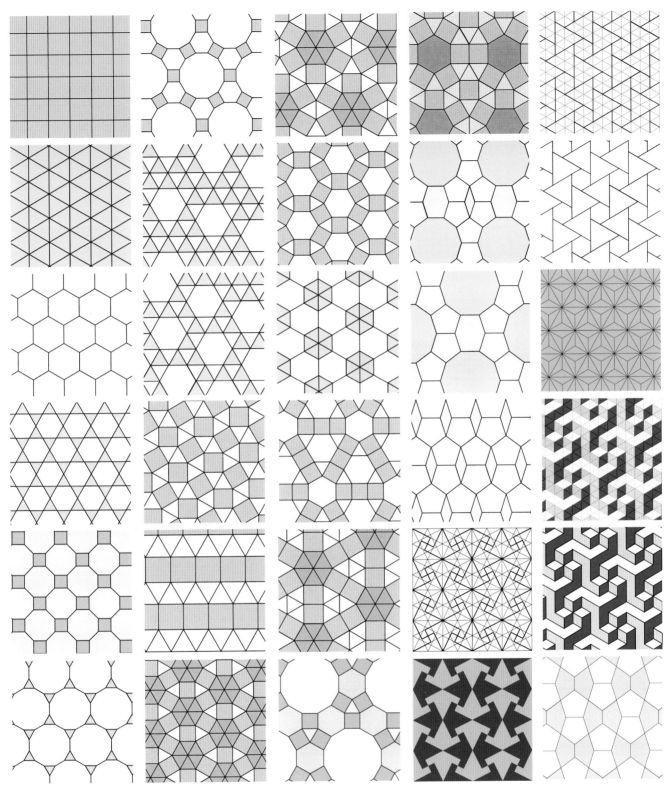

11.5 Regular and semi-regular tessellations composed of regular polygons

CORE 1 MODULE

A first example of a shape-changing polyhedron is that of a core consisting of four 45° rhombi connected edge to edge rotationally around a common 45° vertex. Call this 'core 1' (see fig. 11.6). Core 1 can be tessellated along the x axis and combined with squares (see fig. 11.7).

Core 1 extended Adding polygons within the basic core produces an extended core. In the example shown in fig. 11.8 the core is extended with squares in the x and y axis directions but also combined with external squares. Fig. 11.9 shows an extended and combined core in the x, y and z directions, creating an enclosed shell. Fig. 11.10 shows extensions and interlaced tessellations.

Notes

(i) The term 'extension' is used when polygons are added within a core.

(ii) The term 'combined' is used when polygons are added external to a core.

(iii) The term 'shell' is used when a module fully encloses a 3D space.

(iv) 'Modules' are defined as 3D units that can be duplicated and combined in a multiplicity of ways.

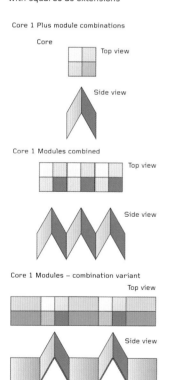

11.6 Core 1 is composed of 45° rhombi with squares as extensions

Core 1 Plus module combinations

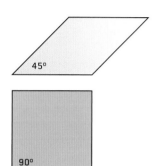

Core 1 Modules combined

Core 1 Modules – combination variant

11.7 Core 1 module consists of four 45° rhombi. Combinations are along the x axis

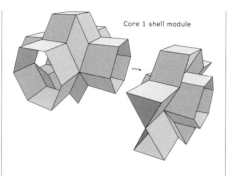

Core 1 shell module

11.8 Core 1 module extended and combined along x and y axis

Core 1 Module combinations

Combination 1   Top view

Side view

Combination 2   Top view

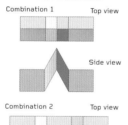

Side view

Combination 3   Top view

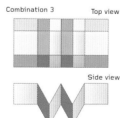

Side view

11.9 Core 1 shell module extended and combined in x, y and z axis. Shows one shape-change

Core 1 shell module and a combination

Module

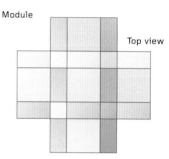

Top view

Side view

Combination   Top view

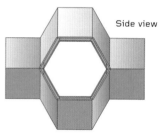

Side view

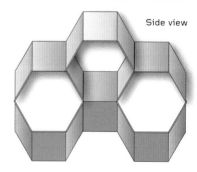

11.10 Core 1 shell module extended and combined along the x, y and z axis

Core 1 module equilibrium positions

When moving a shape-changer the polyhedra will move through points of equilibrium where, in those positions, there is a level of balance or equilibrium (see fig. 11.11). Equilibrium points have a structural stability and are good positions to add a triangulation if there is a need to fix the position of the shape-changer. See also the later paragraph on the flexibility of hinges (p.258).

Core 1 shell module — eight equilibrium positions

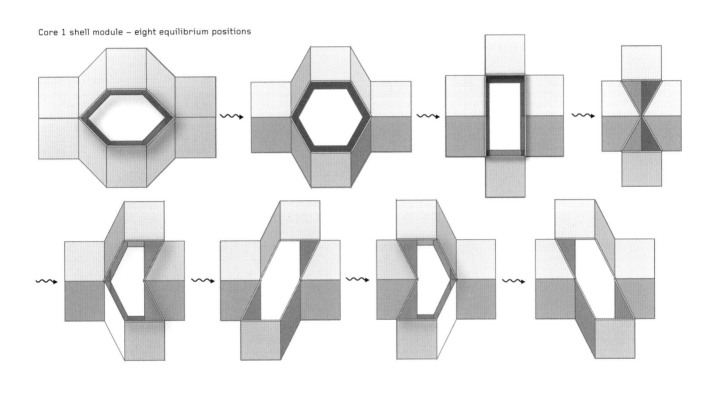

Two Core 1 shell modules combined — three of eight equilibrium positions

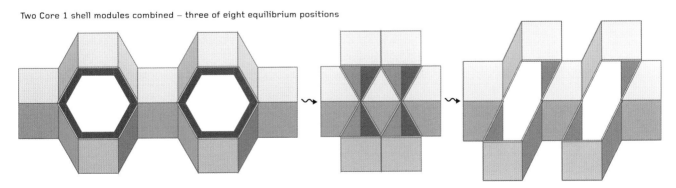

11.11 Core 1 shell module equilibrium positions as individual shells (x 8) and as two shell combinations (x 3)

Core 1 shell module combination
equilibrium positions

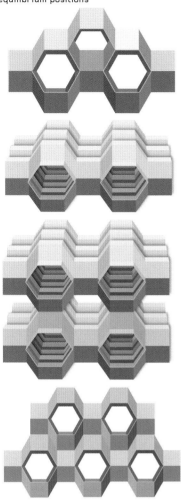

11.12 Core 1 shell module – stacking
and extending retaining shape-changing
characteristics

Core 1 shell module
rotated combination

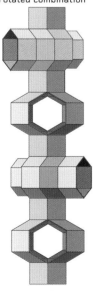

11.13 Core 1 shell combined and rotated.
The rotation prevents shape-change

Combining and extending modules

An example of a shell module combination
is shown in fig. 11.13, where the core 1
shell module is replicated and rotationally
combined. The rotation opposes the
lateral shape-change characteristics.

Combinations appear to be infinite

There are so many ways in which shape-
changer modules can be extended and
combined. For example, the core 1 shell
module can be extended internally and
combined with other polygons along the
x, y and z axis, or stacked as shown in
fig. 11.12. The core 1 shell module can be
further extended and combined across
a plane, or vertically, in nested or tower
forms (see figs 11.12, 11.13 and 11.14).

Core 1 half-shell module combinations

Extended equilibrium
position one

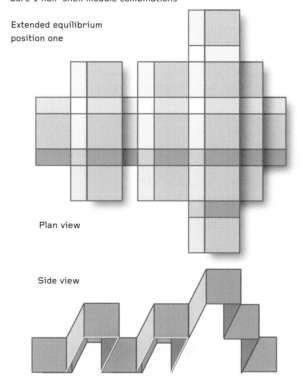

Plan view

Side view

Extended equilibrium
position two

Front view

Plan view

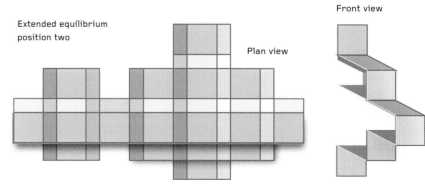

11.14 Core 1 half-shell module – combined along a 2D plane

Shape-changers can walk Combinations of core 1 modules with electro-former flexible hinges can be programmed to move across a two-dimensional surface. Fig. 11.15 shows the core 1 half-shell module in ten 'walking' positions. See also fig. 11.57.

Modules can be combined at angles
Duplicates of the core 1 shell modules combine to create some interesting structures (see fig. 11.16). The fact that the module only shape-changes along one axis means that any combinations that are not along that axis will effectively triangulate the structure and fix its position, and also fix the hexagonal aperture in a regular polygonal form. However, the structure can still be extended in all sorts of ways – for example with hexagonal tunnels, multiple towers, shape-changing sections, combinations with other shape-changing modules, and even combinations with various types of regular and semi-regular polyhedra.

Triangulating shape-changers Shape-changers can freely shape-change from one equilibrium position to another. However, if a space is triangulated by adding a cross beam support, or a solid polygon in an aperture, or combining modules in a way that creates an opposition to the axis of motion, the shape-changer loses its ability to change shape and becomes a fixed structure.

In theory, adding just one triangulation, to a tessellating modular structure, will fix the entire structure, no matter how extensive the structure is, but in practice a number of triangulations will be needed at various stress points depending upon the size, weight, and material characteristics of the construction.

Core 1 half-shell module – moving shape-changer

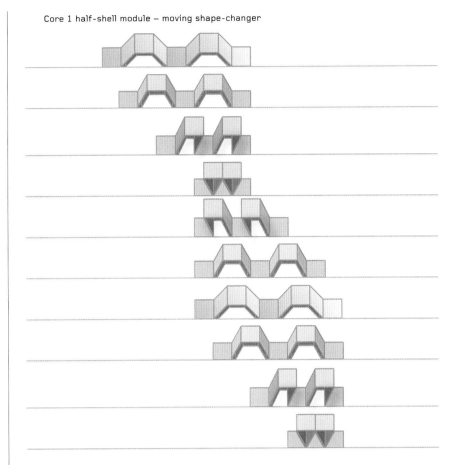

11.15 Core 1 – shape-changers can walk

11.16 Core 1 – modules can be combined at angles

Core 1 shell
module changes
between two
positions

11.17 Core 1 shell modules for The Leonardo Museum

Core 1 shell module combinations

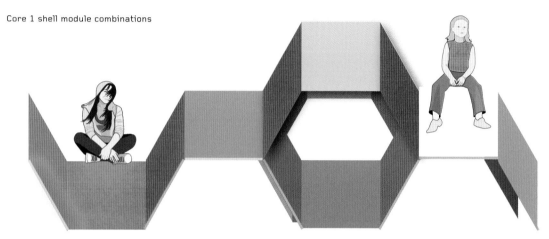

11.18 Core 1 shell module configuration for The Leonardo Museum

Concept for The Leonardo The author was asked by The Leonardo, a science and technology museum in Salt Lake City, Utah, if outside shape-changer structures could be created for visitors to sit on or in, or climb on.

Figs 11.17 and 11.18 show outside possibilities using core 1 shell and half-shell modules. The idea was that smaller shape-changer variants could be transformed by visitors to some preferred arrangement and then the larger outside shape-changer would be configured and triangulated to match that arrangement by museum staff. Alternatively, outside structures could have buffers added to limit the transformations. PolyMetal (manufactured by Nudo Products, Illinois) was specified as an ideal material, being a laminate of aluminium and plastic that is very strong and light. The hinges were designed to be composed of flexible silicone and PolyMetal plates that bolted onto PolyMetal polygonal panels. The shape-changers

illustrated for The Leonardo use only 45° rhombi and squares.

To create a permanent weather-proof shape-changer one concept was to position polygonal panels in a shape-changer configuration and then cover them with a thermoplastic sheet – externally and internally – which, when heat-formed, would create a watertight and flexible connection between the panels.

Scale, sound and light Shape-changer panels can be scaled to be micro or macro sized. So panels can be, for example, metres, centimetres or even microns across. The scale of the panels will significantly alter the reflecting properties of the surfaces as well as the structural possibilities.

Constructing large shape-changers opens up the possibility of creating spaces that will alter the way sound and light reflect on exterior and interior surfaces. The interiors of shape-changers can function

as transformational acoustical environments. In some shape-change positions the angles and distances between opposing panels will create resonant sounds and in other positions dissonant sounds.

Light patterns will also change as the space transforms from one arrangement to another. Of course, the materials selected for the construction, as well as surface treatments, will alter the quality of reflected light and the resonance of reflected sounds. Depending on the overall weight of the shape-changer, the shape-transformation process can be thermoelectric, chemical, hand-powered, hydraulic, photomechanical or electromechanical.

CORE 2 MODULE

The core of the second shape-changer module is constructed using the same 45° rhombi and squares used for the core 1 shell module, but the core alternates two squares with two 45° rhombi (see fig. 11.19).

As with the core 1 module, duplicates of the core 2 module can be combined in a multiplicity of ways: by connecting at the four-sided polygonal apertures, by nesting and by stacking. Modules can be rotated at 90°, one with another, and still shape-change, and further extensions and combinations can be made by adding squares or other polygons.

Core 2 module combinations Core 2 modules can be combined in such a way that the combinations retain their shape-changing characteristics. The fact that the apertures in the core 2 modules are symmetrical quatrilaterals, and in line with the axis of motion, means that quarter-turn rotational combinations do not prevent shape-change.

For the multiple ways that core 2 modules can be combined – stacking, nesting, and connecting about apertures – see figs 11.19 to 11.25.

There are many ways to further combine core 2 modules. In fig. 11.26 the module combinations triangulate, preventing shape-change.

The core 2 module has just two points of equilibrium (see fig. 11.23).

Core 2 module combinations can shape-change in the same way as the module.

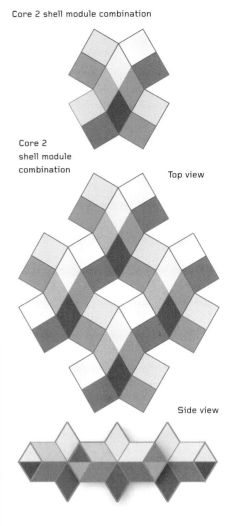

Core 2 plus module combinations

Core

R = 45° rhombus
S = square

Top view

Front view

Core 2 module combinations

Front (half)

Top

Front (full)

11.19 Core 2 module – second combination of 45° rhombi and squares

Core 2 shell module combination

Core 2 shell module combination

Top view

Side view

11.21 Core 2 shell modules stacked and combined

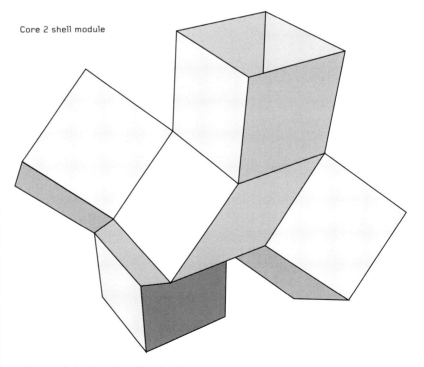

Core 2 shell module

11.20 Core 2 shell module with extension

Core 2 shell module combinations
Nesting combination

Stacked
combination

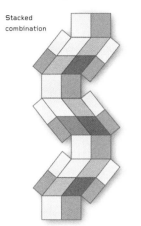

Core 2 shell module equilibrium positions

Equilibrium position one

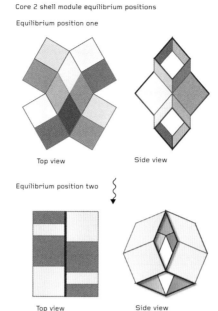

Top view   Side view

Equilibrium position two

Top view   Side view

11.22 Core 2 shell modules combined

11.23 Core 2 shell module in two equilibrium positions

Core 2 shell module equilibrium positions
Combination equilibrium position one

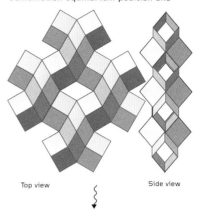

Top view   Side view

Combination equilibrium position two

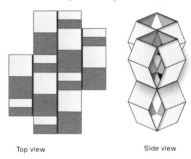

Top view   Side view

11.24 Core 2 shell module combinations in two equilibrium positions

Core 2 shell module combinations

Top view

Fill unit

Top view
with fill unit

Front view
with fill unit

Top view
of central unit

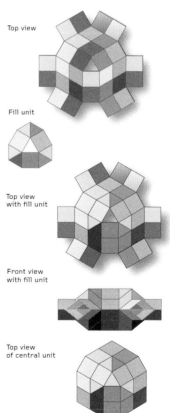

11.25 Core 2 shell module combination

11.26 Core 2 shell module combination with fixed polyhedron insert

FILL UNITS

In fig. 11.26 a fill unit has been added to a core 2 shell module combination; the fill unit is composed of the same square and 45° rhombus shapes used for the core 2 module. Fig. 11.26 shows plan and top views. Fig. 11.27 shows a concept of a portable tentlike structure.

11.27 Core 2 shell module combination with insert as possible application as a tent structure

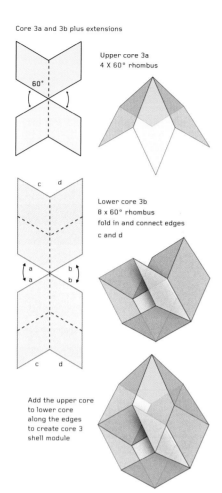

Core 3a and 3b plus extensions

Upper core 3a
4 X 60° rhombus

60°

Lower core 3b
8 x 60° rhombus
fold in and connect edges
c and d

c   d

a   b
a   b

c   d

Add the upper core
to lower core
along the edges
to create core 3
shell module

11.28 Core 3 construction and shell module

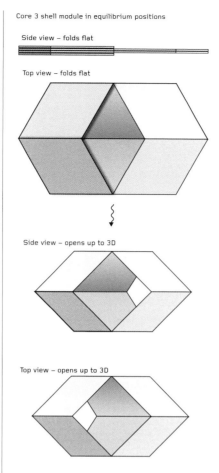

Core 3 shell module in equilibrium positions

Side view – folds flat

Top view – folds flat

Side view – opens up to 3D

Top view – opens up to 3D

11.29 Core 3 shell module equilibrium positions

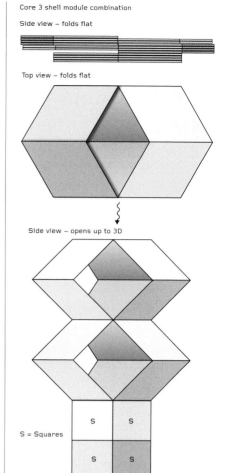

Core 3 shell module combination

Side view – folds flat

Top view – folds flat

Side view – opens up to 3D

S = Squares

S   S

S   S

11.30 Core 3 shell module combined with squares. The module will fold flat with the squares folding up

CORE 3 MODULE

The first two shape-changers, cores 1 and 2 shell modules, are constructed with 45° rhombi and squares. If we use a different rhombus the constructed shape-changer modules will interconnect in new ways determined by the angles of the rhombus.

Core 3 has a similar core structure to core 1, but is assembled with 60° rhombi instead of 45° rhombi.

The assembly of the core 3 module combines an upper and lower core assembly of four 60° rhombi with eight 60° rhombi so that the lower core fits into the upper core. All the rhombi are flexibly connected. The core 3 module has a total of 12 60° rhombi (see figs 11.28 and 11.29).

The core 3 shell module collapses to a flat equilibrium position and shape-changes into an open second equilibrium

position. The second equilibrium position can best be seen when the core 3 shell module is balanced from the top. This balance point creates four square apertures that can be used to interconnect duplicates. As the aperture is four-sided and aligned with two axes of motion then rotational connections do not prevent shape-change.

Connecting duplicates of the core 3 shell module to either, or both, of the square apertures of the module, with connections aligning with either of the two axes of symmetry, creates an indefinite number of structures. The assembled core 3 shell module and combinations of it will fold flat. The core 3 shell module, as with all other modules, can be further extended by adding other polygons. Figs 11.30 and 11.31 are created by adding squares to the core 3 module assembly.

'All things change, nothing is extinguished. There is nothing in the whole world which is permanent. Everything flows onward; all things are brought into being with a changing nature; the ages themselves glide by in constant movement.'
OVID (43 BCE – 17/18 CE)

11.31 Core 3 shell concept application

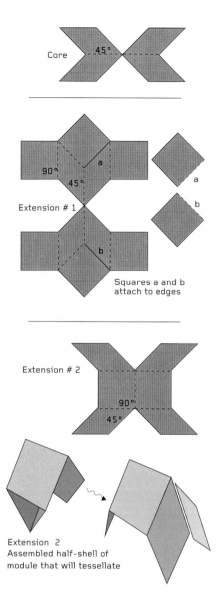

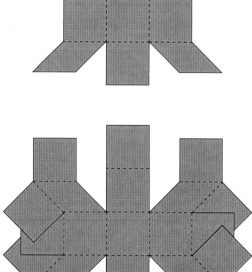

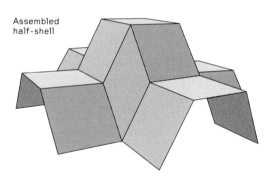

11.32 Core 1 module assembly with an extension

11.33 Core 1 half-shell module assembly

A UNIVERSE OF SHAPE-CHANGERS

The number of 3D shape-changer cores, shell modules, extensions and combinations, using flexibly connected simple polygons, seems endless. Exploring the universe of shape-changers will open up many new avenues of structural study and discovery – for example using 'open' regular or semi-regular polyhedra composed of flexibly connected regular polygons where more than three polygons meet at a vertex. Fig. *11.44* on p.255 shows two 'open' developments from a cuboctahedron. Another example is that of 'open' tessellating cubes composed of flexibly connected squares (fig. 11.46, p.256).

The structural stability of flexibly connected regular and semi-regular polyhedral lattices can be explored as well. We can also ask about other less regular polygonal forms and how they might behave when their composing polygons are flexibly connected.

To provide a number of starting points for further exploration of the shape-changing polyhedral universe the following illustrations of cores composed of regular polygons and equilateral quadrilaterals are presented (see figs 11.32 to 11.46). These cores can be further developed in three-dimensional space, as cores, as shell modules, as extended modules, and in the way they might combine. Extensions and

combinations can remain symmetrical but there will be opportunities to break or change the symmetries. The shape-changer universe has many possibilities and there is much to discover and apply.

The starting points are not drawn as nets but as polygonal maps where joins between polygonal edges are considered to be any sort of flexible connection. Fig. 11.32 shows a basic extension of core 1. Figs 11.33 and 11.34 show the assembly of half-shells of cores 1 and 2, and fig. 11.35 shows a tessellation of core 3.

Some of the shape-changing polyhedra can be grouped by their similarities. For example, the core 1 module shares a similar structure with the core 3 module – differing only in the angles of their

Core 2 half-shell

Core

45°

45°

45°

45°

45°

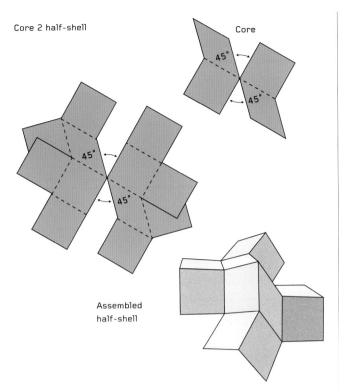

Assembled
half-shell

11.34 Core 2 half-shell assembly extended with squares

Core 3 plus module

Upper core

60°

Lower core

Tessellation of
assembled core 3
shell module

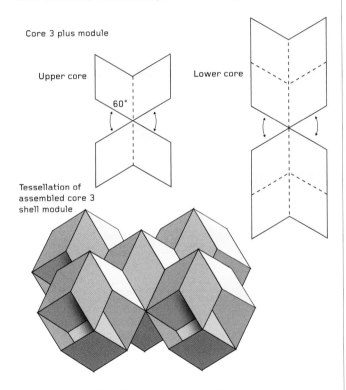

11.35 Core 3 shell module assembly and combinations

Core 3 plus module extensions

Core

60°

Extension 1 (upper)

90°

60°

Extension 2 (lower)

a

b

c

90°

60°

a

b

c

Assembled
upper shell connects
with lower shell.
Connect letter
edges

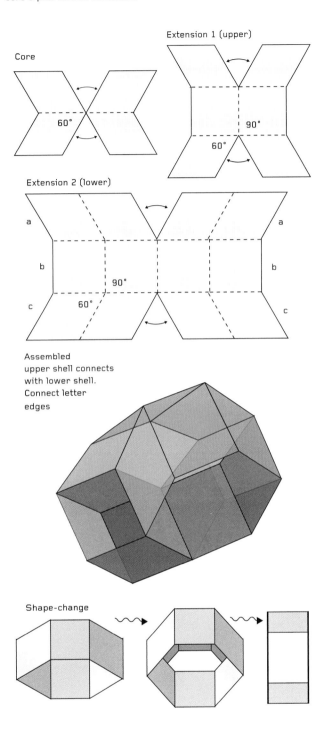

Shape-change

11.36 Core 3 module assembly with square extensions and
equilibrium positions

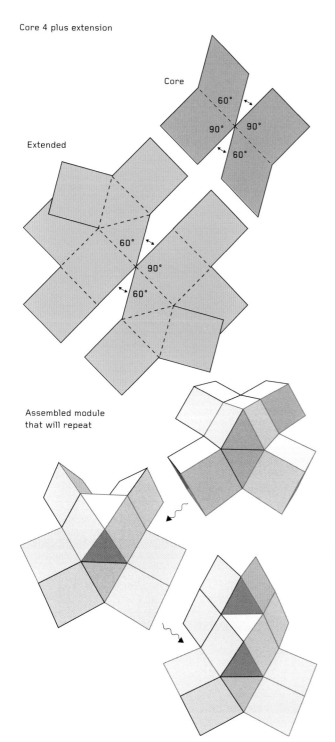

Core 4 plus extension

Core

60°

90° 90°

60°

Extended

60°

90°

60°

Assembled module
that will repeat

11.37 Core 4 half-shell assembly with squares and 60° rhombi

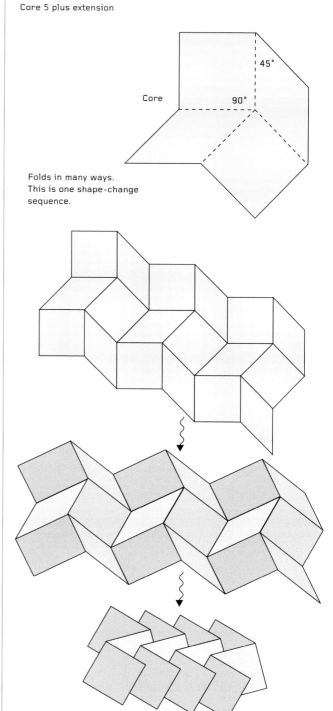

Core 5 plus extension

45°

Core

90°

Folds in many ways.
This is one shape-change
sequence.

11.38 Core 5 flat assembly with squares and 45° rhombi folds
up into 3D

rhombi. The angle differences impact the
way the modules transform and tessellate
in 3D space. Also, some rhombi can be
symmetrically reduced, for example, core
4 and 5 modules are very similar, but the
60° rhombi of the core 4 module have
been divided into two equilateral triangles
in the core 5 module. This division adds
new points about which rotations can

take place. Another variation would be
to divide the squares along a diagonal.

The core 3 extension shown in fig.
11.36 shares properties with the basic
core 3 design, with an interesting
property that when folded flat its 150°
angle corresponds with a dodecagon.

Core 4 (see fig. 11.37) demonstrates
a type of shape-changer that does not

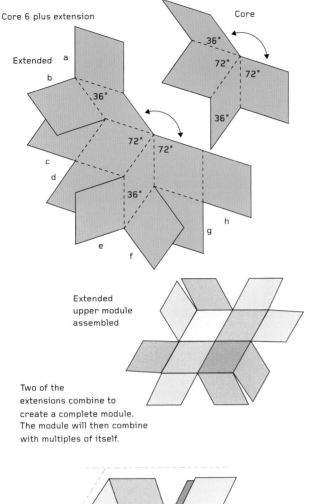

Core 6 plus extension

Core

Extended

a
b

36°

72° 72°

36°

36°

72° 72°

c

d

36°

h

g

e

f

Extended
upper module
assembled

Two of the
extensions combine to
create a complete module.
The module will then combine
with multiples of itself.

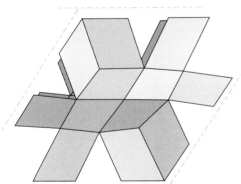

Core 6 modules stacked
in two equilibrium positions

11.39 Core 6 shell module assembly composed of 36° and 72° rhombi

11.40 Core 6 shell modules combined

tessellate but that will transform into various configurations..

Core 5 (see fig. 11.38) is similar to an origami design and will fold up from a 2D surface in a great variety of ways. It will also combine to create 3D shell-type modules with various types of symmetry.

The assembly of core 6 (see fig. 11.39) is shown with just two slightly

different positions of the core shell. The two positions show that, in this case, the rhombi connected to the core shell interfere with each other and thereby restrict the limits of the shape-change. Fig. 11.40 shows one way in which the module will combine.

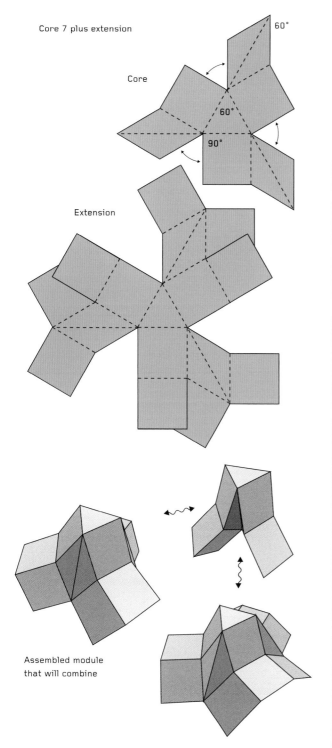

Core 7 plus extension

Core

60°

60°

90°

Extension

Assembled module
that will combine

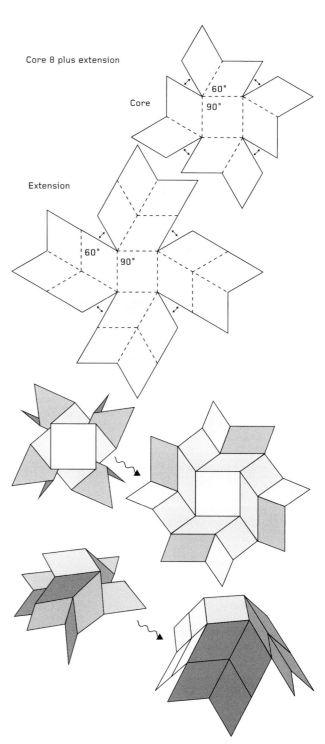

Core 8 plus extension

Core

60°

90°

Extension

60°

90°

11.41 Core 7 half-shell module assembly composed of squares, half 60° rhombi and equilateral triangles

11.42 Core 8 half-shell module assembly composed of 60° rhombi and squares. The module will twist

The fold lines down the middle of the 60° rhombi of the core 7 (see fig. 11.41) module enables the core to fold inside itself as it shape-changes.

Core 8 (see fig. 11.42) module twists as it shape-changes from an open to a closed position.

Core 9 (see fig. 11.43) is an origami-like assembly that folds up into various three-dimensional forms. The core will combine with matching cores in a way similar to a regular tessellation, or combine with a square configuration in a way similar to a semi-regular tessellation. Students at the Institute for Advanced Architecture of Catalonia (IAAC) in Barcelona used core 9 to create shape-changing furniture using

electroactive hinges that connect the polygonal panels. The electroactive hinges fold and unfold when powered (see fig. 11.58).

Core 10 shell module (see fig. 11.44) folds into a shape-changing module that will interconnect with duplicates of itself in ways similar to that of the core 1 module. In one of its equilibrium positions

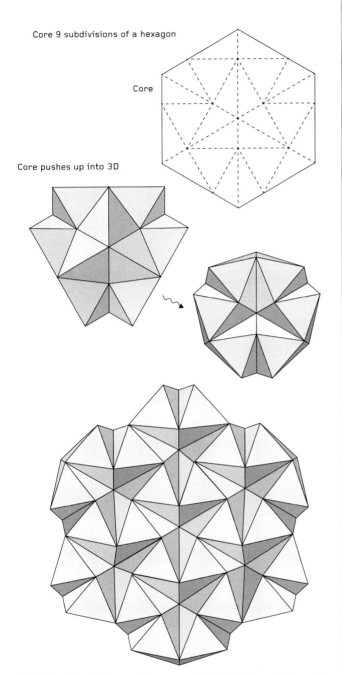

Core 9 subdivisions of a hexagon

Core

Core pushes up into 3D

11.43 Core 9 module assembly composed of subdivisions of a hexagon. Flat sheet folds up to various 3D configurations

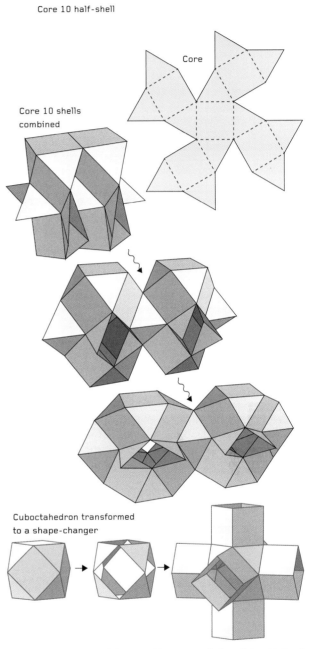

Core 10 half-shell

Core

Core 10 shells combined

Cuboctahedron transformed to a shape-changer

11.44 Core 10 shell module assembly composed of equilateral triangles and squares, with module combinations

Core 11 half-shell

Core 12 shell module showing three of five equilibrium positions

Core

108° 72°

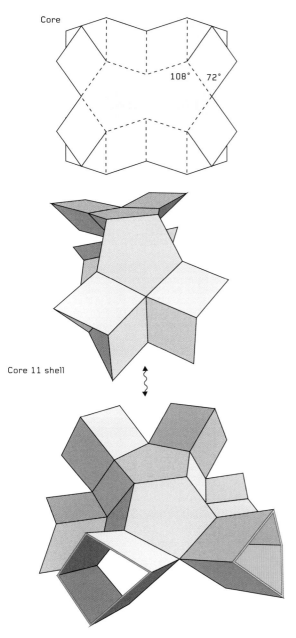

Core 11 shell

11.45 Core 11 shell module assembly composed of pentagons and 72° rhombi

11.46 Core 12 shell module assembly composed of 24 squares with equilibrium positions

the core 10 module matches that of the cuboctahedron. A transformation of a cuboctahedron into a shape-changer is also shown.

The core 11 shell module (see fig. 11.45) does not tessellate but can be extended and combined.

The core 12 shell module (see fig. 11.46) shape-changes from a cubical arrangement to a hexagonal configuration.

Fig. 11.47 shows something different in that it is composed of polyhedra that are flexibly connected and that will fold into the form of a cube and then shape-change into three quarters of a pyramid. Additional polyhedra can be flexibly connected to extend the shape-changing structure.

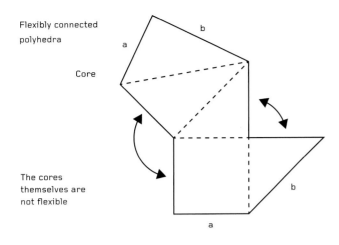

Flexibly connected polyhedra

Core

a

b

b

a

The cores themselves are not flexible

Three assembled cores combine to form a cube. If the cores are flexibly connected on the highlighted edges the assembly will unfold to make three-quarters of a pyramid.

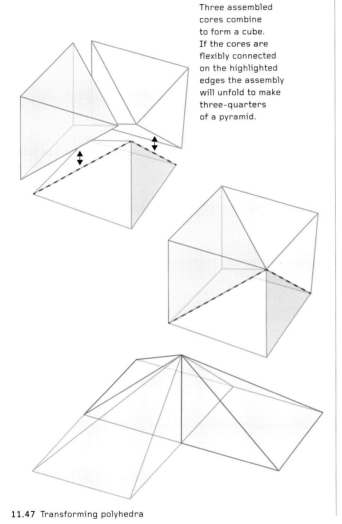

11.47 Transforming polyhedra

11.48 Abstract concept application in Hong Kong harbour

POSSIBLE APPLICATIONS OF SHAPE-CHANGING POLYHEDRA

Shape-changers can be configured to alter solar profiles, reduce or increase internal volumes, and maybe even form structures for cellular materials. Shape-changing polyhedra can be scaled up or down using macro-sized panels for architectural or robotic forms or micro-sized panels that will add shape-changing characteristics to surfaces and materials. Using microcontroller-controlled hydraulics, large shape-changing structures can be programmed to adjust their form to protect themselves from extreme weather (see fig. 11.48), transform their solar profile, or maximize or minimize their internal volume.

The idea that large shape-changer structures can be powered by hydraulics creates the possibility that architectural structures will be assembled in the flat and then shape-changed into one of a number of three-dimensional forms. Applications taking advantage of a fold-flat property with lightweight structures and hand assembly might include tents, storage spaces, emergency shelters and exhibition spaces. Once expanded into three dimensions, shape-changers can be triangulated in various ways to fix their expanded form.

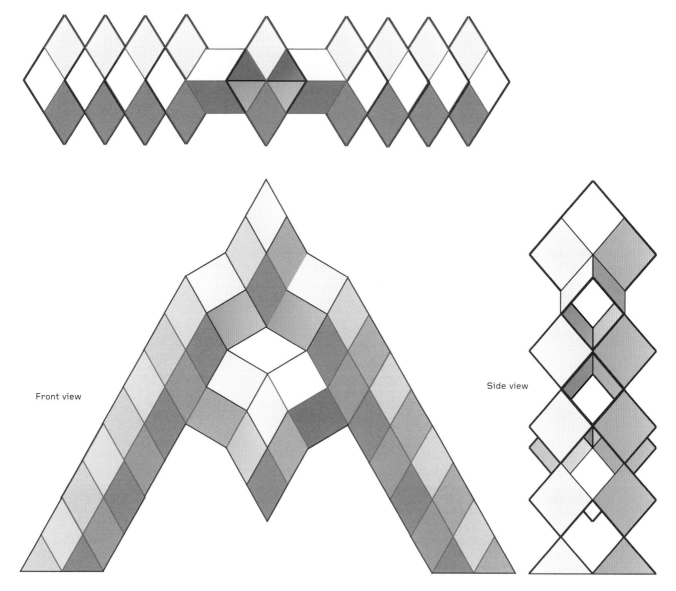

Front view

Side view

11.49 Core 2 shell module combined structure

Flexibility of hinges and rigidity and weight of polygons The nature of a shape-changer is very much determined by the flexibility of the connecting hinges, and the weight, rigidity and strength of the polygonal panels as well as the spacing between them. Flexibility of 100% will result in stable equilibrium positions, meaning that once a module is in an equilibrium position it will stay in it. Flexibilities under 100% will add elasticity to the shape-changer all the way down to 0% flexibility, where hinges will be fixed.

A flexibility of the hinge in the order of 80% will result in a shape-changer that will wobble when touched and that will easily transform from one equilibrium position to another.

The hinge spacing between panels is determined by the thickness of the panels — so that the spacing should be at least equal to the thickness of the material or the combined thickness depending upon the positioning of the hinge.

The weight of the polygonal panels creates stress on the hinges, particularly the lower hinges, so the panels for large structures need to be lightweight if the structures are to fully retain their shape-changing properties. For a similar reason the bigger and heavier the shape-changer then the more rigid the polygonal panels need to be as they will otherwise distort.

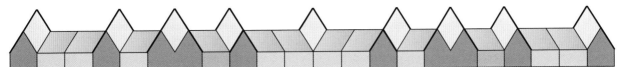

Core 2 shape-changer module combinations

Front view

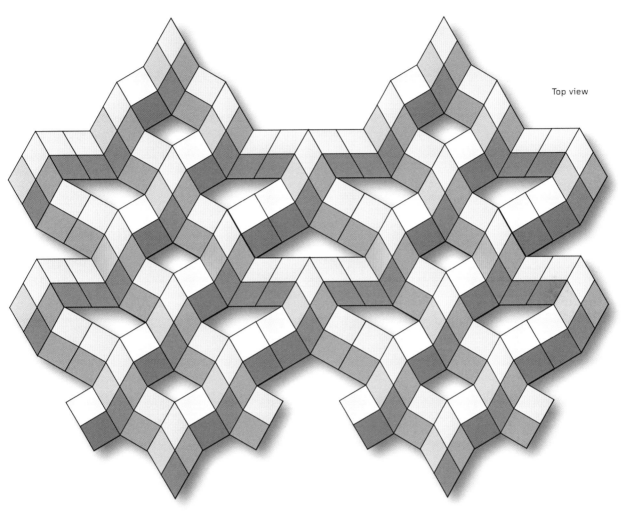

Top view

11.50 Core 2 shell module tessellating structure

'All things must change to something new, to something strange.'

HENRY WADSWORTH LONGFELLOW

(1807–1882)

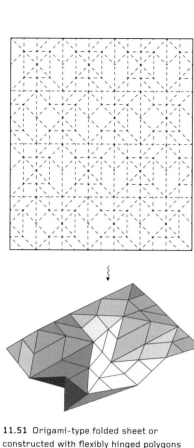

11.51 Origami-type folded sheet or constructed with flexibly hinged polygons

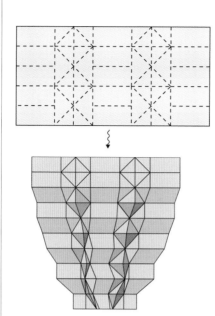

11.52 Origami-type folded sheet or constructed with flexibly hinged polygons

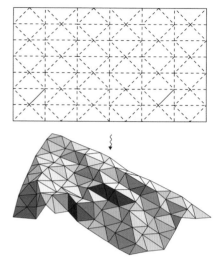

11.53 Origami-type folded sheet or constructed with flexibly hinged polygons. The core tessellates

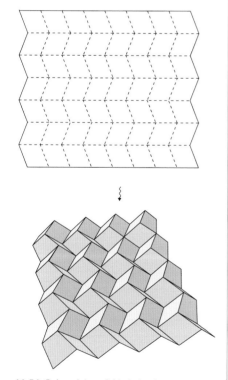

11.54 Origami-type folded sheet or constructed with flexibly hinged polygons

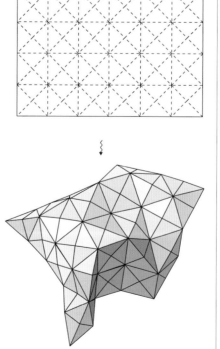

11.55 Origami-type flexibly hinged polygons. MIT application

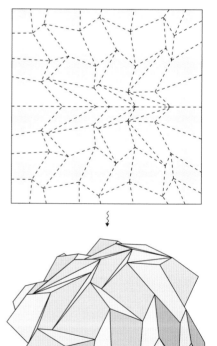

11.56 Origami-type folded sheet or constructed with flexibly hinged polygons

Flat sheet applications Sharing characteristics with the polyhedron shape-changers are origami-like polygonal 2D tessellations that can fold into 3D polyhedra. The 3D forms generated can be random or can repeat, as shown in figs 11.38, 11.43 and 11.51 to 11.56.

Robert Wood of Harvard University and Daniella Rus and Erik Demaine of the Massachusetts Institute of Technology (MIT) have developed a sheet, based on the tessellation shown in fig. 11.55, that has successfully folded itself, using electroformers, into both a paper aeroplane and a traditional origami boat. In theory, the sheet could generate a nearly infinite combination of shapes, just like a person folding paper by hand. The same researchers have developed a self-folding robot prototype that will fold into 3D from a 2D sheet – and then walk away (see fig. 11.57). The prototype uses heat-activated polymers.

At the Institute for Advanced Architecture of Catalonia (IAAC) in Barcelona, students have developed shape-changing furniture using shape-changing polymers/alloys that connect polygonal panels (see fig. 11.58). The core structure of the IAAC design is shown in fig. 11.43.

Technologies currently available for programmed folding and unfolding include the following:

(i) Programmable electroactive and heat-activated polymers that act as controlled hinges and that remember specific shapes and bend back to them after being heat or electrically deformed.

(ii) Thin sheets of shape-memory alloys, such as copper-aluminium-nickel, which, when folded and held in a vice at high temperature, hold an imprinted memory of their folded shape:
(a) a one-way shape-memory alloy, in its cold state, can be bent or stretched and hold those shapes until heated above the transition temperature. Upon heating, the shape changes back to its original. When the metal cools again it remains in the hot (original) shape until deformed again;
(b) a two-way shape-memory alloy remembers two different shapes: one at low temperatures, and one at high

11.57 MIT's fold-up robot

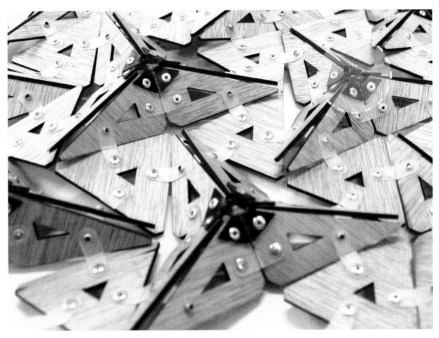

11.58 IAAC's shape-changing furniture

temperatures. Stickers embedded with circuitry trigger the folding. The desired shape can be formed by placing the stickers on the correct actuators in a specific order, in a form of mechanical programming.

The various techniques at present under development could eventually lead to a wide variety of practical shape-shifting objects. Potential applications are endless, and include things such as packages that expand or contract to fit their contents; super-tools that change their shape based on the required function; robots and solar panels that fold up from a single sheet; shape-transforming furniture; and transforming architectural forms.

THE FUTURE OF SHAPE-CHANGERS

The future promises the continued development of shape-changing materials and powered hinges such as electropolymers, shape-memory alloys, Claytronics, hydraulic and pneumatic systems, lightweight servos, and other technologies that will transform our structural world.

More broadly known as programmable matter, Claytronics is an abstract future concept developed by researchers at Carnegie Mellon University in Pittsburgh, Pennsylvania, that combines modular robotics, nanotechnology and computer science to create individual nanometer-scale computers called claytronic atoms, or catoms. These can interact with each other to form tangible, dynamic three-dimensional objects.

TFOT (*The Future of Things*) magazine has reported on various technologies that can change shape, including a flexible computer that could be wrapped round a soda can, or change its shape to better collect data in different situations.

German-based industrial automation company Festo uses servo and cable mechanisms to drive and direct lightweight helium-filled aircraft (see fig. 11.59). The company has also developed shape-changing underwater craft that simulate the swimming motions of fish and dolphins.

The Spidron hexagon shown in fig. 11.60 was first modelled in 1979 by Dániel Erdély, a student of Ernö Rubik, the inventor of the Rubik's Cube. It is a flat geometric figure composed of quadrilaterals each formed from an equilateral triangle and a one-third triangular segment of an equilateral triangle. The 2D Spidron hexagon folds up into a 3D form as shown.

There are shape-changing forms that expand and contract like Chinese lanterns. Fig. 11.61 shows a configuration similar to such a structure.

11.59 Festo, flying manta ray

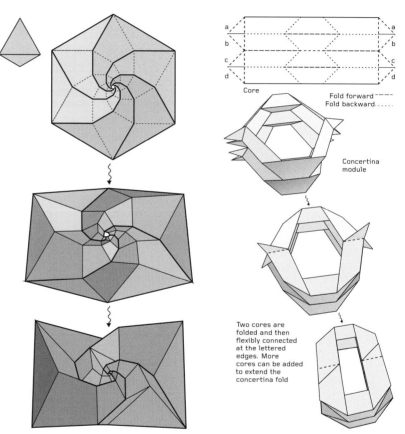

11.60 Dániel Erdély's Spidron

11.61 Lantern-fold or flexibly hinged polygons

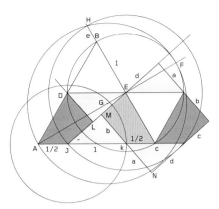

11.62 The Haberdasher's Puzzle tile construction

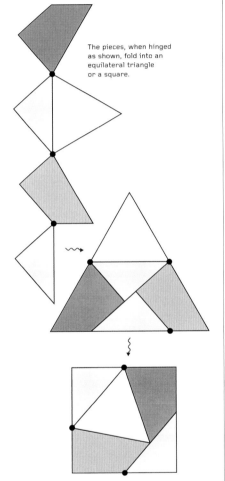

The pieces, when hinged as shown, fold into an equilateral triangle or a square.

11.63 The Haberdasher's Puzzle

11.64 The Haberdasher's Puzzle

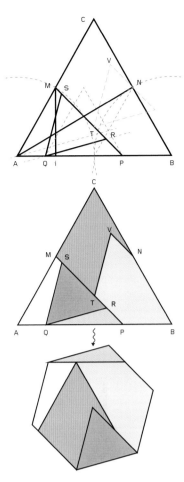

11.65 A Lindgren dissection

The Haberdasher's Puzzle A dissection puzzle is a puzzle in which a set of shapes can be assembled in different ways to produce at least two geometric forms. The earliest known descriptions of dissection puzzles appear in ancient Greece and China. In Greece there was the challenge to create a visual proof of the Pythagorean theorem; in China there were tangrams. In 1903 British mathematician and puzzle creator Henry Dudeney proposed and then developed a solution to the 'Haberdasher's Puzzle' dissection challenge: how do you cut an equilateral triangle into four pieces that can be rearranged to make a square? Dudeney's solution is shown in figs 11.62 and 11.63: when hinged, the shapes can fold into either a square or an equilateral triangle. Fig. 11.64 shows a 2D tessellation of the equilateral triangle arrangement. The construction of the Dudeney solution shown in figs 11.62 and 11.63 works as follows:

Bisect AB in D and BC in E; produce the line AE to F making EF equal to EB; bisect AF in G and describe arc AHF;

produce EB to H, and EH is the length of the side of the required square; from E with distance EH, describe the arc HJ, and make JK equal to BE; now from the points D and K drop perpendiculars on EJ at L and M.

A remarkable feature of the solution is that each of the pieces can be hinged at one vertex, forming a chain that can be folded into the square or the original triangle. Two of the hinges bisect sides of the triangle, while the third hinge and the corner of the large piece on the base cut the base in the approximate ratio 0.982:2:1.018. Dudeney showed just such a model of the solution, made of polished mahogany with brass hinges, at a meeting of the Royal Society in 1905.

The illustration in fig. 11.65 shows one of the dissections of Harry Lindgren, a British/Australian engineer and mathematician. The dissection illustrated is that of an equilateral triangle that can be rearranged as a hexagon.

12. DYNAMIC CIRCLES AND SPHERES

A GEOMETRIC EVOLUTION – A DYNAMIC UNIVERSE

Circles, in all sorts of arrangements, were a common feature of Stone Age art. Ancient Babylonians, Egyptians and Harappans studied their properties. The Greeks and Chinese developed axiomatic definitions of them, as well as of spheres, and their definitions inspired the development of geometry, astronomy and calculus. This chapter explores some of the extraordinary properties of circles and spheres by considering them dynamically – as forms that are in a state of change, where they change size and position, and then combine to create previously unknown close-packing circle and sphere arrangements. From such arrangements new and unique space-filling lattices can be derived for architecture, science and design.

CIRCLES AND SPHERES

It is possible that the circle represents the most perfect form of visual logic and, as such, precedes all others. We see circles in the eyes of our parents at birth. We see the circle of the sun dominating the daytime sky, and the moon at night. Even the ripples from rain drops form circles.

All of the great historical cultures have made use of circles. We see them in the ancient ruins of Göbekli Tepe in eastern Turkey (see p.52); in the remains of Vedic fire altars, with the accompanying need to 'square' the circle (see pp.68–73); in Euclidean circle constructions; and in celestial navigation and theories of gravity and radiation.

Spheres, from a visual logic point of view, are the optimum extension of a circle in three-dimensional space. We can see spheres in soap bubbles, frog's eggs, and fruit such as oranges and cherries, but the idea that such things as the sun, atoms and paths of radiation have sphere-like properties necessitated a fairly sophisticated development of visual logic, deduction and observation.

Spheres appear all around us because matter tends to adopt this structurally efficient form. Stresses are evenly distributed on a sphere's surface both internally and externally; spheres have a smaller surface area per unit volume than any other shape; and energy transference at the surface of a sphere is at a minimum. Gravity also acts through the centre of mass, meaning that everything around a centre point is pulled inwards. Consequently, the arrangement or shape that enables the maximum amount of matter to get as close as possible to the centre is a sphere. Also, energy generated from a point source emanates at the same rate (unless obstructed) and therefore emanates as an expanding spherical form. Soap bubbles are spherical because there is an attractive force (surface tension) that pulls the water molecules into the tightest possible grouping. And the tightest possible grouping that any collection of particles can achieve is to pack together into a sphere, whether

12.1 Golden ratio spheres

12.2 The human iris

12.3 *Clivia nobilis* berries

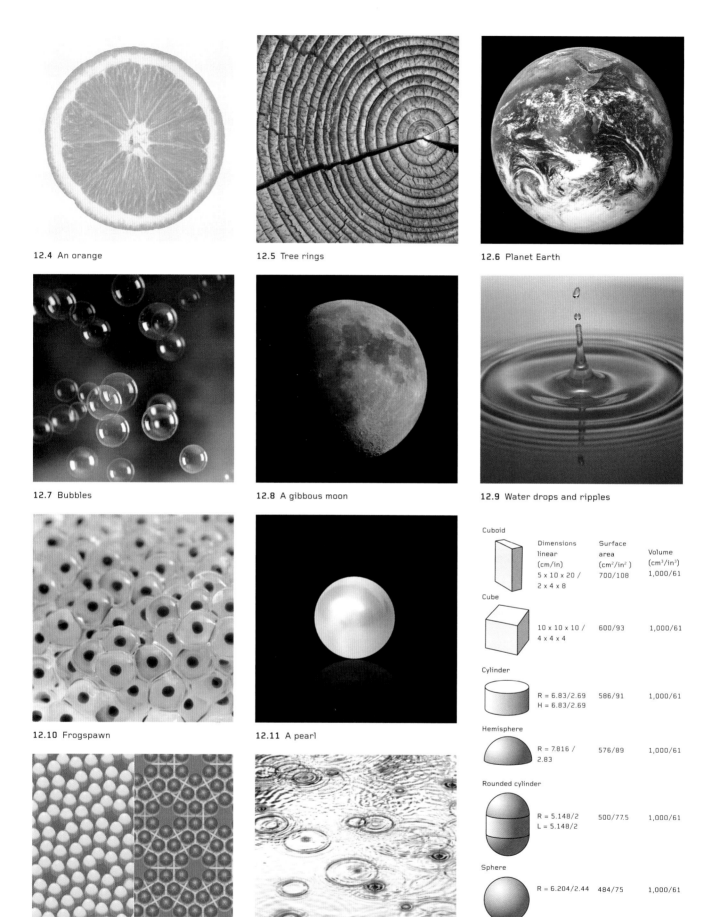

12.4 An orange

12.5 Tree rings

12.6 Planet Earth

12.7 Bubbles

12.8 A gibbous moon

12.9 Water drops and ripples

12.10 Frogspawn

12.11 A pearl

	Dimensions linear (cm/in)	Surface area (cm²/in²)	Volume (cm³/in³)
Cuboid	5 x 10 x 20 / 2 x 4 x 8	700/108	1,000/61
Cube	10 x 10 x 10 / 4 x 4 x 4	600/93	1,000/61
Cylinder	R = 6.83/2.69 H = 6.83/2.69	586/91	1,000/61
Hemisphere	R = 7.816 / 2.83	576/89	1,000/61
Rounded cylinder	R = 5.148/2 L = 5.148/2	500/77.5	1,000/61
Sphere	R = 6.204/2.44	484/75	1,000/61

12.12 Atoms on the face of a crystal

12.13 Ripples in water

12.14 Space-efficient geometrical solids

they are the electron clouds surrounding an atom or the gelatinous material that surrounds a frog's embryos in frogspawn. See figs 12.2 to 12.13.

Fig. 12.14 shows the comparative spatial efficiences of geometrical solids with the sphere as the most efficient.

Space-efficient geometrical forms applied to architecture Western culture's bias towards building rectangular structures translates to readily available rectangular building materials and associated constructional and technological expertise. When hemispherical or spherical geodesics have been constructed using standard rectangular building techniques they have often leaked, wasted materials, and presented constructional and aesthetic design challenges when accommodating rectangular doors, windows and fittings. Construction methods and materials need to be as efficient as the forms that are to be constructed, and many new materials are now available that make building spherical, hemispherical and otherwise curved architectural forms possible.

The Monolithic Dome Institute, based in Texas, constructs domes for housing or virtually any other use with a tough 'Airform' that after inflation is lined with insulating materials, steel-reinforcing lattices, and sprayed-on Shotcrete (a fast-hardening concrete). Projected moon base construction is

envisioned with inflatables covered in moon dust fused by mobile 3D printers. Inflatables as orbital space stations or as space vehicles makes sense because they can be compacted for transit off the Earth's surface and inflated once in space.

Figs 12.15 to 12.21 show examples of circles and spheres in architecture.

Cylinder (fig. 12.15): The Rivergate Tower in Tampa, Florida, designed by Harry Wolf with proportions based on the Fibonacci series.

Toroid (fig. 12.16): The Nautilus-X is a multi-mission space exploration vehicle concept developed by engineers Mark Holderman and Edward Henderson of NASA's Technology Applications Assessment Team.

Dome (fig. 12.17): The Centro de la Familia de Utah, hosting a Migrant Head Start Center, comprises a complex of four monolithic domes designed by architect Leland A. Gray.

Dome (fig. 12.18): Industrial partners including renowned architects Foster and Partners have joined with the European Space Agency (ESA) to test the

12.15 Rivergate Tower, Tampa, Florida, USA

12.17 Centro de la Familia de Utah, Genola, Utah, USA

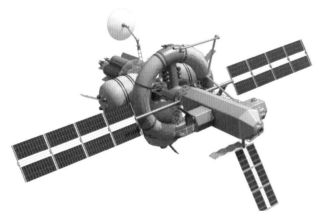

12.16 The Nautilus-X concept space vehicle with inflatable structures

12.18 Lunar outpost concept dome

feasibility of fusing lunar soil to create lunar habitats. The core elements are an inflatable dome and cylindrical modules that can be transported uninflated to the moon's surface. Once inflated, the dome and cylindrical forms are to be covered with layers of lunar regolith (loose, dustlike layer that covers rock) particles that are then fused by a robot-operated 3D laser printer to create a protective ceramic shell.

Sphere (fig. 12.19): Aquapods are fish farm habitats developed by Ocean Farm Technology Inc., and are constructed with a synthetic wood geodesic lattice that is covered with a copper alloy mesh, and equipped with ballast tanks.

Sphere (fig. 12.20): The Triton 3300/3 made by Triton Submarines is a three-person submarine with a diving depth of up to 1,000 m (3,300 ft).

Sphere (fig. 12.21): The Bigelow Expandable Activity Module (BEAM) is an expandable space station module being developed by Bigelow Aerospace, under contract to NASA.

CLOSE-PACKING SPHERES

Close-packed spheres are arrangements of spheres that take up the greatest possible fraction of a three-dimensional space. Given any sort of attractive force, spheres will tend to close-pack whether they are the boundaries of atoms or frogspawn. To achieve the maximum density of close-packing, spheres will adopt positions whereby a maximum number will touch each other and thereby triangulating their centres. Close-packing arrangements and their corresponding lattices appear in nature, from honeycombs and flies' eyes to the packing of atoms and molecules, and have been of use in creating new materials, architectural structures, tube and cylinder configurations for transporting people, fluids and gases, and much more. Certain hexagonal and cubic close-packings of equal-sized spheres have been known for millennia.

Structurally, close-packed spheres are stable and space-efficient, while their centres and contact points create infinite space-filling lattices. Lattices derived from close-packed arrangements of molecules and atoms, or any close-packed arrangements, form many types of polyhedron. Close-packed structures

12.19 Aquapod fish farm habitats

12.20 Triton 3300/3 submarine

12.21 Bigelow Expandable Activity Module

make some of the most space-efficient lattices possible.

There has been a fascination with close-packing arrangements of circles and spheres for centuries, if not millennia, as can be seen in the works of Euclid (325–265 BCE) and René Descartes (1596–1650), and more recently in the works of Frederick Soddy (1877–1956), Paul Koebe (1882–1945), Evgeny Andreev (b. 1944) and William Thurston (1946–91). The author's interest in the subject was initially triggered by the works of Jules Borgoin (1838–1908) and the close-packing circle constructions used in ancient Islamic designs (see chapter 7). Following in the steps of Borgoin, interest focused on close-packing arrangements within symmetrical cells or clusters that would interconnect and fill space infinitely. The study of close-packed circle and sphere arrangements within cells or clusters that will fill space, at micro or macro scales, opens up the possibility of an extraordinary new range of structural lattices from which a vast range of internal and external structural forms can be extracted, each with its own properties of light, sound, spatial efficiency, structural integrity, interconnecting spaces and spatial variations. So architectural spaces such as exhibition areas, a space station module, or creative office or living spaces can be extracted from an almost infinite number of three-dimensional polygonal spaces. Areas can be interconnected with latticed corridors to other three-dimensional polygonal spaces, all within the same close-packing lattice – a circumstance that will bring with it its own harmony and sense of design integrity. In other words it will open up structural opportunites never dreamed of before and provide a paradigm shift from the proportional harmonies envisioned by architects and thinkers such as Vitruvius and Le Corbusier.

We live in an age of new technologies in which we can actually create structures out of individual atoms or out of nanoparticles. We can 3D print or laser fuse particles to create integrated, one-piece structures no longer limited by traditional modular building materials. We can even use microbes to bind particles into structures (see chapter 13). The

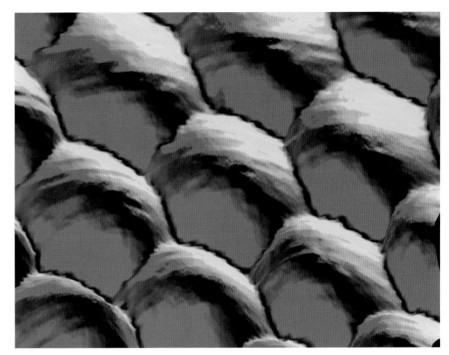

12.22 Don Eigler, *Blue Platinum* – IBM scanning tunnelling microscope image of atoms on the surface of platinum

12.23 A honeycomb shows a close-packing arrangement

new types of close-packing arrangement described in this chapter can be used to generate lattices that be rigid, or that can twist, bend or stretch. These properties have the potential to have an impact on everything from architectural spaces to aircraft design.

DYNAMIC CLOSE-PACKING SPHERE GEOMETRY

As with all the geometries described in this book, there are latent possibilities for close-packing circles and spheres. In the past, three-dimensional applications have been primarily linked to static arrangements of close-packing circles and spheres. What if we consider close-packing circles and spheres of different sizes and allow them to dynamically change from one close-packing relationship to another?

The 'dynamic sphere geometry' developed by the author starting in the late 1960s generates new and unique close-packing circle and sphere arrangements. It is based on algorithmic steps and defined parameters by which circles and spheres are allowed to change size and position within imposed limitations of symmetry and momentum. The parameters of the geometry can be changed, new limits imposed, and new symmetries, non-symmetries and the like created to explore a broad range of sphere arrangements.

The geometry can serve to 'hunt' indefinitely for new and unique geometrical arrangements and unique correspondences in two- and three-dimensional space.

The dynamic close-packing sphere geometry is a little complex when considering spheres moving around and changing size in three-dimensional space, but in two dimensions the dynamics are easier to understand, making the transition to thinking in three dimensions a lot easier. So we will start in two dimensions with just one set of algorithms, and then look at some of the surprising close-packing arrangements generated.

The following first set of algorithms is given descriptively rather than specifically:

(i) The building blocks of the geometry, in the first case, are defined as circles that constantly change position and size, from infinitely small to infinitely large, according to characteristics equivalent to the laws of momentum.

(ii) The disposition of the system is towards stability and conservation of energy. This is represented

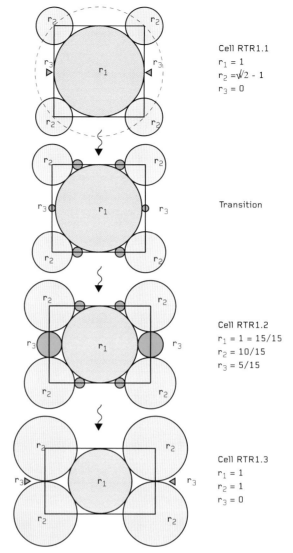

Cell RTR1.1
$r_1 = 1$
$r_2 = \sqrt{2} - 1$
$r_3 = 0$

Transition

Cell RTR1.2
$r_1 = 1 = 15/15$
$r_2 = 10/15$
$r_3 = 5/15$

Cell RTR1.3
$r_1 = 1$
$r_2 = 1$
$r_3 = 0$

12.24 A first close-packing sequence of circles

by a disposition towards close-packing. However, the 'momentum' of the geometry is such that circles can transform through unstable, non-close-packing arrangements, towards new, close-packing arrangements, and then on again.

(iii) The boundaries of the system are represented by lines of symmetry – so either circle centres fall on lines of symmetry, or centres and circumferences are contained within lines of symmetry. Also, circles preserve their own surface/circumference integrity, so that circumferences are not allowed to overlap or penetrate each other. If a circle is increasing in size it will force other circles into reducing their size and/or changing their position.

(iv) The dynamics of the system are such that circles with primary momentum

dominate their space until they have reached the limits of their growth, which is determined by the limits of symmetry that have been imposed. Within this set of rules and limits, circles only build momentum and grow into significance if dominating circles have reached their limits, or if there is an immediate close-packing 'need' for their existence.

(v) Any rule applied to the system can be changed.

For an example of an algorithmic set see chapter 14.

First 2D sequence We will start by looking at a start-up sequence (see fig. 12.24). The constraining symmetry is that of a rectangle – of which a square is a special case. Cell RTR1.1 represents one 'cell' of a plane of close-packing circles contained within a square symmetry. According to the principles of the geometry, this particular arrangement just represents a moment in time when close-packing has occurred. In the example we can say that the four corner circles, r_2, have the momentum, and will therefore grow towards new and different close-packing relationships until they reach the parameters of their maximum growth. r_3 is also allowed to grow (fill space) but has no priority of growth. Other limitations imposed for this start-up sequence are that the r_1 circle retains contact with one set of opposite sides of the containing rectangular symmetry, and that the vertices of the rectangle maintain contact with a circumscribed circle (not shown). The first start-up sequence includes a moment of transition as the first close-packing arrangement, cell RTR1.1, transforms to the next close-packing arrangement, cell RTR1.2.

Once a new close-packing arrangement has been generated by the geometry,

the properties of the packing can be examined. As it happens, cell RTR1.2 is unique in that the circles are all in whole number relationships.

Note: The wiggly arrow that appears in many illustrations indicates transition periods between close-packing arrangements where circles are changing size and position but in positions that are not stable.

In fig. 12.25 we see the first 2D sequence completed. The circumscribed circle is used to control the relative proportions of the cells and is shown surrounding cell RTR1.1. The first sequence continues where r_3 (blue) is given the first priority of growth and grows through the close-packing cells RTR1.2, RTR1.3 and RTR1.4, where it reaches its maximum growth by touching the top and bottom points of the rectangular symmetry. In cell RTR1.4, r_2 is squeezed out of existence but returns

after r_4 (green) is given a priority of growth, growing through close-packings RTR1.5, RTR1.6 and RTR1.7, where it reaches its maximum growth. To complete the possibilities within this cell sequence, r_2 can be given a priority of growth, but this is not shown. As mentioned, cell RTR1.2 circles are in whole number relationships. Cells RTR1.1 and RTR1.4 will generate a lattice of squares and octagons – a semi-regular tessellation. Cell RTR1.7 will generate a square and equilateral triangle lattice – another semi-regular tessellation. Cell RTR1.6 generates a tessellating rectangular lattice, the golden rectangle. (The 'golden' packing is described on pp.135–37.)

The equations for the close-packing circle cells in the first sequence are shown overleaf. See p.284 and figs 12.55 and 12.56 for the three-dimensional 'golden sphere' close-packing equivalent of RTR1.6.

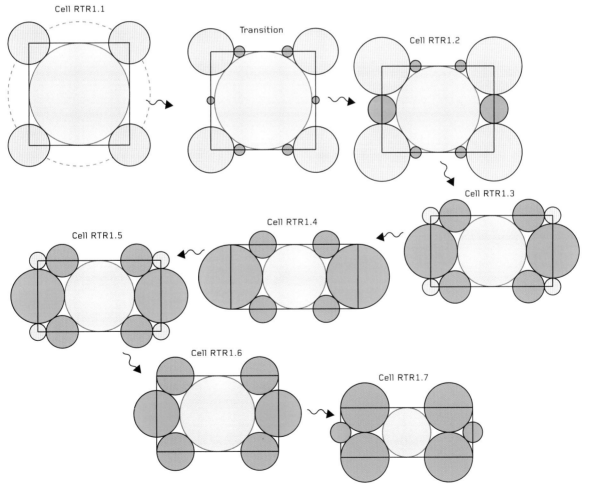

12.25 A first close-packing complete sequence

Cell RTR1.1

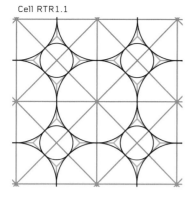

Cell RTR1.2

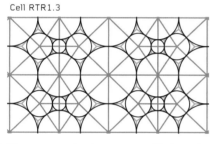

Cell RTR1.3

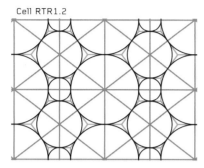

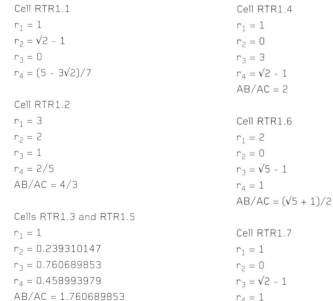

Cell RTR1.4

Cell RTR1.5

Cell RTR1.6

Cell RTR1.7

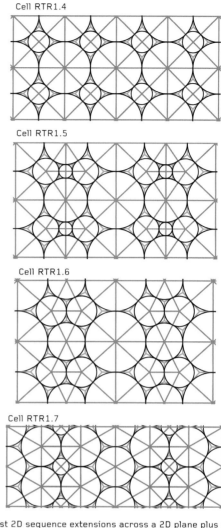

12.26 First 2D sequence extensions across a 2D plane plus circle centre lattices

12.27 First 2D sequence extensions across a 2D plane plus circle centre lattices

Cell RTR1.1
$r_1 = 1$
$r_2 = \sqrt{2} - 1$
$r_3 = 0$
$r_4 = (5 - 3\sqrt{2})/7$

Cell RTR1.2
$r_1 = 3$
$r_2 = 2$
$r_3 = 1$
$r_4 = 2/5$
$AB/AC = 4/3$

Cells RTR1.3 and RTR1.5
$r_1 = 1$
$r_2 = 0.239310147$
$r_3 = 0.760689853$
$r_4 = 0.458993979$
$AB/AC = 1.760689853$

Cell RTR1.4
$r_1 = 1$
$r_2 = 0$
$r_3 = 3$
$r_4 = \sqrt{2} - 1$
$AB/AC = 2$

Cell RTR1.6
$r_1 = 2$
$r_2 = 0$
$r_3 = \sqrt{5} - 1$
$r_4 = 1$
$AB/AC = (\sqrt{5} + 1)/2$

Cell RTR1.7
$r_1 = 1$
$r_2 = 0$
$r_3 = \sqrt{2} - 1$
$r_4 = 1$
$AB/AC = 1 + \sqrt{3}$

The cells of the first 2D sequence, RTR1.1 to RTR1.7, tessellate infinitely across a 2D plane. The lattices of the cells are the lines that connect circle centres, circle contact points and tangents at circle contact points. Lattices reveal the structural characteristics of the circle packings and how the relationships between circles change from one close-packing to another. Simple circle centre to circle centre lattices are shown in figs 12.26 and 12.27.

Variations of sequences Following
the basic principle that close-packing
circle sequences can be generated
from any 2D cell by allowing new circle
growth, according to changeable sets
of parameters, then an almost infinite
number of potential close-packing circle
arrangements can be generated. For
example, cell RTR1.6 from sequence
RTR1 can be used to generate a new
sequence, as shown in fig. 12.28.

Examples of parameters that limit or
direct change include any symmetrical
or non-symmetrical boundary; the
circumferences of the circles; the nature
of the start-up close-packing cell in 2D
space; the dynamics of the system as
to the circles that are given the most
energy; the elasticity and 'bounce' of
the circles; and how strictly the rules
of close-packing are imposed.

Once new close-packing circle cells
have been generated then lattices, internal
structures and polygons can be extracted.
Also, new variations can be added, such as
the way the circles can be accommodated
in 2D space: for example, they can be
given a surface tension and allowed, like
soap bubbles, to fuse to form even more
economical space-filling structures.

Algorithms See p.318 for a set of
algorithms needed to generate a basic
close-packing sequence.

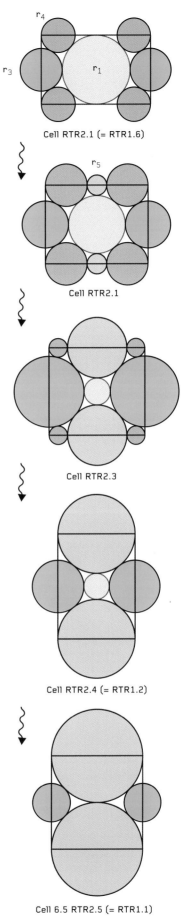

Cell RTR2.1 (= RTR1.6)

Cell RTR2.1

Cell RTR2.3

Cell RTR2.4 (= RTR1.2)

Cell 6.5 RTR2.5 (= RTR1.1)

12.28 Using a cell from the first sequence to generate a new sequence

Extending 2D sequences To demonstrate just how large the close-packing universe can be, the illustrations in figs 12.29, 12.30 12.32 and 12.33 show square symmetry sequences, a single hexagonal packing, and a short hexagonal sequence. Fig. 12.31 shows the extensions across the plane and circle centre lattices for the fig. 12.30 sequence.

Square symmetry sequence S1

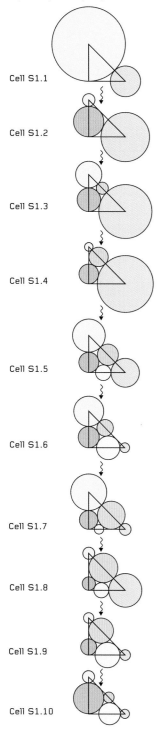

Cell S1.1

Cell S1.2

Cell S1.3

Cell S1.4

Cell S1.5

Cell S1.6

Cell S1.7

Cell S1.8

Cell S1.9

Cell S1.10

12.30 A sequence generated within square cells

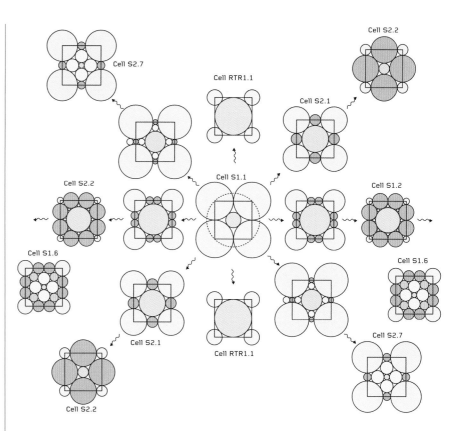

12.29 Sequence S1 generated within square cells

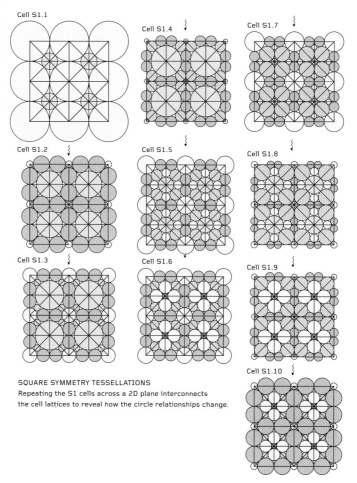

SQUARE SYMMETRY TESSELLATIONS
Repeating the S1 cells across a 2D plane interconnects the cell lattices to reveal how the circle relationships change.

12.31 The sequence of fig. 12.30 extended across the plane plus circle centre lattices

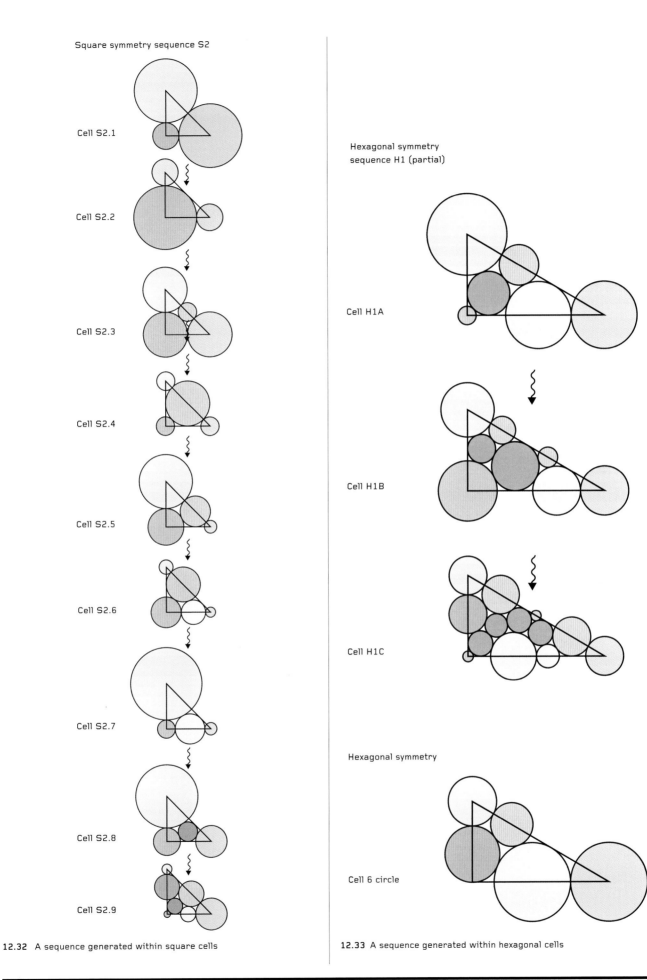

Square symmetry sequence S2

Cell S2.1

Cell S2.2

Cell S2.3

Cell S2.4

Cell S2.5

Cell S2.6

Cell S2.7

Cell S2.8

Cell S2.9

12.32 A sequence generated within square cells

Hexagonal symmetry
sequence H1 (partial)

Cell H1A

Cell H1B

Cell H1C

Hexagonal symmetry

Cell 6 circle

12.33 A sequence generated within hexagonal cells

Square symmetry sequence S1.5 circles

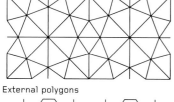

Circle centre connections

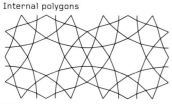

External polygons

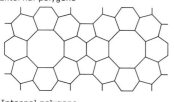

Internal polygons

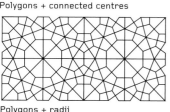

Polygons + connected centres

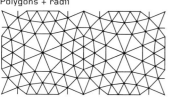

Polygons + radii

12.34 Square symmetry sequence S1.5

Square symmetry sequence S1.5

Internal polygons + radii

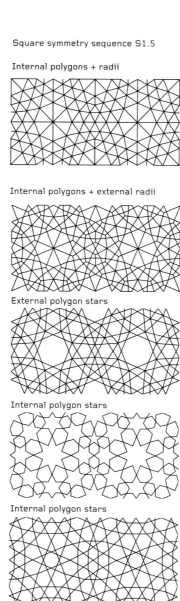

Internal polygons + external radii

External polygon stars

Internal polygon stars

Internal polygon stars

External polygon radii

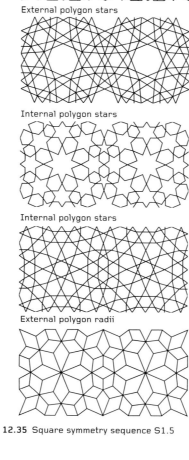

12.35 Square symmetry sequence S1.5

Square symmetry sequence S1.6

Circles

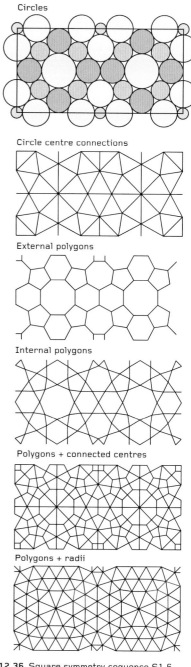

Circle centre connections

External polygons

Internal polygons

Polygons + connected centres

Polygons + radii

12.36 Square symmetry sequence S1.6

Individual cell lattices Comparing different cell lattices reveals some of the relationships between close-packing circles, and how they change as the cells transform from one close-packing arrangement into another. Lattices can also be analysed for their structural properties.

The lattices of cells S1.5 and S1.6 show how the circle connections change between two cells of the square symmetry sequence S1. (See figs 12.34, 12.35, 12.36 and 12.37.)

Square symmetry sequence S1.6

Internal polygons + radii

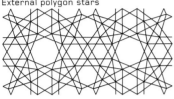

Internal polygons + external radii

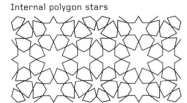

External polygon stars

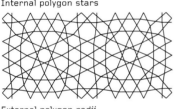

Internal polygon stars

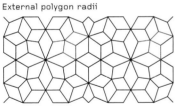

Internal polygon stars

External polygon radii

12.37 Square symmetry sequence S1.6

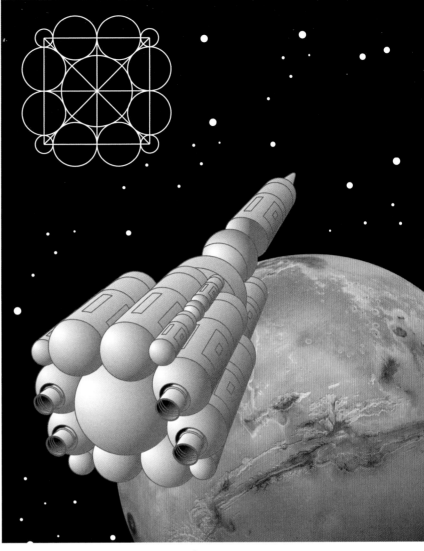

12.38 Rocket tank and booster arrangement

A universe of close-packing circles

It is unclear just how many close-packing circle arrangements can be generated by the dynamic close-packing sphere geometry – there are possibly hundreds of thousands that have structures of interest.

The structure of each generated close-packing circle cell will have unique characteristics that can be explored by looking at generated lattices and also by exploring corresponding 3D close-packing cylinder and sphere arrangements.

The applications are endless: for creating all sorts of 2D and 3D structures for architecture, for cellular materials, for sphere and cylinder arrangements, for off-planet or undersea structures, for rocket booster or fuel cell arrangements, and for various types of product design.

Triangular prism 3D
sequence TP1

Cluster TP1.1

Cluster TP1.2

Cluster TP1.3

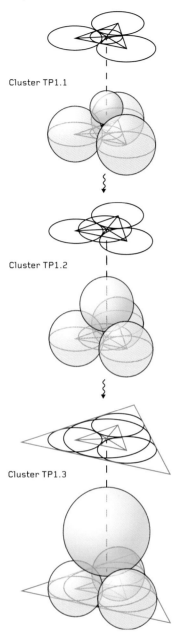

12.39 3D cluster sequence TP1

Hexagonal prism
sequence HP1

Cluster HP1.1

Cluster HP1.2

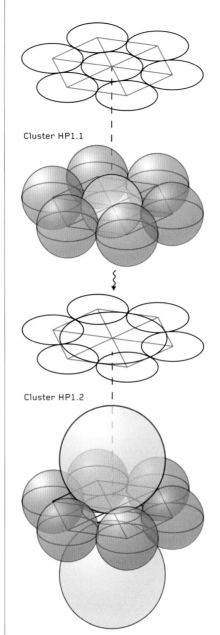

12.40 3D cluster sequence HP1

Cluster HP1.3

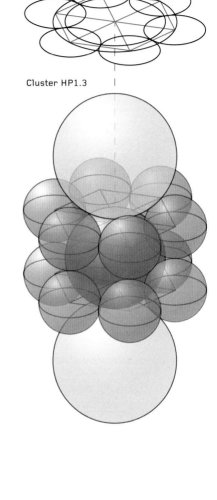

THREE-DIMENSIONAL CLOSE-PACKING SPHERE SEQUENCES

Three-dimensional close-packing sphere sequences develop in ways similar to circle sequences, but the complexity is greater as close-packings in 3D need more concurrence than in 2D. To differentiate arrangements of close-packing spheres from close-packing circle cells, the unit close-packing sphere arrangements are called clusters.

Close-packing clusters of spheres can be generated within 3D space symmetries, such as triangular or hexagonal prisms, where the prisms are equivalent to the 2D constraining symmetries such as squares and equilateral triangles.

The TP1 illustration (see fig. 12.39) shows how a simple four-sphere cluster sequence can be generated by limiting sphere growth and positioning by the symmetrical boundaries of a triangular prism. TP1.1 and TP1.2 do close-pack, with TP1.2 the classic tetrahedral packing. TP1.3 does not strictly close-pack but it is a transitional arrangement whereby triangulated sphere clusters can scale up or down infinitely.

In fig. 12.40, the HP1 sequence is constrained by a hexagonal prism. HP1.1 is again the classic tetrahedral packing. HP1.2 does not close-pack as there is a space between the two larger spheres of $\sqrt{(2 \times \sqrt{3})} - \sqrt{3}$. HP1.3 close-packs with sphere ratios $(\sqrt{5} - 1)$, 1, 2. The close-packing will tessellate infinitely and has three-planes with the golden ratio $(\sqrt{5} + 1)/2$ and two planes with regular hexagonal symmetries. As with all sphere packings, lattices can be extracted.

The HP2 sequence shown in fig. 12.41 is generated within a hexagonal prism, and shows how a new sequence can be generated if new spheres are allowed to grow within contact points of the

HP1 sequence. Unlike the HP2.2 cluster, HP2.1 only close-packs across the shown planes and does not close-pack within the inner domains of the containing hexagonal prism.

True close-packing 3D arrangements of spheres are comparatively rare and are usually unexpected – such as with the centralized sphere clusters shown in figs 12.50 to 12.52. To further explore close-packing in 3D space with spheres of equal and unequal sizes requires a great deal of computer processing. Successive approximation is generally the best way to go, as it is much easier to incrementally alter the size or position of spheres than to derive equations. Adding 'directional' commands will make processing more efficient. The more spheres that there are in play the more redirects will be required.

Note that the parameters for sphere sequences generated can be changed so that spheres change size and position within all sorts of symmetries. Other variations can include centred growth, sphere penetration, sphere distortion and non-symmetry.

Experiential algorithms Earlier in the chapter the parameters of the dynamic circle geometry were defined, and in chapter 14 there is a corresponding set of algorithms – and neither match any known experiential event. The author is in the process of creating another set of algorithms for the sphere geometry that will model what we know of the dynamics of ions and their size shifts and transformations when combining to form matter – where the size of ions varies significantly according to the loss or gain of electrons as much as to their position in the periodic table. An experiential algorithmic set will add a whole new dimension to the geometry.

Parallels in crystalline materials and definitions There are parallels between the dynamic sphere geometry and atomic alignments. This is relevant because a method to directly compare the sizes and positions of spheres in a spherical packing with actual atoms means that the geometry can be used to determine optimum atomic configurations for various applications, such as for optimum material strength or flexibility. However,

an exact comparison with the spherical clouds of electrons (which surround the nucleus of an atom) may never be possible as, according to Heisenberg's uncertainty principle, the sizes and positions of isolated atoms cannot be measured – and yet there is a method by which we can estimate the size of an atom, particularly in metals, by assuming that the radius is half the distance between adjacent atoms (known as metallic radii).

Just as spheres in the geometry can be of different sizes and change size and position, so too can atoms be of different sizes, determined by the number of electrons in their electron clouds. Atoms can also change size with changed energy states or by losing or gaining electrons, and change position electromagnetically. Atoms become larger as we go down a column of the periodic table, and they become smaller as we go across a row of the table. Spin rates also have an impact on an atom's size, as does an atom's ionic state. A negative ion is defined as having more electrons than a neutral atom and a positive ion fewer. When an atom loses an electron, the lost electron no longer contributes to shielding the other electrons from the positive charge of the nucleus; consequently, the other electrons are more strongly attracted to the nucleus, and the radius of the atom gets smaller. Similarly, when an electron is added to an atom, the added electron effectively shields the other electrons from the nucleus, with the result that the size of the atom increases.

As an illustration of atoms of different sizes, fig. 12.42 depicts an idealized face-centred cubic unit cell for a compound of large and small ions, and represents NaCl (sodium chloride, or salt). While the cubic planes do close-pack, the spherical domains at the centre of the cube do not.

Fig. 12.43 is an imaginative representation showing different sizes and positions of atoms modelling the crystalline atomic structure of pyrrhotite 4C. The arrangement was inspired by the Atomium building in Brussels.

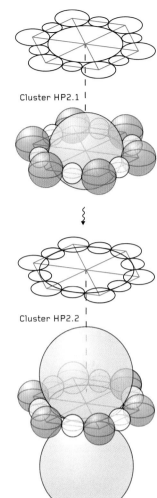

Hexagonal prism sequence HP2

Cluster HP2.1

Cluster HP2.2

12.41 3D cluster sequence HP2

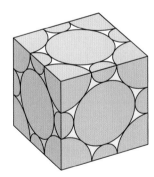

12.42 Face-centred cubic compound cell

12.43 3D model of pyrrhotite 4C

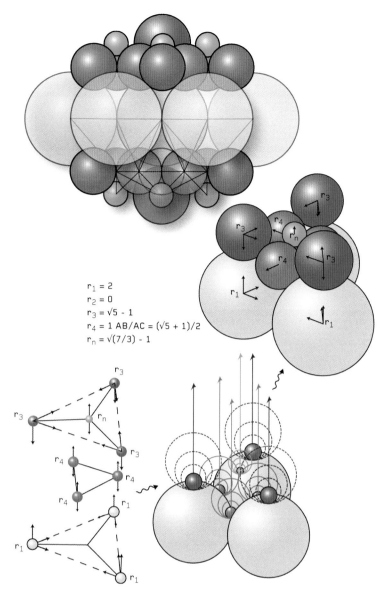

$r_1 = 2$
$r_2 = 0$
$r_3 = \sqrt{5} - 1$
$r_4 = 1$ $AB/AC = (\sqrt{5} + 1)/2$
$r_n = \sqrt{(7/3)} - 1$

12.44 Cluster HP1.3 transforming within an equilateral prism

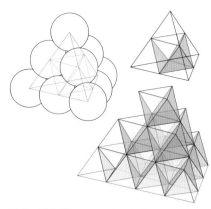

12.45 3D lattice generated by TP1.2 – a tetrahedral and octahedral packing

12.46 A skyscraper-like structure extracted from the lattice grid of TP1.2

The dynamics of 3D sequences

The three-dimensional symmetrical boundaries for clusters can be prisms, cubes or other 3D forms. Fig. 12.44 shows how spheres can change size and move within an equilateral triangular prism. In the example shown, the generated cluster is that of HP1.3 and is the 3D equivalent of RTR1.6. HP1.3 is in fact the golden ratio sphere packing, with three planes in the golden ratio and two planes corresponding to a tessellation of regular hexagons. Potential arrangements for this start point also include that of a tetrahedral close-packing of spheres.

A constraint that can be added to the geometry is that of maintaining a total additive sphere volume within bounding symmetries, so that the total volume of one close-packing arrangement equals that of another. Similar constraints can be added across planes and can be of volume or cross-sectional area, or even of surface area.

Fig. 12.45 shows how a close-packing arrangement of spheres, TP1.2 (see fig. 12.57), can be extended to create a tetrahedon-octahedron lattice that can be applied structurally to an architectural form. The structure is similar to a design concept developed by Singaporean architect Tan Bing Hui of an octahedral-tetrahedral building intended as a new urban community centre in the area of Singapore's Marina Bay (see fig. 12.46).

Fig. 12.47 shows part of a three-dimensional sequence that is generated following various parameter sets. By changing the parameters, different sphere packings can be generated. The drawing shows how a 3D development of cell S1.4 can transform into cluster HP1.3, where the containing symmetry is that of a hexagonal prism. As in fig. 12.45, these packings can generate lattices for structural applications.

Extending 2D cells into 3D clusters

There may be more than one type of 3D cluster development of a 2D cell; but clusters may not close-pack.

(i) 3D close-packings may, or may not, be exact.

(ii) 3D close-packings may, or may not, tessellate.

(iii) 3D close-packings may extend infinitely within a containing sphere.

(iv) Non-close packing 3D sphere clusters may be generated with interesting structural properties.

Figs 12.47 and 12.48 show how cell RTR1.1 can be extended into 3D sphere clusters within cubic, or hexagonal prism, symmetries.

Figs 12.49, 12.50 and 12.51 show how the circles of cell RTR1.2 can be developed as a sphere cluster that will pack within an escribed sphere as well as within an equilateral triangular or hexagonal prism. The spheres do not close-pack in the prisms, only in the escribed sphere. Structurally the sphere packings are of interest because of the whole number relationships of the lattices connecting the sphere centres. The circles of cell RTR1.2 can also be extruded into cylinders (see fig. 12.53).

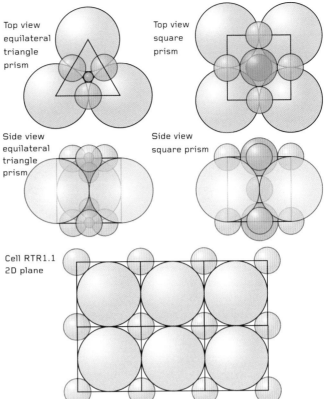

CELL RTR1.1
3D development within triangle and square prisms

Top view equilateral triangle prism

Top view square prism

Side view equilateral triangle prism

Side view square prism

Cell RTR1.1 2D plane

12.48 Cell RTR1.1 extension into 3D clusters

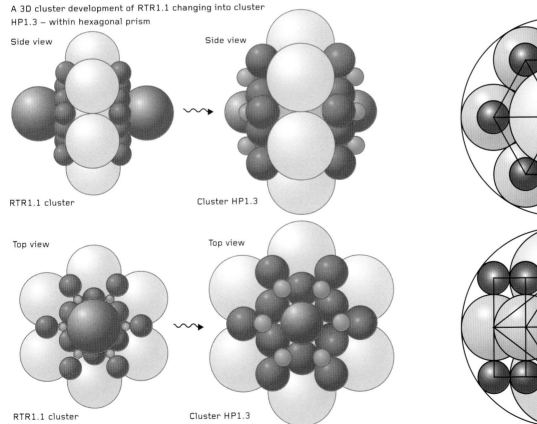

A 3D cluster development of RTR1.1 changing into cluster HP1.3 – within hexagonal prism

Side view

Side view

RTR1.1 cluster

Cluster HP1.3

Top view

Top view

RTR1.1 cluster

Cluster HP1.3

12.47 Cluster development of cell RTR1.1 changing into cluster HP1.3

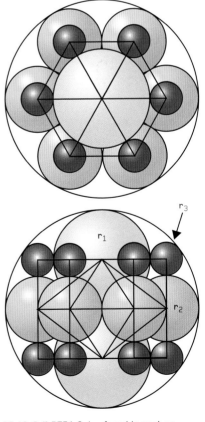

r_3

r_1

r_2

12.49 Cell RTR1.2 developed to pack as spheres within a sphere

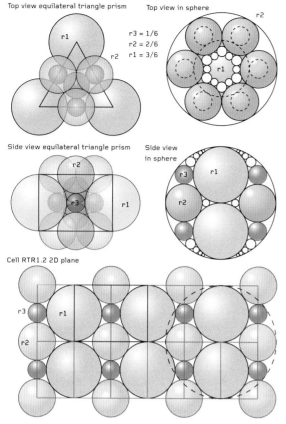

Top view equilateral triangle prism

Top view in sphere

r3 = 1/6
r2 = 2/6
r1 = 3/6

Side view equilateral triangle prism

Side view in sphere

Cell RTR1.2 2D plane

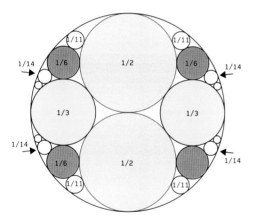

12.50 RTR1.2 packing within an equilateral triangular prism and within a sphere

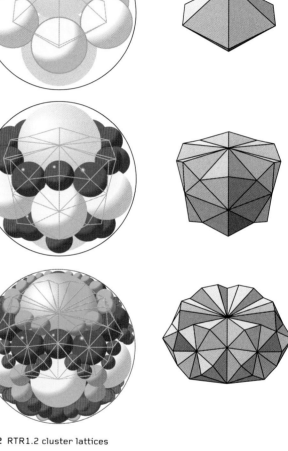

12.52 RTR1.2 cluster lattices

12.51 RTR1.2 and the 'bowl of integers'

Centralized sphere clusters

The centralized sphere cluster that corresponds with RTR1.2 (see fig. 12.50) contains spheres that continue infinitely in whole number relationships (see fig. 12.51). The cluster matches that of British radiochemist Frederick Soddy's 'bowl of integers' (1937) – a packing arrangement of spheres within a containing sphere that has the unique property that the diameter of every sphere in the containing sphere is in a whole number ratio relationship with every other sphere.

The classic 'bowl of integers' is constructed within a hollow sphere of 1 unit diameter (a diameter of, for example, 1 micron or 1 metre). If two spheres with a diameter of 1/2 unit are placed inside the sphere with the diameter of 1 unit then they will touch each other at the exact centre of the bowl and also exactly touch the extremities of the containing 1 unit sphere, with all three centres aligned. Six spheres of diameter 1/3 unit will now fit exactly in the gap between the two 1/2 unit spheres and the containing 1 unit sphere. The unique

property of the 'bowl of integers' is that the diameter of every sphere that can be theoretically packed into the containing sphere will have diameters that are in whole number ratios, one with another: 1:2, 1:3, 1:6, etc. (see fig. 12.51). The proof of the whole number relationship is credited to René Descartes (1643). One application for the ratios in the 'bowl of integers', as with any sphere packing, is that of creating the densest possible concentration of particles – for example, in the aggregate used to make concrete a typical recipe for very dense mixtures

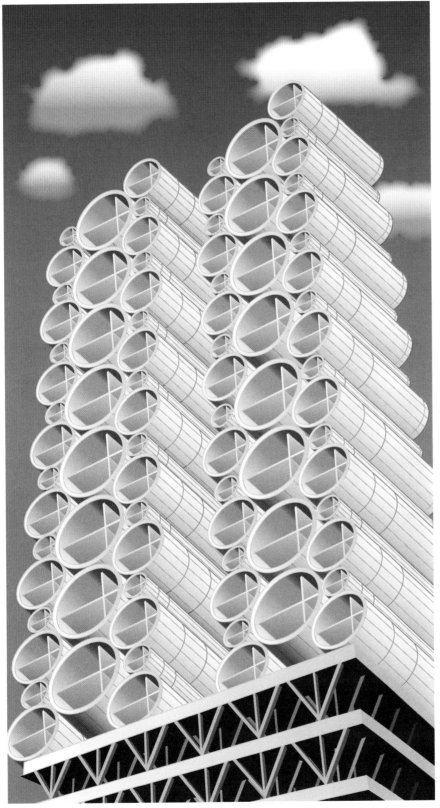

12.53 RTR1.2 low-cost cylinder accommodation skyscraper

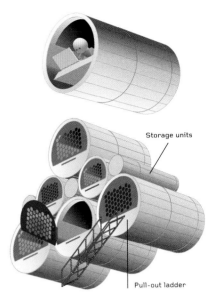

Storage units

Pull-out ladder

12.54 RTR1.2 low-cost cylinder accommodation

starts with grains of a given size and then mixes them with grains of smaller and smaller sizes in prescribed ratios of size and quantity.

Fig. 12.52 shows lattices generated by the 'bowl of integers', where the lattice lines connect the sphere centres and will all be in whole number lengths, making them useful for creating structures, particularly as the lattices will tessellate in three dimensions.

Cell packings extruded into cylinder arrangements Two-dimensional close-packing circle arrangements can be extruded into cylinder packings. Figs 12.53 and 12.54 show possible applications of RTR1.2 with concrete cylinder diameters of 1, 2 and 3 units. The application could be used as inexpensive accommodation with the following features:

· air circulation and filtering options with breeze-like variations or constant flows;
· OLED-wrapped video display with internet, TV and environmental options to coincide with air flow;
· lighting options that include natural light spectrums and directed light with infrared to simulate sunshine;
· sound options that include environmental sound effects;
· option of complete external sound insulation;
· external view options;
· security, size and storage options.

Cluster HP1.3

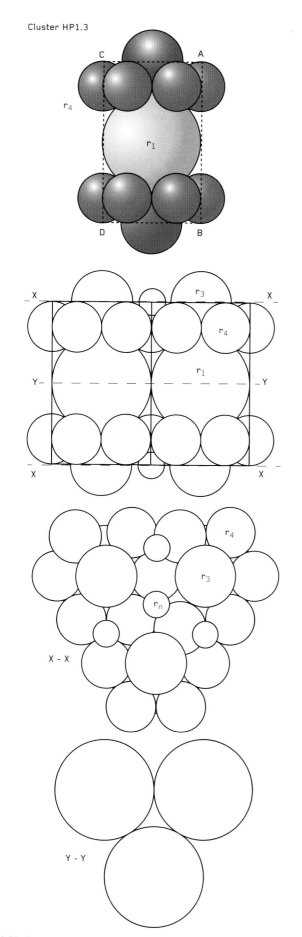

Golden ratio spheres Cell RTR1.6, of the first sequence shown (see pp.270–71), is most interesting in that it corresponds with the close-packing sphere cluster HP1.3, which close-packs within a hexagonal prism and has three planes with golden ratio proportions, as well as two planes with a hexagonal ratio proportion (see fig. 12.55).

Fig. 12.56 shows how cell RTR1.6 extends into three dimensions with multiple planes that pass through it. The drawing also shows how the golden sphere packing can be generated within an equilateral triangle or hexagonal prism. The golden sphere packing can also be used to start other 3D sequences in a way similar to its 2D cell (see fig. 12.28).

W - W plane (cells RTR1.6)

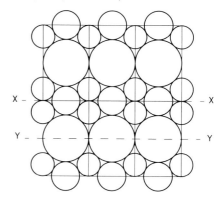

X - X plane

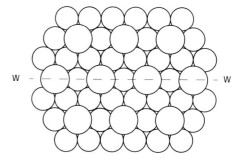

Y - Y plane

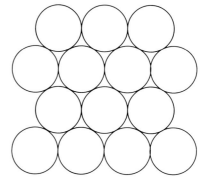

12.55 Golden ratio spheres

12.56 Golden ratio spheres

3D sequences with changed parameters

Fig. 12.57 shows an alternative 3D sequence, where the containing symmetry of cluster TP1.2 is that of a hexagonal sphere packing; a cube is one of the lattices generated by the packing, and the cube transforms into cluster HP1.3. The 3D sequence shown can be preceded by a 3D packing that corresponds with RTR1.1. The significance here is that of cubic packing transforming into a tetrahedron-octahedron close-packing and then into a triangular prism close-packing. The cube packing shown is similar to that of the crystalline structure of sodium chloride (see fig. 12.58).

'Circles touch and move; still touching they grow and roll, and where they touch they spawn. Great ones hold apart for a time, their offspring between; they touch again gladly, and without domination. They fill the universe, cause and consequence tumbling and rolling, yet always leaving room to dance and multiply. The circles compass birth and death with joy.'

BOB BURN

after seeing an animation of the dynamic sphere geometry at the ATM (Association of Teachers of Mathematics) conference, Lancaster University, 1976

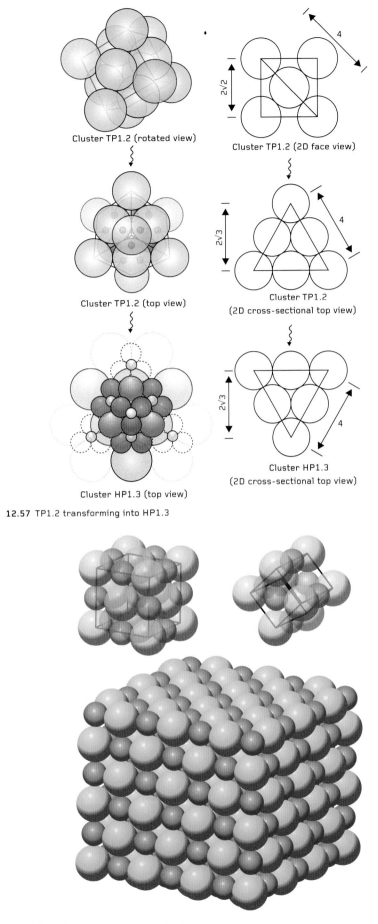

Cluster TP1.2 (rotated view)

Cluster TP1.2 (2D face view)

Cluster TP1.2 (top view)

Cluster TP1.2 (2D cross-sectional top view)

Cluster HP1.3 (top view)

Cluster HP1.3 (2D cross-sectional top view)

12.57 TP1.2 transforming into HP1.3

12.58 Crystal structure of sodium chloride

Double tetrahedron / octahedron packing

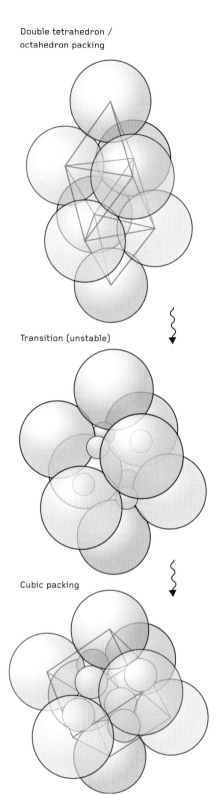

Transition (unstable)

Cubic packing

12.59 Regular polyhedron sequence

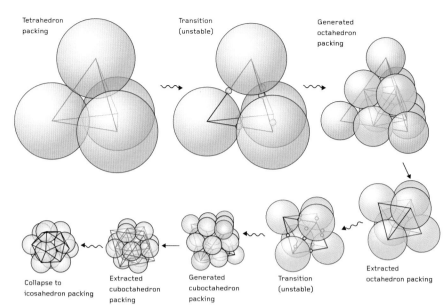

Tetrahedron packing → Transition (unstable) → Generated octahedron packing → Extracted octahedron packing → Transition (unstable) → Generated cuboctahedron packing → Extracted cuboctahedron packing → Collapse to icosahedron packing

12.60 Regular polyhedron sequence

Regular polyhedron sequences Of the many sequences that can be generated by the dynamic close-packing sphere system there is a group of sequences with transformations of close-packing sphere arrangements that have regular polyhedral lattices. In fig. 12.59 a double-tetrahedron and octahedron close-packing sphere arrangement transforms into a cubic packing that close-packs only on the planes of the faces of the cube. The middle packing is a transformational and unstable phase between the first and third packings.

In fig. 12.60 a single tetrahedron packing transforms into an icosahedron.

The examples show that at least some Platonic solids can be transformed, one into another, with the dynamic geometry and that the cube is less stable than the tetrahedron-octahedron packing.

Nancy Stetson art studio The studio was built for a friend of the author's, Nancy Stetson, in Boulder, Colorado (see figs 12.61 and 12.62) in 1986. The design objective was to create an art studio that would enhance the qualities of sight and sound. To meet the design objectives we calculated that an eight-segmented curve, generated by the proportions of a golden rectangle, would reflect and focus sounds into the space of nine 60 cm (24 in) diameter spheres. The spheres would be positioned under each of the eight roof segments at about 1.8 m (6 ft) above the floor level. After

construction we found that the effect was subtle but noticeable to the point that a person could close his or her eyes and walk around the room to find the sound-spheres generated by the natural air pressure of the environment – without any generated sound sources. We also found that whispered words uttered within the central sound-sphere could be clearly heard in each of the surrounding sound-spheres. The architect for the project was Philip Tabb of Boulder, Colorado. The author developed the concept and provided the inner dimensions.

Sphere-packing variations It is evident that the parameters of the dynamic sphere geometry can be varied in a huge number of ways. Spheres can just touch, or can combine in the way of soap bubbles or otherwise change shape. The dynamics of the system can be altered in any way and the start-up containing symmetries can be of almost any type.

If a generated close-packing arrangement is of particular interest – like the golden sphere packing, HP1.3 – then other variations can be investigated. Cluster HP1.3 has two rings of six r4 spheres. If one ring is removed, and the altered clusters are then arranged in a polar opposite way to each other in 3D space, then the clusters can rotate, one against the other. If the removed rings are replaced then the structure becomes rigid (see fig. 12.63).

12.61 Nancy Stetson art studio, Boulder, Colorado, USA

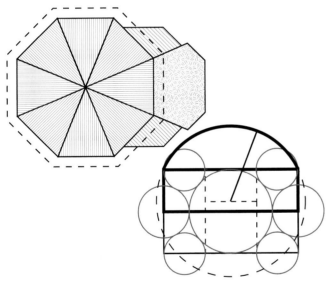

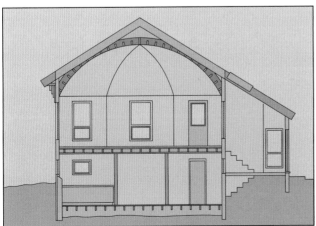

12.62 Nancy Stetson art studio, Boulder, Colorado, USA

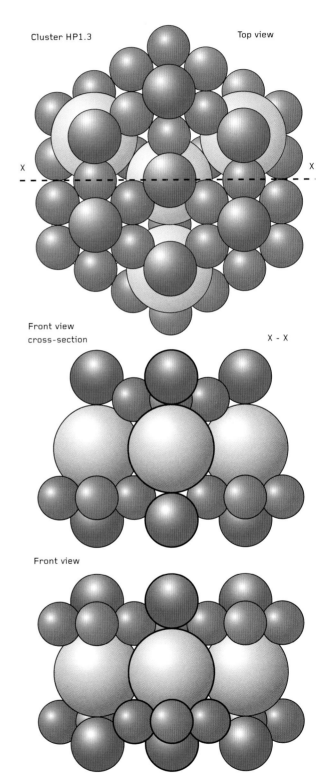

Cluster HP1.3   Top view

X   X

Front view
cross-section   X - X

Front view

12.63 Sphere cluster HP1.3 with alternate R4 spheres removed

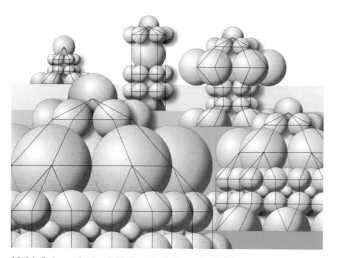

12.64 Sphere cluster HP1.3 with circle centre lattices

12.65 HP1.3 lattice structures

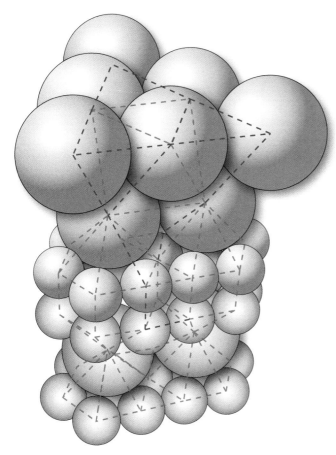

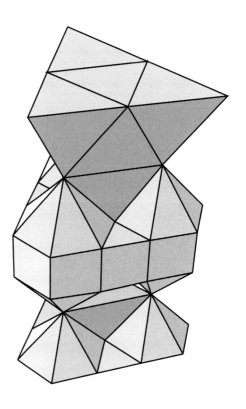

12.66 Alternating HP1.3 and TP1.2 sphere packings and lattices

Lattices Lattices can be drawn connecting sphere centres, and polyhedra can be generated by creating mini-planes at sphere contact points.

Fig. 12.64 shows lattices that can be generated by cluster HP1.3, and figs 12.65 and 12.66 show how some of the lattices might be used to create architectural spaces. Fig. 12.66 shows how the sphere packing HP1.3 can be 'layer cake' alternated with the sphere packing TP1.2.

Applying spherical lattice structures to a home layout A typical room network in a standard Western home is shown in fig. 12.67. The network varies according to need and wealth with more or fewer living spaces, bedrooms, bathrooms, garages and so on. Size is another variation, as is the nature and type of interconnecting links such as corridors, landings, hallways and stairs.

Figs 12.68 and 12.69 show a development of the typical room network mapped onto lattices generated by sphere packings HP1.3 and TP1.2 (see fig. 12.66). The structures are unique in that every point corresponds with the lattice generated by connecting the sphere centres of the close-packing arrangements with the packing generated by the dynamic sphere geometry. All proportions are subservient to the 3D lattice, so that the design can be further developed, in 3D, by following the lattice to create regular and irregular polyhedral forms.

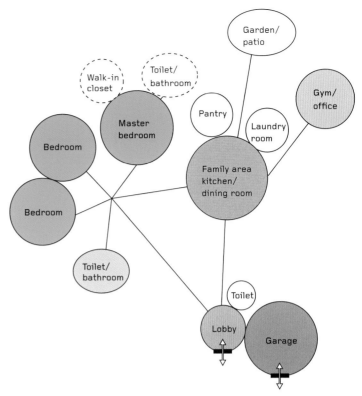

12.67 Typical Western home interconnections

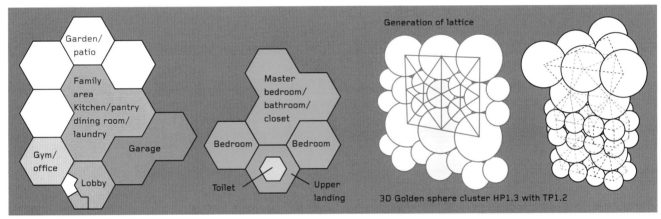

12.68 Architectural application of HP1.3 and TP1.2 sphere lattices

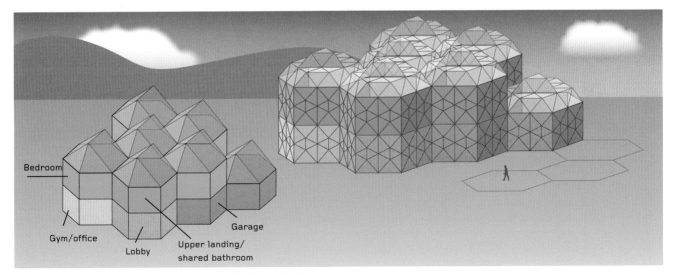

12.69 Floor layout of fig. 12.68 and the associated sphere packing

12.70 Amazon biodomes (artist's rendering)

Biosphere environments Global design company NBBJ has designed a three-sphere structure for Amazon to be built in Seattle, Washington, adjacent to the company's corporate headquarters (see fig. 12.70). The biosphere design combines an internal environment of trees and plants with workspaces, conference rooms and a canteen. In a way the concept provides an idealized, weather-protected, country environment within which people will conduct business, communicate and be creative. NBBJ describes its practices as 'computational design', and has, as much as possible, tried to anticipate and simulate how the structure's occupants will experience and use the spaces enclosed by the spheres. It will be interesting to see how the use of the space evolves; in some ways it seems

like a country village environment where people will work in the equivalent of cottage gardens or on park benches, meet in village halls, rendezvous in the local pub and enjoy walking across village greens. Certainly with its fresh air, maximum amount of daylight, and open spaces, it will be a healthier environment than working in a poorly lit rectangular box, but as to whether it will promote more effective and creative work practices is at this point unknown. Even so, it is an interesting experiment.

The faceted and intersecting spherical forms are to be made of glass and are to be supported by an internal dodecagonal lattice of steel struts. Internally there will be open spaces from the ground level to the top of the domes as well as several floors of workspaces.

Coincidences In fig. 12.71, diagram A shows a method for constructing a pentagon and a decagon using the golden circle packing, cell RTR1.6, seen on p. 271. Golden sphere packings (see HP1.3 on pp. 278 and 280) have many coincidences in three-dimensional space but also over its two-dimensional planes. Diagram B shows one of the planes of the golden sphere packing where the spheres appear as circles on the two-dimensional plane (see p. 284). The illustrations show a correspondence between the golden circle packing and an arrangement of decagons, C and D. The correspondences are interesting in that they echo a hexagonal packing on the plane – a concurrence with other planes in the HP1.3 sphere packing. Diagram E shows how spheres of the golden sphere packing can be circumscribed

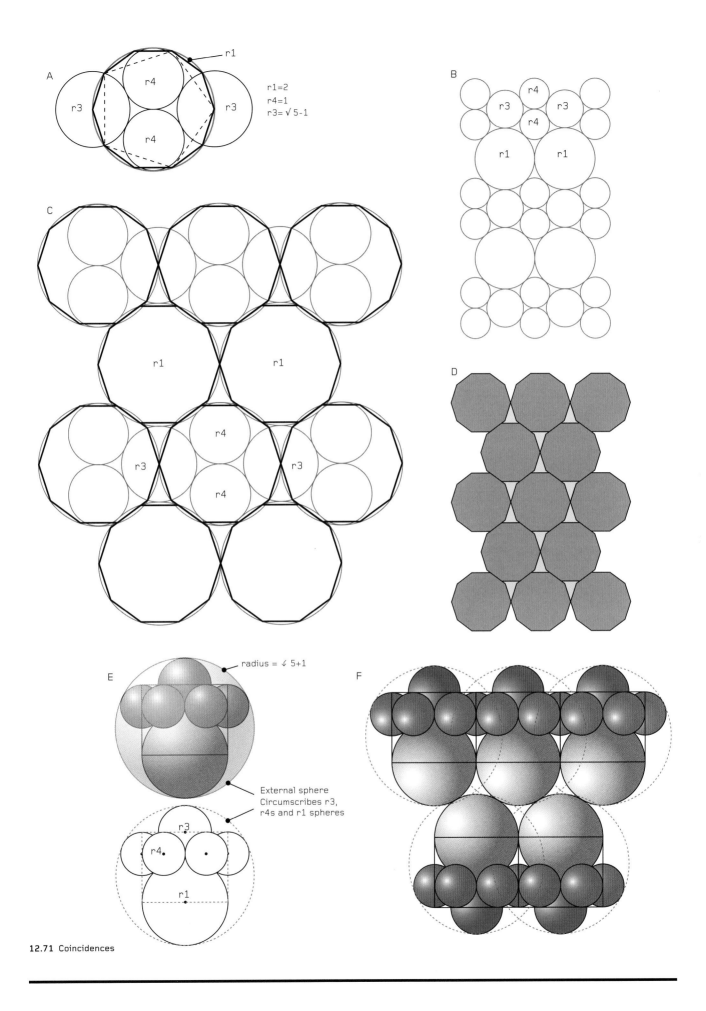

A

r1

r3   r4

r4   r3

r1=2
r4=1
r3=√5-1

B

r4
r3   r3
r4
r1   r1

C

r1   r1

r4
r3   r3
r4

D

E

radius = √5+1

External sphere
Circumscribes r3,
r4s and r1 spheres

r3
r4
r1

F

12.71 Coincidences

by a surrounding sphere, and F shows an example of how the E packing can be arranged three-dimensionally.

Dynamic sphere geometry: a starting point When first programming the dynamic sphere geometry, the circle and sphere packings generated were, mostly, a surprise, but the sequences generated were relatively simple and the parameters were not complex. The author has not had time to create more sophisticated 3D programs and has tended to just calculate out the close-packings and then generate them with 3D animation software, in particular Lightwave 3D. This approach does not reveal much in the way of surprises and is a slow process. Students may be inspired to develop new and more sophisticated 3D programs whereby all sorts of 3D clusters will be generated and all sorts of parameters explored, including energy levels for spheres, sphere penetration and distortion, the use of symmetrical boundaries of all sorts, and also non-symmetrical boundaries. The key to the programming is really that of successive approximation, so that the program should essentially be able to take care of the mathematics.

Future applications Close-packing arrangements and associated lattices generated by the geometry can be used in ways that best suit the application domain.

(i) For architectural groupings, lattices can be selected with a particular ratio range of lengths for ease of construction; polygonal lattice planes can be selected on the basis of acoustical or light-reflecting/absorbing properties; polyhedra can be extracted from the lattice according to their space-filling properties.

(ii) For new material development, sphere packings can be selected on the basis of matching manufactured particle distribution.

(iii) For spacecraft designs, sphere arrangements can be selected on the basis of function and optimum packing.

(iv) For cellular or nanomaterial development, different packings can be selected that will combine across common planes, so that structures of different types can be combined to make materials that, for example, are rigid in some parts and flexible in others – i.e. they will bend, rotate and so on.

(v) Molecular manufacturing is the name given to a specific type of 'bottom-up' construction technology. As its name implies, molecular manufacturing will be achieved when we are able to build things from the molecule up and able to rearrange matter with atomic precision. This technology currently only exists in labs, but once it becomes widely available we should have a thorough and inexpensive system for controlling of the structure of matter.

(vi) Close-packing circle formations can represent hemispherical packings or they can be extruded to form close-packing cylinders of various types with applications for tubular containers, conduits, cables, space rockets, fuel containers, inflatables end even high-rise apartment dwellings (see fig. 12.53).

ALTAIR DESIGNS

In the 1970s, working with Dr Ensor Holiday, the author developed numerous variations on close-packing circle designs, some of which were extraordinarily complex and time-consuming to complete. Prints were made of the close-packing circle lattices and some found their way into the hands of children. The unique visual property of the designs is that, like cracks on a wall, they can conjure all sorts of images in the mind's eye. The fact that they are based on close-packing circles, repeating in square and hexagonal symmetries, means that any shape 'found' can be found again and again – rotated, reflected and translated. It turned out that both children and adults loved colouring the designs and came up with an immense diversity of imagination. The same design might be seen as a landscape by some, a flock of birds by others, or as abstract patterns, faces, wild animals, flowers and many other things. The designs were eventually published in a series of books under the name of Altair Designs by Longman Press around 1973.

Figs 12.72 to 12.74 show lattices generated by close-packing circle arrangements, together with designs derived from each lattice.

12.72 Based on circle cell H1A lattice

12.73 Based on circle cell H1B lattice

12.74 Based on circle cell S2.5 lattice

13. THE FUTURE OF 3D GEOMETRY

NEW APPLICATIONS, NEW NEEDS, NEW CONCEPTS

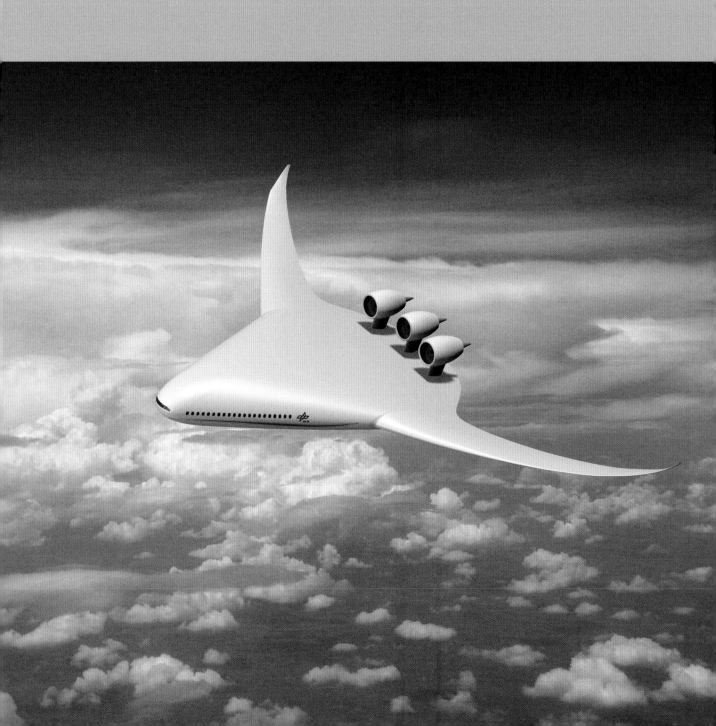

The future will bring new technologies, new materials, new discoveries, new enterprises and new values – but also old problems such as diminishing global resources, climate change, population growth and pollution. New technologies will enable us to create radically different types of 3D space and open up the possibility of paradigm shifts in our modelling systems. New types of logic will allow us to generate dynamic 3D lattices from which a whole new generation of structural forms can be derived.

Let us consider how geometrical concepts might evolve in the future. As ever, concepts will be influenced by the materials at hand, by available technologies and by local cultures.

Our counting and geometric systems rely on a human process of simplification that matches our brain's limited sensing and data-processing capabilities. Historically we have simplified an observed event to create a sort of distilled model that could be managed and understood by our processing and communication abilities. As our ability to observe events developed, our models and languages became more complex to accommodate the new variables we observed, or had seen before and now wanted to accommodate. In the 21st century our means to observe events has increased dramatically, as have our technological ambitions to more accurately model, predict and control events – to the point that the required data processing has outstripped our mental abilities and we are reliant on machines to process data for us.

Our reliance on computers has led to their evolution from simple computational data-processing machines to machines that have all sorts of data inputs and outputs as well as advanced processing capabilities. Computers now process data from file inputs, from sensors, from image and audio files and from energy inputs; and data outputs create digital images, animations and visual simulations, and serve to direct machines as well as manage communications traffic and much more.

As the computer's data-processing and modelling capabilities continue to increase and outputs become more sophisticated and diverse, so too will our ability to explore new concepts that are less reliant on historical mental models that had to be simple for our limited minds and senses to understand and process.

Future conceptual models may, therefore, become less reliant on current geometries and mathematical languages. For example, it is possible that we will no longer have a need for the concept of a sphere but will instead use a different type of conceptual model that defines boundaries, matter and energy levels, vibrations, and external forces such as wind or gravity. The current languages of equations may also become defunct, to be replaced with such things as 'successive approximation' routines, where a computer, linked to inputs, will process data to create outputs that are reliant on input correspondences rather than on simulating equations and conceptual models. If this is the case then our inventiveness will be more to do with how we direct our computers, how we program them, how we enhance their sensors, and what we do with their outputs.

If future education is based more on variables and less on static and simplified models then it will become unrecognizable from today's point of view. On the other hand, there is a reason that planets and bubbles tend to be sphere-like, that the surface of water flattens, and that energetic matter tends to follow spiral-like formations – so the historical logic may not be thrown out completely but just understood in a very different way. Also, basic human needs will still have to be met, and we may yet have a few years of using currently recognizable models of atoms, weather maps, and the like. It is thought-provoking to note that computers already have the capacity to observe better than we can and are held back only by the limits of the programming routines that we have created.

13.1 German Aerospace Centre blended wing body (BWB) aircraft concept

New parameters Maybe it is time to consider a set of human parameters, for future structural design, that might survive new and game-changing technologies. Here are ten possible parameters:

(i) that structures empower the human spirit and meet functional requirements – see 'Functional and emotional needs';

(ii) that structures be transformable in terms of space and function – see 'Shape-changing structures';

(iii) that structures maximize volume against surface area – see Fig. 12.14;

(iv) that structures be constructed with minimum energy costs;

(v) that structures be spatially efficient and adjustable according to human needs, interacting with higher level sensing technologies – see 'Sensing technologies';

(vi) that structural materials be optimum for their space – see page 267;

(vii) that structures be environmentally friendly;

(viii) that durability matches required timeframe;

(ix) that structures be energy-efficient;

(x) that habitable units be transformable, interlinking locally and remotely – see, 'Modular material structures'.

The ten points have been written with the goal of starting a thought process that might provide some sort of foundation when all else changes. As the old constraints of our logical thought processes fall away and our material and computational environment evolves, then the ten points might serve as a starting point for the types of parameter that we might still wish to adhere to. They will hopefully hold true for structures of the future and might apply to many types of form that use current static geometries, new shape-changing and dynamic geometries, but also organic geometries that, up to this point, may not have been thought of as geometries at all. After all, a plant conforms to many of the ten points and it is not inconceivable that future structures might be created organically or chemically. We have already mentioned 3D printing that can use, to a degree, on-site materials to produce any sort of

structural form – which might be rigid, flexible, modular or cellular...

Functional and emotional needs Mention was made earlier about culturally integrated geometries; about broad sensory applications for geometrical forms (see chapter 5); about the impact of proportions and interconnecting spaces (see chapter 8); on geometry in dance, and on sound control. In fact, this book contains many references to the emotional impact of geometric forms.

In our present age, function overshadows emotional need to the point that most people would not really understand the absence of emotional geometry until they enter, say, the circle of Stonehenge or a medieval cathedral, or walk along a tree-lined avenue or stand on a beach looking at the ocean. Functional design is determined by cost, ease of manufacture, and old-fashioned concepts of what work or living spaces should conform to. Changes are beginning to occur, but there is not much in the way of a science applied to structural accommodation for humans, and most people live and work in rectangular boxes and sit in chairs facing a TV or a computer screen or a dining table. If we start with a clean palette, with new geometries, new perceptions of old geometries, new technologies and new human needs and circumstances, then we can move away from old mindsets and consider spaces that accommodate us in a more holistic way. The possibility is that spaces will move away from just providing for consumers, for audiences, and for production-line activities; rather, spaces of the future might be designed to promote human well-being, creativity and positive social interaction, and also allow for privacy; spaces that allow people to navigate more organically and less functionally, that do not conserve and propagate noise, that enhance the senses, that elevate the soul. There is not much science for these goals, though there are precedents in the past.

One of the interesting challenges of the future, when we will be able to generate any sort of structural form, will be to decide what is most aesthetically pleasing. In nature form follows natural dynamics and constraints and, in many

cases, future designs will have similar constraints and end structural forms will have an equivalent 'natural' form, but there will be progressively many more types of structural form that can challenge 'natural' constraints – in the same way that an abstract sculpture made of marble can do. So, then, what will be the aesthetic criteria for structural forms of the future that challenge and even negate natural constraints? This sort of challenge might put us back on the path that started with ideas of divine proportions – but what else?

Harmony in modularity Beauty or harmony has been equated to proportional systems and to conformity to particular grids, as seen in the works of Vitruvius and Le Corbusier, for example. Modularity has not generally been equated to beauty but it commonly occurs in nature and in today's architecture, for example in steel-structured rectangular box frames. Modularity does provide a sense of uniformity and thereby a type of harmony. Modular structures can also be scaled up or down by adding or subtracting modular units within an overall three-dimensional lattice – and, in this way, modularity does create an organic equivalence, much as a plant's cellular structure can expand or contract. In architecture the idea of organic modularity could be applied by creating modular constructs where individual modules can be added or subtracted, or interconnected in new ways. To upscale an accommodation space, for example, new links or modules could be added to a grid, while to downscale accommodation modules could be removed. Conceptually this is illustrated in fig. 13.2, where blue cubes would be the units of one accommodation space, yellow another and green another. Of course, a cubic grid is pretty unimaginative but any 3D modular environment lattice would be effective. Linking remotely positioned modules presents a problem that could be overcome by rearranging, by adding external conduits, or by adding an internal interconnecting core system.

Modular structures based on close-packing polyhedra lattices Any tessellating polyhedra and their

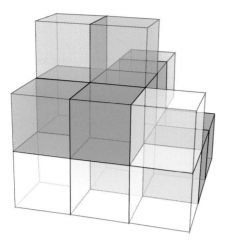

13.2 Cubic 3D lattice structure showing modular groups

associated lattices can be used to abstract modules or other 3D forms - as can lattices generated by the dynamic sphere geometry featured in chapter 12. The advantage is that modules can be moved, added or subtracted within the lattice. Polyhedron lattices as a whole, rather than just cubic or rectangular lattices, can provide more interesting and creative interconnected spaces, different subdivision possibilities, and new types of support structure. Figs 13.3, 13.4 and 13.5 show structures based on (i) rhombic dodecahedra, (ii) truncated octahedra, cuboctahedra and truncated tetrahedra, and (iii) truncated cuboctahedra and octahedra. (See the polyhedra in chapter 5 for other possible combinations.) Fig. 13.6 shows a structure subtracted from a tetrahedron and octahedron lattice. In chapter 12, fig. 12.65 shows structures abstracted from a 'golden rectangle' sphere packing lattice, and fig. 12.46 shows structures abstracted from an octahedron and tetrahedron lattice.

Modular material structures With new cellular materials (including nanomaterials) and laminates, structures can be much lighter and stronger. This can translate to structures that extend through 3D space in ways that currently seem improbable.

Fig. 13.7 shows a bubble-like structure developed using sphere units. A structural form such as this could be serviced by conduits of some type to interconnect sphere units and spaces.

13.3 Tessellating rhombic dodecahedra

13.5 Tessellating cuboctahedra and octahedra

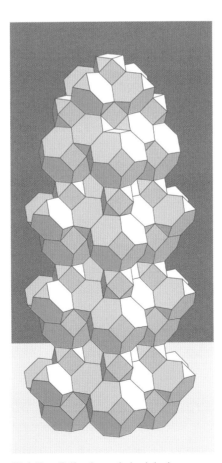

13.4 Tessellating truncated octahedra, cuboctahedra, truncated tetrahedra

13.6 A structure subtracted from a tetrahedron and octahedron lattice

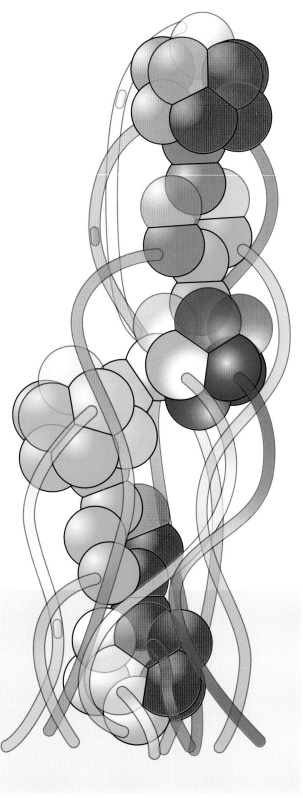

13.7 Tetrahedral sphere structure

13.8 Sphere and cubic lattice sky-high concept skyscrapers (for sphere lattice see p.288, fig. 12.66)

Such structures could also be built in a zero- or low-gravity environment.

For architectural applications conduits might use maglev-type propulsion pods designed to transport occupants horizontally, vertically or at angles between occupancy units or to or from the ground. Units, or parts of units, could be transparent or opaque, or adjustable transparent—opaque; occupants might trade occupation units to increase or decrease their occupancy volume; occupant units might be adjacent or separated.

New-generation structures using modular/cellular materials One of the main reasons that manmade structures tend to be built in a simple vertical fashion, and not be suspended sideways without support, is to do with the loads and stresses that materials can withstand. Forming materials with internal lattice and cell structures generates much higher strength-to-weight ratios than conventional materials and opens up possibilities for new types of space-filling structure (see fig. 13.8).

Cellular materials can be organic, inorganic or man-made. Cells can range in size from a few nanometres to millimetres or even larger. In a sense triangular framing (timber, steel...) performs the same thing, so 'cells' can be almost as large as the imagination can make them. The opportunity for 3D thinkers is to apply innovative cellular structures to create materials with 'designer' properties, in terms of structural characteristics: strength to weight, rigidity, flexibility, specific shape-changing or rotational properties, and so on, and also for properties such as conductivity, bonding, and other, currently unimaginable, applications. The development of new types of cellular material creates a paradigm shift with the potential to revolutionize architecture, transport, medical equipment, computers, solar cells and much more.

Examples of types of cellular material include the following:

1. Cellular materials

Materials with internal cellular or lattice-like structures evolved with organic life forms and we can see them in everything from bones to trees. Many inorganic materials also have internal cellular and internal lattice structures such as pumice and vesicular basalt. The distinguishing feature of these materials is, generally, a high strength-to-weight ratio, depending on whether the cells are open or filled with a lighter material. The arrangement and regularity of the cellular forms, and the materials within which they form, determine the strength-to-weight ratios as well as the potential properties of cellular material. Pumice, for example, is a porous volcanic rock composed of a volcanic glass with irregularly sized and shaped air pockets (typically less than 1 mm [$1/25$ in] in size) formed during the cooling process – making pumice not only a rock that floats but also a perfect aggregate for making concrete. At the other end of the internal cell spectrum with regular cells is graphene, which has cellular spaces of a few nanometres and high purity; in fact pure graphene can be formed by a single layer of carbon atoms arranged in a hexagonal array.

2. Carbon-based cellular materials

Three materials in particular provide very high strength-to weight ratios: carbon fibre, graphene and carbon nanotubes. All are composed of carbon atoms: carbon fibre comprises a polymer formed of carbon chains stretched into fibres (5–10 microns); graphene is a single layer of carbon atoms hexagonally arranged; and carbon nanotubes are cylindrical hollow fibres of single hexagonal lattices of carbon atoms.

Carbon fibre is a well-established material, while graphene and carbon nanotubes are relatively new, but all have extraordinarily high strength-to-weight ratios. The tensile strength of carbon fibre is about 3.5 times that of steel yet it is 4.5 times less dense. According to researchers at Rice University in Houston, Texas, carbon nanotubes are about 100 times stronger than steel at one sixth the weight. Both graphene and carbon nanotubes are electrically conductive – so both can serve to support weight and transmit data and electrical power.

These new materials hold great promise and will potentially revolutionize architecture – for example, the strength-to-weight ratio of carbon nanotubes could even make viable the concept of a space elevator (see p.307). However, the materials are still under development and researchers around the world are working to make their manufacture more efficient and less costly.

3. 3D-printed particulate and fused structures

Metallic or silicon particles can be suspended within a resin that can be hardened with laser-directed heat, creating a shaped material that has many of the characteristics of the suspended particles. Using much higher laser-directed temperatures silicon or metallic particles can be fused together to create a level of particle bonding that almost replicates the crystalline structure of pure materials. As lasers harden particle-suspended resins, or fuse particles, to form shapes, cellular structures can be laser-formed within them. Current 3D laser lithography can print at resolutions as small as 100 nanometres. 3D printer technologies on the horizon include two-photon laser curers and a femtosecond laser, both of which can fuse metallic particles at even higher resolutions. The cellular material possibilities created by new generation 3D laser printers heralds powerful new constructional opportunities.

4. Bioformed particle materials

Microbes such as *bacillus pasteurii* can be used to manufacture binding agents, such as calcium carbonate, to quickly (within hours or days) bind particles to create solid and durable structures. *Bacillus pasteurii* needs to be directed and fed with a nitrogen compound found in urine (urea, $CO(NH_2)_2$), calcium chloride, yeast extract and water. Swedish architect Magnus Larsson wants to halt the marching sands of desertification by using microbes to bind sand to create protective walls. Henk Jonkers at the Delft University of Technology in the Netherlands and Ginger Dosier at the American University of Sharjah in the United Arab Emirates suggest using microbes either to heal degraded concrete structures or to produce moulded bricks. There are still challenges to make the process practical, including managing the high amount of ammonia produced. See figs 13.9 and

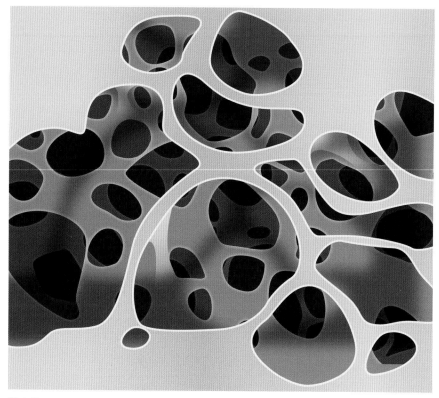

13.9 Representation of a bioformed construction

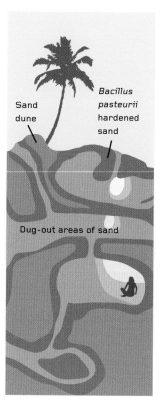

Sand dune

Bacillus pasteurii hardened sand

Dug-out areas of sand

13.10 *Bacillus pasteurii* hardened sand dune concept dwelling inspired by Aglaia Konrad

13.10 (a possible bioform application based on a design by Aglaia Konrad).

5. Organic material structures
Rather in the way that our bodies manufacture bones, programmed living cells may in the future be used to manufacture all sorts of materials. Scientists have been working on generating complex and interactive structures by programming cells using the fact that some genes can turn on or off parts of a genome. According to Professor Lingchong You at Duke University, North Carolina, 'In theory you can put a number of protein-expressing genes under the control of elaborate self-organizing genetic circuits. Once you have that, every cell could carry the blueprint of the design you want to make.' At Massachusetts Institute of Technology (MIT) Professor Timothy Lu and his team programmed bacteria to grow an electrical switch, and are now working on a living glue.

Portable structures Portable structures can be defined by the way they are made to move – by, for example, towing, carrying, flying or floating – as well as by the materials from which they are constructed and by the type of

construction. Tents fit the description, but so too do inflatable structures, seeds, aircraft, cereal boxes, boats, 3D structures that fold flat, caravans, and many types of prefabricated building, including structures assembled with modular panels that connect and easily disconnect. It is also conceivable that membrane-like structures could be generated from liquids that quickly harden and that can be dissolved, and that structures could be grown and even have the flexibility of plants.

A very different means of generating portable structures might be by using a replicator, such as a hybrid 3D printer.

With new materials, increasingly large pre-assembled structures can be hand carried by an individual or individuals. We have seen such structures as those constructed for human-powered flight (for example by MIT students using combinations of carbon-fibre foam and Mylar), but with new cellular materials the possibilities for more durable structures increase to the point that new types of application can be considered, such as hand-carried, pre-assembled work or accommodation spaces, with the advantage that no construction or assembly would be needed.

A drawback of portable accommodation, no matter how constructed, is the requirement to accommodate power, water, sewage and heating. It is conceivable that, in the future, portable dwellings will stack in areas where land supply is short, and where utilities can be easily accessed. Alternatively, it may be that individual power-generating systems will become so lightweight that they can easily be added to portable dwellings. Also, the means to package and recycle waste of all sorts will become portably efficient.

Water, food and physical space, then, may become the last hurdles to true portability – assuming air is not overly polluted. Many readers will have heard of the tubelike structures rented to weary travellers in Tokyo – and without much imagination one can imagine that such microhabitations will become more the norm in densely populated urban areas.

Shape-changing structures Shape-changing structures can change shape, position or orientation – and in this way have an organic equivalence, and thereby a beauty of sorts. Shape-changing structures might fold or otherwise move into a down position when the environment changes, or simply move to a different geographical location. In the architectural concept drawing shown in fig. 13.11, the individual floors of the building freely rotate so that inhabitants can rotate their floor for specific landscape views or set the rotation to automatically follow the sun, a star position or the moon. It would be possible to build skyscrapers that change shape provided the construction materials were light and strong enough – as would be the case, say, with new carbon-based materials. See fig. 13.12 for an illustration of the shape-changer core 1 shell module and its eight equilibrium positions from chapter 11 (see p.241, fig. 11.11).

A modular construction using the shape-changer core 1 shell module would change shape in a corresponding fashion, from very tall to a more compacted configuration.

Shape-change characteristics might be of use during the construction of a building, so that it could be assembled in a compact configuration and then expanded. In the case of the core 1 shell module, an assembled construction could be transformed into any one of the eight equilibrium positions, and then could be triangulated to fix the structure.

To prepare for severe weather conditions, structures assembled with shape-changer modules could be compacted (see figs 13.13 and 13.14). Contents and people would have to be configured for the change and any occupants alerted to move out of the structure or into safe zones during transformation. New sensing technologies would alert operators to any possible dangers.

The shape-changers shown here are conceptual. As the shape-change polygons can be of any size then overall structures could well look curved rather than angular – using very small polygons – even to the point that the shape-change polygons were hardly visible to the naked eye.

A future computer responding to a minimalistic human habitat requirement – as a weather-, temperature- and humidity-protected space – might offer a solution of a bubble-like structure composed of a lightweight, digitally interactive, transparent material with

13.11 Represents a shape-changing building

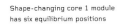

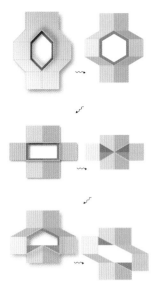

13.12 Shape-changing core 1 shell module

13.13 Shape-changing core 1 shell module combination structure shown in different equilibrium positions

13.14 Shape-changing core 1 shell module combination structure shown in different equilibrium positions

13.15 'Spirit of Dubai', inflatable structure, United Arab Emirates

13.16 The 'Crystal Bubble', by Bubble Tree

shape-changing areas that respond to monitored human needs, shape-changing to provide a toilet, a sink, a shower, a bed, a chair and a work area. It is possible that such a solution could be recycled or reconfigured every day.

Sensing technologies In the future, sensing technologies will likely be integral to structures such that the positions and conditions of people, animals, furniture, food and so on can be monitored. The theremin effect (named after one of the first electronic musical instruments, the theremin, invented in 1920), exploits changes in a magnetic field caused by the movement of a human body, where the position of any moving organic form can be triangulated; RF (radio-frequency) tags can be used to monitor the presence and rough location of items in a house; ultraviolet sensors can monitor heat signatures; pixel data can be processed to monitor changes in images and many light spectrums; audio sensor data can also be processed to monitor and respond to changes. In the future, local and remote sensing equipment will be able to prepare and adjust a structure to be best configured for changes in sunlight, heat, cold, wind, air quality and so on, but also monitor and respond to human needs.

Inflatable structures Inflatable structures have evolved considerably over the years. Almost 2,000 years ago in China, paper lanterns were floated, inflated by hot air from burning oil or wax, and used to signal military manoeuvres. It was not until 1709 that a

European floated a similar sort of device. In the mid-18th century, the Scottish chemist Joseph Black proposed that a balloon filled with hydrogen would be able to rise in the air. In 1783 the Montgolfier brothers in France demonstrated the first hot-air balloon manned flight. The primary applications for inflatable structures were for transport, for military purposes such as bombing, and to serve as elevated observation posts.

The main limitation of forced- and heated-air-inflated structures is that fans must continue to blow or burners burn, or the structures will quickly collapse. The advantages are many, including speed of inflation from a relatively compact form, minimum use of materials, unobstructed interior spaces, and portability. The alternatives to forced- or heated-air-inflated structures are structures with a gas that is sealed in to maintain a three-dimensional form or to provide a pressure differential between an inside gas-filled structure and an outside space.

The developmental history of materials selected to enclose gas starts with simple inflated balloons made from such things as pig's bladders. Materials transitioned to rubber and then on to plastics of various sorts, with materials selected on the basis of impact and fire resistance, air impermeability and cost.

The 'Spirit of Dubai' was a rib-inflated pavilion constructed in 2007 in the United Arab Emirates by the UK company Tectoniks (see fig. 13.15). The Bubble Tree company in Nanterre, France, manufactures clear plastic inflatable habitats using a silent fan that blows

in air and an airlock system that helps keep the air inside (see fig. 13.16). The company 2HD constructed a rib inflatable for the Lille Métropole Museum of Modern Art in 2010 (see figs 13.17 and 13.18).

NASA and Bigelow Aerospace inflatable space habitats (see fig. 13.19) use gas-enclosing materials that are layered to provide strength and air impermeability, such as woven Kevlar, Veetran for impact and structural strength, the ceramic fabric Nextel for flame protection, and woven polymers for air impermeability.

Future possibilities of inflatables We have already seen inflatable structures in space as well as on the ground where the internal gas pressure is greater than the external pressure. The air pressure differential is key to determining effective material combinations. For example, consider how a weather balloon stretches as the ratio of interior to exterior pressure changes with altitude. For habitable inflatable environments the internal air pressure range should be similar to that of the surface of the Earth. An influencing factor is water, as in lower or higher air pressure environments water evaporates more quickly or slowly. Anyone in a low-pressure environment, for example at 1,800 m (6,000 ft) and above, will notice how quickly their skin dries and their eyes get irritated.

As materials continue to evolve, the possibilities of inflatables are enormous. As with air bubbles, inflatables naturally adopt a spherical form depending upon the flexibility of their surfaces. Tori and cylinders with hemispherical ends are

13.17 Lille Métropole Museum of Modern Art inflatable – interior view

13.18 Lille Métropole Museum of Modern Art inflatable – exterior view

13.19 Bigelow Expandable Activity Module (BEAM) attached to the International Space Station

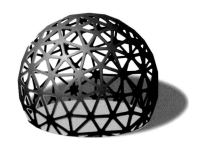

13.20 University of Kassel-inspired airbeam structure

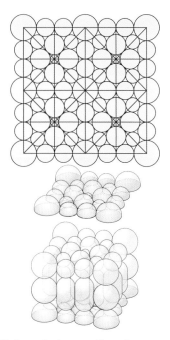

13.21 Dynamic close-packing sphere inflatable cell arrangement

(i)

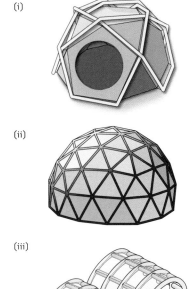

(ii)

(iii)

13.22 Inflatable frame structures

also 3D shapes naturally adopted by inflatable forms with flexible skins. Other possibilities might involve bubble-like forms where surfaces interact to form spherical cellular structures.

Flexible skins with an embedded membrane structure could be inflated with air, covered with a metal reinforcing lattice, and then spray coated with a concrete mixture such as UHPC (Ultra-high- performance concrete). Once the concrete mix has hardened, a solid concrete skeleton will be formed, allowing the flexible skin to be removed. Researchers at the University of Kassel, Germany, have been exploring new synergies of constructions and materials, including a combination of membrane constructions and concrete. An equivalent form of manufacturing for extraterrestrial habitats might be to use fused planetary silicates constructed over inflatables for extra protection from harmful radiation. Orbital or interplanetary craft might be constructed substantially out of inflatable structures.

Airframe inflatable structures Airframe inflatable structures have developed rapidly in recent times, finding applications in a variety of new engineering projects ranging from military tents in Iraq and Afghanistan to antennas in outer space. The technology has significantly reduced the transportable weight and volume and the setup time. Using layered woven materials, airframes can be strong to the point that they can support the weight of a truck, or more, and their lattice structures can be as varied as this book has shown.

Fig. 13.20 shows one example of how a geodesic lattice could serve as an airbeam framework. The design was inspired by a University of Kassel structure.

Dynamic close-packing circle geometry can be used to generate inflatable cell packings – in fig. 13.21 this is a fairly complex arrangement of cells.

Fig. 13.23 is a close-up view of the previously mentioned airbeam inflatable for the Lille Métropole Museum of Modern Art designed by 2HD from Nottingham in England.

Fig. 13.22 shows concept drawings that represent: (i) an airframe support structure for a tent where inflating the frame automatically creates the inner tent structure. The design shown is a copy of

13.23 Close-up view of the Lille Métropole Museum of Modern Art inflatable

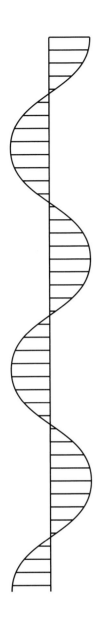

13.24 A wave-like skyscraper concept

a six-person geodesic dome by German company Heimplanet; (ii) an airframe structure with soft fabric or plastic panels that inflates as one to create a dome structure; (iii) an airframe with clear plastic panels that inflates to form a greenhouse-like structure.

THE FUTURE OF 3D FORM

There is really no limit to the way that future forms might evolve. We already have artificial structures that walk, and without much imagination buildings could walk or roll too – and even entire towns.

It may be that most forms will be expected to change shape in the future. A cereal box might self-collapse and change its position and then recycle itself. On a larger scale, vehicles might change shape for a variety of reasons. For example, aircraft wings might change state from rigid to flexible, then change form, and then change back again to a rigid form. Ocean, land and space vehicles might change shape to accommodate external conditions. The technologies to accomplish shape change are already under development (see p.262).

In the future, structures might flow in graceful waves, like a calm ocean, or grow, plant-like, changing form to accommodate solar and weather conditions.

Aesthetically the classic geometric forms might continue to serve as an expression of an abstract ideal – becoming more symbolic than truly structurally efficient. The following examples attempt to show just a faint glimmer of what might be, or in some cases already is, possible.

13.25 Parametric Dunes

13.26 University of Calgary wave forms

Fig 13.24 demonstrates that any starting point can serve to create a 3D structure – in this case one based on a wave form. The rendering is of a futuristic skyscraper where each floor disc can rotate around the interconnecting elevator column, either freely or in concert with all the other floor discs.

Wave-like 3D structures Fig. 13.25 is an example of a possible architectural structure. Known as 'Parametric Dunes', the concept structure was generated by SMD Arquitectes in Barcelona.

The Parametric Dunes looks aesthetically pleasing probably because of the wave-like form. One can imagine using electromechanical hinges or shape-transforming materials to animate the waves. Maybe, to enclose the spaces defined by the Parametric Dunes, transparent cellular materials that can change their surface area could be added to the sides (see chapter 11).

The structure in fig. 13.26 was generated by students at the University of Calgary, Canada, and exhibited in 2010 at the university's Kasian Gallery. As with the Parametric Dunes, the wave form

is shown as an example of a possible architectural formation. The project is described as follows: 'Although digital fabrication has allowed architects and designers to explore more complex geometries, one of the byproducts has been a lack of attention to material waste. Often digitally fabricated projects are generated from a top-down logic with the parameters of typical material sheet sizes being subordinated to the end of the design process. This project attempts to reverse that logic by starting from the basic material dimensions and then generating a series of components

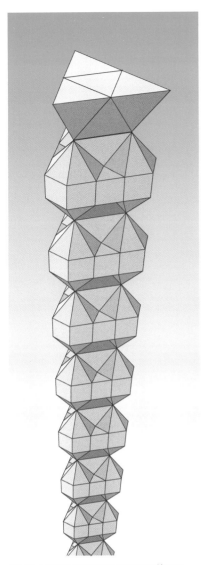

13.27 Lattice structure representing a sky-high habitat

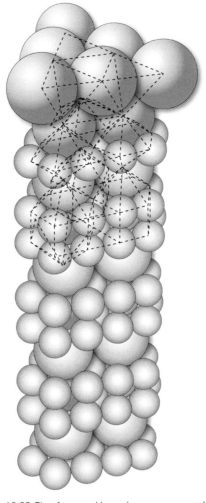

13.28 The close-packing sphere arrangement used to generate the fig. 13.27 lattice

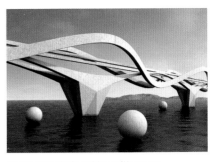

13.29 Futuristic bridge with spans necessitating new materials

13.30 Futuristic skyscraper designed by Christian Hahn

13.31 CCTV Headquarters, Beijing, 2012

that will minimize material waste during CNC cutting while still producing an undulating, light-filtering screen in the gallery.'

Unrestricted 3D dimensions Space elevators are putative transportation systems constructed from ribbon-like cables or tethers anchored to the surface of the Earth that extend into space. Science fiction writer Arthur C. Clarke went a step further by imagining space elevators linked to off-planet, halo-like megastructures that would circle the Earth and accommodate entire cities and various types of habitat.

The illustration in fig. 13.27 is constructed from lattices derived from the golden sphere packing shown in fig. 13.28, and is designed to conceptually show an incredibly tall, tower-like structure – maybe something that is miles high to provide a suborbital platform – a structure that may be possible with new nanomaterials. Fig. 13.29 shows a concept drawing of a futuristic bridge with spans that would be almost impossible to construct with conventional building materials.

Fig. 13.30 shows a futuristic skyscraper design for Battery Park, New York, by German architect Christian Hahn, where the outer organic structure might be manufactured using bioformed particle materials.

Fig. 13.31 shows the CCTV Headquarters in Beijing, by Rem Koolhaas and Ole Scheeren of OMA, completed in 2012.

The conceptual buildings shown in figs 13.27 and 13.30 pose a question with regard to the challenges of creating a

13.32 Northrop Grumman X-47B

13.34 NASA commercial supersonic concept aircraft

13.33 Sierra Nevada 'Dream Chaser'

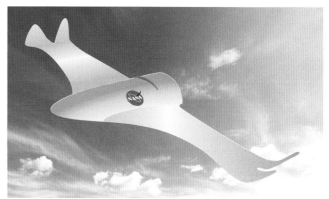

13.35 NASA shape-changing wing concept aircraft

visually acceptable 'look' when almost anything is possible. As architects stretch the boundaries with new materials and methodologies, their designs might take some adjustment to be appreciated.

Future 3D forms Structures of the future will be designed for all sorts of applications, from architecture to product and vehicle design. Aircraft designs considered for the future demonstrate how 3D structures might evolve to best accommodate natural and man-made forces (see figs 13.32 to 13.35). Aircraft can already be shaped to reduce their radar signature and coloured to reduce optical visibility. Planes with adjustable wing surfaces and variable thrust vectoring systems have been designed to increase manoeuvrability. The future holds the possibility of surfaces that will change shape using materials that will ripple, twist and change size, and that will respond to, and be powered by, various types of energy. New technologies will trickle down from military to civilian use so that shape and surface change

become a possible feature of almost any structural form. Other new material technologies will include cellular material development, surface laminates, smart surfaces and so on.

Future concepts of 3D beauty Earlier we considered what might be the aesthetic criteria for 3D structural forms of the future. The question could be rephrased as: 'What will be the concept of beauty in the future, when almost anything is possible?'

The answer may well be to do with dynamics as much as with static form. Beauty in the present and the past has been associated with natural forms, nostalgia, ideas of grandeur and functionality, but also with the so-called divine, or otherwise idealized, proportions. Historically, when creating physical structures, or a model of an event, we have created relatively static forms, or forms with very predictable dynamics, that are either easy to conceptualize (such as a rectangular box or the Rutherford model of the atom), or physically easy to construct (such as

those made out of wood, stone or steel). Streamlining is another factor that has influenced design over thousands of years, with progressively more science applied to it, from Phoenician galleys to flying machines.

Now let us imagine a world where computer-generated routines can, with enhanced sensors, more thoroughly explore the nature of quantum effects in multiple dimensions and spectrums; a world where structures can be built that are no longer dependent on modular building blocks and their stress, strain and loadbearing characteristics (steel girders, bricks and so on); and where materials can change shape to accommodate local environmental conditions. In this imagined world, streamlined structural forms will be able to ripple, bend, bloat and shrink, and materials with internal lattice-like structures will have vastly improved loadbearing characteristics, as already heralded by carbon fibre, carbon nanotubes, graphene and the like.

So what of beauty in the future?

Architecturally, the 1950s can be seen to characterize a mishmash approach to beauty, at least in postwar Europe. Styles ranged from Bauhaus-influenced and ideas of what 'modern' architecture should be, to remnants of classicism or to a strict utilitarianism that was primarily dependent upon inexpensive building materials and speed of construction.

In the future, to eliminate such a mishmash of designs, we might argue for a thematic approach, where some geographical areas are, say, devoted to cursive forms that change shape, others to classicism where individuals need to hold on to what they believe are their cultural traditions, or still others where all structures have a natural efficiency of form, or where structures stretch the visual imagination.

For areas devoted to natural forms that change shape we might have entire cities with structures that move like ocean waves, or whose organically shaped buildings rise out of the ground, blow in the wind, and sink back down in extreme weather. In more classic areas themes could be that of a Moroccan kasbah, Ancient Greece, or a medieval English village; ancient structures would be mimicked with new materials and technologies. Areas where towering structures are required to economize on land usage might use new generations of nanomaterials and cellular materials, allowing them to rise to incredible heights and then spread out to form layers.

It would be advantageous to agree on the sort of forms that can be considered 'beautiful'. One definition might include structures that harmoniously integrate into the natural environment, or are removed from it by being constructed up in the clouds or under the ocean. The idea of natural curves is also appealing.

Structures that mimic mud buildings like those in Timbuktu, or even the melted Art Nouveau architectures of Gaudí, would appeal to many people. Forms that have a natural efficiency, such as hemispheres, also have their appeal. Symbolism would probably work for many in the tradition of medieval cathedrals or Greek temples – proportioned, for example, to mimic an idealized human body. A city built of Platonic and Archimedean geometric forms might be interesting.

Enhancing the human spirit Enhancing the human spirit is not the same as addressing how to define beauty. Enhancing the spirit is about enhancing the sensation of 'life', of making an environment that inspires creativity and effective human relationships – a space that 'inspires the soul'.

Many of the elements that would create a space that would 'enhance the soul' have been mentioned in this book, and much comes down to an individual's culture and sense of self, so that it is difficult to generalize. Spiritual symbolism is important to many, as is family or ancestral history. Spiritual symbolism abounds in all cultures, including, for example, images of the tau, the lotus flower, the star of David, the cross, the crescent moon, and innumerable other examples. Family symbolism can be characterized by totem poles, tribal patterns, and family portraits, photographs, videos and, soon, holograms. Enhancing the soul through physical structures, and even through our conceptual models, is much more than triggering associations with symbols or conceptual models: it is more about physical experiences that trigger emotional and physiological responses – such as how we experience sound, light and touch, how we feel in harmony with the spaces that surround us, how we can move through the spaces we inhabit, and how we feel connected to the universe that surrounds us. There may well also be a functional aspect linked to how adaptable a physical structure is: can we easily change it, or will it change for us?

Prior to creating fixed dwellings, early humans underwent a life of wandering and migration, a life close to the physical world with all its natural beauties and dangers. We survived by adapting to our environments and by creating community groups through rituals of dance and music – as well as of self-interest. Today we have largely internalized or displaced the physical experiences of our ancestors through abstract entertainment and fantasy, giving up our lives to a structured work environment and establishing a sense of security by way of financial and medical assets. Family and community support have significantly been replaced by institutions.

The author proposes that enhancing the human spirit through 3D structures will entail paying respect to our pre-fixed-habitation lifestyles and to our innate modelling dispositions, but also to what is now possible given new technologies, needs and environmental conditions. For our very survival, let us create structural environments that will promote awareness and creativity so that we are not caught in a metaphorical beehive, hanging from a tree that is about to be chopped down. We have little choice as human beings but to evolve in a changing world.

Key elements in models and physical structures that enhance perception
The following list includes practical ideas as well as others that are imaginative or fanciful. Note that no science supports the list, it is simply based on the author's intuition.

1. Internal spaces should not be defined primarily by rectangles. Internal spaces influence and orient people. Living in the classic rectangular box imposes a strict left-right-up-down environment on a human being whose roots are wedded to experiences of the sky, forest canopies, caves, open deserts and temporary shelters. To place a human in a fixed rectangular box is arguably unnatural.
2. We should explore the impact on people of changeable cursive and non-rectangular internal environments: how do they make a person feel and behave? At the moment almost everything is rectangular, from rooms to doors, floors, windows and computer screens. We even use rectangular picture frames to integrate our pieces of art into our rectangular environments. If we consider rock paintings we will notice that artists have not drawn rectangles around their images. We will also notice that images have been created on irregular surfaces, with irregularities often used to add an experiential dimension.
3. Non-rectangular spaces can be substantially cursive or composed of angled polygonal panels and yet still have areas composed of vertical

and horizontal surfaces – and floors can still be horizontal, much as with a forest or cave. Cursive forms are often more stable than rectangular boxes, and forms can be explored that have a natural equilibrium. Stacking, or otherwise connecting, non-rectangular 3D forms can easily be accomplished, as has been shown in this book. New materials and technologies make a a great many 3D forms possible that were not possible in the past, and the only limitations are not having enough scientific data, experience or imagination to best utilize them.

4. The interconnections of spaces can be used to help change a person's mood and give them time to adjust from one space to another. Corridors in medieval monasteries were used to walk, to pause and to contemplate. Today's rectangular corridors generally have no function other than functionally connecting rooms. In some cases corridors are decorated with paintings or photos but their strict Cartesian x, y, z proportions only encourage rapid transitions between spaces.

5. External rectangular structures make no statement except for utilitarianism – they have no implicit symbolism, they make no attempt to blend in with a natural environment, and they make a statement that straight lines in vertical and horizontal grids are essential to our everyday lives. Entering such buildings, we expect to be oriented in internal x, y, z lattices. Rectangular skyscrapers represent the pinnacle of the architectural occupation of the rectangles. Even their materials and surfaces stand in stark contrast to what was once a natural environment. An external form could be used to demonstrate other principles, such as equilibrium, efficiency or inventiveness of form and structure, exploration of spatial structures, natural forms or organic structures, and dynamics such as motion, history and even symbolism.

6. Dynamics and movement, within and without a space, is also critical for enhancing our perceptions. We have become used to static environments, whereas our ancestors were used to changing environments, to portable or temporary structures, and often to wandering lifestyles. We are entering a time when accommodating structures can move if we wish them to – literally walk away, rotate or swirl in wave-like patterns. There is no reason why interior structures, fittings and furniture cannot freely move whether by hand or automatically.

7. External views should be available to all when occupying a structure. This is one justification for spanning out into the clouds. Exposure to natural light is beneficial to health, as is the capacity for far vision as well as close vision. Colours have also been shown to impact mood.

8. With OLEDs, printed speakers and circuits, we now have the capability to make almost any surface a multimedia surface. It is also possible, with sensors, to have an internal space that responds to its occupants, to know where they are in the space, to provide for their material needs, to educate them or otherwise stimulate or challenge them. At a voice command a surface could change – a new colour, a pattern, a communication, a piece of art, a project, the news… Any and all surfaces can have this capability, though it is to be hoped that such multimedia experiences are not used to replace physical experiences, nor used to control our ideas and behaviour.

9. Much as the external aspect of a rectangular skyscraper can make a subtle or gross statement about how we should behave and navigate through our working lives, so too can an internal space be used to bias or limit perception and to encourage addictive behaviours. Architects and designers of the future should consider how they are playing a part in the emotional, physical and mental development of the occupants and users of their 3D creations – since the means to influence many facets of human experience, inside and outside an architectural space, can so easily be abused. Humans might be entering the equivalent of the Minotaur's labyrinth, but they could also be entering something new, that enhances and makes more valuable their life experiences.

Expanding our sensory environment

We have already passed many of our processing tasks over to computers and this trend will only increase. We have also increased our sensor capabilities far beyond those of our natural human senses – sensitivity to expanded energy spectrums and magnetic fields, for example. We are in the process of connecting this enhanced sensor capability to new generations of computers with more diverse types of circuit architecture, such as those inspired by human neural structures, with the possibility of computers with 100 trillion 'neurosynaptic cores', where each corelet might have hundreds of inputs and outputs, as envisioned in IBM's SyNAPSE project. Here, the outputs and inputs will be used to connect the cores to each other, and each corelet will have a different function. This means that once a cognitive computer is a reality, it can be utilized for applications involving pattern recognition and other problems involving sifting through very large amounts of data.

The developments in computer sensor and processing capabilities, whatever the circuit architecture, make us consider how human visual logic, and logic in general, might evolve in the future. In earlier chapters the idea was put forward that our various human logical systems evolved in the way they did because of the limits of our human sensing and processing capabilities. To overcome our natural limits we construct visual models of our surroundings – so, although our eyes focus only on a relatively narrow field, we create mental constructs for the balance. If we had more and expanded senses, and if we also had greater processing and memory capabilities, we might not need to model many observed events, or we might easily create a whole range of models for the same event.

In the future we may be able to hook ourselves into computers so that we can 'see' what they 'see', communicate using their sensor capabilities, and control events through them, such as operating machines and so on. In a sense this is already happening, but in the not-too-distant future the computer–human link is likely to become more integrated and radically change the way we think, communicate and control events.

THE FUTURE OF VISUAL LOGIC: A SUMMARY

Setting the stage In geometry our concept of the space we inhabit has been the stage within which we work to model the things we observe, or wish to create. For many centuries, our concept of space was that it was uniform, unchanging, with north, south, east and west directions. This was a space that could be organized in square and cubic grids and within which every point could be determined in terms of three dimensions. As time passed, new needs and challenges arose, and with them our sense of space evolved – space could be infinite, it could be distorted, its dimensions might be customized to accommodate new types of variable or new ways of quantifying it. We now even have concepts of multidimensional space and of space that is integrated with time – Einstein's 'space-time'.

Current technologies, hardware and software Technologies have greatly enhanced our ability to observe events, in all sorts of energy spectrums, as well as to process and store information, and we can only expect the enhancements to continue. Three-dimensional modelling software has also evolved, by which we can not only design structures but also model the materials that they are made of and how they will react to various environmental conditions. We can see how structures will respond to light, sound, air pressure and much more. We can place our digital structures in simulated environments, and even animate them through periods of time. We can also directly translate our digital structures into real three-dimensional objects, rendering them in all sorts of materials – and all of these capabilities can only improve, with more and more realism and accuracy.

Future technologies A future when computers are so powerful that they will be better than humans at evaluating three-dimensional structures and then manufacturing them. A future when human decisions will revolve around costs of manufacture, use of resources, operational requirements and real-estate placement. Also, hopefully, a future where human decisions regarding digitally produced habitats, and other designs, will involve quality-of-life decisions and preserving ecosystems and the environment.

The actors on the future stage A statement has been made in this book about the current lack of an architectural science that determines and evaluates the human impact of architectural 'space' – meaning the actual shape and nature of architectural and design space as well as its interconnectivity. A science that has researched the impacts of architectural and design spaces upon life, upon human enhancement, empowerment, creativity and positive social interaction. A science that covers much more than ergonomics and catering for standard human functions such as entertainment and basic sculptural and design aesthetics. Current solutions are based on economics and ergonomics as well as the availability of standard and mostly rectangular building materials; and aesthetics are often based on sculptural appearances and what might look good in *Architectural Digest*. An ideal future would be when the computer interface accepts inputs regarding economic and basic functional requirements and then prompts options regarding the 'human' nature of the spaces required and their interconnectivity – where the computer would draw from scientifically supported space options of which a number might include some of the proportional and shape-changing lattices presented in this book. Future computer capabilities should be so powerful, with vast processing and storage capabilities, libraries of structural options and sensor-based and data information interfaces, that they should provide an 'intelligent' response and even a dialogue regarding a human design initiative. Human contributions would be to work on improving all the facets of the computer environment but also to take new leaps of imagination and creativity on the basis that the fabric of computer intelligence was still based on current human invention. Of course, even that is likely to change as computers become more intelligent and creative than humans – when one hopes they will still serve human needs and well-being.

A NOTE FROM THE AUTHOR

Technologies, hardware and software
Over the years I have used various tools, technologies and software to develop geometrical structures – going from using Rotring pens, compasses, rulers, drafting film, slide rules, logarithm tables and mechanical calculators, to using Fortran, a programming language and an IBM 370 computer to animate geometric concepts on film, and AutoCAD software.

Today I use SolidWorks and Rhino CAD software; LightWave 3D for animations; MultiGen Creator for simulations; Adobe Illustrator to create illustrations and to develop concepts; Wolfram Mathematica to model equations; SharePoint for data management; and much more. I am in awe of the current software platforms, my mind boggling over how many functions they now have; and I anxiously await new generations. A challenge for newbies will be that of immersing themselves into even one platform. As words of advice I would recommend a knowledge of code and algorithms, the development of a broad perspective regarding the computer hardware and software environment, a matching of personal interests, skills and creative dispositions with a few software platforms, and then an immersion in a few, but remembering to think outside the box, to continue to question relevance of one's actions, to continue to research and observe – and to always remain a logical, and even an algorithmic, thinker who is as quick to pick up a pencil and a piece of paper, hike along the mountaintops and enjoy being human as to spend time talking to a machine.

14. ADDITIONAL THOUGHTS AND IDEAS

SANGAKU, REULEAUX TRIANGLE, MUSIC, HEROD'S MOSAIC, ALGORITHMS

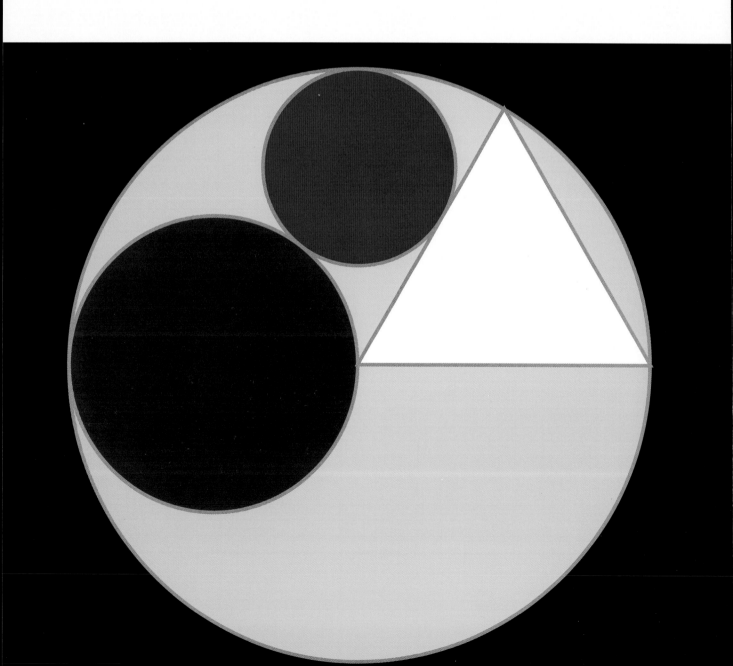

The concepts in this short chapter range from constant-diameter triangles to musical notes in hexagonal grids.

SANGAKU PUZZLE

Sangaku are votive tablets offered in Shinto shrines and sometimes Buddhist temples in Japan. Sangaku images are presented without explanation and simply without any construction or notation. The earliest Sangaku tablets found date back to the beginning of the 17th century.

Description In fig. 14.1a, the green circle (O_1) circumscribes the red (O_2) and blue (O_3) circles and an isosceles triangle. The base of the isosceles triangle and the centre of the red circle stand on the diameter of the green circle. An interpretation of the puzzle is to demonstrate that O_3D is perpendicular to the diameter of the green circle AC.

Considerations DH and DB are tangent to the blue circle with centre O_3 and radius p; triangle O_3DF is a right-angled triangle; and the blue circle is internally tangent to the green circle.

The challenge We shall prove that the blue circle can be drawn so it is tangent to the red circle, and, consequently, also tangent to the isosceles triangle at F.

(i)
$O_1A = R$; $O_2A = r$; $O_3F = p$; $\beta = 90° - \alpha$

(ii)
$CB = DB$
$2DE = 2R - 2r$
$DE = EC = R - r$

$O_1O_3 = R - p$
$O_1D = 2r - R$
$O_1E = O_1D + DE = r = O_2A$
$O_2O_3 = r + p$

(iii) Secant-tangent theorem
Euclid, *Elements*, Book 3, Prop. 36: If a tangent segment and a secant segment are drawn to a circle from an exterior point, then the square of the measure of the tangent segment is equal to the product of the measures of the secant segment and its external secant segment.
$t^2 = p(p + 2r)$ (see fig. 14.1b)

(iv) $t^2 + O_1D^2 = O_1O_3{}^2$
$t^2 + (2r - R)^2 = (R - p)^2$

(v) Solving equations (iii) and (iv)
$t = 2r\sqrt{[2R(R - r)]}/ (R + r)$ and
$p = 2r(R - r)/(R + r)$
we have shown that the blue circle can be drawn so as to be tangent to both the green and the red circles.

(vi) Pythagorean theorem
(a) $BE = \sqrt{(O_1B^2 - O_1E^2)} = \sqrt{(O_1A^2 - O_1E^2)} = \sqrt{(R^2 - r^2)}$ and
(b) $DB^2 = BE^2 + DE^2 = (R^2 - r^2) + (R - r)^2$
$DB = \sqrt{[2R(R - r)]}$

(vii) By comparing
(a) $(p/t)^2 = p^2/t^2 = [2r(R - r)]^2 / 4r^2[2R(R - r)] = [2r(R - r)]^2 / 4rR[2r(R - r)] = (R - r) / 2R$, and
(b) $(DE/DB)^2 = DE^2/DB^2 = (R - r)^2 / 2R(R - r) = (R - r) / 2R$
we have proved that triangle DO_3F is similar to triangle CBE, and consequently, F must lie on line DB.

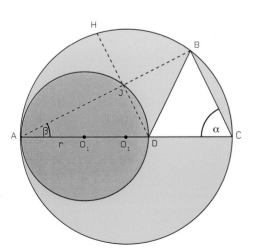

14.1a Sangaku puzzle, Gunma Prefecture, Japan, 1803

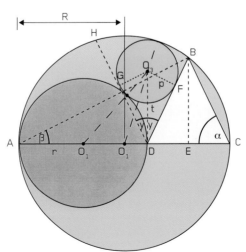

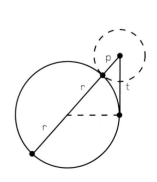

14.1b Secant-tangent theorem

14.2 Window in the Church of Our Lady, Bruges, Belgium

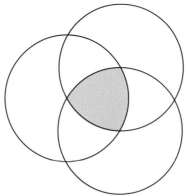

14.3 Construction of a Reuleaux triangle

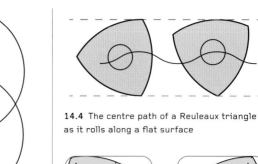

14.4 The centre path of a Reuleaux triangle as it rolls along a flat surface

14.5 The actual path of the centre is not a perfect circle

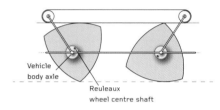

Vehicle body axle
Reuleaux wheel centre shaft

14.8 Possible wheel-drive mechanism

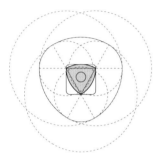

14.6 An extension to the Reuleaux wheel construction

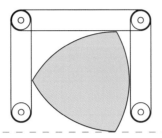
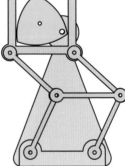

14.7 Possible wheel-drive mechanism

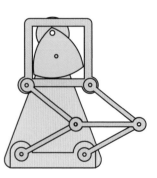

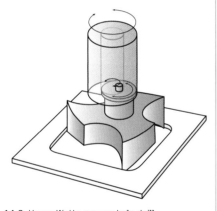

14.9 Harry Watts square hole drill

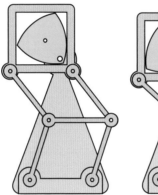

14.10 Luch 2 film advance mechanism

THE REULEAUX TRIANGLE

Franz Reuleaux was a 19th-century German engineer who pioneered the study of machines for translating one type of motion into another. The Reuleaux triangle is named after him, though knowledge of it predates him.

A Reuleaux triangle is formed from the intersection of three circles, each having its centre on the boundary of the other two. It is a curve of constant width.

Fig. 14.2 shows a window in the 14th-century Church of Our Lady in Bruges, Belgium. The curved triangle appears to have been constructed in the same way

as the Reuleaux triangle.

The construction of the Reuleaux triangle is shown in fig. 14.3 – and the diameter of the shape is constant. If the Reuleaux triangle is rolled along a flat horizontal surface then its height above the surface will stay at the same level; however, the centre point will follow the path of a wave as it rolls along (see fig. 14.4). The actual centre path is not quite circular. An approximate circular centre path is shown in fig. 14.5. Possible wheel-drive mechanisms using the circular path are shown in figs 14.6 and 14.7. A construction of an extension

to the Reuleaux triangle is shown in fig. 14.6 – also of constant width.

Reuleaux polygons have many applications, such as in the Wankel engine, British coinage, and guitar picks. The Reuleaux triangle will rotate to trace a square with rounded corners, an application of which is the Harry Watts square drill bit that will drill square holes with rounded corners (see fig. 14.9). Another use is in the film advance mechanism in the Soviet Luch 2 8mm film projector (see fig. 14.10).

In Reuleaux scooters, the wheels of the scooter shown in fig. 14.10 are the

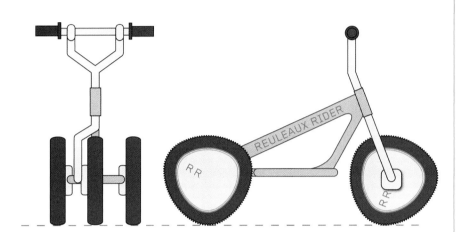

14.11 A Reuleaux scooter concept

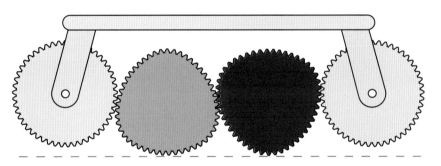

14.12 A Reuleaux rolling wheel concept

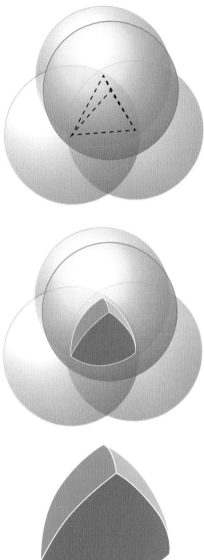

14.13 Meissner tetrahedron

same shape as the extended Reuleaux triangle shown in fig. 14.6. A compensating mechanism using the circular approximation path shown in fig. 14.5 will only help dampen the wave-like motion. The wheel concept shown in fig. 14.12 may well work and stay horizontal.

A mechanism to fully compensate for the up and down motion was patented by Erich John Brandeau in 2011, while in 2009 Guan Baihua of Qingdao, China, invented a bicycle whose back wheel is a Reuleaux triangle and whose front wheel is a pentagonal curve of constant width.

Meissner tetrahedron The intersection of four spheres of radius x, centred at the vertices of a regular tetrahedron of x side length, is called the Reuleaux tetrahedron, but the width of the surface is not constant, varying by up to about 2.5%. The Reuleaux tetrahedron can, however, be made into a surface of constant width by replacing its edge arcs with curved surface patches: this modified form is called a Meissner tetrahedron (see fig. 14.13). There are many ways to generate solids of equal diameter that are not spheres. Equal-sized solids can serve as bearings, in

a similar way to equal-sized spheres. The Danish and German mathematicians Tommy Bonnesen and Werner Fenchel in their 1934 theory of convex bodies conjectured that the Meissner tetrahedron has the minimum volume of all shapes of constant width.

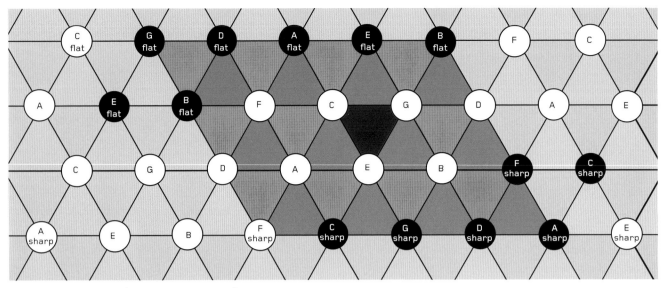

14.14 A triads triangular (also known as hexagonal) keyboard

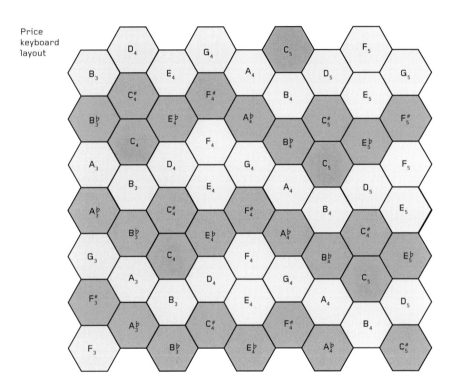

Price keyboard layout

14.15 The Price hexagonal keyboard

PATTERNS IN MUSICAL SCALES

Non-linear arrangements, such as hexagonal or triangular tessellations, can be used to place musical notes in various types of harmonic groups.

Neo-Riemannian theory is a loose collection of ideas aimed at relating harmonies directly to each other. Initially these were major and minor triads (sets of three notes that can be stacked vertically in thirds, producing chords).

A major triad is A, C sharp, E
A minor triad is A, C, E
B major triad is B, D sharp, F sharp

B minor triad is B, D, F sharp
C major triad is C, E, G
C minor triad is C sharp, E, G sharp
D major triad is D, F sharp, A;
D minor trid is D, F, A
E major triad is E, G sharp, B
E minor triad is E, G, B
F major triad is F, A, C
F minor triad is F, A flat, C
G major triad is G, B, D
G minor triad is G, B flat, D

The major and minor triads can be arranged on a triangular grid with two notes in common and third notes (with semitonal shifts) positioned opposite each other. Once a core triangulation of triads has been built then other triads can be arranged around them (see fig. 14.14).

The Price keyboard layout (see fig. 14.15) has a diatonic (traditional) scale following a horizontal path and a semitone scale on the vertical, making the chromatic (proceeding by semitones) scale easier to play. Other hexagonal keyboard layouts include the Gerhard and Maupin; both, theoretically, make diatonic and chromatic scales and triads easier to play than on a standard piano keyboard.

14.16 Mosaic floor at Herod's Western Palace, Masada, Israel

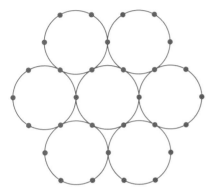

14.17 The core geometric construction of Herod's mosaic

14.18 The construction of Herod's mosaic

HEROD'S MOSAIC

Fragments of a mosaic floor survive in the remains of King Herod the Great's Western Palace (see fig. 14.16). The palace forms part of the massive Masada fortifications located on top of a rock plateau at the western end of the Judaean desert, overlooking the Dead Sea. Herod constructed the palace built between 37 and 31 BCE.

The circle design at the centre of the mosaic is based on seven primary equal-sized circles – six about one (see fig. 14.17).

Each of the primary seven circles has six equal-sized circles drawn with centres on their circumferences and equidistant and positioned on primary contact points (see fig. 14.18). Fig. 14.19 shows the completed design.

14.19 The completed Herod's mosaic

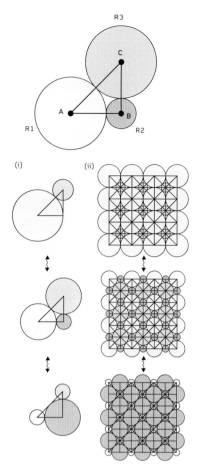

14.20 A dynamic circle algorithm

DYNAMIC CLOSE-PACKING CIRCLE ALGORITHMS

The close-packed circle cells and sphere clusters shown in chapter 12 can be generated with algorithmic steps that apply a successive approximation logic. The logic basically steps through sizes and positions of circles and spheres within set parameters (see fig. 14.20).

First sequence The sequence in fig. 14.20 is presented in two ways: (i) as unit right-isosceles triangles and (ii) as extended tessellated square cells.

Circle circumference x values are calculated as $x = a + r\cos(\theta)$ – with θ values 0 to 2π.

Circle circumference y values are calculated as $y = b + r\sin(\theta)$ – with θ values 0 to 2π.

(a, b) are coordinate positions of circle centres – in this first sequence coordinates (a, b) will all fall on the vertices of symmetry, points a, b and c.

Boundaries of circle circumference values (x, y) are the containing lines of symmetry – in this case the right-

isosceles triangle ABC. So, for R1 the boundary is BC where $x = 1$; for R2 the boundary is AC where $x = y$; and for R3 the boundary is AB where $y = 0$.

First sequence, see drawing (i) where R2 is given the priority of growth:

(a)
R1 circle centre values
The (a_1, b_1) coordinates are $a_1 = 0$, $b_1 = 0$. The R1 circumference coordinate limits are $(x_1 [0 \text{ to } \pm 1], y_1 [0 \text{ to } \pm 1])$.
R2 circle centre values
The (a_2, b_2) coordinates are $a_2 = 1$, $b_2 = 0$. The R2 circumference coordinate limits are $(x_2 [1 \text{ to } 1 \pm \sqrt{0.5}], y_2 [0 \text{ to } \pm \sqrt{0.5}])$.
R3 circle centre values
The (a_3, b_3) coordinates are $a_3 = 1$, $b_3 = 1$. The R3 circumference coordinate limits are $(x_3 [1 \text{ to } 1 \pm 1], y_3 [1 \text{ to } (1 \pm 1)]$.

(b)
$x_1[0 \text{ to } \pm 1] = 0 + r_1[1 - \sqrt{0.5} \text{ to } 1] \cos(\theta)$
$y_1[0 \text{ to } \pm 1] = 0 + r_1[1 - \sqrt{0.5} \text{ to } 1] \sin(\theta)$

(c)
$x_2[1 \text{ to } 1 \pm \sqrt{0.5}] = 1 + r_2[0 \text{ to } \sqrt{0.5}] \cos(\theta)$
$y_2[0 \text{ to } \pm \sqrt{0.5}] = 0 + r_2[0 \text{ to } \sqrt{0.5}] \sin(\theta)$

(d)
$x_3[1 \text{ to } 1 \pm 1] = 1 + r_3[(1 - \sqrt{0.5}) \text{ to } 1] \cos(\theta)$
$y_3[0 \text{ to } \pm 1] = 1 + r_3[(1 - \sqrt{0.5}) \text{ to } 1] \sin(\theta)$

(e) Start R1 with $r_1 = 1$, and R2 with $r_2 = 0$, and R3 with $r_3 = 1 - \sqrt{0.5}$.

(f) Step values of r_2 in small positive increments while maintaining $r_1 + r_2 = 1$. At the same time step values in small negative increments while maintaining $r_3 + r_2 = 1$.

(g) At each step value of R1, R2 and R3 check concurrence of (x_3, y_3) with (x_1, y_1) calculating using (b) and (d). When concurrence then signify a second 'close-pack'.

(h) R2 continues to grow until it reaches its maximum size at $r_2 = \sqrt{0.5}$. At this point R2 reaches its symmetrical opposite across AC and, as R2 has maintained a contact with R3 and 1, this is a third 'close-pack' position.

(i) If the sequence continued then R3 would be given the priority of growth and grow until R3 = 1.

THE DYNAMIC CLOSE-PACKING CIRCLE GEOMETRY

A few examples of ways to compare or control circle and sphere sizes during the transformations of circle size and position during the generation of a dynamic sequence are shown in figs 14.21, 14.22, 14.23 and 14.24.

RADII OF CIRCLES IN PROPORTION
TO CIRCLE $r1 = 1$

Cell RTR1.1
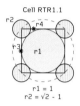
$r1 = 1$
$r2 = \sqrt{2} - 1$

Cell RTR1.2
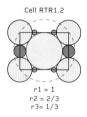
$r1 = 1$
$r2 = 2/3$
$r3 = 1/3$

Cell RTR1.3 and RTR1.5

$r1 = 1$
$r2 = 0.239310147$
$r3 = 0.760689853$
$r4 = 0.458993979$

Cell RTR1.4
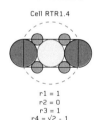
$r1 = 1$
$r2 = 0$
$r3 = 1$
$r4 = \sqrt{2} - 1$

Cell RTR1.6

$r1 = 1$
$r2 = 0$
$r3 = (\sqrt{5} - 1)/2$
$r4 = 0.5$

Cell RTR1.7
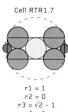
$r1 = 1$
$r2 = 0$
$r3 = \sqrt{2} - 1$
$r4 = 1$

14.21 Radii in proportion to circle R1

Column 1

AREAS OF CIRCLES WITHIN CELLS
WITH RADIUS OF r1 AS A CONSTANT

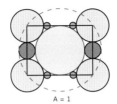

$$\text{area} = \pi\,(r1^2 + r2^2)$$
$$\text{area} = \pi\,(4 - 2\sqrt{2}) = \pi\,(1.17157...)$$

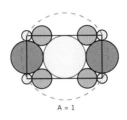

$$\text{area} = \pi\,(r1^2 + r2^2 + r3^2)$$
$$\text{area} = \pi\,(1 + 4/9 + 1/9)$$
$$= \pi\,(1 + 5/9) = \pi\,(1.5555...)$$

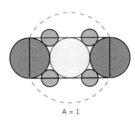

$$\text{area} = \pi\,(r1^2 + r2^2 + r3^2 + 2r4^2) = \pi\,(2.05726)$$

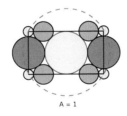

$$\text{area} = \pi\,(r1^2 + r3^2 + 2r4^2)$$
$$\text{area} = \pi\,(1 + 1 + 2(3 - 2\sqrt{2})) = \pi\,(2.343146...)$$

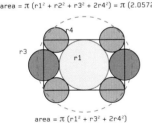

$$\text{area} = \pi\,(r1^2 + r2^2 + r3^2 + 2r4^2) = \pi\,(2.05726)$$

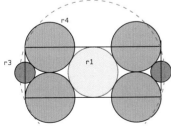

$$\text{area} = \pi\,(r1^2 + r3^2 + 2r4^2)$$
$$\text{area} = \pi\,(1 + (0.381966) + 0.5) = \pi\,(1.881966)$$

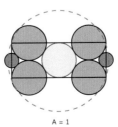

$$\text{area} = \pi\,(r1^2 + r3^2 + 2r4^2)$$
$$\text{area} = \pi\,(1 + (\sqrt{2}-1)^2 + 2) = \pi\,(3.17157...)$$

14.22 Area of circles within cells with R1 as a constant

Column 2

RADII AND CELL SIZE IN PROPORTION WITH
TOTAL CIRCLE AREA WITHIN CELL = 1
(The logic can be applied to sphere volume
within the cell)

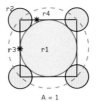

A = 1

[series of figures each labelled]

A = 1

A = 1

A = 1

A = 1

A = 1

A = 1

14.23 Radii and cell size in proportion with
the total circle area

Column 3

BY VOLUME (V) ABOUT SYMMETRICAL
BOUNDARY (RECTANGULAR) ON 2D PLANE.

V = 1
$$\text{Volume} = 4/3\pi\,(r1^3 + r2^3)$$
$$= 4/3\pi\,(1 + (\sqrt{2}-1)^3)$$
$$= 4/3\pi\,(1.0711...)$$

V = 1
$$\text{Volume} = 4/3\pi\,(r1^3 + r2^3 + r3^3)$$
$$= 4/3\pi\,(1 + 8/27 + 1/27)$$
$$V = 4/3\pi\,(1.3333)$$

14.24 By volume about a symmetrical
boundary

FIBONACCI AND GOLDEN RATIO

The following equations relate to proving
the convergence of the Fibonacci
sequence with the golden ratio.

Sum of all integers The following proof
is based on a method attributed to 19th-
century German mathematician Carl
Gauss, whose logic considered the first
100 numbers as follows:
$$1 + 2 + 3 + 4 + ... + 97 + 98 + 99 + 100$$
The sum of the largest and the smallest
= 101, the second largest and second
smallest = 101, etc.
The pattern continues to the nth value,
so the sum of all pairs = n(n + 1)/2.

Sum of all squares
Let $S = 1^2 + 2^2 + 3^2 + ... + n^2$

Cubic equations expand as follows:
$$(1 + 1)^3 = 1^3 + 3 \times 1^2 + 3 \times 1 + 1$$
$$(2 + 1)^3 = 2^3 + 3 \times 2^2 + 3 \times 2 + 1$$
$$(3 + 1)^3 = 3^3 + 3 \times 3^2 + 3 \times 3 + 1...$$
$$(n + 1)^3 = n^3 + 3 \times n^2 + 3 \times n + 1$$
If we add these cubic equations we get:
$$(1 + 1)^3 + (2 + 1)^3 + (3 + 1)^3 + ...+ (n + 1)^3$$
$$= 1^3 + 2^3 + 3^3 + ...n^3 + 3(1^2 + 2^2 + 3^2 + ...n^2)$$
$$+ 3(1 + 2 + 3 + n) + 1 + 1 + 1...1$$
After simplification and substitution for
S, and equation for the sum of all positive
integers, we get:
$$2^3 + 3^3 + 4^3 + ...+ (n + 1)^3 = 1^3 + 2^3 + 3^3$$
$$+ ...+n^3 + 3S + 3/2n(n + 1) + n$$
After subtracting the sum of cubes we
get:
$$3S = (n + 1)^3 - 3/2n(n + 1) - n - 1 \text{ and}$$
$$S = n(n + 1)(2n + 1)/6$$

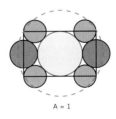

G L O S S A R Y

Underlined words have their own entry.

algorithm A very specific set of instructions that follow a step-by-step logic to accomplish an end purpose. Algorithms are used to map out the logic of a computer program, although the ideas behind them predate computers.

Archimedean solids Any one of 13 geometric solids composed of more than one regular polygon, first described by Archimedes.

axiom A basic assumption that is taken to be true, to serve as a premise or starting point for further reasoning and arguments.

close-packing circles An arrangement of circles (of equal or varying sizes) on a given surface such that no overlapping occurs and so that all circles touch one another in triangulated groups.

close-packing spheres An arrangement of spheres (of equal or varying sizes) in three-dimensional space such that no overlapping occurs and so that all circles touch one another in tetrahedral groups (not necessarily regular tetrahedral groups).

conchoid (below) A curve whose name means 'shell form'. The conchoid of Nicomedes is a curve derived from a fixed point, a fixed straight line and a moving line, where the moving line rotates around and through the fixed point and a position on the moving line is restricted to follow the straight line. Conchoid curves are generated by other points on the moving line. Variations of conchoid curves can be generated by replacing the fixed straight line with a curve.

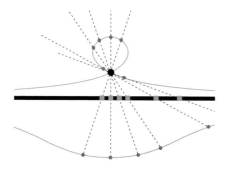

curve of constant width A shape whose height or width between two equidistant parallel lines, or surfaces, is always the same.

geodesic dome A dome constructed from convex polyhedra that approximate a sphere or hemisphere. Typically geodesic domes are constructed from triangular lattices that are rigid and that distribute the structural stress throughout the structure. The term 'geodesic' is derived from 'geodesy' – the science of measuring the size and shape of the Earth and the shortest distance between two points on the Earth's surface.

golden ratio A proportion between two lengths that is considered to be harmonious when expressed as the side lengths of a rectangle (the golden rectangle) or in the dimensional proportions of associated objects or features. See phi.

incommensurable numbers Two numbers are incommensurable with each other if their ratio cannot be written as a rational number.

irrational number An irrational number cannot be expressed as a ratio between two whole numbers and it cannot be written as a simple fraction because it cannot be expressed as a finite number when written as a decimal – meaning that the numbers in the decimal go on forever, without repeating.

lattice An arrangement of lines that connect points. These lines can be structural or purely geometric.

magnitude The relative size of an object. The Greeks distinguished between numerical magnitudes (natural numbers) and geometric magnitudes (continuous quantities) on the grounds that whole numbers cannot be divided but geometrical magnitudes can. An example is the diagonal of a square, where its magnitude is the ratio of the diagonal to the side of the square, leaving no need to define the irrational length that we know as the square root of 2.

micron A millionth part of a metre.

nanomaterial A material having particles or constituents of nanoscale dimensions, or one that is produced by nanotechnology. A nanometre is one billionth of a metre (0.000000001 m).

non-periodic tiling A tiling that lacks translational symmetry, meaning that the tiles fit together but do not form a repeating pattern. Also known as aperiodic tiling.

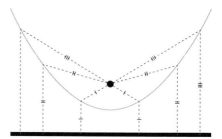

parabolic curve (above) A curve where any point on the curve is at an equal distance from a fixed point and a fixed straight line.

paraboloid A solid generated by the rotation of a parabola around its axis of symmetry.

phi (φ) The golden ratio. The limit of the ratios of successive terms in the Fibonacci additive sequence: 1, 1, 2, 3, 5, 8, 13, 21, … (or any Fibonacci-like sequence). The 'mean and extreme' ratio described by Euclid as the ratio of two parts of a divided line where the length of the whole line to the greater part is at the same ratio as the greater part is to the lesser part. A ratio expressed by $(\sqrt{5} + 1)/2$. An irrational number, 1.6180339887…

pi (π) The ratio of a circle's circumference to its diameter. The ratio is not that of a rational number, as its value extends to infinity without repeats: 3.14159265358979 3238462643383279502…

Platonic solid Any one of five geometric solids composed of regular polygons of one type – equilateral triangles, squares or pentagons. The five Platonic solids are the tetrahedron (four faces), cube (six), octahedron (eight), dodecahedron (12) and icosahedron (20).

polygon A plane figure with at least three straight sides and angles. A regular polygon has equal sides and angles.

polyhedron A three-dimensional solid with flat polygonal faces.

Pythagorean ratio Any number ratio associated with the Pythagoreans, such as the ratios of Pythagorean triples: 5:4:3 and 13:12:5 for example; or in music the ratios of divisions of a string that create octaves, fourths and fifths: 2:1, 4:3, 3:2.

Pythagorean theorem The theorem states that the side lengths of a right-angled triangle are in the ratio $a^2 = b^2 + c^2$. Also expressed as the square of the hypotenuse (the side opposite the right angle) is equal to the sum of the square of the other two sides.

Pythagorean triple The side lengths of right-angled triangles with whole number ratios 5, 4, 3; 13, 12, 5; 25, 24, 7; etc, where the side lengths fall within the general rule that the square of the hypotenuse equals the sum of the squares of the other two sides (Pythagorean theorem).

quantum (mechanics, universe, effects) Initially based on the behaviour of subatomic quantum particles (with both wave-like and particle-like behaviour) that could not be explained with classical physics. The quantum universe is a place where energy states change in steps (quanta) and not continuously — and where quantum particles can be in two or more places at once with their positions in a probabilistic haze. It is a place where the act of observing the energy state of one particle influences the energy state of another particle (if they have previously become entangled), no matter how far away it is.

rational numbers Numbers that can be written as a whole number ratio or as a whole number fraction, such as 1:12 (1/12) or 3,657,212:5,121 (3,657,212/5,121).

real numbers All positive and negative whole numbers and rational and irrational numbers.

secant A straight line that cuts a curve in two or more parts.

tessellation An arrangement of shapes closely fitted together, especially of polygons in a repeated pattern without gaps or overlapping.

tetractys A triangular arrangement of ten points arranged in four rows: one in the first, two in the second, three in the third and four in the fourth. The tetractys was a mystical symbol of the Pythagoreans expressing the first four triangular numbers, the primary Pythagorean musical and planetary ratios, and much more.

toroid A three-dimensional form that resembles a torus or doughnut.

torus A three-dimensional form that can be generated by rotating a circle around a straight line such that the same two opposite edges of the circle remain equidistant from the line and on the same plane.

triangular number Triangular numbers can be represented by a triangular grid of dots, where each subsequent row of dots has one number more than the previous row. The start of the triangular number sequence begins with the units 1; 1 + 2; 1 + 2 + 3; 1 + 2 + 3 + 4… These units are added progressively to create the triangular numbers 1; 3; 6; 10…

unit triangle A right-angled triangle tile that, when repeated by reflection and rotation, will build a tessellating polygon. A unit triangle may include the smallest possible pattern element that when repeated will cover a surface.

REFERENCES

Preface and Introduction

Bronowski, J., *The Ascent of Man*, BBC Books, London, 2011 (first published 1973).

Bryson, B., *A Short History of Nearly Everything*, Broadway Books, New York, 2004.

Hawking, S., *A Brief History of Time*, Bantam Press, London, 1998 (first published 1968).

McGurk, H., J. MacDonald, 'Hearing Lips and Seeing Voices', *Nature*, Vol. 264, Issue 5588, pp. 746–748, Berlin, 1976.

Rae, A., *Quantum Physics: A Beginner's Guide*, Oneworld Publications, London, 2005.

Russell, B., *History of Western Philosophy*, Routledge, Abingdon-On-Thames, 2004 (first published 1946).

Sagan, C., *Billions & Billions: Thoughts on Life and Death at the Brink of the Millennium*, Random House Inc., New York, 1997.

Visual Logic

Bogoshi, J., K. Naidoo, J. Webb, 'The Oldest Mathematical Artifact', *The Mathematical Gazette*, The Mathematical Association, Vol. 71: No. 458, Leicester, 1987.

Buzen, J., *Rethinking Randomness*, CreateSpace, North Charleston, 2015.

Conway, J. H., H. Burgiel, C. Goodman-Strauss, *The Symmetries of Things*, A. K. Peters Ltd, Natick, 2008.

Einstein, A., *Relativity: The Special and General Theory*, Dover Publications Inc., Mineola, 2009 (first published 1916).

Gardner, M., *The Magic and Mystery of Numbers*, Scientific American, New York, 2014.

Gullberg, J., P. Hilton, *Mathematics: From the Birth of Numbers*, W.W. Norton and Company, New York, 1997.

Premack, D., 'Animal Cognition', *Annual Review of Psychology*, Vol. 34, pp. 351–362, University of Pennsylvania, Philadelphia, 1983.

Robson, E., 'Words and Pictures: New Light on Plimpton 322', *American Mathematical Monthly*, The Mathematical Association of America, Vol. 109, No, 2. Washington DC, 2002.

VISUAL LOGIC THROUGH TIME
Neolithic Geometries

Burrows, R., *Labyrinths*, Apple Inc. iBook, 2012.

Clottes, J., *What is Paleolithic Art: Cave Paintings and the Dawn of Human Creativity*, University of Chicago Press, 2016.

Couprie, D. L., *Heaven and Earth in Ancient Greek Cosmology: From Thales to Heraclides Ponticus*, Springer Science + Business Media LLC, New York, 2011.

Kern, H., *Through the Labyrinth: Designs and Meanings Over 5000 Years*, Prestel Publishing, New York and London, 2000.

Saward, J., *Labyrinths and Mazes: A Complete Guide to Magical Paths of the World*, Lark Books, New York, 2003.

von Petzinger, G., *The First Signs: Unlocking the Mysteries of the World's Oldest Symbols*, Atria Books, New York, 2017.

The River Cultures

Brandenburg, R., K. Nevenzeel, 'The Nine Chapters on the History of Chinese Mathematics', *Kapteyn Astronomical Institute*, University of Groningen, 2007.

Coomaraswamy, A. K., *Essays in Early Indian Architecture: Early Indian Architecture and Art, Migration and Diffusion*, Indira Gandhi National Centre for the Arts and Oxford University Press, New Delhi, 1992.

Friberg, J., *A Remarkable Collection of Babylonian Mathematical Texts: Manuscripts in the Schøyen Collection: Cuneiform Texts*, Springer-Verlag New York Inc., 2007.

Garlake, P., *Early Art and Architecture of Africa*, Oxford University Press, 2002.

Kak, S., 'The Astronomy of the Age of Geometric Altars', *Quarterly Journal of the Royal Astronomical Society*, Vol. 36, pp. 385–395, Baton Rouge, 1995.

Robins, G., C. Shute, *The Rhind Mathematical Papyrus: An Ancient Egyptian Text*, Dover Publications, Mineola, 1990.

Standaert N., 'Ancient Chinese Ritual Dances', *Asian Library Journal*, 12–1, Princeton University, 2005.

Wilhelm, R. and C. F. Baynes (trans.), *I Ching or Book of Changes*, Arkana / Penguin, London, 1989 (the original text dates from 1000 BCE).

The Americas

Aveni, A. E. (ed.), *Native American Astronomy*, University of Texas Press, Austin and London, 1977.

Closs, M. P., *Native American Mathematics*, University of Texas Press, Austin, 1986.

Monroe, J. G., R. A. Williamson, *They Dance in the Sky: Native American Star Myths*, Houghton Mifflin Harcourt, Boston, 1987.

Nabokov, P., R. Easton, *Native American Architecture*, Oxford University Press, 1989.

Williamson, R. A., *Living the Sky: The Cosmos of the American Indian*, Houghton Mifflin Harcourt, Boston, 1984.

The Pythagoreans

Burrows, R., 'Animations of the Pythagorean Theorem in Circles', *rogerburrowsimages.com*.

Couprie, D. L., *op. cit.*

Critchlow, K., *Order in Space: A Design Source Book*, Thames & Hudson, London, 2000 (first published 1969).

Densmore, D. (ed.), T. L. Heath (trans.), *Euclid's Elements*, Green Lion Press, Santa Fe, 2002 (the original text was written in c. 300 BCE).

Ferguson, K., *The Music of Pythagoras: How an Ancient Brotherhood Cracked the Code of the Universe and Lit the Path From Antiquity to Outer Space*, Walker & Company, New York, 2008.

Gorman, P., *Pythagoras: A Life*, Routledge and Kegan Paul Ltd, London, 1978.

Lundy, M., D. Sutton, A. Ashton, J. Martineau, J. Martineau, *Quadrivium: Number Geometry Music Heaven*, Wooden Books, Glastonbury, 2010.

Plato, T. K. Johansen (ed.), D. Lee (trans.) *Timaeus and Critias*, Penguin Classics, London, 2008 (the original texts date from c.360 BCE).

Sieden, S., *Buckminster Fuller's Universe: His Life and Work*, Basic Books, New York, 2000.

Vitruvius Pollio, M., M. Morgan (trans.), *De Architectura – The Ten Books on Architecture*, Harvard University Press, Cambridge, MA, 1914 (the original text dates from between 30 and 15 BCE).

European Tribal Geometry

Bain, G., *Celtic Art: The Methods of Construction*, Constable & Robinson, London, 1977.

Geometries of the Early Islamic Period

3d Mekenlar.com, '3D tour of the Umayyad mosque in Damascus, and Other Mosques', www.3dmekanlar.com/en/umayyad-mosque.html.

Bourgoin, J., *Les Arts Arabes*, Institute of the National History of Art, Paris, 1873.

Calvert, A., *Moorish Remains in Spain*, John Lane Company, London, 1906. A PDF is available at: searchformecca.com/downloads/moorishremainsin00calvrich.pdf.

Harmsen, S., *Algorithmic Computer Reconstructions of Stalactite Vaults – Muqarnas – in Islamic Architecture*, University of Heidelberg, 2006. This is an English edition.

Jones, O., *The Grammar of Ornament: A Visual Reference of Form and Colour in Architecture and the Decorative Arts*, Princeton University Press, 2001 (first published 1856).

Lane, E. W., *Arabic–English Lexicon*, The Islamic Texts Society, Cambridge, 1984 (first published 1863). A PDF can be downloaded from www.tyndalearchive.com/tabs/lane.

Rice, D. T., *Islamic Art*, Thames & Hudson, London, 1975 (first published 1965).

Shah, I., *The Sufis*, ISF Publishing, London, 2014 (first published 1964).

The Renaissance

Cohen, J., T. Benton, J. Tittensor (trans.), *Le Corbusier Le Grand: MIDI Edition*, Phaidon Press, London, 2008.

DaVinci, L., L. Pacioli (trans.), *De Divina Proportione*, CreateSpace Independent Publishing Platform, 2014 (the original text dates from 1498). A PDF can be found at: issuu.com/s.c.williams-library/docs/ de_divina_proportione.

Greenblatt, S., *The Swerve: How the Renaissance Began*, Vintage Books, New York, 2012.

Huppert, A. C., *Becoming an Architect in Renaissance Italy: Art, Science, and the Career of Baldassarre Peruzzi*, Yale University Press, New Haven, 2015.

Wade, D., *Fantastic Geometry: Polyhedra and the Artistic Imagination in the Renaissance*, The Squeeze Press, Open Library, 2012.

OUT OF THE PAST – INTO THE FUTURE

Aiello, C., *eVolo Skyscrapers 2: 150 New Projects Redefine Building High*, eVolo, Los Angeles, 2014.

Ching, F. D. K., *Architecture: Form, Space, and Order*, John Wiley & Sons, Hoboken, 2014 (first published 2007).

Fox Weber, N., *The Bauhaus Group: Six Masters of Modernism*, Yale University Press, New Haven, 2011.

Pottmann, H., A. Asperl, M. Hofer, A. Kilian, *Architectural Geometry*, Bentley Institute Press, Exton, 2007.

Salingaros, N. A., *Twelve Lectures on Architecture: Algorithmic Sustainable Design*, ISI Distributed Titles, Wilmington, 2010.

Fractals

DeMars, D., 'Fractal Domains User Manual', *Fractal Domains.com*, 2004.

Moon, B., H. V. Jagadish, C. Faloutsos, J. H. Saltz, 'Analysis of the Clustering Properties of the Hilbert Space-Filling Curve', *IEEE Transactions and Knowledge and Data Engineering*, Vol. 13, Issue 1, pp. 124–141, Washington DC, 2001.

Shape-Changers

Burrows, R., 'Movie Clips of the Shape-Change Geometry', *rogerburrowsimages.com*.

Festo AG, *www.festo.com* (Aqua Ray, Air Ray video clips, 2014), Festo Pneumatic and Electrical Automation Technologies, Esslingen am Neckar, Germany.

Dynamic Circles and Spheres

Burrows, R., *Images Design Book Series*, Running Press, Philadelphia, 1992–2010.

Burrows, R., 'Sphere Animations', *rogerburrowsimages.com*.

Collins, C. R., K. Stephenson, 'A Circle Packing Algorithm', *Computational Geometry: Theory and Applications*, Vol. 25, pp. 233–256, Elsevier, Amsterdam, 2003.

Holiday, E., R. Burrows, *Altair Designs*, Wooden Books, Glastonbury, and Bloomsbury, New York, 2009.

Holiday, E., R. Burrows, R. Penrose, J. Martineau, K. Haifa, *Crystal Cave: The Ultimate Geometric Colouring Book*,

Bloomsbury, New York, and Wooden Books, Glastonbury, 2015.

Stephenson, K., *Introduction to Circle Packing: The Theory of Discrete Analytic Functions*, Cambridge University Press, New York, 2005.

The Future of 3D Geometry

Adrover, E. R., *Deployable Structures*, Laurence King Publishing, London, 2015.

Aiello, C., *eVolo, Issue 6: Digital and Parametric Architecture*, eVolo, Los Angeles, 2014.

Blanciak, F., *Siteless: 1001 Building Forms*, The MIT Press, Cambridge, MA, 2008.

Fortmeyer, R., C. Linn, *Kinetic Architecture: Designs for Active Envelopes*, Images Publishing Group, Mulgrave, 2014.

Krauel, J., *Inflatable Art, Architecture & Design*, Links International, Barcelona, 2014.

Lim, J., *Bio-Structural: Analogues in Architecture*, BIS Publishers, Amsterdam, 2011.

Marcovitz, H., *What is the Future of 3D Printing?* ReferencePoint Press, San Diego, 2016.

Seedhouse, E., *Bigelow Aerospace: Colonizing Space One Module at a Time*, Springer Praxis Books, New York, 2014.

Vance, A., *Elon Musk: Tesla, Space X, and the Quest for a Fantastic Future*, Ecco Press, New York, 2015.

Wimpenny, D. I., P. M. Pandey, L. J. Kumar (eds), *Advances in 3D Printing & Additive Manufacturing Technologies*, Springer Science + Business Media LLC, Singapore, 2017.

Additional Thoughts and Ideas

Fukagawa, H., T. Rothman, *Sacred Mathematics: Japanese Temple Geometry*, Princeton University Press, 2008.

Lewin, D., *Generalized Musical Intervals and Transformations*, Oxford University Press, 1993.

PICTURE CREDITS

All artwork and photographs © Roger Burrows, unless otherwise noted.

000.1: Dale O'Dell / Alamy; 00.1: Wjarek / Shutterstock; 00.2: Oleg Golovnev / Shutterstock; 00.3: Suronin / Shutterstock; 00.4: PRISMA ARCHIVO / Alamy; 00.5: Froaringus; 00.6: Graham Moore 999 / Shutterstock; 00.7: Pecold / Shutterstock; 00.8: Merrydolla / Shutterstock; 00.9: MMiche / iStock; 00.11: Danishkhan / iStock; 00.12: ESA / NASA; 00.13: Zhi Zheng / Evolo; 1.1: ESA / NASA / Martin Kornmesser; 1.6: Plimpton Collection, Cuneiform Tablet 322, Rare Book and Manuscript Library, Columbia University; 1.7: ESA / NASA; 1.9: Oleg Seleznev / Shutterstock; 1.11: Toni Flap / iStock; 1.15: T. Cook after William Hogarth; 1.17: NASA; 1.18: NASA; 1.19 (clockwise from top): Pierre Stéphane Dumas / www.bubbletree.fr; Steven Maltby / Shutterstock; Pi-Lens / Shutterstock; photo © Andrew Churches; Edward Fielding / Shutterstock; Roger Burrows; Naaman Abreu / Shutterstock; Roger Burrows; Vovashevchuk / iStock; 1.20 (clockwise from top left): Lissandra Melo / Shutterstock; Roger Burrows; Merydola / Shutterstock; Paul Wishart / Shutterstock; Francesca Moscatelli / Shutterstock; Wallpaper Safari / TaosPueblo; Silvertone Photography / Craig Sheiles Homes Design Team; Roger Burrows; Michael Jantzen; Ermingut / iStock; Thomas Mølvig / Henning Larson Architects; PlusOne / Shutterstock; Anthony Gibbons Design Ltd.; Feng Li / iStock; Karol Kozlowski / Shutterstock; Plo3 / Shutterstock; Boris-B / Shutterstock; Coy Cunaplus / Shutterstock; Muracciole Jean-Marie; 1.21 (clockwise from bottom left): Dirk Ercken / Shutterstock; Everett Historical / Shutterstock; Eldin / Shutterstock; Mmiche / iStock; Suronin / Shutterstock; Amy Nicole Harris / Shutterstock; Borisb17 / Shutterstock; Everett Historical / Shutterstock; Marzolino / Shutterstock; jx1306 / Shutterstock; public domain; Phant / Shutterstock; Paul Wishart / Shutterstock; 1000 Words / Shutterstock; Chubykin Arkady / Shutterstock; Yulia B. / Shutterstock; Tupungato / Shutterstock; 2.1: National Geographic Creative / Alamy; 2.8: imagestock / iStock; 2.9: Froaringus; 2.10: Mordolff / iStock; 2.13: Halebid2; 2.20: Hemis / Alamy; 2.23: Photo © Adrian Fletcher, www.paradoxplace.com; 2.25: Fulcanelli / Shutterstock; 2.27: Jesse Kraft / Alamy; 2.37: Turtix / Shutterstock; 2.55 dbimages / Alamy; 2.62: Anton Sokolov / iStock; 2.64: Pecold / Shutterstock; 2.65: Aflo Co. Ltd. / Alamy; 3.1: Dan Breckwoldt / iStock; 3.2: Ismoon; 3.19: Rogers Fund, 1923. Gallery 117, OASC. The Metropolitan Museum of Art; 3.20: Double P. / iStock; 3.21: Trustees of the British Museum, 00037564001; 3.61: Benjamin Mercer

/ Shutterstock; 3.64: Cozyta / Shutterstock; 3.71: Fidor Selivanov / Shutterstock; 3.75: Trustees of the British Museum, 00123559001; 4.1: Vadim Petrakov / Shutterstock; 4.4: Jeffrey M. Frank / Shutterstock; 4.5: Pop_Gino / Adobe Stock; 4.6: Jeffrey M. Frank / Shutterstock; 4.8: Zack Frank / Shutterstock; 4.12: Don Mammoser / Shutterstock; 4.13: Uwe Albert-Thiele / Adobe Stock; 4.14: Spacaj / Shutterstock; 4.15: Melastmohican / Adobe Stock; 4.29: Dr Tomas Garcia-Salgado; 4.30: Peter Zaharov / Shutterstock; 4.31: Hashirama / Shutterstock; 4.34: Olga Kot / Shutterstock; 4.37: Matyas Rehak / Shutterstock; 4.43: Olga Kot / Shutterstock; 4.44: Wollertz / Shutterstock; 4.45: Pawel Cebo / Shutterstock; 5.1: Viacheslav Lopatin / Shutterstock; 5.31: Janaka Dharmasena; 5.39: NokHoOkNoi / Shutterstock; 5.69: Ashmolean Museum, Oxford (l-r: AN1927.2727; AN1927.2728; AN1927.2729; AN1927.2730; AN1927.2731); 5.91: Meunlerd / Shutterstock; 5.97: Lefteris Papaulakis / Shutterstock; 5.99: Carmen Avram / Shutterstock; 5.100: Passion Images / Shutterstock; 5.102: Florin Stana / Shutterstock; 5.103: MMiche / iStock; 6.1: Trustees of the British Museum, 00080784001; 6.2: The Board of Trinity College Library, Dublin, Ireland. *The Book Of Kells*, Folio 34R; 6.3: National Museum of Scotland; 6.4: Sergejus Lamanosovas / Shutterstock; 6.5: Johnbod; 6.9: Gallofoto / Shutterstock; 6.10a: Wlad74 / Shutterstock; 6.10b: Pecold / Shutterstock; 6.11: The Board of Trinity College, Dublin, Ireland. *The Book of Kells*, Folio 28R; 6.12: The Board of Trinity College, Dublin, Ireland. *The Book of Durrow*, Folio 85v; 6.13: The Board of Trinity College, Dublin, Ireland. *The Book of Kells*, Folio 34R; 6.15: The Board of Trinity College, Dublin, Ireland. *The Book of Kells*, Folio 34R; 6.16: The Board of Trinity College, Dublin, Ireland. *The Book of Kells*, Folio 34R; 6.17: The Board of Trinity College, Dublin, Ireland. *The Book of Durrow*, Folio 192v; 6.18: The Board of Trinity College, Dublin, Ireland. *The Book of Durrow*, Folio 3v; 6.26: Yael Yolovitch, Israel Antiquities Authority; 6.27: National Museum of Scotland; 6.30: jx1306 / Shutterstock; 6.31: Ricochet64 / Shutterstock; 6.32: Spumador / Shutterstock; 6.33: Eirik Irgens Johnsen / University of Oslo; 7.1: Artography / Shutterstock; 7.5: Dick Osseman; 7.10: Mehmetcan / Shutterstock; 7.54: Daud Sutton; 7.79: Alessandro0770 / Shutterstock; 7.91: Javarman / Shutterstock; 7.93: Artography / Shutterstock; 7.95: Anton Ivanov / Shutterstock; 7.96: Aztec Images / Shutterstock; 7.97: Heidelberg University; 7.103: Rob Pinney / Alamy; 7.104: Casual Builder; 7.105: Casual Builder; 7.106: Daud Sutton; 8.1: AugustSnow / Alamy; 8.2: S-F / Shutterstock;

8.4: Paolo Uccello; 8.5: Peter Barritt / Alamy; 8.9: Art Collection 3 / Alamy; 8.16: Jean-Pol Grandmont; 8.17: Universitaria / Shutterstock; 8.18: Claudiodivizia / iStock; 8.20: LWilk / iStock; 8.21: Netfalls / Shutterstock; 8.22: Scirocco340 / Shutterstock; 8.29: Alpineguide / Alamy; 8.30: Claudio Zaccherini / Shutterstock; 8.31: Lnu / Shutterstock; 8.32: Anton Ivanov / Shutterstock; 8.33: Maciej Czekajewski / Shutterstock; 8.34: Woe / Shutterstock; 8.35: Anibal Trejo / Shutterstock; 8.36: Eleonoracerna / Shutterstock; 8.37: Nataliia Kasian / Shutterstock; 8.38: Mike Dotta / Shutterstock; 8.39: Claudio Divizia / Shutterstock; 8.40: MartineDF / Shutterstock; 9.1: CoolR / Shutterstock; 9.2: NASA; 9.18: Csp / Shutterstock; 9.19: martinwimmer / iStock; 9.20: Jose L Vilchez / Shutterstock; 9.21: Xseon / Shutterstock; 9.22: Leica Camera AG; 9.23: The Digital Michelangelo Project, Stanford University; 10.1: Helen's Photos / Shutterstock; 10.7: Iserp / Shutterstock; 10.9: 3dredraw / Shutterstock; 10.10: Prudkov / Shutterstock; 11.57: WYSS Institute, Harvard University; 11.58: Barcelona Institute for Advanced Architecture; 11.59: Festo AG & Co. KG; 12.2: Grafissimo / iStock; 13.3: Emily Goodwin / Shutterstock; 12.4: Dimitris66 / iStock; 12.5: Gateway / iStock; 12.6: NASA; 12.7: Markross / iStock; 12.8: Claudio Divizia / Shutterstock; 12.9: Markross / iStock; 12.10: Alasdair James / iStock; 12.11: Yuri Arcurs / iStock; 12.13: Mr Twister / iStock; 12.15: Harry Wolf; 12.16: NASA / Mark Holderman and Edward Henderson; 12.17: Leland A. Gray; 12.18: ESA, Foster and Partners; 12.19: Ocean Farm Technology Inc.; 12.20: Triton Submarines LLC., Model 3300 / 3; 12.21: © Bigelow Aerospace LLC; 12.22: IBM; 12.23: Irochka T / iStock; 12.38: NASA; 12.70: NBBJ / image courtesy of the Seattle City Council; 13.1: DLR; 13.15: Tectonics; 13.16: Pierre Stéphane Dumas, www.bubbletree.fr; 13.17: Yves Morfouace, designed by 2HD Ltd.; 13.18: Yves Morfouace, designed by 2HD Ltd.; 13.19: image © Bigelow Aerospace LLC; 13.23: Yves Morfouace, designed by 2HD Ltd; 13.25: Research architectural works from the Advanced Design & Digital Architecture Masters in Elisava, developed by Irene Per, Xavier Montoya and Oriol Carrasco, tutored by Jordi Truco, Marco Verde, Luis Fraguada and Marcel Bilurbina; 13.26: University of Calgary; 13.29: xyzproject / 123 RF; 13.30: eVolo / Christian Hahn; 13.31: TonyV3112 / Shutterstock; 13.32: Northrop Grumman; 13.33: Sierra Nevada Corporation; 13.34: NASA; 13.35: author rendering of NASA aircraft with shape-changing wing.

ACKNOWLEDGMENTS

Much of the content in this book is original and has been gathered from my own experience visiting sites and considering the logic of artefacts and architectural structures. Some of my ideas were developed with the help and encouragement of friends and colleagues from the past, particularly the mathematician and psychologist Ensor Holiday, the theoretical physicist David Bohm (1917–1992), the botanist and anthropologist Francis Huxley (1923–2016) and the photographer, filmmaker and *I Ching* expert Mario DeGrossi (1941–2013). Many of my ideas were developed laterally, a process influenced by the lectures of the psychologist and inventor Edward DeBono (1933–) at the University of London.

I was introduced to ideas about the ABJAD system by author and teacher Idries Shah (1924–1996), and was inspired to write the America chapter by Tomas Garcia-Salgado of the School of Architecture at the Universidad National Autonomade de Mexico. Thanks to Ricky Cheung and Josephine Lai for translating Chinese text and I am also grateful for the help of Andrew Simoson at King University, Anthony McCormick at the University of Waterloo and Joe Pennacchio at the University of Notre Dame, who checked my mathematics. Thanks to Keith Critchlow for his encouraging review of an early version of the manuscript. Keith was Professor of Architecture at the Architectural Association in London. Also thanks to Jeff Buzen, Gordon McKay Lecturer on Computer Science at Harvard University, for his encouragement. My wife, Lauren Nadler, has been a wonderful support during the whole process of creating this book, including her design work on its first incarnation. Thanks also go to her intern editor, Julia Bell, for last-minute proofreading.

At Thames & Hudson I would very much like to thank Lucas Dietrich, who championed my work from the start, and who pushed me to add more chapters on the history of the development of visual logic and geometry, and Fleur Jones for assisting in the impossible task of drawing together all of the elements of *3D Thinking* and making the work look as good as it does. Thanks are also due to Kirsty Seymour-Ure for her detailed and creative edit, to the production team at Thames & Hudson, and last, but not least, to the book's designers, Peter Dawson and Namkwan Cho at Grade Design.

INDEX

Page numbers in *italics* refer to figures and captions.